Mastering XMI
Java Programming with
XMI, XML, and UML

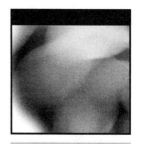

Mastering XMI
Java Programming with
XMI, XML, and UML

Timothy J. Grose
Gary C. Doney
Stephen A. Brodsky, Ph.D.

Wiley Computer Publishing

John Wiley & Sons, Inc.

NEW YORK · CHICHESTER · WEINHEIM · BRISBANE · SINGAPORE · TORONTO

Publisher: Robert Ipsen
Executive Editor: Robert M. Elliott
Developmental Editor: Emilie Herman
Managing Editor: John Atkins
New Media Editor: Brian Snapp
Text Design & Composition: MacAllister Publishing Services, LLC

Designations used by companies to distinguish their products are often claimed as trademarks. In all instances where John Wiley & Sons, Inc., is aware of a claim, the product names appear in initial capital or ALL CAPITAL LETTERS. Readers, however, should contact the appropriate companies for more complete information regarding trademarks and registration.

IBM, DB2, VisualAge, and WebSphere are trademarks or registered trademarks of IBM Corporation in the United States, other countries, or both.

Java and all Java-based trademarks and logos are trademarks of Sun Microsystems, Inc. in the United States and/or other countries.

Microsoft, Windows, and Windows NT are either registered trademarks or trademarks of Microsoft Corporation in the United States and/or other countries.

OMG, Object Management Group, OMG IDL, CORBA, XMI, MOF, CWM, Unified Modeling Language, UML, the UML Cube Logo, Model Driven Architecture, MDA, OMG Model Driven Architecture, OMG MDA, and IIOP are trademarks or registered trademarks of the Object Management Group, Inc., in the United States and other countries. All other names and marks that may appear are used for identification purposes only and may be trademarks of their respective owners.

Pentium is a registered trademark of Intel Corporation.

Walkman is a registered trademark of Sony Corporation.

This book is printed on acid-free paper. ∞

Published by John Wiley & Sons, Inc.

Published simultaneously in Canada.

This publication is designed to provide accurate and authoritative information in regard to the subject matter covered. It is sold with the understanding that the publisher is not engaged in professional services. If professional advice or other expert assistance is required, the services of a competent professional person should be sought.

Library of Congress Cataloging-in-Publication Data:

ISBN: 0-471-38429-1

Printed in the United States of America.

10 9 8 7 6 5 4 3 2 1

Advance Praise for
Mastering XMI

"XMI is a powerful standard for representing objects in XML and it plays key roles in IBM's WebSphere servers and WebSphere Studio application development tools. This book takes the mystery out of XMI, tells why it is important, and shows Java programmers how to use it. Its authors made XMI work for WebSphere and they build on that experience to explain the hows and whys of XMI in an eminently readable and practical way."

Lee R. Nackman
IBM Vice President, Application Development Tools
Member, IBM Academy of Technology

"Model Driven Architecture (MDA) is an appealing vision of how to develop software, but there is little information readily available on how to apply these somewhat abstract ideas in practice. Timothy Grose, Gary Doney, and Stephen Brodsky remedy this deficiency by producing a comprehensive, grounded, and detailed handbook on how to use XMI to create and integrate MDA applications using Java, XML, and UML. The CD contains a wealth of supporting information, including a full-featured trial edition of IBM's WebSphere Studio Application Developer. This book is an essential read for any developer serious about applying the principles of Model Driven Architecture in real software development projects."

Steve J. Cook
IBM Distinguished Engineer
Member, IBM Academy of Technology

"The convergence of modeling technologies into the UML that the OMG drove home in 1997 has finally made software design and architecture a mainstream activity. The convergence of the UML itself with the startling rise of XML is the obvious next step: the communication of metamodels (and objects in general) clearly relies on universal data formats such as XML. This explains the rapid uptake of XMI in the software development community. This masterful book gives everything the serious application developer needs, start to finish—from motivation, through explanation, to clear, concise examples using XMI with Java. As the Model Driven Architecture (MDA) sweeps the mess of software heterogeneity under the rug, XMI at MDA's core ensures interoperability across tools and applications. And there's no better way to learn the details than this book."

Richard Mark Soley, Ph.D.
Chairman and CEO, Object Management Group, Inc.

2001 OMG Press Advisory Board

Karen D. Boucher
Executive Vice President
The Standish Group

Carol C. Burt
President and Chief Executive
   Officer
2AB, Inc.

Sridhar Iyengar
Unisys Fellow
Unisys Corporation

Cris Kobryn
Chief Technologist
Telelogic

Nilo Mitra, Ph.D.
Principal System Engineer
Ericsson

Jon Siegel, Ph.D.
Director, Technology Transfer
Object Management Group, Inc.

Richard Mark Soley, Ph.D.
Chairman and Chief Executive
   Officer
Object Management Group, Inc.

Sheldon C. Sutton
Principal Information Systems
   Engineer
The MITRE Corporation

Ron Zahavi
Chief Technology Officer
AxTechnology

OMG Press Books in Print

(For complete information about current and upcoming titles, go to www.wiley.com/compbooks/omg/.)

- *Building Business Objects* by Peter Eeles and Oliver Sims, ISBN: 0-471-19176-0.

- *Business Component Factory: A Comprehensive Overview of Component-Based Development for the Enterprise* by Peter Herzum and Oliver Sims, ISBN: 0-471-32760-3.

- *Business Modeling with UML: Business Patterns at Work* by Hans-Erik Eriksson and Magnus Penker, ISBN: 0-471-29551-5.

- *CORBA 3 Fundamentals and Programming, 2nd Edition* by Jon Siegel, ISBN: 0-471-29518-3.

- *CORBA Design Patterns* by Thomas J. Mowbray and Raphael C. Malveau, ISBN: 0-471-15882-8.

- *Enterprise Application Integration with CORBA: Component and Web-Based Solutions* by Ron Zahavi, ISBN: 0-471-32720-4.

- *Enterprise Java with UML* by C.T. Arrington, ISBN: 0-471-38680-4.

- *Enterprise Security with EJB and CORBA* by Bret Hartman, Donald J. Flinn, and Konstantin Beznosov, ISBN: 0-471-15076-2.

- *The Essential CORBA: Systems Integration Using Distributed Objects* by Thomas J. Mowbray and Ron Zahavi, ISBN: 0-471-10611-9.

- *Instant CORBA* by Robert Orfali, Dan Harkey, and Jeri Edwards, ISBN: 0-471-18333-4.

- *Integrating CORBA and COM Applications* by Michael Rosen and David Curtis, ISBN: 0-471-19827-7.

- *Java Programming with CORBA, Third Edition* by Gerald Brose, Andreas Vogel, and Keith Duddy, ISBN: 0-471-24765-0.

- *The Object Technology Casebook: Lessons from Award-Winning Business Applications* by Paul Harmon and William Morrisey, ISBN: 0-471-14717-6.

- *The Object Technology Revolution* by Michael Guttman and Jason Matthews, ISBN: 0-471-60679-0.

- *Programming with Enterprise JavaBeans, JTS, and OTS: Building Distributed Transactions with Java and C++* by Andreas Vogel and Madhavan Rangarao, ISBN: 0-471-31972-4.

- *Programming with Java IDL* by Geoffrey Lewis, Steven Barber, and Ellen Siegel, ISBN: 0-471-24797-9.

- *Quick CORBA 3* by Jon Siegel, ISBN: 0-471-38935-8.

- *UML Toolkit* by Hans-Erik Eriksson and Magnus Penker, ISBN: 0-471-19161-2.

About the OMG

The Object Management Group (OMG) is an open membership, not-for-profit consortium that produces and maintains computer industry specifications for interoperable applications. To achieve this goal, the OMG specifies open standards for every aspect of distributed computing from analysis and design, through infrastructure, to application objects and components defined on virtually every enterprise middleware platform. OMG's membership roster includes virtually every large company in the computer industry, and hundreds of smaller ones. Most of the companies that shape enterprise and Internet computing today are represented on OMG's Board of Directors.

OMG's flagship specification, and the basis for future OMG specifications, is the multi-platform Model Driven Architecture (MDA). Unifying the modeling and middleware spaces, the MDA supports applications over their entire lifecycle from Analysis and Design, through implementation and deployment, to maintenance and evolution. Based on normative, platform-independent Unified Modeling Language (UML) models, MDA-based applications and standards may be expressed and implemented, equivalently, on multiple middleware platforms; implementation are produced automatically, for the most part, by MDA-enabled tools that also generate cross-platform invocations, making for a truly interoperable environment. Because the UML models remain stable as the technological landscape changes around them over time, MDA-based development maximizes software ROI as it integrates applications across the enterprise, and one enterprise with another. Adopted by members as the basis for OMG specifications in September 2001, the MDA is truly a unique advance in distributed computing. To learn more about the MDA, see www.omg.org/mda.

OMG's modeling specifications form the foundation for the MDA. These include the UML, the MetaObject Facility (MOF), XML Metadata Interchange (XMI), and the Common Warehouse Metamodel (CWM). The industry's standard for representation of analysis and design, the UML defines Use Case and Activity diagrams for requirements gathering, Class and Object diagrams for design, Package and Subsystem diagrams for deployment, and six other diagram types. The MOF defines a standard metamodel for applications, allowing UML models to be interchanged among tools and repositories; and XMI standardizes the format for these interchanges. Finally, CWM establishes metamodels in the field of data warehousing, completing OMG's standardization in the modeling space.

The Common Object Request Broker Architecture (CORBA) is OMG's vendor-neutral, system-independent middleware standard. Based on the OMG/ISO Interface Definition language (OMG IDL) and the Internet Inter-ORB Protocol (IIOP), CORBA is a mature technology represented on the market by more than 70 ORBs (Object Request Brokers) plus hundreds of other products. Scalable to Internet and Enterprise levels, CORBA more than meets business computing requirements through its robust services-providing directory, distributed event handling, transactionality, fault tolerance, and security. Specialized versions of CORBA form the basis for distributed Realtime computing, and distributed embedded systems.

Building on this foundation, OMG Domain Facilities standardize common objects throughout the supply and service chains in industries such as Telecommunications, Healthcare, Manufacturing, Transportation, Finance/Insurance, Biotechnology, Utilities, Space, and Military and Civil Defense Logistics. OMG members are now extending these Domain Facilities, originally written in OMG IDL and restricted to CORBA, into the MDA by constructing UML models corresponding to their underlying architecture; standard MDA procedures will then produce standards and implementations on such platforms as Web Services, XML/SOAP, Enterprise JavaBeans, and others. OMG's first MDA-based specification, the Gene Expression Facility, was adopted less than six months after the organization embraced the MDA; based on a detailed UML model, this specification is implemented entirely in the popular language XML.

In summary, the OMG provides the computing industry with an open, vendor-neutral, proven process for establishing and promoting standards. OMG makes all of its specifications available without charge from its Web site, www.omg.org. Delegates from the hundreds of OMG member companies convene at week-long meetings held five times each year at varying sites around the world, to advance OMG technologies. The OMG welcomes guests to their meetings; for an invitation, send your email request to info@omg.org or see www.omg.org/news/meetings/tc/guest.htm.

Membership in OMG is open to any company, educational institution, or government agency. For more information on the OMG, contact OMG headquarters by telephone at +1-781-444-0404, by fax at +1-781-444-0320, by email to info@omg.org, or on the Web at www.omg.org.

For Nancy
—Tim Grose

For my mother and father
—Gary Doney

For Sharon and Alicia
—Stephen Brodsky

Contents

List of Figures, Code and Tables

Figures

Source Code and XML Examples

Tables

Acknowledgments

The authors wish to thank the many people who contributed to XMI and to this book: Donald Baisley, Daniel Berg, Dr. Arne Berre, Juergen Boldt, Frank Budinsky, Daniel Chang, Magnus Christerson, Dr. Steven J. Cook, Dr. Stephen Crawley, Philippe Desfray, Dr. Ravi Dirckze, Tom Doucher, Keith Duddy, Raymond Ellersick, David Frankel, Jun Ginbayashi, Alexander Glebov, Mike Golding, Jask Greenfield, Craig Hayman, Shyh-Mei Ho, Anita Huang, Hsin-Liang Huang, Mario Jeckle, G. K. Kalsa, Gary Karasiuk, Dr. John Knapman, Cris Kobryn, Rich Kulp, Suresh Kumar, Malvina Lai, Christina Lau, Martin Matula, Simon McBride, John McLean, Ed Merks, Chuck Mosher, Dr. Gene Mutschler, Lee Nackman, Martin Nally, Van Pham, Dr. Robert Phippen, Woody Pidcock, Kevin Poole, Dr. Kerry Raymond, Jim Rhyne, Scott Rich, Pete Rivett, James Rumbaugh, Danny Sabbah, Ashit Sawney, Marc-Thomas Schmidt, Dr. Jon Siegel, Harm Sluiman, Dr. Richard Soley, Dave Stringer, Peter Thomas, Tony Tsai, Celia Tung, Leo Uzcategui, Shu Wang, and Andrew Watson.

The authors would also like to thank Barbara Price for designing the MDA application in Chapter 10, and Kyle Brown for contributing the EJB material used in Chapter 11.

Tim wishes to thank his mother and father, Harryette and Jim Grose, his sister Cindy, and his brothers, Mike and Dan, for all their support through the years. He also thanks Nancy Z. Liu for her patience and understanding while this book was being written.

Gary wishes to thank his mother and father, Lillian and Charles Doney, and his sister Karen, for all their support and encouragement through the years.

Introduction

The conveniences of our modern, daily lives are made possible by standards. Already today you may have made a phone call on your cell phone, sent or received a fax from a friend or business associate, or read some email, possibly including attachments that could be viewed with applications that were already on your computer. Perhaps you decided to listen to some music recorded on a favorite CD. You had your choice of playing it on the sound system in your home, your car stereo, your CD Walkman, or even the CD-ROM drive in your computer. When you bought that CD at the music store or perhaps over the Web, you didn't need to worry that it would not play on any of those four devices. You didn't need to worry about buying a special adapter to be able to play it. You knew it would work on all of them because the musical information on the CD was written in a standard way. Like musical CDs, many modern conveniences at your disposal provide you with benefits and a freedom of choice because they are designed and built to work with accepted industry standards.

XMI, which stands for Extensible Markup Language (XML) Metadata Interchange, is the standard for representing object-oriented information using XML. The Object Management Group (OMG), an industry-wide consortium that promotes standards for enabling interoperability among heterogeneous systems, adopted XMI 1.0 in February of 1999. XMI 1.0 was developed in response to the OMG's Request for Publication (RFP) for a stream-based standard to represent object-oriented information and was supported by 29 industry-leading companies. Because of XMI's capability to represent many forms of object-oriented information, software that supports XMI can be used to provide lightweight integration among Java applications, the Web, XML, and different kinds of models.

XMI has evolved following the OMG's open process and procedures. Thus far, four versions of XMI have been submitted to the OMG. In addition to XMI 1.0, XMI 1.1, which provides support for XML namespaces, was adopted in February of 2000. XMI 2.0 is the most recent version, and the version upon which this book is based. XMI 1.2 and XMI 2.0 were adopted by the OMG in November of 2001. XMI 2.0 provides support for XML schemas and supports reverse engineering from schemas, documents, and DTDs. (If you are unfamiliar with namespaces, Document Type Definitions [DTDs] or schemas at this point, do not be concerned. We explain these terms in detail in the early chapters of this book.) Finally, there is still some ongoing work on the earlier versions of XMI in resolving outstanding issues.

Depending on your experience, you probably have some familiarity with the concept of an object in the programming sense of the word. If you've been working with Java, you know that objects (along with the classes that describe them) are the fundamental units of organization in the language. When your Java programs run, the Java virtual machine creates objects that carry out the programming instructions in the methods that you have written. If you've worked with a visual modeling tool, you may have created classes and objects using the Unified Modeling Language (UML) or a similar methodology. You may also have worked with objects if you have done programming with languages like C++ and Smalltalk.

If you've been working with objects, you probably also know that there are many different ways to represent them. The tools that you have worked with probably have some special file format that they use to save your models or instances of your objects. These formats probably work well for the tools that use them, and you may have never thought there was a need for any other way to represent the objects that you have been working with. You probably reasoned that as long as the application that needed your objects was able to access them, there was no need for a different way to represent them.

However, the computing world today is changing rapidly. More than ever, interoperability is becoming a key requirement. Advances in communications technology and the rapid growth of the Web have provided more demand, as well as opportunities, for systems that work together. As a result, the data those systems depend on need to be shared in ways that were not thought of when the systems were originally developed. Although in some cases it is possible to build customized software bridges from one application to another, the only cost-effective way to enable object-oriented data to be shared universally is through the use of a standard way of representing it.

Let's consider a simple, hypothetical scenario from everyday life that illustrates how standards expand the freedom you have in making choices. Suppose you decide to buy a new vacuum cleaner. You look at the ones available in several local department stores, but can't quite decide which one to buy. Then, late one evening, you see an infomercial for a new vacuum cleaner sold exclusively by mail order—the new, revolutionary Vac-o-matic. As the infomercial explains, the Vac-o-matic is made exclusively by Vactron Corporation. What makes the Vac-o-matic special from other vacuums is its use of revolutionary sound blast technology. The infomercial explains that the Vac-o-matic has a new space-age component that emits a special sound through its patented sonic dirt blaster as it glides across the carpet. Researchers at Vactron claim that the sonic dirt blaster helps to shake dirt loose from the carpet fibers, thereby enabling the Vac-o-matic to collect up to 10 percent more dirt than a conventional vacuum cleaner. Also, Vactron claims that anecdotal reports from early adopters indicate that the special sound may have a calming effect on household pets and small children.

You immediately decide that the Vac-o-matic is for you, and call the 800 number shown on the infomercial. You speak to someone named Carol at Vactron, and she takes your order. In a few days, your new Vac-o-matic arrives. As promised, it comes with 10 free filter bags. The instructions explain that you should change the filter bag in your Vac-o-matic after every use to avoid damaging the delicate components in the sonic dirt blaster.

The first time you use your Vac-o-matic, you are impressed with how easy it is to use, and your carpeting looks great. However, you notice that your dog seems disturbed by the sound the Vac-o-matic makes, and that he starts to howl every time you turn it on. Alarmed that something may be wrong with your Vac-o-matic, you call Vactron. Carol answers the phone and listens to your concern. To check if your Vac-o-matic has a problem, Carol asks you to turn it on and place the receiver of the phone near your Vac-o-matic so she can listen to it. To your relief, Carol tells you that your Vac-o-matic is fine. The problem, she says, must be with your dog. However, she tells you that other customers who have had similar problems have found that placing their dogs outside while they vacuum usually stops the howling. You are somewhat concerned, but decide that this is what you'll need to do.

After a couple of months, you run out of the filter bags that came with your Vac-o-matic and decide to pick some up at the store. After checking in three local department stores, you find out that none of them stocks replacement bags for the Vac-o-matic. One of the sales managers at the last store you go to explains that the filter bags for the Vac-o-matic are different from other filter bags they sell. Moreover, they do not work with any of the other vacuums on the market. He also relates that since so few Vac-o-matics are sold, stocking filter bags for them is not cost effective. He suggests that you call Vactron to see if they have them available by mail order.

When you get home, you call Vactron and again you talk to Carol. Carol explains that they included a special mail order form in the box that your Vac-o-matic was shipped in. Although they don't take orders for replacement bags over the phone, you can use this form to order them through the mail. After you get off the phone, you search through your Vac-o-matic's packaging materials and find the filter bag order form at the bottom of the box. You find out that replacement filter bags are available only in quantities of 100, are much more expensive than the filter bags you saw at your local stores, and that you will need to wait six to eight weeks for them to arrive. Since you can't use your Vac-o-matic without one of the special filter bags, you decide to order them from Vactron.

After a couple of months, your replacement filter bags arrive, and you again start using your Vac-o-matic. However, this time you notice a strange, high-pitched sound coming from the motor. Alarmed, you call Vactron and speak with Carol again. Carol asks you to describe the sound, and when you do, she tells you that most likely the vortex in your sonic dirt blaster has given out. She tells you that the only way you can get it fixed is to send your Vac-o-matic back so that one of their repairmen can take a look at it. She also tells you that it would be pointless to take it to a local repair shop, since they would only have standard tools, and specially made tools that only Vactron has are required to work on the Vac-o-matic's sonic dirt blaster.

At this point, you ask Carol if you can have a refund, since you've now decided that the Vac-o-matic isn't for you after all. Although it may be a wonderful machine, it's too different from anything else to be practical to maintain. Carol says she understands how you feel, but since it is now past the warranty period, Vactron is unable to give you a refund. However, she does say that Vactron will allow you to trade in your Vac-o-matic towards the purchase of their new vacuum, the Vac-o-*magic*. Carol explains that the vortex in the Vac-o-matic's sonic dirt blaster frequently goes bad because it uses twirl-a-whirl technology. The vortex in the Vac-o-magic's sonic dirt blaster, however, is made with their new, proprietary spin-a-tron technology and therefore is much more durable. She also tells you that with the trade-in value for your Vac-o-matic, you would only need to pay $299.99 to get a Vac-o-magic.

After quickly thinking this over, you tell Carol that you've decided not to upgrade at this point. Instead you will purchase a vacuum made by a more reputable manufacturer. You go to the local department store where you can actually try out the vacuum cleaners. You find one that you like, and you make sure that the store stocks replacement filter bags that you can use with it. To your surprise, there are many manufacturers that make filter bags for your new vacuum because the filter bag is based on a standard and can be used in other vacuum cleaners. You now have a choice of manufacturers to choose from. You can also decide on the quantity you want to buy, and what's more, you can buy them from a nearby store when you need them. Further, if you have a problem with your new vacuum, you can take it to one of the several repair shops located in your hometown, because it doesn't require special tools to open and repair it. All of this is possible because you moved away from a machine based on proprietary technology to one based on widely adopted standards.

As this hypothetical scenario illustrates, making a choice that locks you into the proprietary technology of one company can have profound repercussions down the line, although the choice to use open standards has many benefits. Open standards level the playing field by removing the barriers that lock customers into one company's vision of the marketplace. When open technologies are utilized, all vendors are free to create new tools and applications that work together with existing products, thus providing greater value. As a result, customers enjoy a large array of choices and possess the freedom to select the tools, systems, and products that best meet their needs. In a similar way, XMI, as an adopted industry standard, brings the same kinds of benefits to users of object technology through its capability to facilitate the exchange of data, enhance application integration, and achieve a level of program interoperability not available with proprietary data formats.

Although the M in XMI stands for meta data, you can use XMI in your applications, even though you may be unfamiliar with the term meta data or not think that your applications use it. The distinction between meta data and data is useful for some applications, especially those involving multiple levels of abstraction for the data, but it is less vital for applications that work with data at only one level of abstraction. Even if your application works with data at one level of abstraction, you will still benefit from using XMI. In this book we'll show how XMI and modeling are part of an overall model-driven architecture that integrates Java, software models, XML, and the Web.

As you learn more about the power of XMI in this book, you will see why IBM and other leading software companies have adopted XMI as a fundamental technology for their application tools. IBM's WebSphere Studio Application Developer, included on the CD-ROM with this book, and DB2 Universal Database Warehouse Manager both use XMI. As of the writing of this book, XMI is already in use by the products of over a dozen software companies.

Overview of This Book

Most likely you have chosen to read this book because you are trying to decide if XMI is right for the technology you are developing and, if so, how you can get started using it. You want to know what XMI is about and how you can start writing applications that both create and read XMI files. We believe people learn best by seeing examples and by doing. As such, this is very much a practical, hands-on book. Throughout the text, we've included sample programs written in Java that show you how to create and read XMI files.

The general format that we follow is to introduce a concept, explain it in detail, and then show example programs, models, or XMI information that illustrate that concept. Most of the programs we include are one or two pages long, and where they are longer, we have tried to develop them in a step-like way to make it easier for you to follow them. Additionally, we've included comments throughout the programs' source listings that tie them back to the concepts or algorithms discussed in the text that precedes them. We feel this is the best way to facilitate your understanding of the concepts and to help you move from knowledge to implementation in your own development efforts.

In addition to discussing XMI, we provide some information on a number of related technologies. Among these are UML, the OMG's Meta Object Facility (MOF), XML (including DTDs and schemas), and two XML Application Programming Interfaces (APIs)—the Document Object Model (DOM), and the Simple API for XML (SAX). Since a complete discussion of any one of these topics is worthy of at least one book on its own, we do not attempt to cover all the details of these topics; rather we provide enough background and detail for you to understand how these technologies relate to XMI, and to follow the examples we present. To help you delve deeper into these topics, we've provided a list of references to related documents and specifications that have additional information.

As you will learn, XMI is based on the OMG's MOF. MOF provides a hierarchy that enables you to represent information at progressively higher levels of abstraction. Currently, the OMG is working to align UML 2.0 and MOF 2.0, and we expect this alignment to happen in the very near future. As a result, it should be possible to use UML and MOF models as if they are the same. Because the common capabilities of UML and MOF are sufficient for the models we present to help you understand XMI, and because many people already know UML and have worked with UML tools, we will be using UML examples throughout this book to explain XMI. In Chapter 10, we explain MOF, the Model Driven Architecture (MDA), and how UML fits into it. Because the examples we present in this book are not dependent on being at a certain level in the MOF hierarchy, it is sufficient for us to use UML.

Finally, as we mentioned earlier, XMI has evolved following the OMG's open process. This book is based upon the most recent version, XMI 2.0. Although we do not specifically cover XMI 1.0, 1.1, and 1.2, there are cases where we do explain differences between the current version and the previous versions if it is relevant to the topic. The OMG will continue to revise XMI in the future. Although we have made every attempt to make this book reflect the XMI 2.0 specification in its current form, we anticipate some changes may occur as the specification continues to evolve along with the XML, MOF, and UML technologies.

How This Book Is Organized

This book contains the following two parts:

- Part One, "XMI Explained"
- Part Two, "How to Use XMI"

Part One provides an overview of what XMI is about. We also include an introduction to XML and UML, two technologies you need to know to understand XMI and the sample models we use in this book. Part One includes the following three chapters:

- Chapter 1, "XMI: Representing Objects in XML," explains that XMI provides a standard way for you to represent objects in XML. In this chapter, we develop the motivation for using XMI by showing how the existence of a standard way of representing objects in XML eliminates ambiguities that arise when no such standard exists. We also explain how XMI facilitates the integration of different tools that work with objects, and we discuss other related benefits of utilizing the XMI standard.

- Chapter 2, "Related Standards: XML and UML," provides basic introductions to the concepts in XML and UML that you will need to know in order to understand XMI and the examples we present in this book. Our coverage of XML includes elements, attributes, namespaces, DTDs, and schemas. For UML, our coverage includes classes, objects, attributes, associations, association ends, and packages. If you are already familiar with either XML or UML, you may wish to skip those sections in this chapter or to skim them lightly as a review.

- Chapter 3, "XMI Concepts," covers the details of representing object-oriented information in XMI 2.0. Building on our introduction to UML in Chapter 2, we explain how to represent concepts in the UML object model in XML according to the XMI standard. We also cover the issues related to creating XMI schemas. Finally, we examine the elements and attributes provided by the XMI model, and how they can be used to represent additional information in XMI documents. Included among these are extensions, differences (additions, deletions, and replacements), and details about the data in the document, such as the model that the data is based on.

In Part Two, we utilize the understanding of XMI you have gained in Part One to help you learn how to use XMI in your own Java applications. In Part Two, we introduce a general development process you can use, detail guidelines you should follow when developing your models for use with XMI, and step through some programming examples that work with software designed for XML and XMI. Part Two includes the following eight chapters:

- Chapter 4, "Creating Your XMI Process," covers a five-step development process that we recommend you follow if you decide to utilize XMI in your development projects. The process is presented in a generic form that you can tailor as necessary to meet your needs. To give you a better understanding of how the process works, we walk through an application of the process by developing a model for a simple application, and then generate an XMI schema for the model we have developed. Additionally, we show Java code that is generated from the model.

- Chapter 5, "Creating Models for XMI," begins by detailing issues involving UML modeling and XMI. Following that, we present some general algorithms for reverse engineering UML models from XML documents, DTDs, and schemas.

- Chapter 6, "Creating and Reading Simple XMI Documents with Standard XML APIs," covers how you can use a couple of standard XML interfaces, DOM and SAX, to read and write XMI files. We also introduce a car rental agency model that we use in this chapter as well as some of the chapters that follow. If you are not interested in learning to work with standard XML interfaces and instead prefer to learn about software designed especially to work with XMI, you may wish to skip or lightly skim this chapter. You should, however, read the car rental agency model example covered in the beginning of this chapter so that you can follow the examples that utilize it later in this book.

- Chapter 7, "Creating and Reading Simple XMI Documents with the XMI Framework," introduces software designed to work with XMI that is included with this book. At the beginning of the chapter, we introduce the Java Object Bridge (JOB). We show how this very simple interface can be used to read and write XMI files that contain representations of Java programming objects. Next, we introduce the XMI Framework, which provides an API designed to work with XMI. We demonstrate how you can use the Framework API to read and write XMI files, and how you can represent your UML models within the Framework.

- Chapter 8, "Creating and Reading Advanced XMI Documents with the XMI Framework," builds upon the introduction to the XMI Framework that we provided in Chapter 7. In this chapter, we present programming examples that utilize some of the more advanced features of XMI. Among the topics we cover are XML namespaces, XMI extensions, the use of ZIP files, and cross-file references.

- Chapter 9, "XMI Schemas," explains how you can use the XMI Framework to generate a schema for one of your models and how to do validation when loading an XMI document using the Framework. The chapter also details the type of errors that validation detects and explains how choosing different XMI options for generating schemas affects validation.

- Chapter 10, "Model Driven Architecture (MDA) and XMI," provides an introduction to the MDA approach to developing software. In the early part of this chapter, we explain what the goals of MDA are and give an overview of the MOF's taxonomy for representing different levels of information abstraction. We next develop an example using a modeling methodology other than UML [the Flow Composition Model (FCM)]. We show how this example can be represented in XMI, thereby enabling information sharing that is key to the MDA approach.

- Chapter 11, "A Real-World Use of XMI: WebSphere Studio Application Developer," explores how XMI is being used in IBM's WebSphere Studio Application Developer, which is included on the CD-ROM. In this chapter we first examine how XMI is being used in a tool that provides the capability to specify a mapping either from one XML DTD to another or from one XML schema to another. Then we look at how XMI is used in an example involving Enterprise JavaBeans (EJBs).

An appendix is also included that contains in-depth information on the XMI Framework that supplements the material on the Framework provided in Chapters 7, 8, and 9.

Who Should Read This Book

This book is primarily written for Java software developers who are considering using XMI. Because XMI is based on XML, and because most of the modeling we do in this book is based on UML, previous experience with XML, UML, or both will help you understand this book. However, in Chapter 2, we provide an introduction to the features in XML and UML that are needed to understand the contents of this book, so prior knowledge of XML and UML is not required. If you feel fairly comfortable with these two topics, you may choose to skip Chapter 2 or to focus only on the areas where your knowledge is limited.

The example programs that we present are all written in Java. To understand the examples, you should have some prior experience programming in Java, or at least be comfortable with the syntax of the language. You do not need to have experience with advanced features in Java. As long as you understand concepts like classes, interfaces, flow-of-control constructs, and inheritance, you should be able to follow all the examples we present. Although in some cases we make passing mention of more advanced Java concepts like serialization and reflection, you do not need to know these concepts to benefit from the examples in this book. If you have had previous experience with a language that has a syntax similar to Java's (such as C++), you can probably still understand the general flow of the examples, although you may need to learn more about Java to run them on your own system.

If you are not a software developer, but are interested in learning what XMI is about and whether it's a technology you or your organization should consider using, you may still benefit from reading this book. In particular, the first two chapters, which introduce XMI, XML, and UML, provide a good overview of these technologies and should give you a sense of what XMI is all about and how using it can help you. In addition, you may benefit from reading Chapter 10, which describes MDA, a new software development approach that utilizes XMI. Finally, you may benefit from reading Chapter 11, which describes how XMI is being used in WebSphere Studio Application Developer.

Mastering XMI contains 11 chapters. Although reading all the chapters is certainly one way we intended for this book to be read, we show a chapter-by-chapter roadmap in Figure I.1 that you might find helpful in determining the best path for you to take as you read this book. In the roadmap, we show which sections of the book we consider to be optional material. Depending on your background or your needs, you may choose to skip those sections or skim them lightly. For example, Chapter 2 contains introductions to XML and UML for readers who are either new to those areas or have limited experience with them. If you have considerable experience with either or both of those areas, you may choose to skip those sections.

If you are primarily interested in getting a quick introduction to what XMI is about, and you do not intend to do any programming that uses XMI, you can follow the overview roadmap shown in Figure I.2. Following this path will give you an idea of why XMI is valuable without covering the details of how to represent information in XMI or how to write programs that work with XMI.

What's on the CD-ROM

A CD-ROM is included with this book. The CD-ROM includes the following:

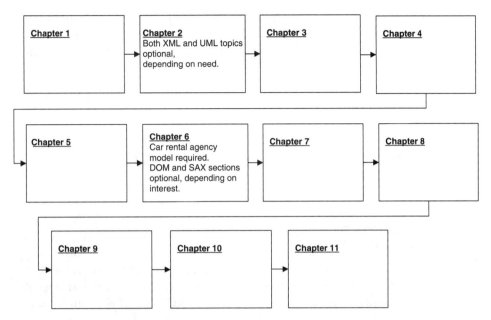

Figure I.1 *Mastering XMI* roadmap.

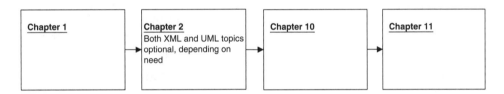

Figure I.2 *Mastering XMI* overview roadmap.

- A full-featured trial edition of WebSphere Studio Application Developer, a Java 2 Platform Enterprise Edition (J2EE)-compliant server-side Java tool, focusing on relational databases, Web site building, Web services, and EJB development, deployment, and profiling. It also contains all the functionality of IBM's WebSphere Studio Site Developer.

- The example programs we present in this book. These include examples from Chapters 6, 7, 8, and 9.

- The XMI Framework, which provides an API for reading and writing XMI files. We cover examples that utilize the XMI Framework in Chapters 7, 8, and 9.

- The JOB, which converts between the objects that you create in your Java programs and XMI. We present examples with JOB in Chapter 7.

- The *XML4J-J-bin.3.2.1.zip* file for IBM's XML4J parser (which includes all the capabilities of the Apache Software Foundation's Xerces Java XML Parser) Version 3.2.1. The XML4J Parser is used to run the examples we present in Chapters 6, 7, 8, and 9.

See the *Readme.htm* file in the root directory of the CD-ROM for the installation instructions for the software on this CD-ROM.

What You Will Need to Use the CD-ROM

The following covers the requirements for running the programs on the CD-ROM that are included with *Mastering XMI*. Note that these requirements are not the same for all the software on the CD-ROM. In general, the requirements to run IBM's WebSphere Studio Application Developer exceed those of the other software included on the CD-ROM. Therefore, if your system meets the requirements to run WebSphere Studio Application Developer, you will also be able to run the other programs included on the CD-ROM on your system.

The following are the requirements for running the XMI Framework, JOB, and the programming examples in this book. These requirements are also adequate for running the XML4J Parser included on the CD-ROM:

- The minimum hardware is equivalent to a Pentium, at 90 MHz, with 64 MB of RAM. The recommended hardware is equivalent to or greater than a Pentium II, at 300 MHz, with 128 MB of RAM.
- Windows 2000, Windows ME, Windows 98, or Windows NT 4.0 with Service Pack 6a or higher.
- JDK 1.2.2 or above.

WebSphere Studio Application Developer has the following software and hardware prerequisites:

- Windows 2000, Windows ME, Windows 98, or Windows NT 4.0 with Service Pack 6a or higher.
- Microsoft Internet Explorer 5.5 or higher.
- TCP/IP installed and configured.
- A mouse or an alternative pointing device.
- Pentium II processor or higher recommended.
- SVGA (800 × 600) display or higher (1024 × 768 recommended).
- 256 MB RAM minimum.

■ Disk space requirements: 400 MB minimum (based on the NT File System [NTFS], actual disk space on the File Allocation Table [FAT] depends on hard [disk] drive size and partitioning).

Additional information on installation, deployment platforms, supported software, and related topics is included with the documentation provided with WebSphere Studio Application Developer. The *Readme.htm* file included on the CD-ROM provides details on how to access this information.

What's on the Companion Web Site

The companion Web site, www.wileybooks.com/compbooks/grose, will include the latest errata, corrections, and updates for *Mastering XMI*; hints, tips, and updates for the XMI Framework and book examples.

A Few Thoughts before You Begin

We are very excited by the promise of open standards like XMI. We have been using XMI and the MDA approach in the software we have developed over the past few years, and we have seen the realization of what open standards can offer in providing value for our customers. It is our hope that by reading this book you will understand what XMI is about so that you can decide if XMI is a good choice for the projects you are either working on now or that you plan to undertake in the future. If you do decide to use XMI, we hope that from seeing the programming examples we present, you'll quickly be able to begin implementing your own applications that utilize XMI, or even develop your own software that supports XMI or works with other XMI tools.

PART One

XMI Explained

*"It is only in the world of objects that we
have time and space and selves."*

T.S. ELIOT

XMI: Representing Objects in XML

XML Metadata Interchange (XMI) is a standard that enables you to express your objects using Extensible Markup Language (XML), the universal format for representing data on the World Wide Web. XMI is much more than a set of serialization rules though. XMI is closely related to modeling standards, enabling you to employ modeling effectively in your XML efforts. XMI 2.0 specifies how to create XML schemas from models, and previous versions of XMI specified how to create XML Document Type Definitions (DTDs) from models. Both schemas and DTDs define the content of XML documents. In addition, XMI specifies how to reverse engineer models from XML documents, XML DTDs, and XML schemas. The primary benefits of XMI include the following:

- XMI provides a standard representation of objects in XML, enabling the effective exchange of objects using XML.

- XMI specifies how to create XML schemas from models.

- XMI enables you to create simple XML documents and make them more advanced as your applications evolve.

- XMI enables you to work with XML without becoming an XML expert; however, you can use your XML expertise to tailor the XML representation of your objects, if you wish.

XMI is necessary because XML is not object-oriented, so it is necessary to map objects to XML. There is more than one way to do this mapping, due to the flexibility of XML. However, the flexibility is also a drawback when it comes to exchanging XML documents. If one tool maps objects to XML one way, and another tool maps objects to XML a different way, it is unlikely that the two tools will be able to properly interpret each other's XML documents. XMI uses models to ensure objects are shared consistently. A tool that uses XMI can exchange objects with other tools that also use XMI.

This chapter describes the benefits of XMI without explaining many details about the specific features of XMI itself. It describes the importance of objects and XML, the gap between objects and XML, how XMI bridges the gap, and the benefits of using XMI. You do not need to be an XML expert or a modeling expert to understand the material in this chapter. Although we provide only brief descriptions of XML and the Unified Modeling Language (UML), a modeling standard, in this chapter, Chapter 2 describes in detail the parts of XML and UML that are relevant to XMI. We explain XMI in detail in Chapter 3.

The Importance of Objects

Many popular programming languages have object-oriented features. Java and C++ are two such languages that are used today in a wide range of applications. Object-oriented features help programmers organize their applications and manage their complexity. Many scripting languages like Perl and Python also provide support for object-oriented programming.

It is desirable to make different applications work effectively with each other. If those applications are written in object-oriented languages, it is desirable for the applications to share objects with each other. If the applications are implemented in the same programming language, but they represent objects differently, it is difficult to share the objects. Therefore, some programming languages provide support for serializing objects in binary form and restoring them. However, this does not make the objects accessible to applications written in other languages. Also, different programming languages have different object-oriented features, which makes sharing objects even more difficult.

To share objects written in different programming languages, it is necessary to define what an object is regardless of the programming language. UML provides such a definition. UML also provides a standard graphical notation for analyzing and designing object-oriented systems. UML can be used regardless of the programming language the system will be implemented in. UML enables programmers to model their applications and then implement the model in the programming language best suited for the application.

UML has been adopted by the Object Management Group (OMG), a software industry consortium that supports the interoperability of object-oriented technology through open standards. Since UML provides a standard definition of what an object is, it can be used to define the objects that are to be shared among applications. Combining UML with a standard way to represent data enables objects to be shared effectively using standards rather than proprietary technology.

The Importance of XML

XML has emerged as a powerful and easy way to save data in files. Because it is a standard, XML enables you to save data in a form that can be accessed by applications other than the ones that created the data. XML software, much of it free, enables you to access the data in XML documents using standard application programming interfaces (APIs). You can also use DTDs and schemas to provide syntactic validation for your XML documents using XML software.

Although we explain the relevant parts of XML in detail in Chapter 2, there are some basic concepts you need to know about XML to understand this chapter. XML represents data using XML elements, which consist of the following parts (see Figure 1.1):

- A start tag, which has a name for the element.
- XML attributes; each attribute has a name and a value.
- Content, which consists of text, other XML elements, or a combination of the two.
- An end tag, which has a name that matches the name of the start tag.

XML documents consist of XML elements. The content of an XML document can be defined using an XML DTD or an XML schema. An XML parser can determine whether a document matches the definitions in an XML DTD or an XML schema using a process called validation. For the purposes of this chapter, you don't need to know the syntax of XML elements, DTDs, or schemas; we explain the syntax in Chapter 2.

XML is flexible. Data can be represented in more than one way. This flexibility is good because it enables you to design an XML representation that is right for your applications, but it causes problems when attempting to share XML documents. To exchange data using XML, you need to do the following:

1. Define the data to be exchanged.
2. Decide how to represent the data in XML.

If you do not define your data, you cannot exchange it with others, regardless of the representation of the data, so the first step is necessary to exchange data using any technology. You might think that the second step is trivial, since XML documents consist of elements and attributes, but if the data is represented in different ways, it complicates the exchange of that data.

For example, consider how to represent data about cars. You want to use XML to represent the year a car was made and the kind of car (sedan, sports car, convertible, and so on). Figure 1.1 shows four valid ways of representing a convertible that was made in the year 2002.

If tools represent the same data differently in XML, it is difficult to exchange the data among the tools. In fact, if there are five different tools, and each tool represents its data differently, regardless of whether the tools use XML, 20 one-way bridges or 10 two-way bridges need to be implemented to exchange data among all the tools. Figure 1.2 illustrates 10 two-way bridges.

If you want to use XML validation with the XML documents to be exchanged, you also need to agree on the DTDs and schemas (these concepts are explained in Chapter 2). Unfortunately, to make DTDs and schemas powerful, you may need to define an order for the contents of XML elements. Defining an order makes it more difficult to produce XML documents than if document producers can pick their own order. It can take a considerable amount of work to create large DTDs and schemas, and it also takes work to reconcile differences in DTDs and schemas.

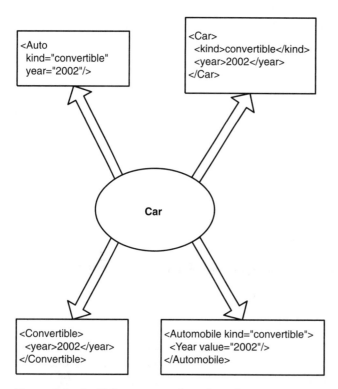

Figure 1.1 An XML representation of car data.

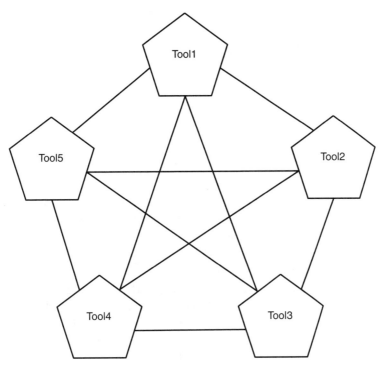

Figure 1.2   The bridges required for different XML representations.

XML is a very successful standard. However, although the original XML standard was small and easily understandable, many additional XML standards have been created. These additional standards enhance certain aspects of XML, such as cross-file linking (the XPointer and XLink specifications), and support multiple elements with the same names (the XML Namespace specification). However, some of these additional standards are not as simple as the original XML standard. For example, the XML schema specification is rather complex, and the World Wide Web Consortium (W3C) wrote a primer to help people understand it. Because of this increasing complexity, it can be difficult to track all of the new developments in XML and effectively adopt new XML technologies. Since XML is a standard for representing data, it is natural to try to build upon it to represent objects.

The Gap between XML and Objects

XML is not object-oriented. XML defines XML elements and XML attributes, not objects. Although XML schemas define types, they do not support such object-oriented features as multiple inheritance, nor do they include an object

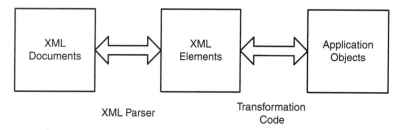

Figure 1.3   Transforming objects to XML elements.

model. Even if you use XML schemas, you still need to map objects to schema features. As we explained in the previous section, if tools represent their data in XML differently, it is difficult to share the data among the tools. The same situation is true for representing objects in XML; if objects are represented differently in XML, it is difficult to share them.

Figure 1.3 illustrates that there are two steps involved when you represent your objects in XML and use a standard XML parser. After a parser reads XML elements from XML documents, you need to transform those XML elements into your objects. In the reverse direction, you need to transform your objects into XML elements that are then saved by an XML parser in XML documents. You need to write this transformation code yourself unless it can be generated automatically for you. If either the application code or the XML representation of your objects changes, you need to update the transformation code. Also, if applications implement this transformation differently, it will be difficult to exchange objects among the applications.

How XMI Bridges the Gap

XMI bridges the gap between objects and XML in several ways. It provides a standard mapping from objects defined by UML to XML. XMI 2.0 also provides a mapping from UML models to XML schemas. Previous versions of XMI provided a mapping from UML models to XML DTDs.

Since XMI defines a mapping between XML and objects, once you define the objects to be exchanged, you do not need to create your own XML representation of the objects if you use XMI. Also, you do not need to implement your own transformation code to transform your objects to XML elements and vice versa; XMI software will do the transformation for you. Since the transformation is standardized, you can exchange your objects with other software that uses XMI.

Figure 1.4 shows how you can work with XMI documents using XMI software by giving the software your application objects; the XMI software puts your objects in XML documents and creates your application objects from XMI

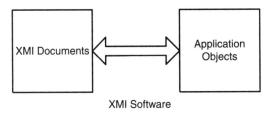

Figure 1.4   Using XMI software.

documents. Although the XMI software probably uses an XML parser to implement this functionality, the XML parser is not exposed to a user of the software. Please note that every XMI document is an XML document, so the application objects are being converted to XML and are restored from XML. These XML documents, however, conform to the XMI standard.

XMI specifies how to create schemas from models. If you know schemas, you have the flexibility to tailor the schemas that are produced.

In the previous section, we saw that there were several ways to represent information about cars in XML. If you model cars in UML, you can use XMI to produce an XML representation, as shown in Figure 1.5. This figure contains a

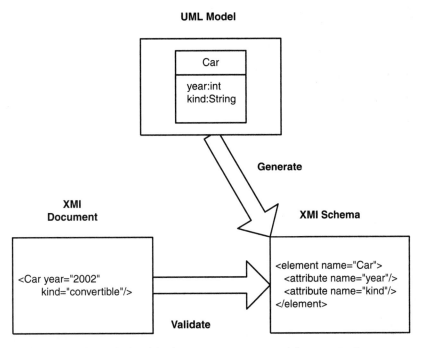

Figure 1.5   The relationship between a UML model, an XMI document, and an XMI schema.

UML model representing a car, the year the car was made, and the kind of car. XMI specifies how to create a schema from the model; only the relevant part of the XMI schema is shown in the figure. XMI also specifies the representation of the particular car; the figure shows the part of an XMI document that represents a convertible made in 2002. You can validate the XMI document with the XMI schema, if you wish.

Another way that XMI bridges the gap between XML and objects is by specifying how to create models from XML documents, DTDs, and schemas. Doing this enables you to use your existing XML assets and to use models to define your software. Once you create the models, you can use them for many purposes, such as generating code and documenting the problem domain.

Benefits of XMI

Now that you know that it is possible for you to use XMI to represent objects in XML, why would you want to use XMI? There are many benefits to using XMI. Here is a list of the ones we explain in the rest of this chapter:

- XMI leverages XML technologies.
- XMI enables you to use modeling with XML.
- Software that supports XMI creates schemas from models.
- Software that supports XMI provides a higher level of abstraction than XML elements and attributes.
- XMI helps you produce XML documents that can be easily exchanged.
- XMI enables you to create simple documents and make more advanced ones as your application evolves.
- XMI enables you to tailor the XML representation of your objects and document your choices in your models.
- XMI enables you to work with data and meta data.

XMI Uses XML

Since XMI uses XML, all of the efforts underway to make XML documents easier to produce and consume will benefit XMI documents as well. XMI does not require you to be an XML expert, however. XMI software can make it easy to produce XMI documents without dealing with XML elements and attributes directly.

As XML technologies are adopted by the W3C, XMI evolves to use them. For example, since XML namespaces were not a recommendation of the W3C when XMI 1.0 was standardized, XMI 1.0 could not use them. However, by the time XMI 1.1 was standardized, the XML Namespace specification was an official recommendation of the W3C, so XMI 1.1 uses XML namespaces to produce more compact XMI documents than was possible with XMI 1.0. Now that XML schemas have been officially adopted as a recommendation by the W3C, XMI 2.0 specifies how to create schemas from UML models as well as how to produce smaller XMI documents than XMI 1.1. XMI will continue to evolve to use future XML technologies, as appropriate.

XMI does not extend XML; it builds upon XML. XML builds upon Unicode, a standard for specifying characters in various languages, in order to represent data. In the same way, XMI builds upon XML to represent objects. Figure 1.6 illustrates this concept. Because XMI builds upon rather than extends XML, every XMI document is an XML document, and every XMI schema is an XML schema. Figure 1.7 illustrates these relationships.

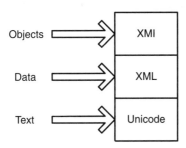

Figure 1.6   XMI builds upon XML.

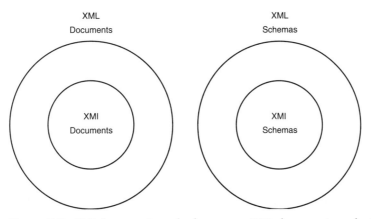

Figure 1.7   XMI documents and schemas are XML documents and schemas.

Modeling and XML

XMI enables you to effectively use modeling with XML.[1] You can design your applications without considering the XML representation of your objects if you wish. If you decide to tailor the XML representation, you can document your decisions in your models.

There are many books that explain the advantages of modeling. Here is a list of some of the main benefits you can enjoy by using modeling when developing software:

- Modeling helps you identify potential problems early in the development cycle when they are easiest to fix.

- Modeling documents your design decisions, which leads to more effective team development since each member of the team understands the design.

- Modeling helps you plan development work.

- Modeling enables you to collect your information in a central place regardless of how that information is implemented in various technologies.

You can use models to provide semantic validation for your XMI documents, because the contents of an XMI document can be matched against a model to determine if it is valid. XMI enables you to unambiguously identify which models define the objects in an XMI document.

You can use XMI as part of a model-driven software architecture. XMI is part of the Model Driven Architecture (MDA) defined by the OMG. In such an architecture, you define models for the problem domain, and then all of your software is based on those models. For example, you can generate programs, database schemas, and so on from the models. Using XMI, you can also generate an XML representation for your models. By basing your software on a model, you can ensure that the different software components are consistent with each other as well as take advantage of the other benefits that modeling provides.

Creating Schemas from Models

You can use XMI to produce XML schemas from UML models. This approach is much easier and less error-prone than generating schemas by hand. Since schemas have many features, it is very likely that two people creating schemas for the same data without using XMI will produce schemas that are different. This difference complicates the exchange of documents that are validated with the schemas. If two people or programs use XMI to produce schemas from a common model, the schemas will be identical.

XMI does not require a single XML representation for your objects. You can tailor the XML representation to suit your needs. The decisions you make to tailor your schemas are documented as part of your models. XMI does not ordinarily impose an order on the contents of the XML elements, but you can impose an order to make your schemas more effective. For example, you can decide that inheritance among the classes in your model will be represented in a schema using the XML schema extension mechanism. Doing so imposes an order on the contents of the XML elements in your documents.

Because the decisions you make about how to tailor the XML representation are made at the model level and are included with the model, two users of XMI will produce identical XML representations from the model. As we have seen already in this chapter, having identical XML representations for objects enables the effective exchange of those objects.

Working with Objects and XML

When you create UML models for use with XMI, you do not need to be concerned about the XML representation of the objects to be defined. In a similar way, software that implements the XMI specification enables you to work with your objects directly, rather than with XML elements and XML attributes. It is possible for XMI software to create your application objects from XMI documents, so you do not need to be aware of how the XMI software transforms XML into your objects.

By allowing you to work with your objects directly, software that implements the XMI specification enables you to use XML without becoming an XML expert. For example, without ever reading the XML schema specification, you can create schemas from your UML models by using software that implements the XMI specification.

Exchanging XML Documents

XMI enables the effective exchange of documents. To exchange objects with others, you create a model that defines the objects and you then derive the XML representation from the model using XMI. This helps you accomplish both steps we described previously that are required for document exchange: defining your data and representing your data in XML. Using UML helps you define your data, while using XMI enables you to easily create the XML representation of your data; you do not need to reconcile different XML representations of your data before exchanging documents.

Consider the case of five tools that want to exchange data. As we saw previously, if each tool has its own data representation, regardless of whether they use

XML or not, 20 bridges need to be built for all the tools to exchange data. As more tools are added, the situation gets even worse. If the tools use XMI, the task of exchanging data is much simpler. If the tool builders create a UML model that defines the objects to be exchanged among the tools, and the tools use XMI, the task of exchanging the objects is much easier. Figure 1.8 illustrates that each tool only needs to deal with the representation of the objects defined by XMI, rather than implementing individual bridges to different tools. In addition, for more tools to exchange objects with the initial tools, each additional tool only needs to support the XMI representation. Also, the UML model that defines the data helps the additional tools understand the objects that are exchanged.

To further aid the exchange of XML documents, XMI provides a mechanism for putting data into XMI documents that is not meant to be shared with other tools. This additional data does not interfere with the objects that are being exchanged. Tools that do not understand the additional data can ignore it.

Evolving Your XML Applications

XMI enables your XML applications to evolve as well. XMI provides an infrastructure for advanced features such as extensions to data, cross-file linking, and identifying objects in various ways. Although these features are available

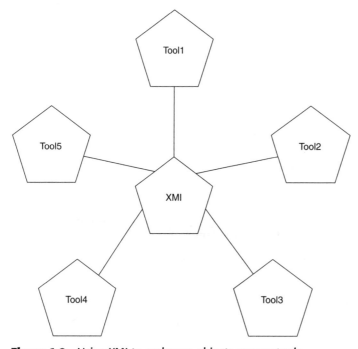

Figure 1.8   Using XMI to exchange objects among tools.

to you, you do not need to use all of them right away. You can start by creating simple documents and then use advanced XMI features in the future if you need to do so.

You can use additional features without creating new schemas. This design enables you to use only the features you need at first, but additional features are available if your applications become more advanced.

XMI Is Flexible

XMI enables you to tailor your XML representation to suit your needs. For example, you can decide to represent data using XML elements or XML attributes. Since you can modify the XML representation to meet your requirements, you can use XMI to optimize the XML representation for your applications. When you do so, the decisions that you make are documented as part of your models.

XMI creates an effective XML representation for your objects even if you decide not to optimize it for your applications. This enables you to use software that supports XMI without requiring XML expertise.

XMI and Meta Data

Although the letter M in XMI stands for meta data, XMI enables you to work with data as well. Often, whether something is considered data or meta data depends on the applications using the data. For example, from one point of view, a model can be considered to be meta data that is defining objects. However, for a modeling tool, a model is simply input data, not meta data.

XMI enables you to transmit models using XML as well as instances of those models. We already saw that XMI specifies how to create schemas from models. To use XMI with models, you need to define a metamodel, that is, a definition of models. For example, the UML specification defines UML models using a UML model; that UML model is a metamodel. A particular UML model is simply an instance of the UML metamodel. You can also use XMI to transmit metamodels. Table 1.1 shows examples of data and meta data that XMI can handle.

Table 1.1   XMI Works with Meta Data and Data

META DATA	DATA
Classes	Objects
Metamodels	Models
Database schemas	Database tables

MOF

Since XMI is related to MOF, which specifies how to express meta data and how to implement meta data repositories, you can use XMI to develop sophisticated meta data software if you wish. MOF also enables meta data at various levels of abstraction to be linked together. XMI works at all levels of the metamodel architecture defined by MOF. However, XMI works well for data as well as for meta data, so you can use XMI even if you are not working with meta data. In addition, there is a standard mapping from MOF models to Java. The Java Metadata API (JMI) standard was developed as part of the Java Community Process. Using JMI enables you to use a standard if you generate Java code from a MOF model.

Summary

XMI enables you to work with objects as well as serialize and deserialize them using XML. XMI also enables you to operate at a higher level of abstraction than XML elements and XML attributes, and you can use XMI with data or meta data. XMI specifies how to produce XML schemas from UML models, enabling you to use a model-driven architecture for producing XML. One of the great benefits of XMI is that you can use XMI software without becoming an XML expert. However, you can also tailor the schemas and documents if you do know XML. Now that you know in general what XMI can do for you, you can begin to learn the details of XMI.

Related Standards: XML and UML

Before we explain the details of XML Metadata Interchange (XMI), you need to know about two related standards: the Extensible Markup Language (XML) and the Unified Modeling Language (UML). You need to know about XML because XMI is based on XML; XMI uses XML to save and load objects from documents. You need to know about UML because it defines the structure of objects and classes, and we use that definition to explain how XMI represents objects and classes in XML.

You will not become an expert in either XML or UML by reading this chapter. We provide you with basic information about both standards to help you understand the material in the rest of the book. Since this chapter focuses on aspects of XML and UML that are directly relevant to XMI, we do not explain other parts of the XML specifications or the UML specifications. For more information, read the XML and UML specifications or books about them.

You may want to refer to only the sections that you are unfamiliar with. You can skip all of the XML part, but we encourage you to read the *Mapping Data to XML* section even if you know about XML, since it contains material that highlights the value of using XMI. Even if you are familiar with UML, you might want to read the parts of the UML section that discuss object models, and you might want to skim the UML section to understand the terms we use to describe constructs in the UML object model. The rest of the book uses the terminology and graphical notation from the UML section. Once you understand some of the basic concepts of XML and UML, you can begin to learn about XMI, which is explained in detail in Chapter 3.

XML

You can skip most of this section if you are an XML expert, but you should read the section entitled *Mapping Data to XML*. If you are unfamiliar with XML, you should be able to learn enough from this section to understand the examples in this book. We focus on the aspects of XML that are relevant to XMI, so you should read an XML book or the XML specifications for information about other aspects of XML. The information in this section comes from the XML specification (W3C, 2000) unless otherwise indicated.

The Basics

XML specifies a way to format data in a file. XML documents consist of *elements*, where each element represents some data. An element consists of a *start tag*, *content*, and an *end tag*. The content and end tag are not always present. A start tag begins with the less than (<) character and ends with the greater than (>) character. An end tag begins with the </ characters and ends with the > character. Both start tags and end tags have names, and the name of the end tag matches the name of the corresponding start tag. Here is the general form of an XML element:

```
<name attributes>content</name>
```

The text *<name attributes>* is a start tag. The *name* names the data represented by the element, and *attributes* is an optional list of attributes and their values. The element's *content* may include text, elements, or both text and elements. The text *</name>* is the end tag for the element. You may omit the end tag if there is no content by using the following format:

```
<name attributes/>
```

Here is an example of legal XML elements:

```
<specification title="Long and Dull">
   <author name="Ima Geek"/>
   <author name="Ura Geek, Jr."/>
</specification>
<comment>A wonderful cure for insomnia</comment>
```

There are four XML elements. The *specification* element has an attribute called *title* and its value is *Long and Dull*. The *specification* element's content consists of two *author* elements, each of which has an attribute called *name*. The *comment* element has text in its content. (Any resemblance to actual specifications and authors is, of course, completely unintentional.)

Elements must be nested; the start and end tags for an element must both be at the top level of an XML document, or both be in the content of the same XML element. The following is illegal XML:

```
<container>
  <contained>
</container>
</contained>
```

It is illegal because the start tag for the *container* element is at the top level, but the end tag for the *container* element is in the content of the *contained* element. It is also illegal because the start tag for the *contained* element is in the content of the *container* element, but the end tag for the *contained* element is at the top level.

XML restricts the characters that can be used in tag names and attribute names. Tag names and attribute names may include letters, digits, and the hyphen (-), underscore (_), period (.), and colon (:) characters, but they must begin with a letter, _, or :. Other punctuation marks and whitespace are not allowed. The : character has a special meaning, which we explain in the following section, *Namespaces*.

Since some characters, such as < and >, define markup in an XML document, you need to specify them in a particular form if you want them to be interpreted as text rather than as the beginning and ending of tags. There are two ways to do so. You can use XML entities to specify the characters in the content of XML elements, or you can put the characters in a character data (CDATA) section. An XML *entity* is a named sequence of characters, and an XML parser replaces a reference to the entity with the characters when it processes an XML document. A reference to an entity consists of an ampersand (&), the name of the entity, and a semicolon (;). Some entities are predefined, including entities for the characters < and >. The characters in a CDATA section are not treated as XML markup, so the < character is interpreted by an XML parser as the < character in a CDATA section, rather than as the beginning of a start or end tag. Here is an example of both approaches for specifying the text *<notATag>* in the content of an element:

```
<tag>&lt;notATag&gt;</tag>
<tag><![CDATA[<notATag>]]></tag>
```

The entities `&lt;` and `&gt;` represent the characters < and >, respectively. The text `<![CDATA[` begins a CDATA section, and the text `]]>` ends a CDATA section. For complete details about the treatment of characters within an XML document, refer to the XML specification or an XML book.

Namespaces

Now that you know what XML elements look like, consider the following elements that represent an insect and a software defect:

```
<bug name="Moth" description="White">Flies toward light</bug>
<bug name="D10589" description="Data on disk erased.">Fix now</bug>
```

If you include both elements in the same XML document, how does a program distinguish insects from defects? The solution is to use XML *namespaces*. An XML namespace defines the context for XML elements and attributes. A namespace consists of a *namespace prefix* that is used to identify a namespace in an XML document and a *Uniform Resource Identifier* (URI) that serves as a unique identifier for the namespace. Namespaces are declared in XML documents by using attributes that begin with *xmlns:*. The following is an XML document that includes the previous elements and uses namespaces to distinguish them (the *description* attributes and element content are omitted to make the example shorter):

```
<document xmlns:INSECTS="http://buglovers.org"
          xmlns:PROGRAMS="http://software">
   <INSECTS:bug name="Moth"/>
   <PROGRAMS:bug name="D10589"/>
</document>
```

This example includes two namespace declarations, one for insects and one for programs (computer programs). The two namespaces have namespace prefixes of INSECTS and PROGRAMS, and their URIs are *http://buglovers.org* and *http://software*, respectively. Each name for the *bug* XML elements includes the namespace prefix of the namespace for the element. A colon separates the namespace prefix from the rest of the name. A program can use the namespaces to differentiate insects from defects. The namespace declarations are available within the element in which they are declared and any contained elements. In the previous example, both namespaces are declared in the *document* XML element. You can also use namespaces to specify the context of XML attributes.

The namespace prefix can be the empty string in an XML document. This specifies the default namespace. To declare the default namespace, use an XML attribute named *xmlns*. The following example shows how to make the namespace that we defined previously for insects be the default namespace:

```
<document xmlns="http://buglovers.org">
   <bug name="Moth"/>
</document>
```

Since the *bug* XML element does not have a namespace prefix, and a default namespace is declared, it is in the default namespace.

You can use the namespace prefix of a namespace declared in an element in the tag name of that element, as the following XML element demonstrates:

```
<INSECTS:bug name="Moth" xmlns:INSECTS="http://buglovers.org"/>
```

XML Element Relationships

So far, the XML attributes in this chapter have been of type *CDATA* or namespace declarations. The original XML specification included about 10 types of attributes. Now, with XML schemas, there are a wide variety of types in addition to the original ones, as well as standard ways of defining new types based on the standard ones. The schema types include numeric datatypes, datatypes related to time and dates, and so on. They also include types that enable XML elements to be related to each other. Those types include three original ones, *ID*, *IDREF*, and *IDREFS*, and one new one, *anyURI*.

An XML element may have exactly one attribute of type *ID*; this attribute's value is an identifier that distinguishes the XML element from other XML elements in the same document. You can refer to an element by setting the value of an attribute of type *IDREF* to the value of the element's identifier. You can refer to multiple elements by setting the value of an attribute of type *IDREFS* to the values of the elements' identifiers, separated by one or more spaces. Consider the following elements:

```
<student id="S1"/>
<student id="S2"/>
<student id="S3"/>
<class name="Advanced Basket Weaving" students="S1 S2 S3"/>
<class name="Pizza Appreciation" students="S1"/>
```

The type of attribute *id* in each *student* element is *ID,* and the type of attribute *students* in each *class* element is *IDREFS.* It is valid to include only one identifier in an XML attribute of type *IDREFS,* as we have done for the second *class* element in the previous example. Three students are enrolled in the class *Advanced Basket Weaving,* and one student is enrolled in the class *Pizza Appreciation.* The attributes of type *ID* are named *id* in the previous example, but you may use any legal attribute name for attributes of type *ID.*

The values of attributes of type *ID* should be unique within a document; otherwise, it is not possible to determine which element is being referenced from other elements. The following example illustrates this:

```
<student name="Mary" id="S1"/>
<student name="Sue" id="S1"/>
<class name="Pizza Appreciation" students="S1"/>
```

Is Mary or Sue enrolled in the class?

The previous two examples showed how to use XML attributes of the *ID* and *IDREFS* types to refer to XML elements in the same document. Can an XML element refer to an XML element in another document? Yes. An entire XML specification, XLink (W3C, June 2001), is devoted to that topic. XLink enables simple and advanced techniques to be used to make cross-document references. At the time this book is being written, the Object Management Group (OMG) is deciding how to use XLinks in XMI. We describe cross-document references that are very similar to simple XLinks. Please see the final XMI 2.0 specification for a complete description of how to use XLinks with XMI; in the current XMI 2.0 specification, the use of XLinks is optional.

You use an XML attribute of type *anyURI* to specify a link from the XML element that has the attribute to an XML element in another document. You can also use an attribute of this type to link two elements in the same document. Imagine that some *student* XML elements are in an XML document called *students.xml*:

```
<student name="Mary" id="S1"/>
<student name="Sue" id="S2"/>
```

We can refer to the XML element representing Mary by using an attribute of type *anyURI*. We can specify that Mary is a student in the Pizza Appreciation class by putting the following XML elements in an XML document called *classes.xml*:

```
<class name="Pizza Appreciation">
   <student href="students.xml#S1"/>
</class>
```

The *href* attribute is of type *anyURI*. The first part of its value, the part before #, identifies the XML document where the *student* XML element is located, and the second part, the part after #, specifies the identifier of the XML element in that document. In this example, the first part is *students.xml*, the document containing the *student* XML elements, and the second part is *S1*, the identifier of the XML element representing Mary. Please refer to the schema datatype specification or the URI specification for more details about the valid values of XML attributes of type *anyURI*.

You can also use attributes of type *anyURI* to link two elements in the same XML document. For example, if the XML elements in *classes.xml* and *students.xml* are in the same document, you can specify the link from the *student* XML element inside the *class* XML element to the XML element representing Mary this way:

```
<student href="#S1"/>
```

Since no document is specified in the first part of the value of the *href* attribute, the second part contains the identifier of an XML element in the same document. In this case, the identifier is *S1*.

Document Type Definitions

Applications that work with XML data typically use an XML parser to read the contents of XML documents before working with the data. In the previous section, we showed an XML document that contained two XML elements with the same identifier. It would be convenient if the XML parser we use reported this error, so that our application doesn't need to include error-checking code for it. To detect this kind of error, a parser needs to know the types of the XML attributes. Document Type Definitions (DTDs) are one way to specify the types of attributes as well as the valid elements in an XML document and the valid content of those elements. Although schemas have superceded DTDs, we provide a brief description of DTDs to help you understand the material in Chapter 5 on reverse-engineering models from DTDs. If you are not interested in that topic, you can safely skip this section.

Any XML parser is capable of reporting some basic errors that occur in XML documents. For example, if an XML element has an end tag but no start tag, an XML parser will report the error. Other types of errors can only be detected if an XML parser processes a DTD (or schema) that defines an XML document. Parsers that process DTDs and schemas are called *validating parsers*. If an XML document has elements that match the element declarations in a DTD or schema, the document is said to be a valid document.

An element declaration in a DTD consists of the name of the element, the element's content, and the attributes of the element. The general format for an element declaration appears as follows:

```
<!ELEMENT name content>
<!ATTLIST name attribute-decls>
```

The *name* is the tag name, the *content* specifies what can be put inside the tags, and the *ATTLIST*, which is optional, contains attribute declarations (*attribute-decls*) for each attribute of the element.

The content in an element declaration can be *EMPTY* or *ANY*, indicating that the element must be empty or can contain any combination of text or other XML elements, respectively. Here are some examples:

```
<!ELEMENT mustBeEmpty EMPTY>
<!ELEMENT anythingGoes ANY>
```

You can also specify which elements and how many of them can be in the content. You put the names of the elements in the content of element declarations to identify which elements can be included in other elements. You can separate the element names with a comma (,), which means the elements must be in the order specified, or you can use a pipe (|), which means that you can choose which elements appear in the content. Here's an example:

```
<!ELEMENT A EMPTY >
<!ELEMENT B EMPTY >
<!ELEMENT C (A, B) >
<!ELEMENT D (A | B) >
```

Elements *A* and *B* are empty, element *C* contains one *A* element followed by one *B* element, and element *D* contains either one *A* element or one *B* element.

You indicate how many elements can appear in the content of other elements by using XML *multiplicities*. The explicit XML multiplicities are * for 0 or more, + for 1 or more, and ? for 0 or 1. As you can see from the previous example, if you do not specify a multiplicity, the multiplicity is 1. Here are some examples:

```
<!ELEMENT A EMPTY>
<!ELEMENT B (A) >
<!ELEMENT C (A*) >
<!ELEMENT D (A?) >
<!ELEMENT E (A+) >
```

Element *B* contains one *A* element, element *C* contains zero or more *A* elements, element *D* contains zero or one *A* element, and element *E* contains one or more *A* elements.

You can include *#PCDATA* in an element's content to indicate that text is allowed. For example:

```
<!ELEMENT text1 (#PCDATA)>
<!ELEMENT A EMPTY>
<!ELEMENT text2 (#PCDATA | A)* >
```

Element *text1* contains only text, no XML elements. Element *text2* contains any combination of text and *A* elements.

An attribute declaration has the general form:

```
name type default
```

The *name* is the name of the attribute. The values for *type* may be *CDATA*, a set of legal values, *ID*, *IDREF*, or *IDREFS*. You indicate a set of legal values like this:

```
(v1 | v2 | v3)
```

where *v1*, *v2*, and *v3* are the legal values.

The *default*, which is optional, is one of the following:

- #REQUIRED
- #IMPLIED
- #FIXED followed by an attribute value
- An attribute value

Here are some examples of attribute declarations:

```
<!ELEMENT e EMPTY>
<!ATTLIST e
      a1 CDATA "default"
      a2 (v1 | v2 | v3) #IMPLIED
      a3 ID #IMPLIED
      a4 IDREF #IMPLIED
      a5 IDREFS #IMPLIED
      a6 CDATA #FIXED "default"
   >
```

In these examples, attribute *a1* has type character data; a validating XML parser provides the value *default* for it if it does not appear in an XML element *e*. Attributes *a2* through *a5* are optional, and attribute *a6* must be present and must have the value *default*. The value of attribute *a2* must be *v1*, *v2*, or *v3*, if it is present.

You specify the DTD an XML parser uses to validate a document in a DOC-TYPE statement in the document to be validated. Here is the format of a DOC-TYPE statement:

```
<!DOCTYPE name SYSTEM "some.dtd">
```

The *name* is the tag name of the top-level element for the XML document, and *some.dtd* is a URI that specifies the location of the DTD.

You should now have an understanding of some of the basic concepts of DTDs. There are many more details about DTDs that are not covered here. Please consult the XML specification or a book about XML for more details.

Schemas

Schemas are an exciting new development for XML. Schemas replace DTDs, and they enable you to specify more constraints on XML documents than DTDs do. A schema document is an XML document, so you do not need to learn another syntax for specifying constraints. Although XML was originally very simple, schemas are much more complex. They are so complex, in fact, that the World Wide Web Consortium (W3C) has published a primer describing schemas in addition to the two specifications, *XML Schema Part 1: Structures* (W3C, 2001), and *XML Schema Part 2: Datatypes* (W3C, 2001).

There is no way to cover schemas completely in one chapter of a book, let alone part of a chapter. We describe only the aspects of schemas that are relevant to XMI 2.0. As you will see later in the book, XMI 2.0 produces XML schemas and enables you to tailor them in various ways. We describe the features of schemas that XMI uses and the features that you can tailor so you can more easily understand your options for using XMI to produce schemas. We do not attempt to describe all aspects of schemas, however.

Schema Elements

With those caveats, we can begin. Schemas are XML documents. There is a schema namespace that defines the context for the XML elements, and there are attributes that schemas use to declare XML elements and XML attributes. All schema documents have a *schema* XML element as the root XML element. Here is a schema document that does not contain any element or attribute declarations:

```
<xsd:schema xmlns:xsd="http://www.w3.org/2001/XMLSchema"/>
```

In the previous example, as in all examples in this section on schemas, we will use a namespace prefix of *xsd* for the schema namespace to make it clear which elements are defined by the schema specification. If we show parts of schemas, we will still use the *xsd* namespace prefix, although we may omit the *xsd:schema* element so you can focus on the schema construct we are introducing. You may use whatever namespace prefix you wish for the schema namespace in your own schemas.

Element and Type Declarations

You will probably not create too many empty schemas; you will create schemas that have element and type declarations. Each element declared in a schema uses the predefined XML element called *element*. The *name* attribute of that element is the name of the element. Here are some element declarations:

```
<xsd:element name="A"/>
<xsd:element name="B"/>
```

The first element has a name of *A*, and the second element has a name of *B*. XML elements that validate against these schema declarations will have tag names of *A* and *B*, respectively. Since you have not defined any content or attributes for either element, they must be empty and have no attributes. The order in which XML elements are declared in a schema need not match the order of the XML elements in the documents. You can specify an order for elements within the content of XML elements, as the next section describes.

Schemas enable you to declare types. The types themselves do not appear in XML documents, but they are used to declare elements and attributes that do appear in XML documents. There are two kinds of types in schemas, simple types and complex types. Simple types represent data values, whereas complex types represent data that has structure. You can specify the type of an element by using the *type* attribute for the *element* XML element. You declare a complex type by using a *complexType* XML element. The following example declares a complex type called *empty* and specifies that an element *C* is of that type:

```
<xsd:complexType name="empty"/>
<xsd:element name="C" type ="empty"/>
```

Element *C* must not have attributes or content, since none have been defined for it.

You can also declare a type when you declare an element. To do so, you put a *complexType* XML element inside an *element* XML element; the nested complex type is called an *anonymous type* because you do not specify a name for it. The previous declaration of *C* could be written using an anonymous type as follows:

```
<xsd:element name="C">
  <xsd:complexType/>
</xsd:element>
```

Element Content

You specify the content of an XML element by using XML elements in the content of the *complexType* element that defines the type of the XML element. Here is an example of how to specify that a complex type must have three elements, *D*, *E*, and *F*, inside it in that order:

```
<xsd:complexType name="orderedContent">
  <xsd:sequence>
    <xsd:element name="D"/>
    <xsd:element name="E"/>
    <xsd:element name="F"/>
  </xsd:sequence>
</xsd:complexType>
```

Now, if we want an element *G* to have this content, we can declare it as follows:

```
<xsd:element name="G" type="orderedContent"/>
```

In the declaration of the *orderedContent* type, the elements *D*, *E*, and *F* are declared inside the type. The declarations are local; they are not available to other types or element declarations in the same schema. If elements are declared directly in the *schema* element, you can refer to them in the declaration of types and elements in other places in the schema. You use the *ref* attribute of the *element* XML element to refer to an element declared in the schema.

Here is the previous example with the elements *D*, *E*, and *F* declared in the *schema* element and with references to those elements in the declaration of the complex type *orderedContent*:

```
<xsd:schema xmlns:xsd="http://www.w3.org/2001/XMLSchema">
  <xsd:element name="D"/>
  <xsd:element name="E"/>
  <xsd:element name="F"/>
  <xsd:complexType name="orderedContent">
    <xsd:sequence>
      <xsd:element ref="D"/>
      <xsd:element ref="E"/>
      <xsd:element ref="F"/>
    </xsd:sequence>
  </xsd:complexType>
</xsd:schema>
```

You can express alternatives in element content by using the *choice* XML element. If you use *choice*, you specify that one of the elements inside the *xsd:choice* element may appear in the element content. You can specify that multiple choices can be made from among the elements inside the *choice* element by using attributes to express multiplicities, which we explain later. Here is the declaration of a type called *choiceContent* that specifies that one of the elements *H*, *I*, or *J* may appear in the content of elements of type *choiceContent*:

```
<xsd:complexType name="choiceContent">
  <xsd:choice>
    <xsd:element name="H"/>
    <xsd:element name="I"/>
    <xsd:element name="J"/>
  </xsd:choice>
</xsd:complexType>
```

You can nest *sequence* and *choice* elements to express more complicated element content.

You use the *any* element in a *sequence* or *choice* XML element to express content that consists of any XML element that belongs to a namespace. You can specify whether to validate the content or not, depending on the value of the *processContents* attribute. For example, the following declaration of the complexType *anyContent* enables one XML element to appear in the content of XML elements of type *anyContent*, as long as the element is in a namespace:

```
<xsd:complexType name="anyContent">
  <xsd:sequence>
    <xsd:any/>
  </xsd:sequence>
</xsd:complexType>
```

The default value of the *processContents* attribute of the *any* XML element is *strict*, meaning that a validating parser attempts to validate the XML element in the content in the normal way. If there is no declaration for the element in the schema, the parser reports an error. If you set the value of *processContents* to *lax*, the parser will not report an error if the declaration of the XML element cannot be found. However, the parser will still report an error if there is a declaration and the element does not match it. If the value of *processContents* is *skip*, the parser will not attempt to validate the XML element. To specify empty content, you simply do not include a *sequence* or a *choice* element in the declaration of a complex type.

You can specify that content may include text as well as elements by setting the *mixed* attribute for the *complexType* element to *true*. For example, the following type *mixedContent* declares that there must be one element *K* in the content of elements of this type, but text can appear before or after element *K* in the content:

```
<xsd:complexType name="mixedContent" mixed="true">
  <xsd:sequence>
    <xsd:element name="K"/>
  </xsd:sequence>
</xsd:complexType>
```

So far, we have seen how to specify which elements appear in the content of other elements, but we have not seen how to specify how many elements should appear in the content. To specify the number of occurrences of elements in element content, use the *minOccurs* and *maxOccurs* attributes in the *element, sequence,* or *choice* XML elements. The *minOccurs* attribute contains the minimum number of occurrences that are allowed; the *maxOccurs* attribute contains the maximum number of occurrences that are allowed. The *maxOccurs* attribute can be set to a number or to *unbounded*, meaning that there is no restriction on the maximum number of elements that can occur. The default value of both of these attributes is *1*.

Here are some type declarations that demonstrate the use of the *minOccurs* and *maxOccurs* attributes. The following type *doubleContent* declares that the sequence of elements *L* and *M* must be in the content twice:

```
<xsd:complexType name="doubleContent">
  <xsd:sequence minOccurs="2" maxOccurs="2">
    <xsd:element name="L"/>
    <xsd:element name="M"/>
  </xsd:sequence>
</xsd:complexType>
```

Here is an example of an element with content that matches the declaration of *doubleContent*:

```
<someElement>
  <L/>
  <M/>
  <L/>
  <M/>
</someElement>
```

The following declaration of type *orderedContent2* constrains the content to be a sequence of one *N* element followed by two or more *O* elements:

```
<xsd:complexType name="orderedContent2">
  <xsd:sequence>
    <xsd:element name="N" minOccurs="1" maxOccurs="1"/>
    <xsd:element name="O" minOccurs="2" maxOccurs="unbounded"/>
  </xsd:sequence>
</xsd:complexType>
```

The following declaration of type *choiceContent2* constrains the content to be either three *P* elements or three *Q* elements:

```
<xsd:complexType name="choiceContent2">
  <xsd:choice>
    <xsd:element name="P" minOccurs="3" maxOccurs="3"/>
    <xsd:element name="Q" minOccurs="3" maxOccurs="3"/>
  </xsd:choice>
</xsd:complexType>
```

The following declaration of type *choiceContent3* constrains the content to be three elements; any combination of *R* and *S* elements may make up the three required elements:

```
<xsd:complexType name="choiceContent3">
  <xsd:choice minOccurs="3" maxOccurs="3">
    <xsd:element name="R"/>
    <xsd:element name="S"/>
  </xsd:choice>
</xsd:complexType>
```

Attribute Declarations

You can declare attributes as well as elements and element content in schemas. You use the *xsd:attribute* XML element to do so. That element has *name*, *type*, *use*, *default*, and *fixed* attributes that enable you to specify information about the attribute and its values. The *type* must be a simple type, not a complex type. The *use* attribute constrains whether or not an attribute may appear in an element. If the value of the *use* attribute is *required*, the attribute must appear. If *use* is *optional*, the attribute may appear. If *use* is *prohibited*, the attribute must not appear. An XML attribute can never appear more than once in an XML element.

If *use* is *optional*, you may specify a default value for the attribute that the parser will supply if an element does not have the attribute. If the attribute appears in an element, the actual value of the attribute is used, rather than the default one. You specify the default value of an attribute using the *default* XML attribute of the *attribute* XML element. You may also require that an attribute has a specific value by using the *fixed* XML attribute of the *attribute* XML element to hold the fixed value.

You specify attributes after you specify content in a complex type declaration. Here are some examples of attribute declarations:

```
<xsd:complexType name="someAttributesAndContent">
  <xsd:sequence>
    <xsd:element name="T"/>
  </xsd:sequence>
  <xsd:attribute name="a1" type="xsd:string"/>
  <xsd:attribute name="a2" type="xsd:string" use="required"/>
  <xsd:attribute name="a3" type="xsd:string" use="optional"
                 default="MyDefault"/>
  <xsd:attribute name="a4" type="xsd:string" fixed="FixedValue"/>
</xsd:complexType>
```

In this example there are four attribute declarations. All of the attributes have type *string*, which is one of the predefined schema datatypes. The *xsd* namespace prefix is used to identify predefined schema types, just as that prefix is used to identify the elements defined by schemas. Attribute *a1* is optional, because the default value of *use* is *optional*. Attribute *a2* must appear. Attribute *a3* is optional; if it does not appear, a validating parser will supply the value *MyDefault* for it. If it does appear, the parser will use the actual value that appears. Attribute *a4* is also optional; however, if it does appear, it must have the value *FixedValue*.

You use the *anyAttribute* element to indicate that any attribute can appear in an XML element. The *anyAttribute* element has a *processContents* attribute that is used in a similar way to the *processContents* attribute of the *any* element.

The following complex type declaration specifies that any XML element can appear in the content of an XML element of this type in a document, and the element in the document can have any XML attributes:

```
<xsd:complexType name="anyContent">
  <xsd:sequence>
    <xsd:any/>
  </xsd:sequence>
  <xsd:anyAttribute/>
</xsd:complexType>
```

Just like elements, you can declare attributes directly inside the *schema* element and then refer to the declarations in other places in the schema.

Attribute Groups

You can declare XML attributes in a group and then refer to that group in the declaration of complex types. This allows you to reuse groups of attribute declarations rather than refer to the declaration of each attribute. The *attributeGroup* XML element has a *name* attribute for the name of the group. You put attribute declarations inside the *attributeGroup* element.

Here is an example of an attribute group called *MyGroup* that declares attributes *a1* and *a2*. The attribute group is used to declare types *MyType1* and *MyType2*:

```
<xsd:attributeGroup name="MyGroup">
  <xsd:attribute name="a1" type="xsd:string"/>
  <xsd:attribute name="a2" type="xsd:string"/>
</xsd:attributeGroup>

<xsd:complexType name="MyType1">
  <attributeGroup ref="MyGroup"/>
</xsd:complexType>

<xsd:complexType name="MyType2">
  <attributeGroup ref="MyGroup"/>
</xsd:complexType>
```

Namespaces in Schemas

In the examples we have seen so far, we have not used namespaces except to identify the XML elements in a schema that belong to the schema namespace and to identify types that are predefined schema types. You can specify that the top-level elements, types, and attributes in a schema belong to a specific namespace by using the *targetNamespace* attribute of the *schema* XML element. You set the *targetNamespace* attribute to the URI of the namespace that top-level elements, types, and attributes belong to. When you specify a target namespace using the *targetNamespace* attribute, you also need to declare the target namespace for the schema so you can refer to the elements, types, and attributes at the top level using a namespace prefix. For example, consider the following schema:

```
<xsd:schema xmlns:xsd="http://www.w3.org/2001/XMLSchema"
            targetNamespace="http://myURI"
            xmlns:myStuff="http://myURI">
  <xsd:element name="U"/>
  <xsd:complexType name="MyType">
    <xsd:sequence>
      <xsd:element ref="myStuff:U"/>
      <xsd:element name="V"/>
    </xsd:sequence>
  </xsd:complexType>
  <xsd:element name="MyElement" type="myStuff:MyType"/>
</xsd:schema>
```

Notice that we used the namespace prefix *myStuff* to identify the element *U* in the content of *MyType*, and to identify the type of element *MyElement*. Since we specified a target namespace for the schema, without the namespace declaration for the target namespace we would not have been able to refer to them.

Here is a document that conforms to the previous schema. Note the use of the namespace URI and the presence or absence of namespace prefixes for the elements in the document:

```
<p:MyElement xmlns:p="http://myURI"
        xmlns:xsi="http://www.w3.org/2001/XMLSchema-instance"
        xsi:schemaLocation="http://myURI myURI.xsd">
  <p:U/>
  <V/>
</p:MyElement>
```

The namespace that has the prefix *xsi* is the schema instance namespace that is used in several ways in XML documents. One of the ways it is used is to specify a *schemaLocation* attribute that identifies where a schema for a particular namespace can be found. That attribute specifies pairs of URIs and schema documents; in this case, it specifies the URI *http://myURI* and the schema document *myURI.xsd*. The previous schema needs to be in a file called *myURI.xsd*. A parser may use this information to locate a schema, but is not required to do so.

Note that *MyElement* and *U* use the namespace prefix *p*, but element *V* does not. This is because the element *V* was declared locally, whereas the elements *MyElement* and *U* were declared at the top level. Note also that the namespace prefix *p* is used in the document, whereas the namespace prefix *myStuff* is used in the schema. This works because schemas use the namespace URI, not the prefix, to identify the namespace that is defined in a particular schema.

By default, locally declared elements and attributes must not use a namespace prefix. You can override this behavior by using the *form* attribute on *element* and *attribute* XML elements in a schema though. If *form* is set to *qualified*, the element or attribute must have a namespace prefix in a document. By default, *form* is set to *unqualified*, meaning that the element or attribute must not have a namespace prefix.

Type Extension

We have seen one way to reuse element and type declarations by referring to top-level elements and types in a schema. Another way to reuse types is to specify that a given type inherits the content and attributes from another type, possibly adding its own content and attributes. This capability is called *extension*. You use the *complexContent* and *extension* XML elements to specify that a complex type extends another complex type. Here is an example of a complex type, *MyExtension*, that extends another complex type *MyBase*:

```
<xsd:schema xmlns:xsd="http://www.w3.org/2001/XMLSchema">
  <xsd:complexType name="MyBase">
    <xsd:choice>
      <xsd:element name="Choice1"/>
      <xsd:element name="Choice2"/>
    </xsd:choice>
    <xsd:attribute name="baseAttrib" type="xsd:string"/>
  </xsd:complexType>

  <xsd:complexType name="MyExtension">
    <xsd:complexContent>
      <xsd:extension base="MyBase">
        <xsd:choice>
          <xsd:element name="ExtensionElement1"/>
          <xsd:element name="ExtensionElement2"/>
        </xsd:choice>
        <xsd:attribute name="extensionAttrib" type="xsd:string"/>
      </xsd:extension>
    </xsd:complexContent>
  </xsd:complexType>
</xsd:schema>
```

You should already understand the declaration of complex type *MyBase* from our previous explanations. Type *MyExtension* is declared to be an extension of *MyBase*, so it inherits the content of *MyBase* and the attributes from *MyBase*. It adds one of two XML elements to the content of *MyBase* and attribute *extensionAttrib*. Note that the declaration of *MyExtension* is equivalent to the following declaration:

```
<xsd:complexType name="MyExtension">
  <xsd:sequence>
    <xsd:choice>
      <xsd:element name="Choice1"/>
      <xsd:element name="Choice2"/>
    </xsd:choice>
    <xsd:choice>
      <xsd:element name="ExtensionElement1"/>
      <xsd:element name="ExtensionElement2"/>
    </xsd:choice>
  </xsd:sequence>
  <xsd:attribute name="baseAttrib" type="xsd:string"/>
  <xsd:attribute name="extensionAttrib" type="xsd:string"/>
</xsd:complexType>
```

The content from the extended type appears first, followed by the content declared locally. This means that in an element of type *MyExtension*, a *Choice1* or *Choice2* element must appear before an *ExtensionElement1* or *ExtensionElement2* element.

Schema Import

You can use XML elements, types, and attributes from other schemas when creating your own schemas. To do so, use the *import* XML element. This element enables you to specify which other schemas a particular schema depends on. The *import* XML element has a *namespace* attribute and its value is the URI of the target namespace of the schema being imported. You can also use the *schemaLocation* attribute to identify the file for the imported schema. XMI uses the import mechanism in the schemas it produces because there is a schema that defines XML elements and attributes pertaining to XMI, and schemas that XMI produces will import that schema to use the elements and attributes defined in it.

Mapping Data to XML

There is frequently more than one way to map your data to XML, so you must choose how to do it. If you are producing XML documents for your own use, it may not matter how you map your data to XML. However, if you plan to exchange XML documents, you need to ensure that all parties involved understand how the data to be exchanged is represented in the XML documents. For example, if your program puts some data in an XML attribute, but another program expects the data to be an XML element, the other program will not find the data. Two of the most common decisions you will need to make when considering how to put your data in an XML document are whether to use XML elements or XML attributes for your data and how to represent containment in XML.

For string values, you can use XML attributes to store them, or you can put them in the content of XML elements. For example, here are two ways to represent names of authors:

```
<author name="I. M. Geek"/>


<author>
    <name>I. M. Geek</name>
</author>
```

The first way is shorter than the second and may be easier for programs to process because standard interfaces to XML parsers, such as the Document Object Model (DOM) and Simple API for XML (SAX), enable you to access the attributes of an XML element before accessing the content. We explain DOM and SAX in Chapter 6. The second way may be desirable, though, if the data is not a simple string. For example, if it is important to split the name into its parts (first name, middle initial, and last name), you should probably put the name into XML either this way:

```
<author>
    <name firstName="I" middleInitial="M" lastName="Geek"/>
</author>
```

or this way:

```
<author>
    <name>
        <firstName>I</firstName>
        <middleInitial>M</middleInitial>
        <lastName>Geek</lastName>
    </name>
</author>
```

rather than parsing the value of a *name* attribute to get the parts of the name.

Representing containment is another issue you will face when mapping your data to XML. There are two basic approaches you can use. The first approach is to use the textual containment of XML elements to represent logical containment. This approach may be done in a couple of ways. The contained elements may be put directly in a container element, or they may be put in elements that indicate their relationship to their container element. As an example of the first way, if you want to indicate that a car contains an engine and a radio, you can represent it very simply in XML as follows:

```
<car>
   <engine/>
   <radio/>
</car>
```

As an example of the second way, if you also need to indicate that the engine is a critical part for the car (while the radio is not), you could represent it in XML in this way:

```
<car>
   <criticalPart>
      <engine/>
   </criticalPart>
   <noncriticalPart>
      <radio/>
   </noncriticalPart>
</car>
```

The second approach to representing containment uses attributes that have an *ID*, *IDREF*, or *IDREFS* type. With this approach, you indicate that an element contains another element by giving it an attribute with a value that is the same as the identifier of the contained element. For example, using this approach, you can represent the previous example in XML like this:

```
<engine id="E1"/>
<radio id="R1"/>
<car criticalPart="E1" noncriticalPart="R1"/>
```

In this example, the value of the *car* element's *criticalPart* attribute, *E1*, is the same as the value of the *engine* element's *id* attribute. This indicates that the engine is contained by the car. Similarly, the value of the car element's *noncriticalPart* attribute, *R1*, is the same as the value of the *radio* element's *id* attribute, indicating that the radio is also contained by the car.

Since there are at least three ways in XML to specify that a car contains an engine and a radio, you can see that it is important to agree not only on what data to exchange, but also how that data will be represented in XML. The mapping of data (in particular, object-oriented data) to XML is precisely the issue that XMI addresses.

UML

To use XMI, your data must be in objects or be mapped to objects. Most object-oriented systems implement the concepts of classes, instances, and inheritance, among others. Java implements all of these concepts, for example. These concepts are defined by object models, and UML is an example of such a model. Another object model, the Meta Object Facility (MOF), is the object model for XMI. Since UML and MOF are closely aligned, and the OMG is working to make them even more closely aligned in the future, you do not need to know about MOF to use XMI. UML models can be mapped to MOF models, so we use UML models in this book rather than MOF models.

The object-oriented concepts that are relevant to XMI are the concepts that describe the state of objects. Behavioral aspects of objects, such as their methods, are not part of an object's state, so it is not necessary to preserve them. For example, the state of a Java object is the value of its fields. UML defines the state of objects, too. UML also defines a graphical notation for UML models that is convenient for accurately defining your data.

An object's identity may be related to an object's state or it may be separate. XMI provides a standard mechanism for identifying objects, so you do not need to create your own means of specifying an object's identity in your models, although you may do so if you wish. Although you need to map your data to objects, you can represent the values of simple and complex datatypes using XMI.

Chapter 5 contains more information about the issues involved in defining your data using UML models; the remainder of this chapter presents the object-oriented concepts of Java and UML that you need to know to understand the rest of the book.

The Java Object Model

The Java Language Specification (Gosling, 2000) completely defines the Java object model, which consists of classes, objects (instances), inheritance, interfaces, and primitive types, among other things. Each of these concepts is also present in the UML object model, so we briefly consider how Java implements these concepts before discussing UML.

Java classes consist of fields, methods, and constructors. Fields are variables that have types. The types of fields are either primitive types such as *int*, *double*, or *char*, or reference types such as arrays, classes, and interfaces. Methods consist of a name, a return type, parameters, and a body. Java classes, fields, methods, and constructors have visibility modifiers as well, but they are not relevant to XMI so we won't cover them here.

Java supports single inheritance between classes. The members of a class consist of the locally declared members for the class as well as the inherited members. A Java class can implement more than one interface, even though it can only inherit from a single class.

Java classes can be grouped in packages. The qualified name of a class consists of the name of the package containing the class followed by a . and the name of the class. You can use qualified names to distinguish between two classes with the same names in different packages.

Java objects are instances of classes. When a class is instantiated, an instance variable is created in the instance for each of the nonstatic fields in the class. The instance variables hold the values that comprise the state of an object. You can invoke instance methods on an object if the visibility modifier of the method enables you to do so in a particular scope.

The UML Object Model

The Java language provides a definition of objects and classes; other programming languages have other definitions. An object model can be used to define objects independent of their implementation in a particular programming language. UML is an example of such an object model. It also provides a useful graphical notation for specifying object-oriented programming systems. UML defines many concepts, but only a few of the basic concepts that are related to the structure of classes and objects are relevant to XMI.

UML models can be implemented in programming languages. In this section, we include Java implementations of some simple UML models to help you understand UML concepts, and to help you understand the relationship between UML models and programming languages.

Only the parts of UML that are relevant to XMI are explained here. There are many excellent books that describe UML and how to use it if you want more information about UML and how to create models using it.

Table 2.1 lists the concepts in UML that are relevant to XMI and the corresponding Java concept, if there is one.

Many of the UML concepts correspond to Java language features, although UML has several concepts such as multiple inheritance and associations that

Table 2.1   UML and Java Comparison

UML CONCEPT	JAVA CONCEPT
Class	Class
Attribute	Field
Association	None
Association end	None
Single inheritance	Inheritance
Multiple inheritance	None
Instance	Instance
Package	Package
Datatype	Primitive type

are not part of the Java language. The UML concepts that are not in the Java language can be implemented in Java though.

In Java, a class consists of members; in UML, a class consists of features. The two kinds of features are *structural* and *behavioral*. One kind of structural feature is an attribute, which corresponds to a Java field. An attribute has a type and multiplicity. Like Java, UML classes and features have visibility modifiers, which are not relevant to XMI, so we do not explain them. The multiplicity of an attribute indicates the number of values for the attribute that an instance of the class can hold. The multiplicity can be a single number, such as *1*, or a range of numbers, such as *2..4*. More than one range of numbers can be used. The * symbol is used to represent unbounded. You can specify a multiplicity of 0 or more as *0..** or as *. Table 2.2 shows some examples of how multiplicities can be specified.

Consider a simple UML model that consists of one class, *C1*, that has an attribute *a* with a multiplicity of *0..**. The type of *a* is a primitive datatype, *integer*. This UML class can be implemented in Java as follows:

```
public class C1 {
  int a[];
}
```

The attribute can also be implemented using one of the collection classes in the *java.util* package:

```
import java.util.*;

public class C1 {
  Collection a;
}
```

This implementation of the class requires that each *int* value be represented by an instance of the Java *Integer* class, since the values of primitive types cannot be added to collections in Java.

Table 2.2   Multiplicity Examples

MULTIPLICITY	MEANING
1	Exactly 1
1..1	Exactly 1
0..*	0 or more
*	0 or more
0..1	0 or 1
1..4, 7..10	1 to 4 or 7 to 10

There are several behavioral features of UML classes, such as operations and methods. However, since they are not relevant to XMI, we do not explain them. Does this mean that XMI cannot be used to save all parts of UML models? No, when a UML model is saved, all parts of the UML model, including any behavioral features of classes, are saved. However, when saving an instance of a UML class, the state of the instance consists of the values of the instance's structural features, not the behavioral features, so only the values of the structural features need to be saved.

A class is represented by a rectangle in UML notation. The rectangle may have three sections: The top section contains the name of the class, the middle section contains the attributes, and the bottom section contains the operations. Not all of these sections need to be displayed in a class diagram. Figure 2.1 illustrates three representations of the same class C, with attributes *a1* and *a2* and operation *o*. Attribute *a1* has a multiplicity of *0..** and type *int*. Attribute *a2* has a multiplicity of *1* and type *float*. The multiplicities and types for the attributes are displayed in the representation on the right in Figure 2.1.

In this book, we often need to make the distinction between a UML attribute that has a type that is a datatype and a UML attribute that has a type that is a class (we explain UML datatypes later). We call a UML attribute with a type that is a datatype a *data attribute*. We call a UML attribute with a type that is a class an *object attribute*. The value of a data attribute is a *data value*. The value of an object attribute is an *object value*.

There is an important difference between an object attribute in UML and a field in Java with a type that is a class. The value of an object attribute in UML has a *composition* relationship to the object that has the value. A composition relationship is a container-part relationship where the part is deleted if the container is deleted, and a part can be in only one container. This means that an object can be the value of only one object attribute in an object. In contrast, a Java field does not have composition semantics, so a Java object can be the value of more than one field.

Consider two UML classes, *F* and *G*, where class *F* has an attribute *attrib* of type *G* and a multiplicity of *1*. They are displayed in Figure 2.2. An implementation of these classes in Java is:

```
// F.java
public class F {
    public G attrib;
```

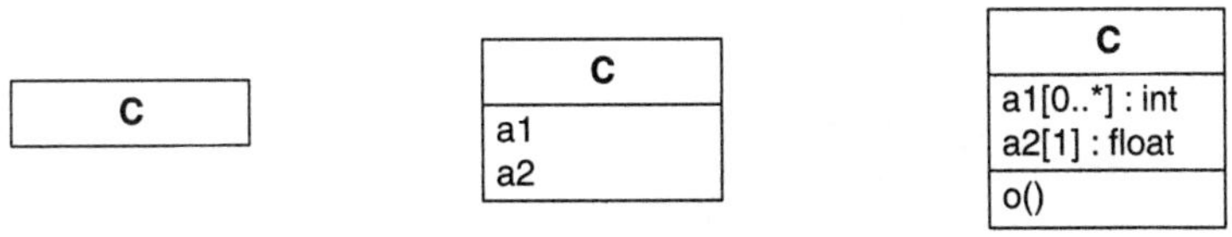

Figure 2.1   UML class notation.

```
}

// G.java
public class G{}
```

It is legal in Java for an instance of *G* to be the value of the *attrib* field for two instances of *F*, as follows:

```
F f1 = new F();
F f2 = new F();
G g = new G();
f1.attrib = g;
f2.attrib = g;
```

However, this violates the composition semantics of object attributes in UML. Because of these semantics, the values of *f1.attrib* and *f2.attrib* cannot both be *g*. The value *g* can only be related to the one instance of *F* that has the value by a composition relationship. The instance of *F* is the container and *g* is the part. The part *g* can only have one container, not two. So, it is illegal for it to be the value of *attrib* for both *f1* and *f2*, because then *g* would have two containers, *f1* and *f2*. Object *g* can be the value of *attrib* in *f1* or *f2*, but not both. The container can change, however. You can set *g* to the value of *attrib* in *f1*, set the value of *attrib* in *f1* to *null*, and then set *g* to the value of *attrib* in *f2*.

UML classes can have one or more superclasses. Each UML class inherits features from its superclasses. Inheritance in UML is represented by arrows between classes. The arrow points from the subclass to the superclass. Figure 2.3 illustrates this notation in a class diagram that specifies that classes *A* and *B* are superclasses of class *C2*.

If you want to implement this model in Java, you need to simulate multiple inheritance. One way to do so is to create an interface for each class and an implementation for each interface. Here is one implementation of this model:

```
// A.java
public interface A {}

// AImpl.java
public class AImpl implements A {}

// B.java
```

F
attrib[1] : G

G

Figure 2.2   Classes F and G.

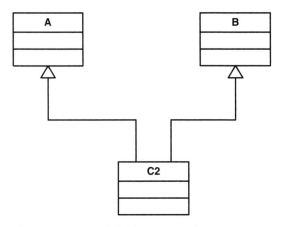

Figure 2.3 UML inheritance notation.

```
public interface B {}

// BImpl.java
public class BImpl implements B {}

// C2.java
public interface C2 extends A, B {}

// C2Impl.java
public class C2Impl implements C2 {}
```

Each UML class has an interface and a Java class that implements the interface. For class *C2*, its implementation, class *C2Impl*, implements the interface for *C2*, which extends the interfaces for *A* and *B*. By doing this, an instance of the *C2Impl* class acts like an instance of *A* and an instance of *B*, although it does not inherit from any class. There are other ways to implement the model in Java as well, but this example demonstrates that multiple inheritance can be simulated in Java when classes implement multiple interfaces.

UML has packages, just like Java, that may contain classes. Packages are represented in UML notation by folders, as demonstrated in Figure 2.4, which contains package *P*.

One relationship between classes is inheritance, which we have already explained. Other relationships between classes can be explicitly represented in UML using associations. Associations in UML are not directly connected to classes; they have association ends that are connected to classes. An association end has a name and *multiplicity*, *navigability*, and *aggregation properties*. The multiplicity of an association end is specified the same way as the multiplicity of an attribute. You can think of navigability as characterizing whether an association end provides the capability of one class to reach, or *navigate* to, the

Figure 2.4   UML package notation.

other class participating in the association. If both ends of the association are navigable, the association appears as a straight line between the two classes. If only one end of the association is navigable, then the navigable end is distinguished with an arrow. The aggregation property is used to indicate no aggregation, aggregation, or composition. We explain aggregation and composition later.

Figure 2.5 includes an association between two classes, *D* and *E*, with ends that are named *r1* and *r2*; *r1* has a multiplicity of *1* and *r2* has a multiplicity of *0..**.

Because of the way that an association end is used, it is scoped *not* by the class that it appears adjacent to in the class diagram, but by the class it appears across from. For example, in Figure 2.5, the end *r1* is in the namespace of class *E*, while the end *r2* is in the namespace of class *D*. Figure 2.6 contains a diagram of the same association displayed in Figure 2.5, except that only *r2* is navigable. Since only *r2* is navigable, it is distinguished by an arrow.

In this case, *r2* is in the namespace of *D*, but *r1* is not in the namespace of *E*, since *r1* is not navigable.

There are many ways to represent associations using Java. Consider the UML diagram in Figure 2.5. A simple way to implement this model in Java is as follows:

```
// D.java
public class D {
  public E[] r2;
}

// E.java
public class E {
  public D r1;
}
```

Since the multiplicity for the association end *r1* is *1*, we can implement it using a field of type *D* in class *E*. Since the multiplicity for the association end *r2* is *0..**, we can implement it using a field of type *E[]* in class *D*. Of course, we probably want the fields to be private or protected and to implement accessor methods on classes *D* and *E* to access the values of *r1* and *r2*, but this simple example demonstrates a direct way to represent associations in Java.

Figure 2.5 UML association notation.

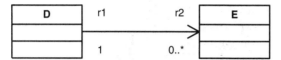

Figure 2.6 UML unidirectional association notation.

In the previous example, instances of class *D* have references to instances of class *E* and vice versa. It is not a requirement that this be the case, however. The model indicates that, given an instance of class *D*, the *r2* end can be used to obtain instances of class *E* and, given an instance of class *E*, the *r1* end can be used to obtain an instance of class *D*. We can also implement the model so that class *D* has no knowledge of class *E* and vice versa, with a third class managing the relationships between instances of *D* and instances of *E*:

```
//D.java
public class D {}

// E.java
public class E {}

// AssociationManager.java
import java.util.HashMap;

public class AssociationManager {
  // key is instance of D, value is array of E
  private HashMap r2;

  // key is instance of E, value is instance of D
  private HashMap r1;

  public AssociationManager() {
    r2 = new HashMap();
    r1 = new HashMap();
  }

  public E[] getR2(D d) { (E[]) return r2.get(d); }
  public D   getR1(E e) { (D) return r1.get(e); }

  public void setR2(D d, E[] e) { r2.put(d, e); }
```

```
    public void setR1(E e, D d)    { r1.put(e, d); }
}
```

In this implementation, the *AssociationManager* class handles the relationship between instances of *D* and instances of *E*. This particular class is very simple, but you can easily imagine many enhancements that can be made to it to extend its capability.

Aggregation indicates a container-part relationship. A part can be in more than one container, and there is no relationship between the life of the part and the life of the container. An aggregation relationship is represented by a clear diamond at the end of the association connected to the container. Figure 2.7 shows that a container has parts. XMI treats an aggregation relationship the same way it treats the relationships in Figures 2.5 and 2.6.

A stronger containment relationship is called *composition*, which indicates that if the container is deleted, the parts are deleted also, and a part can have only one container. This type of relationship is indicated by a solid diamond at the container end, as you can see in Figure 2.8.

Another way to represent composition in UML is by using object attributes, as we discussed earlier in this chapter. In this book, we almost always represent composition using object attributes (the only exception is a model in Chapter 4); we do not use the notation in Figure 2.8. We do this to simplify our discussion of XMI. In your models, you can represent composition either way. Because we use object attributes to represent composition when we discuss association ends in this book, the association ends do not have *aggregation* properties with a value of *composition*.

Figure 2.7   UML aggregation notation.

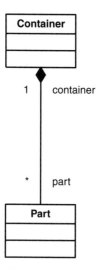

Figure 2.8 UML composition notation.

Figure 2.9 shows a model that is semantically equivalent to the model in Figure 2.8. Class *Container* in Figure 2.9 has an object attribute called *part*.

In Java, you do not explictly control the deletion of objects; the Java garbage collector deletes objects for you. However, you can implement composition in Java by marking part objects as deleted when the container object is deleted. To employ this strategy, you need to implement a delete method for both the container and the part. Source Code 2.1 contains a simple implementation of the UML model in Figure 2.8 (or Figure 2.9).

Using these classes, you can detect whether a container or part is deleted and avoid handling containers or parts that have been deleted. Notice that if a part is added to a container and then removed from it, and the container is deleted, the part is not deleted since it does not belong to the container anymore.

There is one final UML concept that pertains to classes and their parts that is used by XMI. It is called a *tagged value*. A tagged value consists of a tag and a value, and it can be used to specify additional properties for UML constructs. For example, you can specify that an *implementationLanguage* tag for a class has the value *Java*, meaning that the UML class is implemented in Java. XMI uses tagged values to enable you to specify how to tailor XML schemas that are produced from models.

UML contains the concept of an object as well as a class. A UML object is an instance of a UML class. UML objects have *attribute values* and *link ends*, which are instances of association ends.

Objects can be illustrated in UML object diagrams. Each object is represented by a rectangle. The name of the object and the name of the class can be included in the object. Figure 2.10 shows an object diagram representing an object called *obj1* that is an instance of a class *F*.

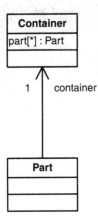

Figure 2.9   UML attribute representing composition.

Figure 2.10   A simple object diagram.

If an object has attribute values, they can be displayed as well. For example, if the same object in Figure 2.10 has two attributes, *a1* and *a2*, and they have values *string* and *2*, respectively, the diagram in Figure 2.11 displays their values.

If two classes have an association between them, instances of the classes can have *links* between them. A link is an instance of an association, and links have *link ends*. In this book, we use the term *reference* for a link end. For example, Figure 2.5 indicates that an instance of class *E* can access one instance of class *D* through its *r1* reference. Similarly, instances of *D* can access zero or more instances of class *E* through their *r2* references.

Links between objects can be shown in an object diagram. Each link is represented by a line between two objects. The names of the references for the link can be shown. Consider three objects, *d1*, *e1*, and *e2*. Object *d1* is an instance of class *D* from Figure 2.5, and *e1* and *e2* are instances of class *E* from Figure 2.5. Objects *e1* and *e2* are related to *d1* via its *r2* references, and *d1* is related to *e1* and *e2* through their *r1* references. This situation is illustrated in the object diagram in Figure 2.12.

So far, we have discussed classes and instances of classes. UML also has a concept very similar to a Java primitive type called a *datatype*. Attributes of classes in UML can have types that are either classes or datatypes. A datatype can be represented in UML notation as a class with a *<<datatype>> stereotype*.

```
// Container.java
import java.util.*;

public class Container {
  private Collection parts;
  private boolean deleted;

  public Container() { parts = new ArrayList(); }

  public void addPart(Part p) { parts.add(p); }
  public void removePart(Part p) { parts.remove(p); }
  public boolean isDeleted() { return deleted; }

  public void delete() {
    deleted = true;
    Iterator p = parts.iterator();

    while(p.hasNext())
      ((Part) p.next()).delete();

    parts = new ArrayList();
  }
}

// Part.java
public class Part {
  private boolean deleted;

  public void delete() { deleted = true; }
  boolean isDeleted()  { return deleted; }
}
```

Source Code 2.1   A simple implementation of *Container* and *Part*.

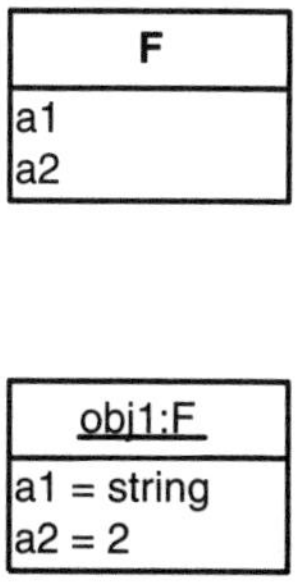

F
a1
a2

obj1:F
a1 = string
a2 = 2

Figure 2.11   Attribute values.

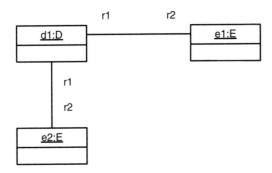

Figure 2.12   Object links.

Figure 2.13   UML datatype notation.

In UML, you can use stereotypes to extend UML with your own constructs, if you wish. Stereotypes also enable you to use the UML notation for a given construct, such as a UML class, to represent another construct. By using a stereotype for a UML class in a UML diagram, you indicate that the construct is actually not a class, but another type of construct. For example, the class diagram in Figure 2.13 contains an *Integer* datatype.

How do you represent this datatype using Java? A natural way to do so is to use the Java *int* primitive type; however, the definition of *Integer* in the diagram may not exactly match the definition of a Java *int*. In general, it is not possible to unambiguously map from arbitrary datatypes in a UML model to concrete datatypes in an implementation of the model. Part of the task of implementing a model is to map the datatypes in the model to the datatypes that are available in the environment in which the model is implemented.

You can also specify *enumerations* in UML; an enumeration is a datatype with a legal value that is restricted to a set of values. To indicate an enumeration, use the enumeration stereotype for a class and add an attribute to the class for each legal value, where the name of the attribute matches the legal value. For example, Figure 2.14 contains a UML diagram for a *Boolean* enumeration that has legal values of *true* and *false*.

Although this particular enumeration maps to a Java *boolean* primitive type, Java does not provide direct support for arbitrary enumerations. Consider an enumeration with the legal values of *v1*, *v2*, and *v3*. This enumeration is the type of an attribute *a* in class *C3*. This model can be implemented in Java as follows:

Figure 2.14 UML enumeration notation.

```
// C3.java
public class C3 {
   private String a;

   public String getA() { return a; }
   public void setA(String value) {
      if (value == null || (!value.equals("v1") && !value.equals("v2")
                        && !value.equals("v3")))
         throw new IllegalArgumentException(value);
      a = value;
   }
}
```

There are other ways to implement this model in Java as well.

Chapter 5 contains suggestions for handling datatypes when you define your objects using UML.

This concludes our tour of the parts of UML that are relevant to XMI. Although there are many concepts in UML, you can see that only a few of them are relevant to XMI, so you do not need to be a UML expert to use XMI.

Object Identity

Regardless of the object model that defines what objects are, object identity is an important concept in many object-oriented applications. An object's identity may depend on an object's state or be independent of it.

Consider how Java handles object identity. Two objects are considered equal using the == operator if the objects are the same object. For example, for a class C, the following lines of Java print *obj1 is equal to obj2*:

```
C obj1 = new C();
C obj2 = obj1;
if (obj1 == obj2)
   System.out.println("obj1 is equal to obj2");
```

This handling of objects is not sufficient for any program that saves objects and restores them, because the restored objects will not be the exact objects that were saved. Instead, they will be copies of them. The state of the restored objects should equal the state of the original objects, even though they are different objects.

Java enables you to specify equality for your objects by implementing the *equals()* method in your classes; its signature is *boolean equals(Object object)*. You can specify that two objects are equal according to the state of the objects. For example, consider a Java class *C* that has two fields, a *String* and an *int*. You can define an *equals()* method for the class that returns *true* if two objects are instances of *C*, and they have the same values for their fields, as follows:

```
public class C {
    private int number;
    private String string;

    public int getNumber() { return number; }
    public String getString() { return string; }

    public void setNumber(int value) { number = value; }
    public void setString(String value) { string = value; }

    public boolean equals(Object object) {
        if (!(object instanceof C))
           return false;
        C obj = ( C ) object;
        return number == obj.number && string.equals(obj.string);
    }
}
```

Given this declaration of class C, the following lines of code print *obj1 equals obj2*:

```
C obj1 = new C();
obj1.setNumber(5);
obj1.setString("s");
C obj2 = new C();
obj2.setNumber(5);
obj2.setString("s");
if (obj1.equals(obj2))
    System.out.println("obj1 equals obj2");
```

In this program, although *obj1* is not the same object as *obj2*, it is equal to *obj2* because its state matches the state of *obj2*. In other contexts, though, it may be expensive to compare the entire state of two objects to determine whether they are equal. It may be possible to distinguish objects based on a subset of their states. For example, for a *Person* class, it may only be necessary to compare two persons' Social Security numbers to determine whether they are the same person, rather than comparing all of the other fields of the *Person* ojects.

As you will see in Chapter 3, XMI uses strings to identify objects, rather than using the entire state of each object. Please see Chapter 3 for more details about how to identify objects using XMI.

Summary

This chapter has discussed two standards that are related to XMI: XML and UML. You have learned some of the basic concepts in both standards that are most relevant to XMI. You saw how to represent data in XML elements and attributes, and how to write schemas that define the legal content of XML elements and the values of XML attributes. You also know the basic constructs of the UML object model that define the state of objects, and you saw that you can use Java to implement UML models. Now that you are familiar with XML and UML, you are ready to learn details about how XMI represents objects in XML.

XMI Concepts

Now that you know the basic concepts of the Extensible Markup Language (XML) and the Unified Modeling Language (UML), you are ready to begin learning the core concepts of XML Metadata Interchange (XMI) itself. We explain the latest version of XMI, XMI 2.0, in this chapter. The Object Management Group (OMG) is currently finalizing XMI 2.0 as we write this book, so there may be some differences between the final specification of XMI 2.0 and the current specification (OMG, 2001). Also, in some cases, we believe there are errors in the current specification that will be fixed in the final specification. We describe in this chapter what we believe XMI 2.0 will be when the final specification is approved by the OMG. We note differences between this chapter and the current specification as we explain XMI.

This chapter explains how XMI works with the UML object model we explained in Chapter 2, and it also describes the XML elements and XML attributes that XMI defines. Before explaining XMI itself, though, we define the terminology we use in this chapter and the rest of the book. The terminology enables us to succinctly refer to parts of the UML object model. We also describe how we represent UML composition in this book. UML enables you to represent composition in two ways; by using only one way in this book, we simplify our discussion of XMI.

After explaining our terminology, this chapter describes the following aspects of XMI:

- Writing objects and their parts using XMI

- Generating schemas from models and how to tailor the schemas XMI creates

- Defining XMI XML elements and attributes using the XMI model

We explain XMI by focusing our discussion on one part of the UML object model at a time. For example, we describe how to write objects using XMI by first describing how to write objects that have no attribute values and no references, then by describing how to write attribute values, and then by discussing how to write references. Similarly, we discuss how to generate schemas for classes with no attributes or association ends; then we discuss how attributes are represented in schemas and we look at association ends. This approach enables us to focus on the issues that pertain to a specific part of the object model, rather than attempt to discuss many issues at the same time.

After we discuss how to generate a schema from a model, we define some XML elements and XML attributes used by XMI in a model, and then derive the corresponding schema from it. We also explain any XMI elements and attributes that we have not yet explained.

As mentioned in the introduction, we describe XMI in terms of the UML object model rather than the Meta Object Facility (MOF) object model, the one used by the XMI specification. We do so for the following reasons:

- UML 2.0 and MOF 2.0 will be closely aligned because the OMG is working to eliminate the differences between the class-modeling capabilities of UML and MOF.

- Since we expect UML and MOF to be closely aligned, we expect that UML models can be transformed into MOF models very easily. Although an MOF model is at a higher level of abstraction than a corresponding UML model, that difference does not matter unless you are writing an application that needs to work with data at different levels of abstraction, such as an MOF repository. We expect that many applications work with data at one level of abstraction that is defined by a model. In these applications, multiple levels of abstraction are not used.

- We believe that more people are familiar with UML than with MOF.

UML Terminology and Use

We define several terms that enable us to refer to parts of the UML object model. Also, we explain our choice for representing UML composition. This simplifies our discussion of XMI. We are not redefining UML; we are simply defining terms to make the discussion of XMI easier to understand.

Classes have attributes and association ends. Using our terminology, there are two kinds of attributes. A *data attribute* is a UML attribute that has a UML datatype as its type. An *object attribute* is a UML attribute that has a class as its type. Each attribute has a corresponding value in an object. A *data value* is the value of a data attribute, and an *object value* is the value of an object attribute. An object value represents UML composition; the object value is contained in the object that has the value, and if the object that has the value is deleted, so is the object value. Because of the composition semantics, only one object has an object value; an object value cannot belong to two objects.

Consider the class diagram in Figure 3.1. The *Car* class has a *part* object attribute and its type is the *Part* class. A *Part* object can be a value (an object value in this case) of the *part* attribute in a particular *Car* object. If the *Car* object is deleted, the *Part* object is deleted also, because of the composition semantics of object attributes and object values. Also, if a *Part* object, *Part1*, is a value of the *part* attribute in a *Car* object, *Part1* cannot be the value of the *part* attribute in any other *Car* objects.

We use the term *reference* for an instance of an association end. A reference represents a relationship between two objects, the object that has the reference and another object, which we call the *referenced object*. The relationship does not represent composition.

In this book, we always use object attributes to represent composition; we do not use associations to do so. We do this merely to simplify the discussion of XMI; in your models, you can use either attributes or associations to represent composition. The choice of how to represent composition in a UML model does not affect how XMI handles composition.

To summarize this discussion, classes have attributes and association ends. Each attribute is either a data attribute or an object attribute. Because we do not use associations to represent composition, the association ends in this book do not have composition semantics. Objects have attribute values and references. Each value is either a data value or an object value. An object value represents a composition relationship between the object that has the value and the object that is the value. A reference is a relationship between the object that has the reference and the referenced object; there are no composition semantics for this relationship.

Figure 3.1 The *Car* class with a *part* object attribute.

Writing Objects Using XMI

This section explains how to write objects and their parts using XMI. We start by explaining how to write objects that have no attribute values or references, focusing on where to put the objects in XML documents and the XML attributes that XMI defines to identify objects. We also introduce the *XMI* XML element, which can be used to hold objects. Then we discuss how to write attribute values and references, and how to refer to objects in different documents. We end this section by explaining how to write additional information with objects, information that is not in attribute values or references. After reading this section, you should be able to write objects in XML using XMI, and you should be able to read XMI documents and understand the objects that are saved in them.

Objects

The simplest objects to write are objects that do not have any attribute values or references. Furthermore, they are not object values themselves. We discuss objects that are object values later.

XMI specifies two alternatives for writing such objects. You can put them in XML documents, where all the XML elements in the document comply with the XMI specification, or you can write them inside any XML element. In the latter case, you could have a single XML document that contains XML elements that are not related to the XMI specification as well as objects serialized using XMI.

In both cases, you need to use the XMI namespace, which is the context for all the XML elements and attributes defined by the XMI specification. The namespace Uniform Resource Identifier (URI) is *http://www.omg.org/XMI*. For the examples in this chapter, we use the namespace prefix *xmi* for this namespace, but you can use any namespace prefix you wish in your documents.

XMI Documents

Because XMI documents are XML documents, you should put the XML processing instruction at the beginning of them. The processing instruction includes the version of XML and identifies the encoding of the characters in the document. We always use *UTF-8* encoding in this book. The XML processing instruction is:

```
<?xml version="1.0" encoding="UTF-8"?>
```

If the encoding is *UTF-8*, the processing instruction is not required in an XML document. We sometimes do not include it in our examples. However, it is probably best to include it in your XMI documents even if it is not required, since the XML specification [World Wide Web Consortium (W3C), 2001] says that you should include it.

One way to write your objects in XMI is to put your objects in an *XMI* XML element that is the root element for an XML document. The *XMI* XML element has an XML attribute called *version* that must have the value *2.0*, and that attribute must use the namespace prefix for the XMI namespace. Here is an empty XMI document:

```
<xmi:XMI xmi:version="2.0" xmlns:xmi="http://www.omg.org/XMI"/>
```

XMI represents each object using an XML element. The tag name of the element corresponds to the name of the class that the object is an instance of. You may use XML namespaces to distinguish classes with the same names. Since your class name may not be a legal XML tag name, you may need to convert from the class name to a legal XML tag name.

Here is how an object that is an instance of a *Car* class can be represented in XMI:

```
<xmi:XMI xmi:version="2.0" xmlns:xmi="http://www.omg.org/XMI">
  <Car/>
</xmi:XMI>
```

You specify the XML namespaces to use with your objects in models, as described in the *Generating Schemas from Models* section of this chapter. You provide the namespace URI for an XML namespace when you specify an XML namespace in a model, so you must choose a namespace prefix to use with that namespace in a particular XMI document. You can choose a different prefix for different documents if you wish. For example, if an XML namespace with a URI of *http://cars* is specified for the *Car* class, you can choose to use a namespace prefix of *cars* for that namespace in an XMI document. Here is an XMI document that uses that namespace:

```
<xmi:XMI xmi:version="2.0" xmlns:xmi="http://www.omg.org/XMI"
                       xmlns:cars="http://cars">
  <cars:Car/>
</xmi:XMI>
```

In UML, like Java, the fully qualified name of a class consists of the name of the class and the name of the package that contains it, along with the packages that contain that package. For example, the class name *p1.p2.Car* is the fully qualified name for a *Car* class that is in package *p2*, where *p2* is contained in package *p1*. You can use the fully qualified names of classes to distinguish two classes with the same name. Class *p1.p2.Car* is different than class *p3.Car*, for example.

If you do not use namespaces, you need to use the fully qualified names of classes to distinguish XML elements corresponding to instances of classes with the same name. This technique may result in very large documents that are rather difficult to read. You should use XML namespaces to distinguish them instead, because the resulting documents are shorter and easier to read. In fact, you should probably provide XML namespaces for your models even if all the class names are unique, so you can put objects defined by different models in the same XMI document without causing name collisions.

For the classes *p1.p2.Car* and *p3.Car*, if you specify a namespace for each class, you can use those namespaces in the tag names of XML elements in an XMI document, rather than using the fully qualified names. If the namespace for the first *Car* class has a URI of *http://car1*, you may decide to use the prefix *car1* for that namespace. If the namespace for the second *Car* class has a URI of *http://car2*, you may decide to use a prefix of *car2* for that namespace. Then an instance of both classes can be written to an XMI document as follows:

```
<xmi:XMI xmi:version="2.0" xmlns:xmi="http://www.omg.org/XMI"
                           xmlns:car1="http://car1"
                           xmlns:car2="http://car2">
  <car1:Car/>
  <car2:Car/>
</xmi:XMI>
```

The first *Car* object is an instance of the class *p1.p2.Car* since the namespace for the *Car* XML element is the namespace for class *p1.p2.Car*. The second *Car* object is an instance of *p3.Car* since its namespace is the namespace for class *p3.Car*.

The *XMI* XML element need not be used if there is only one object at the top level. You can use the *version* XML attribute defined by XMI in the XML element for an object to indicate that the object was serialized using XMI. The following is a legal XMI document with one instance of a *Car* class:

```
<Car xmi:version="2.0" xmlns:xmi="http://www.omg.org/XMI"/>
```

When there is only one object at the top level in the document, you do not need to put that object in an *XMI* XML element, but you may do so if you wish.

XML Documents

You saw in the previous section how the root element of an XMI document is either the *XMI* XML element or an XML element that is an object serialized using XMI. However, these elements do not need to be the root element of a document; you can put them inside other XML elements. This enables you to use XMI with other standards that use XML. You can use XMI to serialize objects in the body of a Simple Object Access Protocol (SOAP) document, for instance.

Here is an example of serializing an instance of a *Car* class inside an *XMI* XML element that is inside another XML element:

```
<containerElement>
  <xmi:XMI xmi:version="2.0" xmlns:xmi="http://www.omg.org/XMI">
    <Car/>
  </xmi:XMI>
  <moreContent/>
</containerElement>
```

Here the same *Car* object is serialized without using an *XMI* XML element. Instead, the *version* XML attribute defined by XMI is placed inside the *Car* element:

```
<containerElement>
  <Car xmi:version="2.0" xmlns:xmi="http://www.omg.org/XMI"/>
  <moreContent/>
</containerElement>
```

You can serialize multiple objects without using an *XMI* XML element if you wish:

```
<containerElement>
  <Car xmi:version="2.0" xmlns:xmi="http://www.omg.org/XMI"/>
  <Car xmi:version="2.0" xmlns:xmi="http://www.omg.org/XMI"/>
  <moreContent/>
</containerElement>
```

To avoid declaring the XMI namespace multiple times, it is more convenient to declare the XMI namespace once in an XML element that contains the XML elements corresponding to the objects, as follows:

```
<containerElement xmlns:xmi="http://www.omg.org/XMI">
  <Car xmi:version="2.0"/>
  <Car xmi:version="2.0"/>
  <moreContent/>
</containerElement>
```

In the previous two examples, you can put any XML elements you wish between the two *Car* XML elements, before them, and after them.

Object Identity

As you saw from the discussion of object identity in Chapter 2, the state of an object consists of its attribute values and references. Two objects with the same state are considered identical. XMI enables you to specify the identity of an object with three XML attributes defined by XMI, rather than using the object's state. Each attribute has different semantics.

The *id* XML attribute has the type *ID*, so its value must be a legal identifier for an XML element. The value of the *id* attribute must be unique within a document, but is not guaranteed to be unique among documents. It is used to specify relationships among objects, as we explain in the following *References* section. XMI enables you to specify another name for this attribute, as we explain in the *Generating Schemas from Models* section later in this chapter.

The *uuid* XML attribute must contain a globally unique identifier; it needs to be unique among all objects regardless of the documents they are saved in. The name *uuid* is an abbreviation for *universally unique identifier*. XMI does not specify the format for the *uuid*, so you can use any algorithm you wish to generate its value. The Distributed Computing Environment (DCE) specification describes an algorithm for generating globally unique identifiers, for example.

The *label* XML attribute contains any other piece of information that you wish to associate with an object. XMI does not define the *label* attribute's value.

The names of these XML attributes must include the namespace prefix for the XMI namespace when the attributes occur in a document. All of these attributes are optional, so you should only use the ones that are needed for your applications. Here are some examples of instances of a *Car* class that use these attributes:

```
<xmi:XMI xmi:version="2.0" xmlns:xmi="http://www.omg.org/XMI"/>
  <Car xmi:id="_1" xmi:uuid="CA 9ABC123" xmi:label="clunker"/>
  <Car xmi:id="_2" xmi:label="clunker"/>
  <Car xmi:id="_3"/>
</xmi:XMI>
```

Note that each of the values of the *id* attributes is unique, as required by XML. Also, since the first *Car* object has a *uuid* attribute with the value *CA 9ABC123*, no other *Car* object should have the same *uuid* attribute value in any other documents. Since XMI does not define the value of the *label* attribute, it is legal for two objects to have the same value for that attribute.

Attribute Values

Now that you know where to put objects in XMI and XML documents, and how to use the XML attributes defined by XMI for identifying objects, you are ready to learn how to represent an object's attribute values. XMI represents attribute values using either XML elements or XML attributes. Recall from Chapter 2 that there are two kinds of UML attribute values: data values and object values. A UML attribute has a multiplicity that defines the number of values for that attribute that can appear in an object. It is possible for an object to have multiple values for the same UML attribute.

XMI enables you to put a UML attribute value either in an XML attribute or an XML element if both of the following conditions are true:

- The value is a data value.

- There can be at most one value for the UML attribute in an object.

XMI requires the use of an XML element to represent a UML attribute value in any of the following cases:

- The value is an object value.

- The value is one of several values for an attribute in an object.

- The value is nil.

First, we explain how XMI represents data values and then we explain how XMI represents object values.

Data Values

XMI specifies that an attribute's data value be put in either an XML attribute or an XML element. If it is put in an XML attribute, the name of the XML attribute is the name of the attribute. Similarly, if it is put in an XML element, the tag name of the XML element is the name of the attribute. If the name of the attribute is not a legal XML attribute name or tag name, you need to convert it to a legal one.

Consider a class *Person* that has an attribute called *name* of type *string*, the XML schema *string* datatype. The multiplicity of the attribute is *0..1*. If an object is an instance of *Person* and has an attribute value of *John Doe* for the *name* attribute, you can serialize the object and its attribute value this way:

```
<Person name="John Doe"/>
```

For brevity, we do not show the enclosing *XMI* XML element for the examples in this section.

You can also serialize the object as follows, using an XML element for the data value:

```
<Person>
  <name>John Doe</name>
</Person>
```

XMI enables you to specify in a model whether a data value is written using an XML element or an XML attribute. Details of how to do so are in a later section on generating schemas from models.

One reason for putting a data value in the content of an XML element rather than an XML attribute is to preserve whitespace. XML parsers normalize whitespace in the values of XML attributes. For example, XML parsers convert tab characters and end-of-line characters to space characters. If your data value contains whitespace that will be normalized, you should put the value in the content of an XML element to preserve the whitespace.

Another reason to use an XML element is to serialize a nil data value. You represent a nil value by setting the *nil* XML attribute in the XML schema instance namespace to *true* on an XML element with empty content. For example, if there is a nil value for the *name* attribute of an instance of the *Person* class, it is serialized this way:

```
<Person xmlns:xsi="http://www.w3.org/2001/XMLSchema-instance">
  <name xsi:nil="true"/>
</Person>
```

The declaration of the schema instance namespace does not need to be in the *Person* XML element; it can be in the root element of the document, for example.

You are required to use XML elements to save data values if an attribute has multiple data values. For example, if a *Person* class has an attribute called *hobby* that has a multiplicity of *0..** and type *string* (the XML schema *string* datatype), the values for the *hobby* attribute in an instance of the *Person* class are written as follows:

```
<Person>
  <hobby>Reading specifications</hobby>
  <hobby>Programming computers</hobby>
  <hobby>Surfing the Internet</hobby>
</Person>
```

Since we are biased, we do not comment on the merit of this person's hobbies.

Object Values

Unlike a data value, an attribute's object value must always be serialized using an XML element rather than an XML attribute. The tag name of the XML element is the name of the attribute. The object value can be in a different XMI document than the object that has the value; we describe how to handle such a case in the *Objects in Different Documents* section. We describe the case where the object value and the object that has the value are in the same document in this section.

For example, consider a *Car* class with an object attribute called *style* that has *Style* as its type, where *Style* is a class. The *Style* class has two data attributes called *make* and *model* of type *String* (which is mapped to the XML schema *string* datatype). Figure 3.2 contains the class diagram for these two classes and the *String* datatype. You can serialize an instance of the *Car* class (and the object value for its *style* attribute) as follows:

```
<Car>
  <style make="Jalopy" model="Deluxe"/>
</Car>
```

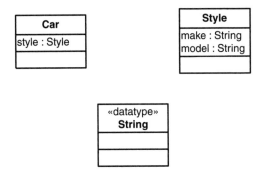

Figure 3.2 The *Car* class with the *style* object attribute.

The XML element *style* represents the value of the *style* attribute for the *Car* object. The value of the *make* attribute in the *Style* object is *Jalopy,* and the value of the *model* attribute in the *Style* object is *Deluxe*. Note that the class name *Style* for the *Style* object is not used as the tag name of the XML element representing the object; the tag name is *style*, the name of the attribute that the *Style* object is a value of.

Since the tag name of an XML element representing an object value is not the name of the class the object value is an instance of, you need to determine the class for the object value by examining the model that defines the objects. If the model has classes that inherit from each other, you may not be able to determine the class for the object value, because the object value may be an instance of one of several classes. In this case, you need to specify the class for the object value using either the *type* XML attribute defined by XMI or the *type* XML attribute defined by the XML schema specification. The following example clarifies this point.

Consider a *Car* class that has an object attribute called *part* with a multiplicity of *0..** and type *Part*. The *Part* class has two subclasses, *Engine* and *Transmission*. The UML class diagram for these classes appears in Figure 3.3.

Now consider a *Car* object that has one value for the *part* attribute. The *Car* object appears as follows:

```
<Car>
  <part/>
</Car>
```

We know that this car has a part, but what kind of part is it? XMI specifies that the class for an object value must be specified if it is a subclass of the class that is the type of the attribute. So, in the previous example, the object value for the *part* attribute is an instance of class *Part* since the type of the *part* attribute is *Part*. If the object value for the *part* attribute is an instance of class *Engine*, it

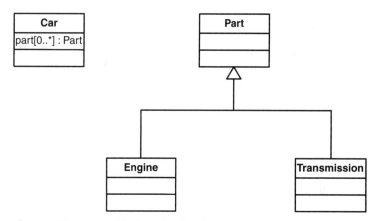

Figure 3.3 A car with three kinds of parts.

is written with an XML attribute called *type*. The following example uses the *type* attribute defined by XMI:

```
<Car>
  <part xmi:type="Engine"/>
</Car>
```

Remember that the namespace associated with the prefix *xmi* is the XMI namespace, and its URI is *http://www.omg.org/XMI*.

If you specify a namespace URI for the *Car, Part, Engine*, and *Transmission* classes, the value of the *type* attribute needs to specify the namespace as well. For example, if you specify the namespace URI *http://cars* for these classes and decide to use the namespace prefix *CAR* for that namespace URI in an XMI document, the *Car* and *Engine* objects in the previous example appear as follows:

```
<xmi:XMI xmi:version="2.0" xmlns:xmi="http://www.omg.org/XMI"
         xmlns:CAR="http://cars"/>
  <CAR:Car>
    <part xmi:type="CAR:Engine"/>
  </CAR:Car>
</xmi:XMI>
```

Note that the *Car* XML element has a tag name that includes the namespace prefix *CAR*, and the value of the *type* attribute also includes that namespace prefix. If we used the *type* attribute in the XML schema instance namespace instead of the *type* attribute in the XMI namespace, the value of the attribute would still be *CAR:Engine*.

When do you use the *type* attribute defined by XMI rather than the *type* attribute defined in the XML schema instance namespace? As you will see in the section *Generating Schemas from Models*, you can use schema extension to represent inheritance. If you choose to do so, you need to use the *type* attribute defined in the XML schema instance namespace. If you do not use schema extension to represent inheritance, you need to use the *type* attribute defined by XMI.

Namespaces and Values

We have seen that XMI uses either an XML attribute or an XML element to represent an attribute value. In each of our examples so far, the names of the XML attributes for attribute values have not included a namespace prefix. Also, the tag names of the XML elements for attribute values have not included a namespace prefix. A namespace prefix may need to be included in these names, though, depending on the schema created from the model.

As we described in Chapter 2, XML schemas can require that namespace prefixes be used in attribute names and in the tag names of XML elements. In XMI schemas, the XML attributes and XML elements for attribute values do not normally require namespace prefixes in their names. However, you can specify in your models that namespace prefixes must be used. Please refer to the *Generating Schemas from Models* section for a complete description of how to specify that namespace prefixes are to be used and how that affects XMI schemas.

References

Like attribute values, XMI serializes references using either XML attributes or XML elements. Recall from the terminology section of this chapter that a reference is an instance of an association end. Because we use object attributes in this book to represent composition rather than association ends, a reference is a relationship between two objects that does not have composition semantics. We use the term *referenced object* for the object that is related to the object that has the reference.

An object may have more than one reference that is an instance of a particular association end. The number of references in an object is constrained by the multiplicity of the association end. XMI serializes the references that are instances of an association end using either an XML attribute to represent all the references or an XML element for each reference.

XMI uses an XML attribute for the references that are instances of an association end if both of the following conditions are true:

- The referenced object of each reference is in the same document as the object that has the reference.

- You use XML attributes of type *ID* and *IDREFS* to refer to objects in the same document.

XMI uses an XML element for each reference in the following situations:

- The referenced object of any of the references that are instances of an association end is in another XMI document.

- You choose to use a URI to refer to objects in the same document (we explain how to specify this choice in a model in the *Generating Schemas from Models* section).

We describe how to use an XML attribute to represent references first and then how to use an XML element to represent references. For both cases, we discuss how to represent a reference that has a referenced object in the same document as the object that has the reference. We also discuss how to represent a reference that has a referenced object in another document in the *Objects in Different Documents* section.

Representing References Using XML Attributes

By default, XMI uses an XML attribute to represent all the references in an object that are instances of a particular association end if all the referenced objects are in the same document as the object that has the references. The name of the attribute is the name of the association end. If the name of the association end is not a legal XML attribute name, you need to convert it to a legal name.

The XML attribute has type *IDREFS*. The value of the attribute consists of the identifiers of the XML elements corresponding to the referenced objects, separated by spaces.

Consider a model consisting of a *Car* class and a *Person* class, with a unidirectional association between the two classes. The association end attached to the *Person* class is called *driver*, and it has a multiplicity of *0..**. The class diagram for this model appears in Figure 3.4.

Consider a *Car* object that has two references that are instances of the association end *driver*. Each reference relates a *Person* object to the *Car* object. The three objects can be written using XMI as follows (excluding the *XMI* XML element):

Figure 3.4 A car has drivers.

```
<Car driver="P1 P2"/>
<Person xmi:id="P1"/>
<Person xmi:id="P2"/>
```

The *driver* XML attribute represents the two *driver* references. The value of the *driver* XML attribute contains the identifiers of the two *Person* XML elements that represent the two *Person* objects related to the *Car* object.

Representing References Using XML Elements

If you specify in a model that URIs are to be used to refer to objects in the same document, XMI represents each reference using an XML element. The tag name of the XML element is the name of the association end that the reference is an instance of. If the name of the association end is not a legal XML tag name, you need to convert it to a legal name. The XML element has an *href* XML attribute that contains a URI *fragment identifier* that references an XML element in the document.

Here is how XMI writes the *Car* and *Person* objects in the previous section using URIs to refer to objects in the same document:

```
<Car>
  <driver href="#P1"/>
  <driver href="#P2"/>
</Car>
<Person xmi:id="P1"/>
<Person xmi:id="P2"/>
```

The two *driver* XML elements inside the *Car* XML element refer to the *Person* XML elements outside the *Car* XML element.

Namespaces and References

We have seen that XMI uses either an XML attribute or an XML element to represent a reference. In each of our examples so far, the names of the XML attributes for references have not included a namespace prefix. Also, the tag names of the XML elements for references have not included a namespace prefix. A namespace prefix may need to be included in these names, though, depending on the schema created from the model.

As we described in Chapter 2, XML schemas can require that namespace prefixes be used in XML attribute names and the tag names of XML elements. In XMI schemas, the XML attributes and XML elements for references do not normally require namespace prefixes in their names. However, you can specify in your models that namespace prefixes must be used. Please see the

Generating Schemas from Models section for a complete description of how to specify that namespace prefixes are to be used and how that affects XMI schemas.

Objects in Different Documents

So far, we have only considered the case where all the objects are saved in one XMI document. XMI gives you the flexibility of saving your objects in different documents. When you use multiple documents, it is possible that a referenced object of a reference or an object value of an attribute is in a different document than the object being serialized. XMI uses an XML element to represent the reference or the object value in this case. The XML element has an *href* attribute with a value that is a URI that points to the XML element corresponding to the referenced object or object value in the other document. The tag name of the XML element is the name of the attribute or the name of the association end corresponding to the reference.

We provide an example of an object value in a different document than the object that has the value. Then we provide examples of references where the referenced objects are in a different document than the object that has the reference.

Object Values in Different Documents

Consider a *Car* object and a *Part* object that are instances of the *Car* class and *Part* class in Figure 3.3. The *Part* object is the object value of the *part* attribute in the *Car* object. You can serialize a *Part* object in the file *parts.xmi*, and the *Car* object in the file *car.xmi*. The *Car* object in *car.xmi* appears as follows:

```
<Car>
  <part href="parts.xmi#P1"/>
</Car>
```

USE OF XLINKS IN XMI

At the time this book is being written, the OMG is considering how to use XLinks from the XLink specification (W3C, 2001) in XMI. It is likely that XMI will enable the use of the attributes defined in the XLink specification in addition to the *href* attribute defined by XMI, as described in this section. If so, you may be able to use an *xlink:href* attribute, where *xlink* is the namespace prefix for the XLink namespace. You may also be able to set the *xlink:type* attribute to the value *simple* to indicate that the XML element is a simple XLink. Also, you may be able to use more sophisticated XLink features than simple XLinks in XMI.

The value of the *href* attribute indicates that the object value is located in *parts.xmi*, and the object value is represented by the XML element with the identifier *P1*.

The *Part* object in *parts.xmi* appears as follows:

```
<Part xmi:id="P1"/>
```

Referenced Objects in Different Documents

Consider an object that has two references that are instances of the same association end. One of the referenced objects is in another document, while the other referenced object is in the same document. Since one of the referenced objects is in another document, XMI requires that each of the references be represented using an XML element. If you choose to use URIs to refer to objects in the same document (as described in the *Generating Schemas from Models* section), each XML element for a reference will have an *href* XML attribute to refer to the XML element for the referenced object. If you do not specify that option, the XML element for the reference with the referenced object in the same document will have an *idref* XML attribute. The *idref* attribute is defined by XMI, and its value is the identifier of the XML element for the referenced object in the same document.

Here is an example. The model in Figure 3.4 specifies that a *Car* object can have *Person* objects related to it using *driver* references. If a particular *Car* object has two *driver* references that relate the *Car* object to two *Person* objects, we can save the *Car* object and one of the *Person* objects in the file *file1.xmi*. We can save the other *Person* object in the file *file2.xmi*. Since one of the *Person* objects is in another document, XMI requires that each *driver* reference be represented by an XML element.

The *Person* object in *file2.xmi* appears as follows:

```
<Person xmi:id="P2"/>
```

The model in Figure 3.4 does not indicate that URIs are to be used to refer to objects in the same document (you can use the XMI tagged value *href* explained later in this chapter to indicate that URIs are to be used to refer to objects in the same document), so the *Car* object and *Person* object in *file1.xmi* appear as follows:

```
<Car>
  <driver xmi:idref="P1"/>
  <driver href="file2.xmi#P2"/>
</Car>
<Person xmi:id="P1"/>
```

The first *driver* XML element has an *idref* XML attribute that contains the identifier of the XML element for the *Person* object saved in *file1.xmi*. The second *driver* XML element has an *href* XML attribute that refers to the *Person* object saved in *file2.xmi*.

If the model in Figure 3.4 indicated that URIs were to be used to refer to objects in the same document, the contents of the *XMI* XML element for *file1.xmi* would appear as follows:

```
<Car>
  <driver href="#P1"/>
  <driver href="file2.xmi#P2"/>
</Car>
<Person xmi:id="P1"/>
```

Note that each XML element for a *driver* reference has an *href* XML attribute that refers to an XML element representing a *Person* object.

Additional Information

So far, we have described how XMI represents objects and their parts. XMI also enables you to put additional information for each object in a document. That additional information does not need to follow the XMI serialization rules; it can be represented using any legal XML elements.

Why would you want to put additional information for an object in a document? Sometimes you may need to store information in a document that is useful to your tool but not to other tools. For example, your tool may display information using a graphical user interface (GUI). You may want to save the GUI information for an object serialized using XMI. It is doubtful that other tools will be able to use the GUI information for your tool, unless you create a model that defines the GUI information. XMI enables you to express this information for each object in such a way that it does not interfere with the information to be exchanged.

You serialize this information using an *Extension* XML element. The *Extension* XML element can be put inside the XML element representing an object. You can put as many *Extension* elements as you wish in the XML element for an object.

The *Extension* XML element has two XML attributes, *extender* and *extenderID*. Both attributes are optional, and the type of both attributes is the XML

EXTENSION ELEMENTS IN THE XMI SPECIFICATION

At the time this book is being written, the XMI specification indicates that an *extension* XML element is to be used rather than an *Extension* XML element. We believe that a future specification will use *Extension* for the tag name rather than *extension*, so we use *Extension* in this book.

schema *string* type. You can use the *extender* XML attribute to identify the tool that created the extension, and you can use the *extenderID* attribute to specify an identifier for the extension that is specific to your tool. By using these attributes, you can distinguish extensions that pertain to your tool from extensions that other tools have serialized with an object.

Consider a tool that displays information about cars using a GUI. The tool takes instances of a *Car* class and displays information about them on a screen. The tool saves *Car* objects in XMI documents. When the *Car* objects are restored from documents, the tool displays the *Car* objects in the same position on the screen as they were when the objects were saved. To support this functionality, the tool can save the position information in an *Extension* XML element for each object. The tool can use the *extender* XML attribute of each *Extension* element to store the name of the tool. If the position information can be expressed as an x-coordinate and a y-coordinate, a particular *Car* object can appear as follows in an XMI document:

```
<Car>
    <xmi:Extension extender="ToolName">
        <GUIInfo x="35" y="17"/>
    </xmi:Extension>
</Car>
```

Notice that you must use the namespace prefix for the XMI namespace in the tag name of the *Extension* XML element. You can put any well-formed XML elements you wish inside an *Extension* XML element.

You are not required to put your *Extension* XML elements inside the objects that the additional information is for. You can put them directly inside an *XMI* XML element and then refer to the objects that the *Extension* XML elements pertain to.

For example, you can serialize the GUI information for the previous *Car* object as follows:

```
<xmi:XMI xmi:version="2.0" xmlns:xmi="http://www.omg.org/XMI" >
  <Car xmi:id="C1"/>
  <xmi:Extension extender="ToolName" extenderID="C1">
    <GUIInfo x="35" y="17"/>
  </xmi:Extension>
</xmi:XMI>
```

In this example, the *extenderID* XML attribute has the identifier of the *Car* that the GUI information pertains to. You can also refer to the *Car* object within the *Extension* XML element. For example, you can use a *car* XML attribute on the *GUIInfo* XML element as follows:

```
<xmi:XMI xmi:version="2.0" xmlns:xmi="http://www.omg.org/XMI" >
  <Car xmi:id="C1"/>
```

```
   <xmi:Extension extender="ToolName">
     <GUIInfo x="35" y="17" car="C1"/>
   </xmi:Extension>
</xmi:XMI>
```

If you anticipate that some of the information you are putting in *Extension* XML elements will be used by other tools, you should consider defining the information in a model. Then the information can be serialized as objects and their parts using the XMI serialization rules, enabling that information to be easily exchanged.

As you will see in *The XMI Model* section of this chapter, putting information in *Extension* elements does not hinder schema validation for XMI documents. Chapter 4 discusses other issues that you should consider when you use *Extension* XML elements.

Generating Schemas from Models

Not only can you use XMI to serialize objects in documents, but you can also use XMI to generate schemas from models. If you are unfamiliar with schemas, you can use XMI to create valid schemas. However, if you are familiar with schemas, you can tailor the schemas that XMI produces. This section describes the schemas that XMI specifies and how you can tailor the schemas for your own purposes.

You specify how to tailor the schemas XMI produces by using tagged values in your models. Recall from Chapter 2 that tagged values are additional properties for UML constructs. Each tagged value consists of a tag and a value. XMI defines tags that affect how XMI creates schemas from models. We describe each tag that can be used with a particular UML construct, the legal values for those tags, and the effect that each value has on the schemas XMI creates. We summarize this information at the end of this section.

Each of the tags defined by XMI contains the prefix *org.omg.xmi*. For brevity in the following discussion, we use tag names that do not include the prefix.

UML MODELS IN XMI DOCUMENTS

Software that implements the XMI specification to generate schemas from models requires that the models be input in a form the software can understand. Some modeling tools enable you to save your models in XMI documents; those documents can then by processed by XMI software to generate schemas. Chapter 9 shows how to use a model in XMI format with the Framework software included on the accompanying CD-ROM.

Keep in mind that you need to use the prefix unless you are using software that automatically adds the prefix for you.

You can also use stereotypes rather than some of the tag values. If a tag has a boolean value, and its default value is *false*, you can specify a stereotype rather than set the tag to *true*. The name of the stereotype is the name of the tag, excluding the *org.omg.xmi* prefix. For example, we explain that the *ordered* tag can be set to *true* for a class. Rather than setting the *ordered* tag to *true*, you can add an <<ordered>> stereotype to the class. Note that you cannot use stereotypes in this manner for tags that do not have boolean values, and you cannot use stereotypes for tags that have a default value of *true*.

We first describe the default schemas that XMI specifies and then we describe how to use tagged values in UML models to tailor the schema representation. Each discussion is organized by UML constructs. We describe how XMI represents packages, classes, datatypes, attributes, association ends, and inheritance in XML schemas.

We strongly urge you to specify XML namespaces in your models so that XMI creates schemas with target namespaces. Since we consider this technique to be very important, we describe how to specify namespaces when we discuss the default representation for packages.

Default XMI Schemas

XMI creates valid XML schemas from models even if you do not tailor the schemas in any way, as long as the names in the model are legal XML tag names and XML attribute names. This section explains how XMI creates XML schemas from models if you choose not to tailor the schemas. However, since we urge you to specify XML namespaces in your models, we explain how to do so when we discuss packages.

Packages

By default, the XML schemas created by XMI do not have target namespaces (if you do not know what a target namespace is, please read the *Schemas* section of Chapter 2). However, you can specify an XML namespace for each package, causing XMI to create schemas with target namespaces. If you do this, there will not be name collisions among the XML tag names in your documents, even if you write objects from different models in the same document. This also prevents name collisions if you have multiple classes with the same names in different packages in your models. Another benefit of using this approach is that XMI creates a schema for each package in your model.

You specify the XML namespace to use for a package by setting values for the *nsURI* and the *nsPrefix* tags in your model. The value of the *nsURI* tag is the XML namespace URI; XMI uses it as the target namespace for the schema created from the package. The value of the *nsPrefix* tag is the namespace prefix that XMI uses in the schema for the package.

Whether or not you specify an XML namespace for each package, each XMI schema imports a schema that defines all of the XML attributes and XML elements in the XMI namespace.

Consider a package called *Cars* with an *nsURI* tag that has the value *http://cars* and with a *nsPrefix* tag that has the value *cars*. The schema corresponding to this package appears as follows:

```
<xsd:schema xmlns:xsd="http://www.w3.org/2001/XMLSchema"
            xmlns:xmi="http://www.omg.org/XMI"
            targetNamespace="http://cars"
            xmlns:cars="http://cars">
  <xsd:import namespace="http://www.omg.org/XMI"
            schemaLocation="xmi20.xsd"/>
</xsd:schema>
```

As we saw in Chapter 2, the schema is contained in a *schema* XML element in a schema namespace defined by the XML Schema specification (W3C, 2001). We always use the namespace prefix *xsd* for that namespace in this book. Because the *nsURI* tag is specified, the schema has a target namespace. We use the prefix *cars* for the target namespace in the schema because that is the value of the *nsPrefix* tag. The *import* XML element makes the declarations in the schema that defines the XMI namespace available in this schema for the *cars* package. The *schemaLocation* attribute indicates that the schema that defines the XMI namespace can be found in the file *xmi20.xsd*. The XMI namespace is declared in this schema with the prefix *xmi*, so the contents of the schema that defines the XMI namespace can be referred to in this schema by using that prefix. We include the file *xmi20.xsd* on the CD-ROM.

Classes

XMI creates a complex type declaration and an element declaration for each class in a model. If you use the *nsURI* and *nsPrefix* tags, as explained in the previous section, each complex type declaration and element declaration corresponding to a class is in the target namespace for the package that the class belongs to. In this section, we consider classes that have no attributes or association ends. We discuss the treatment of attributes and association ends later in this chapter.

Consider a class named *Car* in a package called *Cars* that has a *nsURI* tag with the value *http://cars* and an *nsPrefix* tag with the value *cars*. The XMI schema corresponding to this package appears as follows:

```
<xsd:schema xmlns:xsd="http://www.w3.org/2001/XMLSchema"
            xmlns:xmi="http://www.omg.org/XMI"
```

```
            targetNamespace="http://cars"
            xmlns:cars="http://cars">
  <xsd:import namespace="http://www.omg.org/XMI"/>

  <xsd:complexType name="Car">
    <xsd:choice minOccurs="0" maxOccurs="unbounded">
      <xsd:element ref="xmi:Extension"/>
    </xsd:choice>
    <xsd:attribute ref="xmi:id"/>
    <xsd:attributeGroup ref="xmi:ObjectAttribs"/>
  </xsd:complexType>

  <xsd:element name="Car" type="cars:Car"/>
</xsd:schema>
```

In the previous section, *Packages*, you saw the *schema* XML element, the namespaces declared in it, and the *import* XML element. Now you can see the complex type declaration and the element declaration for the *Car* class. Notice that the declaration of the complex type specifies that the content contains any number of *Extension* XML elements. We discuss how to use the *Extension* XML elements in the *Writing Objects Using XMI* section of this chapter. We also describe the declaration of the *Extension* XML element in *The XMI Model* section of this chapter.

Note that the attribute group *ObjectAttribs* from the schema that defines the XMI namespace is included in the complex type declared for the *Car* class. This attribute group includes the declarations of the XML attributes *uuid*, *label*, *idref*, and *href*. This enables you to use the identity and linking attributes defined by XMI when serializing an object.

You may wonder why the *id* XML attribute is not in the *ObjectAttribs* attribute group. The reason is because you can rename the *id* attribute, as we explain when we describe how you can tailor the representation of classes in XMI schemas. If you rename the *id* attribute, the XML attribute declaration for that attribute replaces the reference to the *id* XML attribute declared in the XMI namespace. It would not be possible to do the replacement if the *id* attribute was in the *ObjectAttribs* attribute group.

XMI declares both an element and a complex type for each class to give you the most options for reusing a schema created by XMI. You can use both the complex type and the element in your schemas by importing the created schema, since the declarations are in the target namespace of the created schema.

Datatypes

XMI maps a UML datatype to an XML schema simple type. The schema type can be one of the predefined schema datatypes or one of your simple types. We discuss how you specify the schema type a UML datatype maps to in the section *Tailoring XMI Schemas*. We describe in this section how XMI represents UML enumerations in schemas.

Recall from Chapter 2 that a UML enumeration consists of a name for the enumeration and literals that are the legal values for the enumeration. XMI creates a simple type for a UML enumeration that restricts the *string* schema datatype. The name of the simple type is the name of the enumeration, and each literal is represented using an *enumeration* XML element in the XML schema namespace. The declaration of the simple type is in the *schema* XML element, so it can be referred to within the schema and by schemas that import the schema.

Consider a UML enumeration called *MyEnum* that has literals *v1*, *v2*, and *v3*. XMI creates the following declaration for it in an XMI schema:

```
<xsd:simpleType name="MyEnum">
  <xsd:restriction base="xsd:string">
    <xsd:enumeration value="v1"/>
    <xsd:enumeration value="v2"/>
    <xsd:enumeration value="v3"/>
  </xsd:restriction>
</xsd:simpleType>
```

Notice that there is an *enumeration* XML element for each enumeration literal. Each literal is put in a *value* XML attribute.

Attributes

By default, XMI creates an XML element declaration for each UML attribute, and possibly an XML attribute declaration as well, depending on the type of the UML attribute and the attribute's multiplicity. We explain how to customize the XMI representation of attributes in the section *Tailoring XMI Schemas*; we explain the default XMI representation of attributes here.

An XML attribute is declared for a UML attribute if the UML attribute has both of the following characteristics:

- The multiplicity of the attribute is *1..1* or *0..1*.
- The attribute is a data attribute (its type is a UML datatype).

Consider a *Person* class that has an attribute called *name*, which has *string* as its type (the *string* XML schema type) and *0..1* as its multiplicity. XMI creates the following complex type declaration for it:

```
<xsd:complexType name="Person">
    <xsd:choice minOccurs="0" maxOccurs="unbounded">
      <xsd:element name="name" type="xsd:string"/>
      <xsd:element ref="xmi:Extension"/>
```

```
        </xsd:choice>
        <xsd:attribute ref="xmi:id"/>
        <xsd:attributeGroup ref="xmi:ObjectAttribs"/>
        <xsd:attribute name="name" type="xsd:string"/>
    </xsd:complexType>
```

XMI also creates an element declaration for the *Person* class, which is not shown here. Notice that there is an XML element declaration for the UML attribute in the content of the complex type as well as an XML attribute declaration. If the maximum multiplicity of the UML attribute is greater than 1, XMI does not create the XML attribute declaration.

Now consider a *Car* class with an attribute called *style,* which has *Style* as its type and *0..1* as its multiplicity. *Style* is a class. The *style* attribute has an XML element declaration but no XML attribute declaration. The complex type declarations for the two classes are as follows:

```
<xsd:complexType name="Style">
    <xsd:choice minOccurs="0" maxOccurs="unbounded">
        <xsd:element ref="xmi:Extension"/>
    </xsd:choice>
    <xsd:attribute ref="xmi:id"/>
    <xsd:attributeGroup ref="xmi:ObjectAttribs"/>
</xsd:complexType>

<xsd:complexType name="Car">
    <xsd:choice minOccurs="0" maxOccurs="unbounded">
      <xsd:element name="style" type="xmi:Any"/>
      <xsd:element ref="xmi:Extension"/>
    </xsd:choice>
    <xsd:attribute ref="xmi:id"/>
    <xsd:attributeGroup ref="xmi:ObjectAttribs"/>
</xsd:complexType>
```

Notice that the XML element declaration for the *style* attribute does not have a type of *Style*, which you might expect. It has a type called *Any*. The *Any* type is declared as follows in the schema that defines the XMI namespace:

```
<xsd:complexType name="Any">
  <xsd:choice minOccurs="0" maxOccurs="unbounded">
    <xsd:any processContents="skip"/>
  </xsd:choice>
  <xsd:anyAttribute processContents="skip"/>
</xsd:complexType>
```

The *Any* type enables any content and any attributes to be used.

The reason we use the *Any* type rather than the *Style* type has to do with the default way that class inheritance is represented in XMI schemas and how it can affect document validation. For example, suppose that you had a subclass

ANY TYPE AND THE XMI SPECIFICATION

The current XMI specification does not define the *Any* type. We have included the *Any* type in the schema that defines the XMI namespace (in the file *xmi20.xsd*). Doing so allows us to refer to the type rather than declaring it multiple times. It is possible that the final XMI specification will not include the *Any* type in the XMI namespace. If that is the case, you can define this type in your own schema and reuse it.

of *Style* called *Substyle*, and that the object value for the *style* attribute in a *Car* object was an instance of *Substyle*. XMI does not use schema extension to represent class inheritance by default, so the *Substyle* type in a schema would not be defined by extending type *Style*. If the *Substyle* class has attributes, and you put the values of those attributes in the XML element *style*, a parser would report a validation error if the type of the *style* element were *Style*. A parser would report a validation error because the *Style* type has declarations for the attributes in the *Style* class, but it does not have declarations for the attributes in the *Substyle* class. If the *Substyle* type in the schema extends the *Style* type in the schema, the type of the *style* XML element can be *Style*. We explain how you specify that schema extension is to be used in the *Tailoring XMI Schemas* section of this chapter. We also provide examples of using schema validation in Chapter 9. Notice also that there is no XML attribute declaration for the *style* UML attribute, since the type of the UML attribute is a class.

Association Ends

XMI creates an XML element declaration and an XML attribute declaration for an association end. The XML element declaration for an association end enables any content and any attributes to be used with the element in a document. Remember that the association ends in this book do not have composition semantics because we represent composition using object attributes instead.

Consider the model in Figure 3.4. In it, there is a class called *Car* that has an association end *driver*. XMI creates the following complex type declaration for the *Car* class:

```
<xsd:complexType name="Car">
   <xsd:choice minOccurs="0" maxOccurs="unbounded">
     <xsd:element name="driver" type="xmi:Any"/>
     <xsd:element ref="xmi:Extension"/>
   </xsd:choice>
   <xsd:attribute ref="xmi:id"/>
```

```
        <xsd:attributeGroup ref="xmi:ObjectAttribs"/>
        <xsd:attribute name="driver" type="xsd:IDREFS"/>
</xsd:complexType>
```

Notice that the type of XML element *driver* is *Any*. Also notice that the type of the XML attribute declared for the association end is *IDREFS*. This enables references to *Person* elements in the same document as a *Car* element. The type of the *driver* XML element is not *Person*, as you might expect. This is because XMI does not use schema extension to represent inheritance unless you choose to do so. If schema extension is not used, and the *driver* XML element declaration has type *Person*, an instance of a subclass of *Person* serialized using the *driver* element in a document may cause schema validation to fail. This reasoning is analogous to the reasoning we used in the previous section, *Attributes*, to explain why the *style* XML element for the *style* object attribute was not given the type of *Style*.

Inheritance

As mentioned previously, by default XMI does not use schema extension to represent inheritance. XMI does not do so because XML schema types can only extend one other type, and UML supports multiple inheritance. This means that by default XMI puts inherited attributes and inherited association ends in the complex type declaration for a class, along with the locally declared ones. We see the effect of using schema extension, and how to tell XMI to use schema extension, in the section *Tailoring XMI Schemas* later in this chapter.

Consider the model in Figure 3.5. The *Driver* class inherits from the *Person* class. XMI maps the *String* datatype to the schema *string* datatype (we explain in *Tailoring XMI Schemas* how you specify this mapping). The default complex type declaration for the *Driver* class includes element declarations and attribute declarations for the inherited *name* UML attribute and inherited *address* association end, as well as the local *driverLicenseNumber* UML attribute and *car* association end. Here is the default complex type declaration for the *Driver* class:

```
<xsd:complexType name="Driver">
    <xsd:choice minOccurs="0" maxOccurs="unbounded">
      <xsd:element name="name" type="xsd:string"/>
      <xsd:element name="driverLicenseNumber" type="xsd:string"/>
      <xsd:element name="address" type="xmi:Any"/>
      <xsd:element name="car" type="xmi:Any"/>
      <xsd:element ref="xmi:Extension"/>
    </xsd:choice>
    <xsd:attribute ref="xmi:id"/>
    <xsd:attributeGroup ref="xmi:ObjectAttribs"/>
```

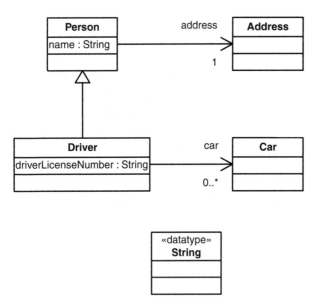

Figure 3.5   The *Driver* class inherits from the *Person* class.

```
    <xsd:attribute name="name" type="xsd:string"/>
    <xsd:attribute name="driverLicenseNumber" type="xsd:string"/>
    <xsd:attribute name="address" type="xsd:IDREFS"/>
    <xsd:attribute name="car" type="xsd:IDREFS"/>
  </xsd:complexType>
```

Tailoring XMI Schemas

This section discusses how to tailor the schema representation for each of the constructs in a UML model. You will learn that XMI is very flexible in its representation of data. XMI defines tags that enable you to specify how you wish the schemas to be tailored by providing values for the tags in your models. We discuss the tags that affect each model construct and then we summarize the tags XMI defines at the end of this section.

Packages

When we discussed packages in the *Default XMI Schemas* section, we explained how to specify namespaces for packages by providing values for the *nsURI* and *nsPrefix* tags. There are other tags defined by XMI that can be specified for packages that affect the classes contained in the packages. We identify those tags when we summarize the tags in the *Tagged Value Summary* section later in this chapter.

Classes

Numerous XMI tags affect the representation of classes in schemas. The tags are:

- *xmiName*
- *idName*
- *contentType*
- *ordered*
- *superClassFirst*

xmiName **Tag**

So far in our discussion, we have seen that XMI uses the names of classes as the names of complex types and the names of elements that correspond to classes. You can use the *xmiName* tag to specify the name to use for a class in a schema. As you may guess, the value of the *xmiName* tag must be a legal XML name. XMI uses the value of the *xmiName* tag as the name of the complex type declaration and the name in the XML element declaration for the class. Using this tag enables you to generate valid schemas without changing the names of classes to make them legal XML names.

For example, if there is a class in a model called *My Class*, and you do not wish to change the name of the class, you can set the value of the *xmiName* tag for the class to *MyClass*.

idName **Tag**

There is at most one XML attribute that has a type of *ID* in a complex type declaration within a schema. By default, XMI uses the XMI *id* attribute defined in the XMI namespace. However, if you provide a value for the *idName* tag, XMI uses that value as the name of the attribute of type *ID* in the complex type for the class. The attribute of type *ID* is declared locally in the complex type declaration, and the attribute declaration replaces the reference to the *id* attribute declaration in the schema that defines the XMI elements and attributes.

Consider a *Car* class with an *idName* tag that has a value of *myId*. The complex type declaration for the *Car* class appears as follows:

```
<xsd:complexType name="Car">
  <xsd:choice minOccurs="0" maxOccurs="unbounded">
    <xsd:element ref="xmi:Extension"/>
  </xsd:choice>
  <xsd:attribute name="myId" type="xsd:ID"/>
  <xsd:attributeGroup ref="xmi:ObjectAttribs"/>
</xsd:complexType>
```

Note that rather than using the *id* attribute in the XMI namespace, an attribute named *myId* is declared locally in the *Car* complex type. The type of the *myId* attribute is *ID*. Also notice that if the XMI *id* attribute had been in the *ObjectAttribs* attribute group, it would not have been possible to replace the declaration of the XMI *id* attribute with another one.

As another example, SOAP uses an XML attribute called *id* that is not in a namespace to identify XML elements. If you set the *idName* tag to *id*, XMI will use the same XML attribute as SOAP to identify XML elements in XMI documents, rather than the *id* attribute in the XMI namespace.

contentType Tag

XMI defines a number of tags that affect the content of the complex type declarations for classes. Many of the tags for UML attributes and association ends affect the content, for example. In this section, we discuss one of the tags that can be used with classes that affect the content: the *contentType* tag. You can provide a value for the *contentType* tag to make the content be *mixed* or *empty*. If the value of the *contentType* tag is *mixed*, the content is mixed. If the value of the *contentType* tag is *empty*, the content is empty.

For a *Car* class with no attributes and no association ends, setting the *contentType* tag to *mixed* results in the following complex type declaration:

```
<xsd:complexType name="Car" mixed="true">
  <xsd:choice minOccurs="0" maxOccurs="unbounded">
    <xsd:element ref="xmi:Extension"/>
  </xsd:choice>
  <xsd:attribute ref="xmi:id"/>
  <xsd:attributeGroup ref="xmi:ObjectAttribs"/>
</xsd:complexType>
```

This enables text to be mixed with elements in the content of *Car* objects in XMI documents.

You may specify that the content of the complex type for a class be empty by setting the *contentType* tag to *empty*. If you do so, XMI still declares XML attributes for UML attributes and association ends, as appropriate, for the class. You cannot set this value for the *contentType* tag if the class has object attributes or data attributes that can have multiple values, because XMI uses XML element declarations in the content of the complex type to represent those constructs.

Setting the *contentType* tag to *empty* for the *Car* class results in the following complex type:

```
<xsd:complexType name="Car">
  <xsd:complexContent/>
</xsd:complexType>
```

If the *Car* class had UML attributes and association ends that resulted in the declaration of XML attributes, those XML attributes would be included in the

Car complex type declaration. Note that this complex type declaration does not enable the use of *Extension* XML elements, since an element with this type may not contain anything.

ordered Tag

We have seen that the element declarations that appear in the content of the complex type declaration for a class are inside a *choice* XML element, so the elements can appear in any order in a document. However, you can specify that the content be ordered by setting the *ordered* tag to *true* for a class. This results in the same element declarations as before; however, they are included in a *sequence* XML element rather than a *choice* XML element.

We have not described the order of the element declarations in the content yet, because the elements have always been in a *choice* XML element. The order is determined by the order of the attributes and association ends in an XMI document containing the model. This order cannot be determined by examining a class diagram. The *Extension* XML element declaration appears last in the content.

Consider the model in Figure 3.6, in which a *Car* class has an attribute called *available* of type *Boolean* (which is mapped to the schema *boolean* datatype as explained later in this chapter) and a *style* association end attached to the *Style* class. If you do not specify a value for the *ordered* tag, the declaration of the complex type for the *Car* class appears as follows:

```
<xsd:complexType name="Car">
  <xsd:choice minOccurs="0" maxOccurs="unbounded">
    <xsd:element name="available" type="xsd:boolean"/>
    <xsd:element name="style" type="xmi:Any"/>
    <xsd:element ref="xmi:Extension"/>
  </xsd:choice>
  <xsd:attribute ref="xmi:id"/>
  <xsd:attributeGroup ref="xmi:ObjectAttribs"/>
  <xsd:attribute name="available" type="xsd:boolean"/>
  <xsd:attribute name="style" type="xsd:IDREFS"/>
</xsd:complexType>
```

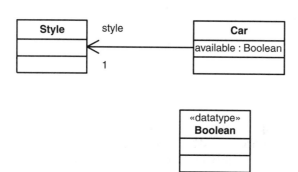

Figure 3.6 The *Car* class with attributes and association ends.

Notice that the element declarations for *available* and *style* are in a *choice* XML element and can appear in any order in a document that validates with this schema.

If the *ordered* tag is set to *true* for the *Car* class, the complex type declaration includes a *sequence* XML element rather than a *choice* XML element. The order in which the *available* and *style* XML elements are declared inside the *sequence* element is determined by the order of the *available* UML attribute and the *style* association end in the XMI document that contains the model. If the *style* association end appears before the *available* UML attribute, the complex type declaration is as follows:

```
<xsd:complexType name="Car">
  <xsd:sequence minOccurs="0" maxOccurs="unbounded">
    <xsd:element name="style" type="xmi:Any"/>
    <xsd:element name="available" type="xsd:boolean"/>
    <xsd:element ref="xmi:Extension"/>
  </xsd:sequence>
  <xsd:attribute ref="xmi:id"/>
  <xsd:attributeGroup ref="ObjectAttribs"/>
  <xsd:attribute name="available" type="xsd:boolean"/>
  <xsd:attribute name="style" type="xsd:IDREFS"/>
</xsd:complexType>
```

Although you do not need to set the *ordered* tag to *true* for the *Car* class, there are some situations that require the *ordered* tag to be set to *true*. We explain those situations later.

superClassFirst Tag

Like the *ordered* tag, the *superClassFirst* tag imposes an ordering on the contents of a complex type declaration for a class. If this tag is set to *true*, XML elements for inherited attributes and association ends must appear before XML elements for local attributes and association ends. The content of the complex type declaration would be identical to the content if schema extension were used to represent inheritance. We believe that the final XMI 2.0 specification will either remove this tag or specify that it can be *true* only if the *useSchemaExtensions* tag is *true*. Please see the *Inheritance* section later in this chapter for a complete description of the effect of setting the *useSchemaExtensions* tag to *true* on XMI schemas.

Datatypes

When we discussed the default representation of a UML datatype in XMI schemas, we mentioned that XMI maps a UML datatype to an XML schema simple type, but we did not explain how this worked. You set the value of the *schemaType* tag to indicate the XML schema simple type to use. The simple type

SCHEMA TYPE MAPPING

As we have explained previously, XMI uses MOF models rather than UML models. MOF defines *Boolean*, *Integer*, *Long*, *Float*, *Double*, and *String* datatypes. XMI maps those MOF datatypes to the schema datatypes *boolean*, *int*, *long*, *float*, *double*, and *string*, respectively. If a UML datatype is mapped to one of the MOF datatypes, the MOF-to-schema datatype mapping should be used.

can be one of the predefined schema datatypes as described in the XML Schema:Datatypes specification (W3C, 2001), or it can be one of your simple types.

The value of the tag consists of the namespace URI for the type followed by # and the name of the type. For example, to specify that a particular UML datatype maps to the schema datatype *int*, you set the *schemaType* tag to the value *http://www.w3.org/2001/XMLSchema#int*. To use a simple type you have defined called *MySimpleType* in a namespace URI *http://myURI*, you set the value of the *schemaType* tag to *http://myURI#MySimpleType*.

If a UML attribute has a datatype for which there is a *schemaType* tag, the schema datatype specified in the value of the *schemaType* tag is the type used in XML element and XML attribute declarations for the UML attribute. Consider the model in Figure 3.6. When we declared the complex type for the *Car* class, we used the schema datatype *boolean* without explaining why XMI mapped the *Boolean* datatype in the model to the schema datatype *boolean*. XMI performs that mapping because the *Boolean* datatype in the model has a *schemaType* tag whose value is *http://www.w3.org/2001/XMLSchema#boolean*. That tag is not shown in the UML diagram in Figure 3.6.

Attributes

There are numerous tags that affect how XMI represents UML attributes in schemas. We describe them and how some of the tags affect each other. The tags are:

- *xmiName*
- *serialize*
- *attribute*
- *element*
- *includeNils*
- *enforceMaximumMultiplicity*

- *enforceMinimumMultiplicity*
- *form*
- *defaultValue*
- *fixedValue*

xmiName Tag

We have already explained the use of the *xmiName* tag with classes. You can also set this tag on UML attributes. The value of the tag is the name that XMI uses for the name of the element declaration and attribute declaration for a UML attribute in schemas.

serialize Tag

There are some situations when you do not want to serialize attribute values. For example, the value of a UML attribute may be derived from other attribute values. Derived attribute values can be computed from other attribute values, so they don't need to be serialized when saving objects. If you set the *serialize* tag to *false* on an attribute, XMI creates neither an XML element declaration nor an XML attribute declaration for the attribute. By default, the value of this tag is *true*.

element and *attribute* Tags

For some UML attributes, XMI creates both an XML element declaration and an XML attribute declaration. You can cause XMI to create only an XML element declaration for a UML attribute. You can also cause XMI to create only an XML attribute declaration for a UML attribute. You cause these effects by providing the value *true* for either the *element* tag or the *attribute* tag. If the *element* tag is *true*, XMI creates only an XML element declaration for the UML attribute. If the *attribute* tag is *true*, XMI creates only an XML attribute declaration for the UML attribute.

XMI imposes some restrictions when using these tags. You cannot set both the *element* tag and the *attribute* tag to *true* for a UML attribute. Since multiple values for an attribute must be represented using XML elements rather than XML attributes, you cannot set the *attribute* tag to *true* for an attribute that can have multiple values. You also cannot set the *attribute* tag to *true* for UML attributes with types that are classes. Finally, you cannot set the *element* tag to *true* for a UML attribute if the class that has the attribute has a value of *empty* for its *contentType* tag.

The use of these tags enables you to customize your XML documents. You can choose to serialize the data for objects in XML elements rather than XML attributes. Or you can choose to serialize the data for objects in XML attributes, which may result in shorter documents but longer start tags for XML elements. XMI provides this flexibility so you can create highly readable documents that are easily integrated with other XML software.

We mentioned that using XML attributes usually results in shorter documents than using XML elements. There are several reasons you might set the *element* tag to *true*, though. XML parsers may not preserve all of the whitespace in an XML attribute value, whereas the whitespace is preserved if it is in the content of an XML element. Also, XML parsers do not preserve the order of XML attributes in an XML element, but the order of XML elements is preserved. Finally, for cross-file references, XML elements must be used.

Consider the model in Figure 3.7. The *Car* class has a UML attribute called *available* of type *Boolean*. Since the *Boolean* datatype in the model has a *schemaType* tag set to *boolean* (the actual value is *http://www.w3.org/2001/XMLSchema#boolean*, but we shortened it to make the diagram easier to understand), XMI uses the *boolean* schema datatype for it.

Here is the complex type for the *Car* class if the *element* tag for attribute *available* is *true*:

```
<xsd:complexType name="Car">
  <xsd:choice minOccurs="0" maxOccurs="unbounded">
    <xsd:element name="available" type="xsd:boolean"/>
    <xsd:element ref="xmi:Extension"/>
  </xsd:choice>
  <xsd:attribute ref="xmi:id"/>
  <xsd:attributeGroup ref="ObjectAttribs"/>
</xsd:complexType>
```

A particular *Car* object for which the *available* attribute has the value *true* is serialized as follows to validate with the previous schema:

```
<Car>
  <available>true</available>
</Car>
```

If the *attribute* tag for the *available* attribute is *true*, the complex type for the *Car* class is as follows:

```
<xsd:complexType name="Car">
  <xsd:choice minOccurs="0" maxOccurs="unbounded">
    <xsd:element ref="xmi:Extension"/>
  </xsd:choice>
```

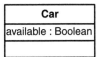

Car
available : Boolean

«datatype»
Boolean
{schemaType = boolean}

Figure 3.7 The *Car* class with the *available* attribute.

```
    <xsd:attribute ref="xmi:id"/>
    <xsd:attributeGroup ref="ObjectAttribs"/>
    <xsd:attribute name="available" type="xsd:boolean"/>
</xsd:complexType>
```

A *Car* object for which the *available* attribute has the value *true* is serialized as follows to validate with the previous schema:

```
<Car available="true"/>
```

includeNils Tag

If you set the *includeNils* tag to *true*, XMI creates XML element declarations that enable nil values to be written in an XMI document. To do this, the XML element declarations must include the XML attribute *nillable* and it must be *true*. For example, for a *Person* class that has an attribute called *name* of type *string* (the schema *string* datatype), if the *includeNils* tag is *true*, the complex type for the *Person* class appears as follows in a schema:

```
<xsd:complexType name="Person">
    <xsd:choice minOccurs="0" maxOccurs="unbounded">
      <xsd:element name="name" type="xsd:string" nillable="true"/>
      <xsd:element ref="xmi:Extension"/>
    </xsd:choice>
    <xsd:attribute ref="xmi:id"/>
    <xsd:attributeGroup ref="xmi:ObjectAttribs"/>
    <xsd:attribute name="name" type="xsd:string"/>
</xsd:complexType>
```

We have seen that the default XML element declaration for attributes does not include the *nillable* XML attribute. The *includeNils* tag cannot be set to *true* if the *attribute* tag is *true*, because nil values must be represented using XML elements. Nor can the *includeNils* tag be set to *true* for a UML attribute belonging to a class that has its *contentType* tag set to *empty*.

Multiplicity Tags

By default, XMI creates an XML element declaration for a UML attribute without using the multiplicity of the UML attribute. Any number of XML elements can appear in the content, regardless of the multiplicity of the UML attribute. XMI uses the multiplicity of a UML attribute if you provide the value *true* for the *enforceMinimumMultiplicity* or *enforceMaximumMultiplicity* tags. You can specify that XMI enforces minimum multiplicities, maximum multiplicities, or both minimum and maximum multiplicities.

If you set either (or both) of these tags to *true* for a UML attribute, the *ordered* tag of the class that the attribute belongs to must have the value *true*, because XML schemas enforce multiplicities correctly only for ordered content. A consequence of setting either (or both) of these tags to *true* is that XMI does not create an XML attribute declaration for the UML attribute unless all of the following conditions are true for the UML attribute:

- Its multiplicity is exactly 1.
- Its type is a datatype.
- Its *attribute* tag is set to *true*.

In this case, XMI creates an XML attribute declaration with a *use* attribute that is set to *required*.

Let's see the effect of using the multiplicity tags on the complex type declaration for a class. Consider a *Person* class that has a UML attribute called *hobby* that has a type of *string* (the schema *string* datatype) and a multiplicity of *1..3*. By default, the complex type declaration for this class appears as follows:

```
<xsd:complexType name="Person">
  <xsd:choice minOccurs="0" maxOccurs="unbounded">
    <xsd:element name="hobby" type="xsd:string"/>
    <xsd:element ref="xmi:Extension"/>
  </xsd:choice>
  <xsd:attribute ref="xmi:id"/>
  <xsd:attributeGroup ref="xmi:ObjectAttribs"/>
</xsd:complexType>
```

Notice that the multiplicity for the UML attribute is not used in the corresponding XML element declaration.

If you set the *enforceMinimumMultiplicity* tag to *true* for the UML attribute *hobby*, the complex type declaration appears as follows:

```
<xsd:complexType name="Person">
  <xsd:sequence>
    <xsd:element name="hobby" type="xsd:string" minOccurs="1"
                 maxOccurs="unbounded"/>
    <xsd:element ref="xmi:Extension" minOccurs="0"
                 maxOccurs="unbounded"/>
  </xsd:sequence>
  <xsd:attribute ref="xmi:id"/>
  <xsd:attributeGroup ref="xmi:ObjectAttribs"/>
</xsd:complexType>
```

Note the presence of a *sequence* XML element rather than a *choice* XML element. The *sequence* XML element is used because we are required to set the *ordered* tag to *true* when we set any of the multiplicity tags to *true*. Also note that the *minOccurs* attribute in the *hobby* XML element declaration is *1*, because the minimum multiplicity of the UML attribute *hobby* is *1*. The maximum multiplicity of *3* is not enforced in this case.

If you instead set the *enforceMaximumMultiplicity* tag to *true* for the UML attribute *hobby*, the complex type declaration appears as follows:

```
<xsd:complexType name="Person">
  <xsd:sequence>
    <xsd:element name="hobby" type="xsd:string" minOccurs="0"
               maxOccurs="3"/>
    <xsd:element ref="xmi:Extension" minOccurs="0"
               maxOccurs="unbounded"/>
  </xsd:sequence>
  <xsd:attribute ref="xmi:id"/>
  <xsd:attributeGroup ref="xmi:ObjectAttribs"/>
</xsd:complexType>
```

Note that, just as for the *enforceMinimumMultiplicity* tag, there is a *sequence* XML element rather than a *choice* XML element. This time, however, the *minOccurs* attribute is *0* and the *maxOccurs* attribute is *3*, because the maximum multiplicity of the UML attribute is 3. The minimum multiplicity of *1* is not enforced in this case.

As you might expect, setting both the *enforceMinimumMultiplicity* and *enforceMaximumMultiplicity* tags to *true* for the UML attribute *hobby* results in the following complex type declaration:

```
<xsd:complexType name="Person">
  <xsd:sequence>
    <xsd:element name="hobby" type="xsd:string" minOccurs="1"
               maxOccurs="3"/>
    <xsd:element ref="xmi:Extension"/>
  </xsd:sequence>
  <xsd:attribute ref="xmi:id"/>
  <xsd:attributeGroup ref="xmi:ObjectAttribs"/>
</xsd:complexType>
```

The value of *minOccurs* is *1* and the value of *maxOccurs* is *3* for the *hobby* XML element, matching the multiplicity of the UML attribute *hobby*.

So far, we have seen that the multiplicity tags affect the XML element declaration corresponding to a UML attribute. The *enforceMinimumMultiplicity* tag can also affect the corresponding XML attribute declaration as well. Consider a *Person* class with a *name* attribute of type *string* (the schema *string* datatype) that has a multiplicity of *1..1*. If the *enforceMinimumMultiplicity* tag is set to *true* for the *name* attribute, and the *attribute* tag is *true* also, the complex type declaration for the class *Person* is as follows:

```
<xsd:complexType name="Person">
  <xsd:choice minOccurs="0" maxOccurs="unbounded">
    <xsd:element ref="xmi:Extension"/>
  </xsd:choice>
  <xsd:attribute ref="xmi:id"/>
  <xsd:attributeGroup ref="xmi:ObjectAttribs"/>
  <xsd:attribute name="name" type="xsd:string" use="required"/>
</xsd:complexType>
```

Notice that the *use* attribute in the XML attribute declaration is set to *required*, meaning that the attribute must appear in *Person* XML elements in documents that validate with the schema.

XMI creates only an element declaration for the *name* UML attribute if you set the *enforceMinimumMultiplicity* tag to *true* as before and also set the *element* tag to *true* for the *name* attribute:

```
<xsd:complexType name="Person">
  <xsd:sequence>
    <xsd:element name="name" type="xsd:string" minOccurs="1"
                 maxOccurs="unbounded"/>
    <xsd:element ref="xmi:Extension"/>
  </xsd:sequence>
  <xsd:attribute ref="xmi:id"/>
  <xsd:attributeGroup ref="xmi:ObjectAttribs"/>
</xsd:complexType>
```

Notice that the *minOccurs* attribute has the value *1*.

Finally, if you set the *enforceMinimumMultiplicity*, *enforceMaximumMultiplicity*, and *element* tags to *true* for the *name* attribute, this is the declaration you get for the *Person* class:

```
<xsd:complexType name="Person">
  <xsd:sequence>
    <xsd:element name="name" type="xsd:string" minOccurs="1"
                 maxOccurs="1"/>
    <xsd:element ref="xmi:Extension"/>
  </xsd:sequence>
  <xsd:attribute ref="xmi:id"/>
  <xsd:attributeGroup ref="xmi:ObjectAttribs"/>
</xsd:complexType>
```

The *enforceMaximumMultiplicity* tag does not apply to UML attributes that have an *attribute* tag with the value *true*, because there can only be one XML attribute with a particular name in an XML element.

form Tag

You can require the use of a namespace prefix in the tag name of an XML element or the name of an XML attribute corresponding to a UML attribute by setting the *form* tag to *qualified*. For example, consider a *Person* class with a *name* attribute of type *string* (the schema *string* datatype) and a multiplicity of *0..1*. If the *form* tag is set to *qualified* for the *name* attribute, the complex type declaration for the class *Person* is as follows:

```
<xsd:complexType name="Person">
  <xsd:choice>
    <xsd:element name="name" type="xsd:string" form="qualified"/>
```

```
        <xsd:element ref="xmi:Extension"/>
      </xsd:choice>
      <xsd:attribute ref="xmi:id"/>
      <xsd:attributeGroup ref="xmi:ObjectAttribs"/>
      <xsd:attribute name="name" type="xsd:string" form="qualified"/>
    </xsd:complexType>
```

Notice the *form* XML attributes in the XML element declaration and the XML attribute declaration for the *name* UML attribute.

Value Tags

The last two tags we discuss that affect UML attributes only affect the XML attribute declarations for them. If you provide a value for the *defaultValue* tag, that value is used as the default value in the XML attribute declaration for the UML attribute. If you provide a value for the *fixedValue* tag, that value is used as the fixed value of the XML attribute declaration for the UML attribute. You may not set a value for both tags, only one of them.

If the *defaultValue* tag is set to *John Doe* for the *name* attribute of the *Person* class, as described in the previous example, the complex type declaration for class *Person* appears as follows:

```
    <xsd:complexType name="Person">
      <xsd:choice>
        <xsd:element name="name" type="xsd:string"/>
        <xsd:element ref="xmi:Extension"/>
      </xsd:choice>
      <xsd:attribute ref="xmi:id"/>
      <xsd:attributeGroup ref="xmi:ObjectAttribs"/>
      <xsd:attribute name="name" type="xsd:string" default="John Doe"/>
    </xsd:complexType>
```

Note that the *default* XML attribute in the XML attribute declaration for the *name* UML attribute has the value *John Doe*.

If the *fixedValue* tag is set to *Required Name* for the *name* attribute of the *Person* class, as described in the previous example, the complex type declaration for class *Person* appears as follows:

```
    <xsd:complexType name="Person">
      <xsd:choice>
        <xsd:element name="name" type="xsd:string"/>
        <xsd:element ref="xmi:Extension"/>
      </xsd:choice>
      <xsd:attribute ref="xmi:id"/>
      <xsd:attributeGroup ref="xmi:ObjectAttribs"/>
      <xsd:attribute name="name" type="xsd:string" fixed="Required Name"/>
    </xsd:complexType>
```

Note that the *fixed* XML attribute in the XML attribute declaration for the *name* UML attribute has the value *Required Name*.

Association Ends

Many of the tags that affect attributes affect association ends as well. There are also two tags that affect association ends that do not affect attributes. Remember that we do not use association ends in this book to represent composition, so the following discussion pertains to association ends that do not represent composition. Here is a list of the tags that affect association ends:

- *xmiName*
- *serialize*
- *attribute*
- *element*
- *enforceMaximumMultiplicity*
- *enforceMinimumMultiplicity*
- *form*
- *remoteOnly*
- *href*

We discuss each of these tags, how they affect the representation of association ends in schemas, and how the tags affect each other.

xmiName Tag

We have already explained the use of the *xmiName* tag with classes and attributes. You can also set this tag on association ends as well. The value of the tag is the name that XMI uses for the name of the element declaration and the attribute declaration for an association end in a schema.

serialize Tag

There are some situations when you do not want to serialize association ends. For example, you might implement a system that automatically sets both references (we use the term *reference* to mean an instance of an association end) for objects if one reference is restored for a bidirectional association. In this case, you do not need to serialize the reference that will be automatically set when the opposite reference is set. If you set the *serialize* tag to *false* on an association end, XMI creates neither an XML element declaration nor an XML attribute declaration for the association end. By default, the value of this tag is *true*.

element and *attribute* Tags

XMI creates both an XML attribute declaration and an XML element declaration for an association end. You can specify whether to generate only an attribute declaration or only an element declaration for an association end. If the *attribute* tag is set to *true*, only an XML attribute declaration is created; if the *element* tag is *true*, only an XML element declaration is created. You cannot set both the *attribute* and *element* tags to *true*. Note that you cannot set the *attribute* tag to *true* if the *href* tag is set to *true* for an association end. We describe the use of the *href* tag later in this section.

Multiplicity Tags

By default, XMI does not use the multiplicity of an association end when it creates an XML element declaration for the association end. If you set the value of the *enforceMinimumMultiplicity* or *enforceMaximumMultiplicity* tags to *true*, XMI will use the multiplicity of the association end.

The consequences of using these tags for an association end are similar to the consequences of using the tags for a UML attribute. First, the *ordered* tag of the class that the association end belongs to must be *true*, so the multiplicity is enforced correctly. Second, XMI creates only an XML element declaration for the association end unless both of the following conditions are true for the association end, in which case XMI creates only an XML attribute for the association end:

- The association end has a multiplicity of *1..1*.
- The *attribute* tag of the association end is set to *true*.

Consider the model shown in Figure 3.8. The *Car* class has an association end called *passenger* with a multiplicity of *1..5*. By default, XMI creates the following complex type declaration for the *Car* class:

```
<xsd:complexType name="Car">
    <xsd:choice minOccurs="0" maxOccurs="unbounded">
      <xsd:element name="passenger" type="xmi:Any"/>
      <xsd:element ref="xmi:Extension"/>
    </xsd:choice>
    <xsd:attribute ref="xmi:id"/>
    <xsd:attributeGroup ref="xmi:ObjectAttribs"/>
    <xsd:element name="passenger" type="xsd:IDREFS"/>
</xsd:complexType>
```

Notice that there can be any number of *passenger* XML elements and any number of identifiers in the *passenger* XML attribute.

If you set the *enforceMinimumMultiplicity* tag to *true* for the *passenger* association end, XMI creates an XML element declaration rather than an XML attribute declaration for the *passenger* association end. The complex type declaration for the *Car* class is as follows:

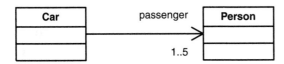

Figure 3.8 A *Car* with passengers.

```
<xsd:complexType name="Car">
    <xsd:sequence>
      <xsd:element name="passenger" type="xmi:Any"
                   minOccurs="1" maxOccurs="unbounded"/>
      <xsd:element ref="xmi:Extension" minOccurs="0"
                   maxOccurs="unbounded"/>
    </xsd:sequence>
    <xsd:attribute ref="xmi:id"/>
    <xsd:attributeGroup ref="xmi:ObjectAttribs"/>
</xsd:complexType>
```

Notice that the *minOccurs* attribute is *1* for the *passenger* XML element.

If you set the *enforceMaximumMultiplicity* tag to *true*, the XML element declaration for the association end has a *maxOccurs* attribute with a value of *5*:

```
<xsd:complexType name="Car">
    <xsd:sequence>
      <xsd:element name"passenger" type="xmi:Any"
                   minOccurs="0" maxOccurs="5"/>
      <xsd:element ref="xmi:Extension" minOccurs="0"
                   maxOccurs="unbounded"/>
    </xsd:sequence>
    <xsd:attribute ref="xmi:id"/>
    <xsd:attributeGroup ref="xmi:ObjectAttribs"/>
</xsd:complexType>
```

If the multiplicity of the *passenger* association end is *1..1*, the *enforceMinimumMultiplicity* tag is set to *true*, the *enforceMaximumMultiplicity* tag is set to *true*, and the *attribute* tag for the *passenger* association end is set to *true*, the complex type declaration is as follows:

```
<xsd:complexType name="Car">
    <xsd:choice minOccurs="0" maxOccurs="unbounded">
      <xsd:element ref="xmi:Extension"/>
    </xsd:choice>
    <xsd:attribute ref="xmi:id"/>
    <xsd:attributeGroup ref="xmi:ObjectAttribs"/>
    <xsd:attribute name="passenger" type="xsd:IDREF" use="required"/>
</xsd:complexType>
```

Notice that the type of the *passenger* XML attribute is *IDREF*, and that attribute must be present.

form Tag

By default, the XML element declaration and the XML attribute declaration, if any, that XMI creates for an association end are declared locally in the complex type declaration for the class that has the association end. This means that you are prohibited from using a namespace prefix in the tag name of the XML element or the name of the attribute. However, if you set the *form* tag to *qualified*, XMI creates an XML element declaration and an XML attribute declaration that have the XML attribute *form* set to *qualified*. This means that a namespace prefix must be used if the XML element or XML attribute appears in a document.

remoteOnly Tag

If you set the *remoteOnly* tag to *true* for an association end, XMI does not create an XML attribute declaration for the association end, just an element declaration. The reason is that a reference (an instance of an association end) will only be serialized in this case if the referenced object is in another document. Since the referenced object is in another document, the reference will be represented in a document by an XML element that has an *href* XML attribute with a value that is a URI that refers to the object in the other document.

Consider the following example. The model in Figure 3.9 includes a *Car* class that has a *driver* association end. The *Person* class has a *car* association end. If you set the *remoteOnly* tag to *true* for the *driver* association end, the complex type declaration for the *Car* class is as follows:

```
<xsd:complexType name="Car">
    <xsd:choice minOccurs="0" maxOccurs="unbounded">
      <xsd:element name="driver" type="xmi:Any"/>
      <xsd:element ref="xmi:Extension"/>
    </xsd:choice>
    <xsd:attribute ref="xmi:id"/>
    <xsd:attributeGroup ref="xmi:ObjectAttribs"/>
</xsd:complexType>
```

Note that there is only an XML element declaration for the *driver* association end.

Now consider a *Car* object and a *Person* object. The *Car* object is related to the *Person* object via a *car* reference. The *Person* object is related to the *Car* object via

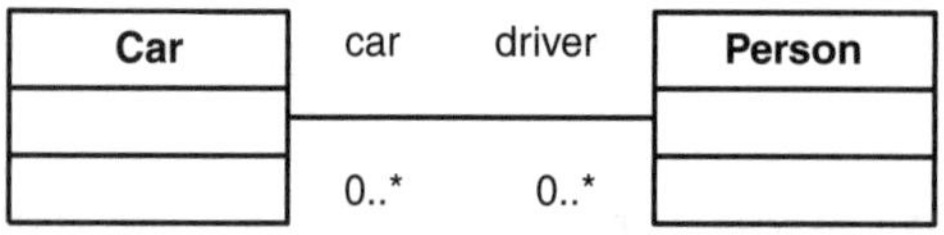

Figure 3.9 A *Car* has a *driver* and a *Person* has a *car*.

a *driver* reference. Because the *remoteOnly* tag is *true* for the *driver* association end, if the *Car* object and the *Person* object are serialized in the same file, they appear as follows:

```
<Person xmi:id="P1" car="C1"/>
<Car xmi:id="C1"/>
```

The *driver* reference for the *Car* object is not serialized because the *Person* object is in the same file as the *Car* object. Notice that the *car* reference is serialized, because references are serialized by default.

If the *Person* object is serialized in the file *person.xmi*, and the *Car* object is serialized in the file *car.xmi*, the *Car* object appears as follows:

```
<Car xmi:id="C1">
  <driver href="person.xmi#P1"/>
</Car>
```

The *driver* reference is serialized in this case because the *Person* object is in a different file than the *Car* object.

Why use the *remoteOnly* tag? The *remoteOnly* tag indicates that a reference is written only when the referenced object is located in another file. You can load the other file to obtain the actual object if you wish, but you are not required to do so. Without the remote object information, you would have no knowledge of the referenced object by loading the file that has the reference.

In the previous example, imagine that your application sets the *driver* reference for a *Car* object whenever the *car* reference for a *Person* object is set. If both objects are in the same file, the *driver* reference for the *Car* is restored even though it is not serialized because it will be restored when the *car* reference for the *Person* is restored.

Consider the case where the *Car* object is in *car.xmi* and the *Person* object is in *person.xmi*. Because the presence of the *Person* object in *person.xmi* is indicated in *car.xmi*, by loading only *car.xmi* it is possible to know the existence of the *driver* reference for the *Car* object. Now you have the option of loading the *person.xmi* file if you wish to fully restore the referenced object. You may be able to avoid loading *person.xmi* though, which would be more efficient than loading both files. If *car.xmi* did not indicate that the *Person* object was saved in *person.xmi*, you would be unaware of the existence of the *driver* reference until both files were loaded.

href Tag

If you set the value of the *href* tag to *true* for an association end, XMI does not create an XML attribute declaration for the association end, just an element declaration. By setting this tag to *true*, you are indicating that URIs are to be used to refer to objects within a document rather than XML IDs. Because of this, each reference corresponding to the association end must be represented by an XML element that has an *href* XML attribute. The value of the *href* attribute is a URI that refers to an XML element in the same document or in another document. Since only XML elements can be used for the references, only an XML element declaration is included in the complex type declaration for the class that has the association end.

Inheritance

You set the *useSchemaExtensions* flag to *true* to cause XMI to use schema extension to represent class inheritance. If the *useSchemaExtensions* flag is *true*, the *superClassFirst* flag must be set to *true* as well. The *useSchemaExtensions* flag affects the XML elements created for UML attributes and UML association ends, as well as the representation of inheritance.

Schema extension cannot be used to represent multiple inheritance. That is a limitation of XML schemas, not of XMI.

Consider the model in Figure 3.5. In the *Default XMI Schemas* section we saw the complex type declaration for the *Driver* class when schema extension is not used. That complex type declaration includes element declarations for the inherited *name* UML attribute and the inherited *address* association end. The default declaration for the *Driver* class is included here so you can compare it to the declaration when you set the tag *useSchemaExtensions* to *true,* which we show next:

```
<xsd:complexType name="Driver">
    <xsd:choice minOccurs="0" maxOccurs="unbounded">
      <xsd:element name="name" type="xsd:string"/>
      <xsd:element name="driverLicenseNumber" type="xsd:string"/>
      <xsd:element name="address" type="xmi:Any"/>
      <xsd:element name="car" type="xmi:Any"/>
      <xsd:element ref="xmi:Extension"/>
    </xsd:choice>
    <xsd:attribute ref="xmi:id"/>
    <xsd:attributeGroup ref="xmi:ObjectAttribs"/>
    <xsd:attribute name="name" type="xsd:string"/>
    <xsd:attribute name="driverLicenseNumber" type="xsd:string"/>
    <xsd:attribute name="address" type="xsd:IDREFS"/>
    <xsd:attribute name="car" type="xsd:IDREFS"/>
</xsd:complexType>
```

Notice that both the local and inherited attributes and association ends are reflected in the declaration. They can appear in any order in the content of the *Driver* type.

Consider what happens if *useSchemaExtensions* is set to *true* for the classes in the model in Figure 3.5, the *nsURI* tag is *http://cars*, and the *nsPrefix* is *cars* for the classes in that model. The declaration of the complex type for the *Driver* class is as follows:

```
<xsd:complexType name="Driver">
  <xsd:extension base="cars:Person">
    <xsd:choice minOccurs="0" maxOccurs="unbounded">
      <xsd:element name="driverLicenseNumber" type="xsd:string"/>
      <xsd:element name="car" type="cars:Car"/>
    </xsd:choice>
    <xsd:attribute ref="xmi:id"/>
    <xsd:attributeGroup ref="xmi:ObjectAttribs"/>
    <xsd:attribute name="driverLicenseNumber" type="xsd:string"/>
    <xsd:attribute name="car" type="xsd:IDREFS"/>
  </xsd:extension>
</xsd:complexType>
```

Notice that the *Driver* complex type extends the *Person* complex type, so there are no declarations for the inherited *name* UML attribute or for the inherited *address* association end. Notice also that the declaration of the XML element for the *car* association end has type *Car*. This is how using schema extension affects the element declarations for association ends.

By using schema extension, more of the schema validation capabilities can be used in your applications. As mentioned before, the type for the *car* XML element in the schema that uses extension is the schema type *Car*, rather than *xmi:Any*. A validating parser can detect illegal information in the *car* XML element with the schema that uses extension, but not with the schema that does not use extension.

Any *Extension* XML elements in the content of an XML element with type *Driver* must appear before an XML element for the local UML attribute *driverLicenseNumber* and the local *car* association end. This is so because of the way that schema extension works. When a type extends a base type in a schema, the elements in the content of the base type must be serialized before the elements in the content of the type that extends the base type. The *Extension* XML element is not included in the content of the *Driver* type because it is included in the content of the base type *Person*, so *Extension* XML elements must appear before the *driverLicenseNumber* and *car* XML elements.

Tagged Value Summary

We summarize our discussion of XMI tags in this section, using tables to present various aspects of the XMI tags. For a detailed discussion of these tags, refer to the previous sections in this chapter.

Table 3.1 enables you to look up the parts of the UML object model that are affected by a given XMI tag.

Table 3.1 XMI Tags and the UML Constructs They Affect

XMI TAG	UML CONSTRUCT
xmiName	Class, attribute, association end
serialize	Attribute, association end
element	Attribute, association end
attribute	Attribute, association end
enforceMaximumMultiplicity	Attribute, association end
enforceMinimumMultiplicity	Attribute, association end
form	Attribute, association end
remoteOnly	Association end
href	Association end
includeNils	Attribute
defaultValue	Attribute
fixedValue	Attribute
nsURI	Package
nsPrefix	Package
useSchemaExtensions	Class
contentType	Class
ordered	Class

Table 3.2 enables you to look up the tags that affect each UML construct.

Table 3.3 contains the scope of each tag. If the scope is package scope, setting the tag on a package makes the tag apply to the classes and their attributes and association ends within the package, as appropriate. If the scope is class scope, setting the tag on a class affects the attributes and association ends belonging to a class. If the scope is for a particular construct, the tag affects only the construct the tag is set on.

By setting tags on a package or class, you avoid setting the same tags repeatedly for classes in the package and for the attributes and association ends belonging to the classes. For example, the *element* tag applies to attributes and association ends. If the *element* tag is set to *true* for a class, the class itself is not affected, but each attribute and association end belonging to the class is treated as if the *element* tag were set to *true* for each of them. Another example is the *contentType* tag. If the *contentType* tag is set to *mixed* in a package, each class in the package is treated as if the *contentType* tag were set to *mixed* for each of them.

Table 3.2   XMI Tags for Each UML Construct

UML CONSTRUCT	XMI TAG
Package	nsURI, nsPrefix
Class	xmiName, useSchemaExtensions, contentType, ordered, superClassFirst
Attribute	xmiName, serialize, element, attribute, enforceMaximumMultiplicity, enforceMinimumMultiplicity, form, includeNils, defaultValue, fixedValue
Association end	xmiName, serialize, element, attribute, enforceMaximumMultiplicity, enforceMinimumMultiplicity, form, remoteOnly, href

Table 3.3   XMI Tags and Their Scope

XMI TAG	PACKAGE SCOPE	CLASS SCOPE	CONSTRUCT SCOPE
xmiName			x
serialize	x	x	x
element	x	x	x
attribute	x	x	x
enforceMaximumMultiplicity	x	x	x
enforceMinimumMultiplicity	x	x	x
form	x	x	x
remoteOnly	x	x	x
href	x	x	x
includeNils	x	x	x
defaultValue			x
fixedValue			x
nsURI	x	x	x
nsPrefix	x	x	x
useSchemaExtensions	x	x	x
contentType	x	x	x
ordered	x	x	x

Table 3.4   XMI Tags and Their Default Values

XMI TAG	DEFAULT VALUE
xmiName	No default value
serialize	*true*
element	*false*
attribute	*false*
enforceMaximumMultiplicity	*false*
enforceMinimumMultiplicity	*false*
form	No default value
remoteOnly	*false*
href	*false*
includeNils	*false*
defaultValue	No default value
fixedValue	No default value
nsURI	No default value
nsPrefix	No default value
useSchemaExtensions	*false*
contentType	*complex*
ordered	*false*

Table 3.4 contains the default values of each tag.

You can use these tables to determine which XMI tags to use to create schemas that are appropriate for your applications.

The XMI Model

Now that you know how XMI generates schemas from models, and how you can tailor the schemas that XMI creates, you are ready to learn about the XMI model, the model that defines many of the XMI elements and attributes. The XMI model gives you information about the contents of an XMI document and the differences between documents. In this section, we explain the XMI model and the schema that is created from the model, so you can understand the schema that is imported by every schema XMI creates. You have already seen some of the XML attributes and elements defined by that schema, particularly the XML attributes defined by XMI for specifying object identity and linking and the *Extension* XML element. XMI also defines XML elements that let you describe a document, identify the model that defines the data in the document, and specify differences in XMI documents.

We describe the XMI model from the bottom up, so that you do not need to refer to information later in the discussion to understand a particular part of the model. All of this information comes from the XMI specification (OMG, 2001).

XML Attribute Declarations

Before we explain the classes in the model from which the XML elements were created, we show the declaration of the XML attributes defined by XMI:

```
<xsd:attribute name="id" type="xsd:ID"/>

<xsd:attributeGroup name="IdentityAttribs">
   <xsd:attribute name="label" type="xsd:string" use="optional"
                  form="qualified"/>
   <xsd:attribute name="uuid" type="xsd:string" use="optional"
                  form="qualified"/>
</xsd:attributeGroup>

<xsd:attributeGroup name="LinkAttribs">
   <xsd:attribute name="href" type="xsd:string" use="optional"/>
   <xsd:attribute name="idref" type="xsd:IDREF" use="optional"
                  form="qualified"/>
</xsd:attributeGroup>

<xsd:attributeGroup name="ObjectAttribs">
   <xsd:attributeGroup ref="IdentityAttribs"/>
   <xsd:attributeGroup ref="LinkAttribs"/>
   <xsd:attribute name="version" type="xsd:string" use="optional"
                  fixed="2.0" form="qualified"/>
   <xsd:attribute name="type" type="xsd:QName" use="optional"
                  form="qualified"/>
</xsd:attributeGroup>
```

You can see the declaration of the identity attributes *id*, *uuid*, and *label*, as well as the linking attributes *href* and *idref*. The *ObjectAttribs* attribute group includes those attribute declarations as well as the declaration of the *version* XML attribute and the *type* XML attribute.

Extension Element

We have already seen the *Extension* XML element used in documents. Figure 3.10 contains the *Extension* class with attributes *extender* and *extenderID*. The *contentType* tag for the *Extension* class is *any*, and the *processContents* tag for the *Extension* class is *lax*. The *attribute* tag for the *Extension* class is *true*. The class declaration and the values of the XMI tags result in the following complex type declaration and element declaration:

```
<xsd:complexType name="Extension">
  <xsd:choice minOccurs="0" maxOccurs="unbounded">
    <xsd:any processContents="lax"/>
  </xsd:choice>
  <xsd:attribute ref="xmi:id"/>
  <xsd:attributeGroup ref="ObjectAttribs"/>
  <xsd:attribute name="extender" type="xsd:string" use="optional"/>
  <xsd:attribute name="extenderID" type="xsd:string" use="optional"/>
</xsd:complexType>

<xsd:element name="Extension" type="Extension"/>
```

You can use any of the object identity or linking attributes for the *Extension* element, as well as the *extender* and *extenderID* attributes. The *Writing Objects Using XMI* section of this chapter contains examples of the *Extension* XML element and its attributes.

Identifying Models

XMI provides the capability to unambiguously identify which models the data in a document conforms to and what the metamodel is for the data. The *Model* and *MetaModel* classes of the XMI model provide these capabilities. Figure 3.11 shows these classes. Each of them inherits from a *PackageReference* class since they each have a *name* and *version* attribute. Since the *useSchemaExtensions* flag is *true* for the XMI model, the declarations for this part of the XMI model are as follows:

```
<xsd:complexType name="PackageReference">
  <xsd:choice minOccurs="0" maxOccurs="unbounded">
    <xsd:element name="name" type="xsd:string"/>
    <xsd:element name="version" type="xsd:string"/>
    <xsd:element ref="Extension"/>
  </xsd:choice>
```

Figure 3.10   The *Extension* class.

```
  <xsd:attribute ref="id"/>
  <xsd:attributeGroup ref="ObjectAttribs"/>
  <xsd:attribute name="name" type="xsd:string" use="optional"/>
  <xsd:attribute name="version" type="xsd:string" use="optional"/>
</xsd:complexType>

<xsd:element name="PackageReference" type="PackageReference"/>

<xsd:complexType name="Model">
  <xsd:complexContent>
    <xsd:extension base="PackageReference"/>
  </xsd:complexContent>
</xsd:complexType>

<xsd:element name="Model" type="Model"/>

<xsd:complexType name="MetaModel">
  <xsd:complexContent>
    <xsd:extension base="PackageReference"/>
  </xsd:complexContent>
</xsd:complexType>

<xsd:element name="MetaModel" type="MetaModel"/>
```

XMI serializes *Model* and *MetaModel* objects the same way as objects defined by your models.

You can use these elements to specify the physical location of a document containing the model or metamodel. You do this by specifying the physical location in the *href* attribute. The *version* attribute enables you to specify which version of models or metamodels is being used in a document.

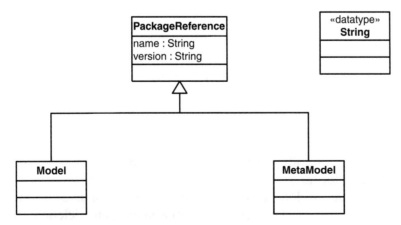

Figure 3.11 Class declarations for identifying models.

IMPORT XML ELEMENT IN XMI SPECIFICATION

The current version of the XMI specification includes a description for an
***Import* XML element. We believe that this element will be removed from the**
final version of the specification, so we do not describe it in this book.

For example, the following *Metamodel* object indicates that the metamodel
for the data in a file is UML version 1.3, which can be found in the file
uml13.xmi:

```
<xmi:MetaModel name="UML" version="1.3" href="uml13.xmi"/>
```

Describing a Document

Figure 3.12 illustrates the *Documentation* class in the XMI model. Since each of
the attributes of the class has a multiplicity of *0..**, the declarations for the class
in the schema are as follows:

```
<xsd:complexType name="Documentation">
  <xsd:choice minOccurs="0" maxOccurs="unbounded">
    <xsd:element name="contact" type="xsd:string"/>
    <xsd:element name="exporter" type="xsd:string"/>
    <xsd:element name="exporterVersion" type="xsd:string"/>
    <xsd:element name="longDescription" type="xsd:string"/>
    <xsd:element name="shortDescription" type="xsd:string"/>
    <xsd:element name="notice" type="xsd:string"/>
    <xsd:element name="owner" type="xsd:string"/>
    <xsd:element ref="Extension"/>
  </xsd:choice>
  <xsd:attribute ref="xmi:id"/>
  <xsd:attributeGroup ref="ObjectAttribs"/>
</xsd:complexType>

<xsd:element name="Documentation" type="Documentation"/>
```

Table 3.5 summarizes the type of information you can include as part of the
documentation for an XMI document.

Differences

XMI enables you to express differences in XMI documents. Figure 3.13 contains the class diagram for this part of the XMI model. We include an association that represents composition in this diagram because it comes from the
XMI specification. You can represent additions, replacements, and deletions of
objects in an XMI document. Here is the declaration for these elements:

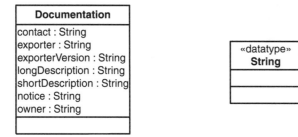

Figure 3.12 The *Documentation* class.

Table 3.5 Documentation Information

NAME	DESCRIPTION
contact	The person to contact with questions about the XMI document
exporter	The name of the tool that produced the XMI document
exporterVersion	The version of the tool that produced the XMI document
longDescription	A long, detailed description of the XMI document
shortDescription	A brief description of the data in the XMI document
notice	Legal disclaimers about the XMI document or copyrights
owner	The owner of the data in the XMI document

```
<xsd:complexType name="Difference">
  <xsd:choice minOccurs="0" maxOccurs="unbounded">
    <xsd:element name="target">
      <xsd:complexType>
        <xsd:choice minOccurs="0" maxOccurs="unbounded">
          <xsd:any processContents="skip"/>
        </xsd:choice>
        <xsd:anyAttribute processContents="skip"/>
      </xsd:complexType>
    </xsd:element>
    <xsd:element name="difference" type="Difference"/>
    <xsd:element name="container" type="Difference"/>
    <xsd:element ref="Extension"/>
  </xsd:choice>
  <xsd:attribute ref="id"/>
  <xsd:attributeGroup ref="ObjectAttribs"/>
  <xsd:attribute name="target" type="xsd:IDREFS" use="optional"/>
  <xsd:attribute name="container" type="xsd:IDREFS" use="optional"/>
</xsd:complexType>
```

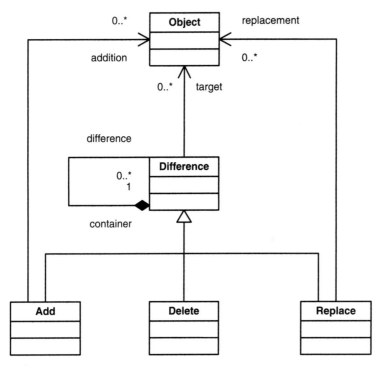

Figure 3.13 Difference classes.

```
<xsd:element name="Difference" type="Difference"/>

<xsd:complexType name="Add">
  <xsd:complexContent>
    <xsd:extension base="Difference">
      <xsd:attribute name="position" type="xsd:string" use="optional"/>
      <xsd:attribute name="addition" type="xsd:IDREFS" use="optional"/>
    </xsd:extension>
  </xsd:complexContent>
</xsd:complexType>

<xsd:element name="Add" type="Add"/>

<xsd:complexType name="Replace">
  <xsd:complexContent>
    <xsd:extension base="Difference">
      <xsd:attribute name="position" type="xsd:string" use="optional"/>
      <xsd:attribute name="replacement" type="xsd:IDREFS"
                     use="optional"/>
    </xsd:extension>
  </xsd:complexContent>
</xsd:complexType>
```

```
<xsd:element name="Replace" type="Replace"/>

<xsd:complexType name="Delete">
  <xsd:complexContent>
    <xsd:extension base="Difference"/>
  </xsd:complexContent>
</xsd:complexType>

<xsd:element name="Delete" type="Delete"/>
```

XMI serializes *Add*, *Replace*, and *Delete* objects in a document the same way as any other objects.

Consider the model in Figure 3.14, in which a *Car* has parts, and there are two kinds of parts, an *Engine* part and a *Cylinder* part. An *Engine* also has parts. The *Part* class has a *name* attribute with a type that is a *String* datatype. The *String* datatype is mapped to the *string* schema datatype because, although not shown in the diagram, its *schemaType* tag is *http://www.w3.org/2001/XMLSchema#string*.

Here is an XMI document in the file *base.xmi* that contains a *Car* object, an *Engine* object, a *Cylinder* object, and a *Part* object:

```
<xmi:XMI xmi:version="2.0" xmlns:xmi="http://www.omg.org/XMI">
  <Car xmi:id="_1">
    <part xmi:id="_2" xmi:type="Engine">
      <part xmi:id="_3" xmi:type="Cylinder"/>
    </part>
    <part xmi:id="_4"/>
  </Car>
</xmi:XMI>
```

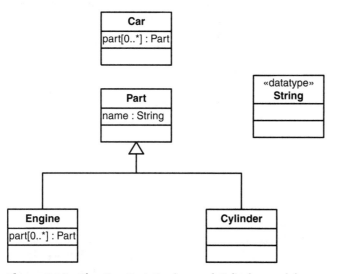

Figure 3.14   The *Car*, *Part*, *Engine*, and *Cylinder* model.

The *Car* object contains the *Engine* object and the *Part* object. The *Engine* object contains the *Cylinder* object. Here is an XMI document that contains a *Delete* object specifying the deletion of the engine:

```
<xmi:XMI xmi:version="2.0" xmlns:xmi="http://www.omg.org/XMI">
  <xmi:Delete>
    <target href="base.xmi#_2"/>
  </xmi:Delete>
</xmi:XMI>
```

Notice that the target of the *Delete* object identifies the XML element in the base document to delete.

Applying the deletion to *base.xmi* results in the following XMI document:

```
<xmi:XMI xmi:version="2.0" xmlns:xmi="http://www.omg.org/XMI">
  <Car xmi:id="_1">
    <part xmi:id="_4"/>
  </Car>
</xmi:XMI>
```

Notice that the *Cylinder* object inside the *Engine* object is deleted when the *Engine* object is deleted, since it is an object value.

You can specify additions to a document as well as deletions. You use an *Add* object to represent an addition to a base document. For each *Add* object, the *target* specifies the XML element that is the container for the XML element to add. The *addition* XML attribute identifies the XML element for the object to add. The *position* XML attribute indicates where in the container XML element the new XML element will be added. If no position is specified, the element is added at the end of the existing content of the XML element that is the target. If a position is specified, the new XML element is added so that it occupies that position inside the content of the target XML element. The first position is indicated with a *1*.

Consider the following base document *base2.xmi*:

```
<xmi:XMI xmi:version="2.0" xmlns:xmi="http://www.omg.org/XMI">
  <Car xmi:id="_1">
    <part xmi:id="P1" name="Part1"/>
    <part xmi:id="P2" name="Part2"/>
    <part xmi:id="P3" name="Part3"/>
  </Car>
</xmi:XMI>
```

The *Car* object has three parts. Now consider how to add new parts to the *Car* object. The part named *NewPart1* is to be added before the existing parts, the part named *NewPart3* is to be added after *Part1* yet before *Part2*, and the part named *NewLastPart* is to be added after *Part3*. Here is the XMI document containing the three *Add* objects representing each addition to the base document:

```
<xmi:XMI xmi:version="2.0" xmlns:xmi="http://www.omg.org/XMI">
  <xmi:Add addition="NP1" position="1">
    <target href="base2.xmi#_1"/>
  </xmi:Add>
  <Part xmi:id="NP1" name="NewPart1"/>
  <xmi:Add addition="NP3" position="2">
    <target href="base2.xmi#_1"/>
  </xmi:Add>
  <Part xmi:id="NP3" name="NewPart3"/>
  <xmi:Add addition="NLP">
    <target href="base2.xmi#_1"/>
  </xmi:Add>
  <Part xmi:id="NLP" name="NewLastPart"/>
</xmi:XMI>
```

The *position* for the first *Add* object is *1* because *NewPart1* is to be added at the beginning of the existing parts for the car. The *position* for the second *Add* object is *2*, because the positions are based on the original document. The *position* for *NewLastPart* is not specified, so that it will be added to the end of the existing parts for the car.

Applying these additions to *base2.xmi* results in the following XMI document:

```
<xmi:XMI xmi:version="2.0" xmlns:xmi="http://www.omg.org/XMI">
  <Car xmi:id="_1">
    <part xmi:id="NP1" name="NewPart1"/>
    <part xmi:id="P1" name="Part1"/>
    <part xmi:id="NP3" name="NewPart3"/>
    <part xmi:id="P2" name="Part2"/>
    <part xmi:id="P3" name="Part3"/>
    <part xmi:id="NLP" name="NewLastPart"/>
  </Car>
</xmi:XMI>
```

You can specify the replacement of an object in a base document using a *Replace* object. The *target* of the *Replace* object is the XML element for the object to replace. The *replacement* of the *Replace* object is the XML element for the new object that will replace the existing object in the base document. The *position* of the *Replace* element indicates where to add the content of the new object in the content of the existing object. The first position is indicated by a *1*. If no position is specified, the content of the new object will be added to the end of the existing content of the object to be replaced in the base document.

Consider how to replace the *Car* object in *base2.xmi* with another *Car* object, making the three parts for the original *Car* object the parts for the new *Car* object. Here is an XMI document with a *Replace* object that indicates that the *Car* object in the base document is to be replaced by the *Car* object with a *xmi:id* of _2.1:

```
<xmi:XMI xmi:version="2.0" xmlns:xmi="http://www.omg.org/XMI">
  <xmi:Replace replacement="_2.1">
    <target href="base2.xmi#_1"/>
  </xmi:Replace>
  <Car xmi:id="_2.1"/>
</xmi:XMI>
```

The result of applying the replacement to the original *base2.xmi* is as follows:

```
<xmi:XMI xmi:version="2.0" xmlns:xmi="http://www.omg.org/XMI">
  <Car xmi:id="_2.1">
    <part xmi:id="P1" name="Part1"/>
    <part xmi:id="P2" name="Part2"/>
    <part xmi:id="P3" name="Part3"/>
  </Car>
</xmi:XMI>
```

The only difference is that the *Car* object has a *xmi:id* of _2.1. The new *Car* object has the same three parts as the original *Car* object.

Now consider replacing the *Car* object in *base2.xmi* with another *Car* object that has a part. The new part is to be added to the beginning of the existing parts of the *Car* object to be replaced. The following XMI document contains the *Replace* object that specifies this difference:

```
<xmi:XMI xmi:version="2.0" xmlns:xmi="http://www.omg.org/XMI">
  <xmi:Replace replacement="_3.1" position="1">
    <target href="base2.xmi#_1"/>
  </xmi:Replace>
  <Car xmi:id="_3.1">
    <part xmi:id="NP1" name="NewPart1"/>
  </Car>
</xmi:XMI>
```

Applying this difference to the original *base2.xmi* document results in the following document:

```
<xmi:XMI xmi:version="2.0" xmlns:xmi="http://www.omg.org/XMI">
  <Car xmi:id="_3.1">
    <part xmi:id="NP1" name="NewPart1"/>
    <part xmi:id="P1" name="Part1"/>
    <part xmi:id="P2" name="Part2"/>
    <part xmi:id="P3" name="Part3"/>
  </Car>
</xmi:XMI>
```

XMI XML Element

Figure 3.15 contains a UML diagram for the *XMI* class. The *contentType* is *any*, and the *processContents* tag is *strict*. All the attributes can have multiple values except for the *version* attribute. The *version* attribute has its *attribute* tag set to *true*, its *form* tag set to *qualified*, its *fixedValue* tag set to *2.0*, and its *enforceMinimumMultiplicity* tag set to *true* (since this tag is set to *true*, the *ordered* tag is *true*; however, the *contentType* tag is *any*, so ordering is not relevant in this case). The declarations for the XMI class appear as follows:

```
<xsd:complexType name="XMI">
  <xsd:choice minOccurs="0" maxOccurs="unbounded">
    <xsd:any processContents="strict"/>
  </xsd:choice>
  <xsd:attribute ref="xmi:id"/>
  <xsd:attributeGroup ref="IdentityAttribs"/>
  <xsd:attributeGroup ref="LinkAttribs"/>
  <xsd:attribute name="type" type="xsd:QName" use="optional"
                 form="qualified"/>
  <xsd:attribute name="version" type="xsd:string" use="required"
                 fixed="2.0" form="qualified"/>
</xsd:complexType>

<xsd:element name="XMI" type="XMI"/>
```

The *XMI* complex type declaration does not use the *ObjectAttribs* attribute group because it defines its own *version* attribute that is required to be present, whereas the *version* attribute in the *ObjectAttribs* group is not required. All the attributes in the *ObjectAttribs* attribute group, except for the *version* attribute, are in the complex type declaration.

The *IdentityAttribs* and *LinkAttribs* attribute groups are used in the declaration of the *ObjectAttribs* attribute group, as described in the *XML Attribute Declarations* section in this chapter.

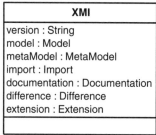

Figure 3.15   The *XMI* class.

XMI serializes *Model, MetaModel, Extension, Difference,* and *Documentation* objects in *XMI* XML elements or in XML documents using the same rules as other objects.

Summary

XMI specifies how to write objects to documents and how to generate schemas from models, and it defines a number of XML elements and attributes. You do not need to know much about XML to use XMI; however, if you do know XML, you can tailor the default XMI representation of objects and the generation of schemas. This flexibility enables you to create XML documents that match your needs.

After reading this chapter, you should have a good idea of how objects are represented in an XMI document and how classes are represented in an XMI schema. You should also be aware of some of the variations that XMI supports in XMI documents and schemas. As you move on into the next part of this book, *How To Use XMI,* we will focus on helping you learn how to use XMI in your applications. At times, you may want to refer back to the information presented in this chapter, either by reviewing the tables that summarize the major concepts or by looking at the sections that describe those concepts in detail.

How to Use XMI

Creating Your XMI Process

There are many ways you can use XML Metadata Interchange (XMI) in your applications. In this chapter, we describe a generic process for using XMI that you can tailor for your own purposes. We chose this process because it is representative of all the processes for using XMI. By examining the process we describe in this chapter, you can devise a process for using XMI that best suits your needs.

As we describe each step in the process, we explain the issues that you should consider when you use XMI. Issues to consider at each stage will be covered in the abstract but will be supported by plenty of pointers to other parts of the book that deal with the issues concretely. We also offer advice about which features of XMI to use in different situations based on our experience using XMI.

After we describe the process, we provide a concrete example of the use of the process. The example demonstrates the use of the entire process. Once you have seen the entire process in action, you can understand how the steps of the process relate to each other so you can decide which steps are appropriate for your situation. Then you can learn details about each step of the process and fit them into your view of the whole process.

Since this chapter describes many aspects of using XMI, it serves as a road map for the rest of the book. The rest of the book provides more details about the issues discussed here as well as concrete examples of XMI. Chapter 5 discusses issues related to modeling your data and reverse engineering models from Extensible Markup Language (XML) documents, Document Type Definition (DTD), and schemas. Chapter 6 discusses how to use XMI with the Simple API for XML (SAX) and the Document Object Model (DOM), two standard XML application programming interfaces (APIs). Chapters 7, 8, and 9 discuss the XMI Framework, an example of software that supports XMI and is included on the accompanying CD-ROM. Chapter 9 also discusses schema validation in more detail to help you decide whether to use validation in your applications. Chapter 10 discusses how XMI fits into a more general strategy for using models in your software development efforts and how XMI works well with meta data. Chapter 11 discusses some of the uses of XMI in the Websphere Studio Application Developer software included on the accompanying CD-ROM. Finally, Appendix A contains documentation about the XMI Framework.

Overview of the XMI Process

The XMI process that we describe here is model-based. This ties in to the Object Management Group's (OMG) Model-Driven Architecture approach, briefly described in Chapter 1 and discussed in more detail in Chapter 10. There are many benefits to modeling your data, but we do not describe all of them here. Please refer to one of the numerous books on Unified Modeling Language (UML) for a full description of the benefits of modeling.

We recommend that you perform the following steps when using XMI:

1. Define your objects using UML.
2. Create an XMI schema (optional).
3. Design your files.
4. Generate code from the model (optional).
5. Implement the application.

This process is illustrated in Figure 4.1. Two of the steps of the process are optional. Creating an XMI schema is optional because XMI does not require you to use XML validation in your applications. Generating code from the model is optional because you can implement your applications any way you wish. Although generating code can be considered part of implementing the application, we place it in its own step because we feel that you should evaluate whether generating code can be useful to you.

The following sections summarize each step and reference chapters in this book that cover related topics in greater detail.

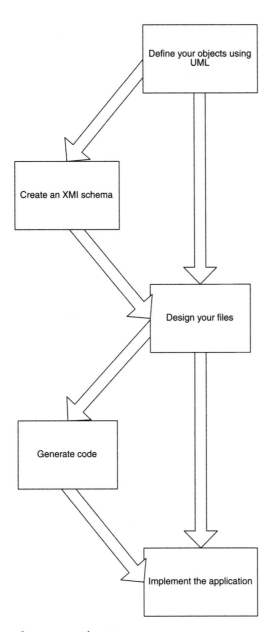

Figure 4.1 The XMI process.

Define Your Objects

Use UML to create a model that defines your objects. You can create a model by analyzing your problem domain, or you can reverse engineer a model from existing software. You do not need to be a UML expert to use XMI. Chapter 2 describes the parts of UML that you need to know to complete this step.

Are we recommending that you model your data in every case? No, we are not. Although we believe that modeling is very useful in most cases, modeling can be too much effort. If you are implementing a very simple system with only a few types of data that are completely defined and understood, you do not anticipate that other people will use your XML files, and the system is unlikely to change or evolve, then you probably do not need to model. You may still use the XMI object serialization rules to create XMI files, even if you do not have a model for your data. However, we strongly recommend that you create a model for your data if:

- Your data has not been precisely defined.
- You expect other people to use the data or to use it in new ways.
- Your system will evolve and grow.

Another reason to create a model is to ensure that XMI documents are correctly interpreted. If a model exists for objects, XMI software can use the model to correctly interpret an XMI document. Chapter 7 provides an example of this situation. XMI software can also perform semantic checking of XMI documents that is not possible without a model.

Once you have created a UML model for your objects, there are several things you need to check to make sure that you can use the model with XMI. Some XMI software may alert you to potential problems with your model and may change your model to be XMI-compliant automatically. Whether you are using software that handles these issues or not, you should be aware of them. Chapter 5 describes in more detail what these issues are, but we briefly explain some of them here.

For example, the names that you use in the model need to be legal XMI names, which generally means that they should be legal XML tag names and XML attribute names. If you have a class called *My Class*, for example, XMI software may attempt to serialize instances of that class using a tag called *My Class*, which is not a legal XML tag name. You can either change the name to *MyClass* or *My_Class* to make it a legal XMI name. The names of classes, attributes, and association ends need to be legal XMI names.

Some modeling tools enable you to have unnamed constructs in your model. For example, they may enable you to create an association between two classes without specifying a name for both association ends. XMI requires that you specify a name for your association ends, and the name must be a legal XMI name.

Another issue is the declaration of the types of attributes. Modeling tools may enable you to use a string to identify the type of an attribute without requiring that the datatype that is named in the string be declared in the model. You should include the datatype declarations in your model, so you can document your datatypes. If you include the declarations, you can document the mapping between your UML datatype declarations and the concrete datatypes in programming languages or XML when you implement the model.

Chapter 5 describes in more detail the issues that you need to consider when creating a UML model for use with XMI. It also describes how to reverse engineer a UML model from existing software.

Create an XMI Schema

XMI does not require you to use XML validation, but you can do so if you wish. XMI software exists to help you create schemas so you do not need to create them manually. Chapter 3 describes default XMI schemas and how you can tailor the schemas XMI software creates. Chapter 9 describes how you can use the XMI Framework to produce schemas from your models and the verification performed by XML validation with XMI schemas. Whether you create an XMI schema depends primarily on whether you decide to use XML validation.

Software is available that creates XMI schemas from UML models. Using software to create your XMI schemas rather than creating XMI schemas manually has many advantages. By using software to create the XMI schemas, you can save time, reduce the number of errors in the schemas, and ensure that the schema matches the UML model. The bigger your models, the more advantageous it is to use software to create your XMI schemas.

There are several issues you need to consider when deciding on whether to use XML validation:

- The source of the XMI files
- Performance
- How tolerant your software is of errors in input data

If other companies create XMI files, if you do not know the source of the XMI files, or if you do not trust the source of the XMI files, XML validation can help you determine if the XMI files are what you expect them to be. If your software will be using XMI files that your own software creates, you probably don't need to use XML validation, although performing XML validation can help you debug your software during the development phase.

If an XML parser performs XML validation when processing an XML file, it takes longer to process the file than if validation is not performed. In fact, it typically takes much longer to validate a document than to parse it. Is performance critical for your application? If it is, XML validation may take too long. Another performance issue to consider is how much data will be in the XMI files your software uses. If there is a lot of data, validation may also take too long. However, if not much data is put in the XMI files, performance may be acceptable even if XML validation is used. If performance is critical, we recommend that you analyze the impact of XML validation on your software's performance before deciding to use XML validation.

Another issue to consider when deciding whether to use XML validation is how much error checking you plan to implement yourself. XML parsers perform XML validation, so if you decide to use validation, you may not need to implement as much checking yourself. However, if your software already does a lot of checking and works well even with unexpected input data, XML validation may not be useful to you. You can also do validation during the development of your application to catch as many errors as possible, and then turn validation off once you are satisfied that your application works correctly.

We recommend that you use XML validation if one or more of the following statements applies to your application:

- The XMI files your software uses come from unknown or unreliable sources.
- Performance is not critical.
- You do not plan to implement error checking.

We recommend that you do not use XML validation if any of the following statements applies to your application:

- The XMI files your software uses come from trusted sources.
- Performance is critical.
- You plan to implement error checking.

Even if you choose not to validate your XMI documents, an XMI schema describes the expected contents of XMI documents, so it can help others produce XMI documents that your software can handle.

Once you make the decision to create an XMI schema, you need to decide whether to tailor the schema or use the default schema specified by XMI. As you saw in Chapter 3, XMI specifies a valid schema without requiring you to tailor the schema. Software that implements the XMI specification allows you to create valid schemas without requiring you to be an expert on XML schemas. However, XMI enables you to use your schema expertise if you wish to tailor the schemas to suit your purposes. By tailoring the schemas, you can affect the content of XMI documents and the checking performed by XML validation. If you are unfamiliar with schemas, it is best to start with the default schemas XMI specifies. As you learn more about schemas, you can tailor the default schemas if necessary.

Here are some of the issues to consider when deciding how to tailor an XMI schema. You can decide whether to represent certain data in XML attributes or elements. Using XML attributes may result in shorter documents and allow more data to be accessed when a start tag is processed by a parser. However, in some situations, an XML parser will normalize XML attribute values, and that normalization may be significant to your applications. For example, an XML parser may convert end-of-line or tab characters to space characters when reading an XML document. If those characters are meaningful to your application, they may be lost unless you put them in the content of an XML element rather than in an XML attribute.

We strongly recommend that you use XML namespaces in your applications and that you specify an XML namespace for each of the packages in your model. Doing so prevents name collisions if data defined by different models is written in the same document. It also prevents name collisions between two classes with the same name in different packages. You can choose not to use XML namespaces if you wish, however.

Default XMI schemas do not use schema extension. You can choose to use schema extension in your schemas if you wish. Doing so allows schema validation to detect more errors than otherwise, but it also imposes a restriction on the order of the content of XML elements. This happens because inherited information needs to be serialized before locally declared information when schema extension is used.

Each of these issues, choosing attributes or elements, namespaces, and schema extension, affects document producers. If you choose not to use XML attributes, document producers must be capable of putting the data in elements rather than attributes and vice versa. If you decide to use schema extension, document producers need to be able to serialize data in the correct order for schema validation to be successful. When you decide how to tailor XMI schemas, be aware of the impact that your choices have on document producers.

Design Your Files

After creating a model and possibly generating a schema from it, you should consider the XMI documents your system will read and write. XMI has many optional features that you may find useful that enable you to do the following things:

- Specifying information that describes your documents
- Creating cross-file references
- Storing additional information by utilizing extensions
- Embedding XMI within XML documents

We explain the issues to consider when deciding whether to use each of these features, and then we provide recommendations for when to use them. Although each of these features is explained in detail in Chapter 3, Chapter 3 does not provide guidance for when to use them. Some XMI software provides support for these features, while some does not. Therefore, you should consider which features you are going to use when you are selecting which XMI software to use. If the software you select does not provide the features you plan to use, you will need to implement support for them yourself. You need to examine the documentation for the XMI software you plan to use to ensure it has the capabilities you need.

To help you decide which features of XMI to use, you should consider how your XMI documents are likely to be used. Do you expect to use XMI documents created only by your software, or will your software use XMI documents produced by other software? How many times will your XMI documents be exchanged? Will your software exchange documents with other software and then receive them again? The answers to these questions can help you determine the features of XMI that you need to use.

Some decisions about the contents of the documents were decided when generating an XMI schema. Refer to the previous section, *Create an XMI Schema*, for more details about how schemas affect document content.

Describing Your Documents

XMI defines some XML elements that enable you to specify information about the objects in an XMI document. The elements include the *Documentation*, *Model*, and *MetaModel* elements. Chapter 3 contains all the details about the information you can specify in these XML elements, so we do not repeat them all here. You can use the *Model* element to unambiguously identify the model that defines your objects, for example. You should consider using this feature if you exchange your XMI documents with other software; the other software might be able to verify that the model you identified is the model that it expects. Another example of information that could be useful if you are working with XMI documents created by different software is the name and version number of the software that produced the XMI document. This information might help you determine the cause of bugs. You should review Chapter 3 for the types of data that XMI enables you to specify in order to decide whether to use these XML elements in your XMI documents.

Cross-File References

Once you know what kind of information you want to put in your XMI documents, you should consider whether to write your objects in a single XMI document or write them in several XMI documents. XMI enables you to group your objects into documents in any fashion you wish, and it provides a way for objects to reference objects in other documents. If the objects are written in several documents, the documents will probably contain references to objects in other documents. Using multiple XMI documents requires more software support than using XMI documents that do not refer to other XMI documents, but if your documents are very large, splitting them into smaller ones might result in significant performance improvements.

The decision to write your objects into multiple documents depends on the size of the XMI documents. It also depends on whether there are logical groupings of objects, whether the documents will be shared, whether it is feasible to update one of the documents without updating others, and whether meaningful work can be done without loading all of the documents. In general, if there is a logical way to group the objects, each group should be written in its own XMI document. If the documents will be shared, having multiple documents can reduce conflicts when more than one application accesses them. If one of the documents can be updated without updating all of them, this can also help to promote sharing. If meaningful work can be done with a subset of the objects, then writing the objects in multiple documents can be very useful. However, if all of the objects need to be available before they can be processed, it may be useful to put them all in a single document, since all of the documents containing the objects would need to be loaded in this case.

This discussion of cross-file references is rather abstract, but Chapter 8 contains a section that describes how cross-file references are handled by a particular implementation of XMI software, and it provides concrete examples. Reading that section can help clarify the issues you need to deal with when working with XMI documents that refer to other XMI documents.

Extensions

Whether or not you use cross-file references, you should consider if you need to store data in your XMI documents that is specific to your software and not meant to be shared with other software. This data can be put in XMI extensions so it does not interfere with data to be shared. An example is user interface information that is only useful for one application. You also need to consider what to do with XMI extensions from other software. Although the XMI specification does not require you to preserve extensions from other tools, doing so makes it easier to exchange documents, especially if you import an XMI document from another tool, modify the information in it, and then send it back to the tool that put the extensions in it. If you do put data into extensions, you need to consider the possibility that other tools will not preserve them.

It is possible to write objects that are defined by different models into one XMI document; doing so does not require you to use extensions. Extensions should be used for data that is not to be shared with other tools. If you put a

considerable amount of data in extensions, consider whether you should be
defining the data in your extensions in models so other tools can use it. You
can also put data in extensions if the data is not defined by a UML model.
Extensions are also a place where you can put XML elements that do not correspond to the XMI specification. See Chapter 8 for concrete examples of using
XMI extensions and how XMI software supports using them.

Embedding XMI

The issues we have considered so far affect how you use XMI in XMI documents, but there is a more basic issue to consider, however. Should you embed
XMI in an XML document? The XMI specification enables you to do so. For
example, you can use XMI to serialize your objects in the body of a Simple
Object Access Protocol (SOAP) document. (SOAP is an XML standard for mes-
saging; it may be replaced by the XML Protocol standard.) This is an example
of using XMI with another XML standard. You may use XMI in your own XML
documents wherever it makes sense to do so. XMI software may provide limited support for this feature, though, so if you do not want to implement XMI
support yourself, you should determine whether XMI software is available to
help you.

Recommendations

We recommend you put information into your XMI documents using the *Documentation*, *Model*, and *MetaModel* elements if any of the following statements
applies to your application:

- You want to unambiguously identify the model that defines your
  objects, especially if there are multiple versions of the model.
- The information you can specify will be used by the application.

We recommend you use cross-file references if any of the following statements applies to your application:

- You can logically place your objects into several groups.
- You are writing many objects to XMI documents.
- You can process a subset of the objects.
- You want to share XMI documents, either across programs or among
  teams.
- You want to version your objects.

We recommend you use XMI extensions if any of the following statements
applies to your application:

- You want to save data that is not to be shared with other tools.
- Some of the data you want to put in XMI documents is not defined by a model.
- You are exchanging XMI documents with software that preserves your extensions.

Generate the Code

After defining your model, possibly generating a schema, and considering some basic issues about the content of your XMI documents, you can begin to implement software that handles the XMI documents. You can implement the software any way you choose, of course. However, you should consider whether it is possible to generate some of the code you need from your model rather than implementing it yourself. One advantage of doing so is that your code will match your model; another advantage is that the code for a specific model may be more efficient than code that handles multiple models. This is because code that handles multiple models might need to be more general and therefore have extra overhead not required by code generated for a specific model. The generated code may also provide support for bidirectional linking, loading objects from XMI documents when they are needed, and enforcing restrictions on references between objects (for example, whether the objects can be referenced and whether the number of references matches the multiplicity of an association end in your model).

You may need to supply additional information in your model to allow code generation to occur. For example, you might need to explicitly map datatypes in your model to datatypes in the language you will use to implement the system. Some XMI software generates code that helps you serialize your objects using XMI. We provide a complete example of this for you in Chapter 8.

Since XMI documents are XML documents, you may be able to make use of software that generates code for specific types of XML documents. For example, if you are working with an XMI schema, you may be able to use software that produces code from an XML schema and that enables you to work with XML documents that validate against that schema.

Implement the System

Although you may be able to generate code from your model, you will probably need to implement at least part of your software yourself. For example, the generated code might provide interfaces that you need to implement yourself, or it might create empty method bodies that you need to write yourself. You need to decide what to implement yourself and what software to use that supports XMI or XML.

CODE GENERATION STANDARD

One advantage of using XMI is that there is a standard way to generate Java code from Meta Object Facility (MOF) models. The Java Metadata Interface Specification (JMI) describes the generation of interfaces that enable the creation of instances of particular MOF models as well as interfaces for saving those instances in XMI documents and loading them. By the time this book is published, this standard may be finalized. You should evaluate whether using JMI can help you implement your applications efficiently. You can also use the MOF to Interface Description Language (IDL) mapping if you are interested in cross-language APIs.

You should investigate whether to use software that supports XMI. You may not need to generate code to use this software. If you have followed the process we describe, the decisions you reached when designing your XMI documents can help you decide what XMI software, if any, is right for you. For example, you may have identified a need for XMI extension support or cross-file reference support. One advantage of using XMI software is that you do not need to become an XMI expert to use it. Another advantage is that you may not need to know much about XML itself to use the XMI software, since XMI software can present an API that is more powerful than XML elements and attributes. Of course, the more you know about XMI and XML, the better your chances of using XMI software effectively. Chapters 7 and 8 contain programs that use XMI software to read and write XMI documents, so you should read those chapters if you are interested in learning what XMI software can do for you.

There are many XML tools available, and many of them are free. There is no need to write your own XML parser unless you cannot find one for the language you are using, or you cannot find one with acceptable performance. You can use standard XML interfaces to read and write XMI documents. If you do so, though, you are responsible for knowing enough about XMI to produce legal XMI documents. Even if you cannot find software with XMI support that suits your needs, you may be able to use XML tools to help you work with XMI documents. When you design your application, you should investigate the available software for XMI and XML to avoid implementing functionality that is already available.

XMI Process Example

Now that you know the steps to follow when using XMI in your applications, you are ready to see the XMI process in action. This section contains an example that describes how two programmers use the XMI process to implement XMI for a practical application. The problem domain will be familiar to most readers. The application that is designed is not intended to represent the state of the art in electronic commerce or business process design. We present it to enhance your understanding of the XMI process so you can effectively use XMI in your applications.

The Situation

A car dealer has just made a deal with a car broker, who makes arrangements to purchase cars from the car dealer on behalf of his clients. In this deal, the car broker submits bids to purchase cars from the car dealer. The sales manager at the car dealer examines the bid and either accepts it or proposes a higher price. The car broker submits another bid if necessary, until the broker and sales manager agree on a price. In addition, the car broker wants to know which cars the car dealer has on the lot, so he does not submit a bid for a car that the dealer needs to order from the factory. The broker and dealer agree to exchange data using computers, rather than telephones or fax machines, in the hope that this approach will increase their efficiency.

The car dealer hires a programmer named Dave to implement the dealer's part of the system. The car broker hires a programmer named Bob to build the broker's part of the system. To avoid confusion about who the programmers work for, D is the first letter of Dave and dealer, and B is the first letter of Bob and broker. After consulting with the dealer and the broker about their needs, the two programmers meet and agree that the inventory and bid information will be exchanged using XML, and that the two types of information will be combined in the XML files that are exchanged.

Next, Dave and Bob begin to decide the details about the information to be exchanged. For brevity, let's assume they decide that the relevant information for each car includes the make, model, year, vehicle identification number (VIN), and options. The options might include air conditioning, power windows, power locks, a CD player, and so on. Finally, Dave and Bob agree to include the bid price from the broker, the offer price from the dealer, and the status of the car (available, sold, or negotiating).

Using this system, the car broker will be able to get an XML file containing the data for all the cars on the dealer's lot. The status of these cars is *available* if they have not yet been sold. When the broker submits a bid, the dealer will get an XML file containing the data for the car being bid on and the bid price. If the sales manager at the car dealer accepts the bid, the manager will send the car broker an XML file with the car's status changed to *sold*. If the sales manager rejects the bid, the manager will send the car broker an XML file with the car's status changed to *negotiating* and a counteroffer for the offer price. This process will continue until the sales manager and the car broker agree on a price or decide to stop negotiating (by changing the car's status from *negotiating* to *available*).

Dave and Bob decide to use XMI to help them with the XML part of their application. The rest of this section describes their actions when they undertake each of the five steps of the XMI process.

Defining the Objects

The first step in using XMI is to create a model that defines the data to be used in an application. Both Dave and Bob create models based on their understanding of the information to be exchanged. Figure 4.2 shows Dave's model, and Figure 4.3 shows Bob's model.

Bob and Dave compare their models and notice several important differences, even though they are not working with much data. Bob put the *make*, *model*, and *year* into a *Style* class, so that information does not need to be duplicated for each car with that style. Also, Bob does not have an attribute on the *Option* class to identify the option, whereas Dave has a *name* attribute for the *Option* class. Bob also included a *date*, *time*, and *dealer* for each car, whereas Dave did not.

There are several differences in the datatypes of the attributes. Bob made the *year* attribute an *int*, whereas Dave made it a *String*. The type of the *bidPrice* and *offerPrice* attributes in Dave's model is *int*, but Bob specified that the type

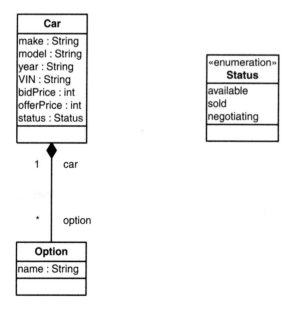

Figure 4.2 Dave's model.

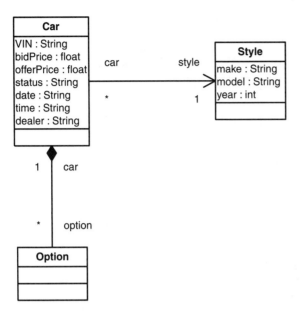

Figure 4.3 Bob's model.

is *float*. Dave defined a *Status* enumeration that has the literals *available, sold,* and *negotiating*. The type of the *status* attribute in Bob's model is *String*.

After comparing the models, Dave and Bob reconcile their models to make them the same. They agree to use Bob's *Style* class and Dave's *Status* enumeration. They also agree that the type for the *year* attribute should be *int*, and the type for the *bidPrice* and *offerPrice* attributes should be *float*. They decide to include a *Date* and a *Time* datatype in their model, and they specify the types of the *date* and *time* attributes accordingly. Taking our advice about modeling datatypes, they include each of the datatypes in the final model. They also include Dave's *Option* class, which includes a *name* attribute to identify each option. Figure 4.4 shows the model they agree to use.

Notice that Dave and Bob are not yet thinking about the XML representation of their data. They are clarifying their understanding of the data to be exchanged. Even for this simple example, you can see that there were some important differences in their understanding of the problem domain. Modeling has helped them resolve these differences before considering implementation details. By resolving differences now, they can avoid rework that might occur if they implemented their application without noticing these differences.

As a result of their modeling efforts, they now have clear documentation about the data to exchange that they can both use when they implement their part of the application. Other people can also use this documentation to understand the data to be exchanged.

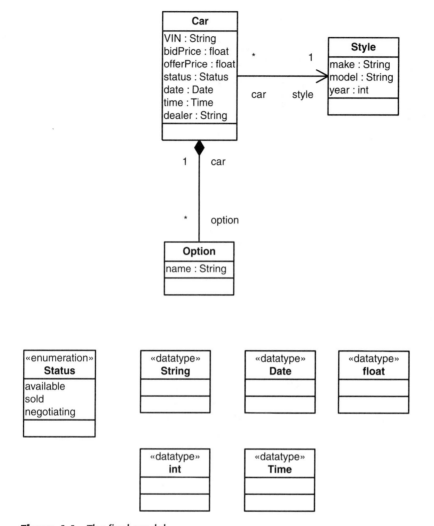

Figure 4.4 The final model.

If Dave and Bob did not use XMI, they might each have created an XML schema and then reconciled their schemas. There are several drawbacks to this approach. Since schemas contain the XML representation of the data, it would have been necessary to analyze all the differences between the two schemas. For each difference, they would need to determine if the difference is a result of a misunderstanding about the data to be exchanged or a difference in the XML representation of the data. Also, they might have begun to consider various other implementation issues, such as whether the schemas might make creating documents more difficult in exchange for doing more validation. Attempting to resolve these issues at the same time as they are resolving differences in their understanding of the data is much more difficult than doing those tasks separately.

Creating an XMI Schema

Now that Dave and Bob have created a UML model for their data, they can use XMI to help them represent the data in XML. Dave and Bob believe that it will be useful to create a schema for their application. Even if they decide not to use XML validation, the schema can still serve as documentation for the expected contents of the XML documents to be exchanged.

Neither Dave nor Bob is an expert on using XML schemas, so they decide to use the default schemas XMI creates. Another reason for using the default schemas is because they do not have strong opinions about whether to use XML elements rather than XML attributes to represent the data. The default schemas give document producers options for using either XML elements or XML attributes in some cases, and Dave and Bob want to keep their options open at this stage in the development of their application.

Dave and Bob both agree that it makes sense to use an XML namespace in their XML documents. Although they do not anticipate mixing their data with other data, by using an XML namespace, they ensure that if it becomes necessary to mix data in the future they will not encounter problems with names that conflict with names they use. They decide to use the XML namespace URI *http://carDealerAndBroker,* and they decide to use the namespace prefix *cdb* for this namespace in their schema. They specify the *org.omg.xmi.nsURI* and *org.omg.xmi.nsPrefix* tags in their model to document their decisions. Since the classes and datatypes are not in a package, they specify these tags for each class and datatype in their model. It would be very useful for a modeling tool that supports XMI to enable them to provide this information once and apply it to each class and datatype, rather than requiring Dave and Bob to manually set the tags for each class and datatype in the model.

Next, Dave and Bob consider the datatypes in their model and the available datatypes that schemas provide. They decide to map their datatypes to schema datatypes, as shown in Table 4.1.

Table 4.1   Datatype Mapping

MODEL DATATYPE	SCHEMA DATATYPE
String	string
Date	date
Time	time
int	int
float	float

Dave and Bob specify the schema datatype in their model using the *org.omg .xmi.schemaType* tag. Since they have included each of the datatypes they use in their model, they can set the value of the *org.omg.xmi.schemaType* tag for each datatype.

We describe how the XMI Framework creates schemas in Chapter 9. Dave and Bob use either the XMI Framework or other XMI software to create the following schema:

```
<?xml version="1.0" encoding="UTF-8"?>
<xsd:schema xmlns:xsd="http://www.w3.org/2001/XMLSchema"
            xmlns:xmi="http://www.omg.org/XMI"
            targetNamespace="http://carDealerAndBroker"
            xmlns:cdb="http://carDealerAndBroker">

<xsd:import namespace="http://www.omg.org/XMI"
            schemaLocation="xmi20.xsd"/>

<xsd:simpleType name="Status">
  <xsd:restriction base="xsd:string">
    <xsd:enumeration value="available"/>
    <xsd:enumeration value="sold"/>
    <xsd:enumeration value="negotiating"/>
  </xsd:restriction>
</xsd:simpleType>

<xsd:annotation>
  <xsd:documentation>CLASS: Car</xsd:documentation>
</xsd:annotation>

<xsd:complexType name="Car">
  <xsd:choice minOccurs="0" maxOccurs="unbounded">
    <xsd:element name="VIN" type="xsd:string"/>
    <xsd:element name="bidPrice" type="xsd:float"/>
    <xsd:element name="offerPrice" type="xsd:float"/>
    <xsd:element name="status" type="cdb:Status"/>
    <xsd:element name="date" type="xsd:date"/>
    <xsd:element name="time" type="xsd:time"/>
    <xsd:element name="dealer" type="xsd:string"/>
    <xsd:element name="style" type="xmi:Any"/>
    <xsd:element name="option" type="xmi:Any"/>
    <xsd:element ref="xmi:Extension"/>
  </xsd:choice>
  <xsd:attribute ref="xmi:id"/>
  <xsd:attributeGroup ref="xmi:ObjectAttribs"/>
  <xsd:attribute name="VIN" type="xsd:string" use="optional"/>
  <xsd:attribute name="bidPrice" type="xsd:float" use="optional"/>
  <xsd:attribute name="offerPrice" type="xsd:float"
                 use="optional"/>
  <xsd:attribute name="status" type="cdb:Status" use="optional"/>
```

```
    <xsd:attribute name="date" type="xsd:date" use="optional"/>
    <xsd:attribute name="time" type="xsd:time" use="optional"/>
    <xsd:attribute name="dealer" type="xsd:string" use="optional"/>
    <xsd:attribute name="style" type="xsd:IDREFS" use="optional"/>
  </xsd:complexType>

  <xsd:element name="Car" type="cdb:Car"/>

  <xsd:annotation>
    <xsd:documentation>CLASS: Option</xsd:documentation>
  </xsd:annotation>

  <xsd:complexType name="Option">
    <xsd:choice minOccurs="0" maxOccurs="unbounded">
      <xsd:element name="name" type="xsd:string"/>
      <xsd:element name="car" type="xmi:Any"/>
      <xsd:element ref="xmi:Extension"/>
    </xsd:choice>
    <xsd:attribute ref="xmi:id"/>
    <xsd:attributeGroup ref="xmi:ObjectAttribs"/>
    <xsd:attribute name="name" type="xsd:string" use="optional"/>
    <xsd:attribute name="car" type="xsd:IDREFS" use="optional"/>
  </xsd:complexType>

  <xsd:element name="Option" type="cdb:Option"/>

  <xsd:annotation>
    <xsd:documentation>CLASS: Style</xsd:documentation>
  </xsd:annotation>

  <xsd:complexType name="Style">
    <xsd:choice minOccurs="0" maxOccurs="unbounded">
      <xsd:element name="make" type="xsd:string"/>
      <xsd:element name="model" type="xsd:string"/>
      <xsd:element name="year" type="xsd:int"/>
      <xsd:element ref="xmi:Extension"/>
    </xsd:choice>
    <xsd:attribute ref="xmi:id"/>
    <xsd:attributeGroup ref="xmi:ObjectAttribs"/>
    <xsd:attribute name="make" type="xsd:string" use="optional"/>
    <xsd:attribute name="model" type="xsd:string" use="optional"/>
    <xsd:attribute name="year" type="xsd:int" use="optional"/>
  </xsd:complexType>

  <xsd:element name="Style" type="cdb:Style"/>

</xsd:schema>
```

If any of the details of this schema are unfamiliar to you, you can find a detailed explanation of XMI schemas in Chapter 3.

The decision to use XMI helped Dave and Bob in generating a schema to represent the data for their system. By agreeing on a model, they avoided the step of reconciling the separate schemas they would have created for the two models they came up with originally. Also, because they utilized XMI software to generate a schema for their combined model, they avoided the effort, and potential errors, of creating a schema manually. They also did not need to become schema experts to create their schema. All that Dave and Bob needed to know was how to specify an XML namespace and how to map their model's datatypes to schema datatypes. The XML namespace and schema datatypes that Dave and Bob chose are included in their model as values of XMI tags, making the results of those decisions available to XMI software and other developers that want to make documents that work with the application that Dave and Bob are developing.

Designing the Files

Now Dave and Bob consider whether they need to use advanced XMI capabilities. After reviewing the kind of information that XMI enables them to put in documents, both of them decide that they should use the *exporter* and *exporter-Version* XML elements inside the XMI *Documentation* XML element to identify their software. This information will make it easy to determine which software created which XMI documents. They determine that the XMI files will not be very large, so they do not plan to use cross-file references. Dave and Bob also cannot think of any information about cars to put in their XML files that is not specified by their UML model, so they do not plan to use extensions.

Dave and Bob both made the same decisions about their XMI files in this case, but if they had not, the XMI files that their parts of the application create would be exchangeable anyway, since they would follow the XMI standard. Also, by using XMI, they gave themselves the opportunity to use advanced XMI functionality in the future without regenerating their schema or impeding the exchange of their files.

Generating the Code

Now that Dave and Bob know what their XMI files will look like, they can begin to consider how to implement their parts of the car purchasing application. Bob decides to implement his part on his own, while Dave decides to use XMI software to implement his part. Since Dave has a UML model of the objects in the XMI files, he decides to use a code generator to generate some of the code for his system. He believes that by automatically creating code from the model, he can ensure that the code will match the model, and he can implement his system quicker than if he implemented all of it by hand.

Dave decides to use the XMI Framework, which provides basic capabilities for reading and writing XMI files and can generate Java code from a UML model. Chapters 7, 8, and 9 provide a description of the capabilities of the XMI Framework and demonstrate its use.

The XMI Framework generates a Java interface and a Java class for each class in the UML model; the generated class implements the generated interface. For each attribute in the model, the Framework generates two accessor methods to get and set the value of the attribute. For example, the following method signatures are generated for the *VIN* attribute for the *Car* class in Dave and Bob's final UML model shown in Figure 4.4:

```
public String getVIN();
public void setVIN(String value);
```

The XMI Framework generates three methods for each association end that is navigable. It ignores the multiplicity of the association end (this is a limitation of the current version of the Framework). Here are the signatures of the three methods corresponding to the *option* association end in the final model:

```
public Collection getOption();
public void addOption(Option object);
public void removeOption(Option object);
```

Now you are ready to look at the interfaces that the XMI Framework makes from the final UML model:

```
// Car.java
package car;

import com.ibm.xmi.framework.*;
import java.util.*;

public interface Car extends XMIObject {
  public String getVIN();
  public void setVIN(String value);

  public float getBidPrice();
  public void setBidPrice(float value);

  public float getOfferPrice();
  public void setOfferPrice(float value);

  public String getStatus();
  public void setStatus(String value);

  public String getDate();
  public void setDate(String value);
```

```
    public String getTime();
    public void setTime(String value);

    public String getDealer();
    public void setDealer(String value);

    public Collection getOption();
    public void addOption(Option object);
    public void removeOption(Option object);

    public Collection getStyle();
    public void addStyle(Style object);
    public void removeStyle(Style object);
} // Car

// Option.java
package car;

import com.ibm.xmi.framework.*;
import java.util.*;

public interface Option extends XMIObject {
  public String getName();
  public void setName(String value);

  public Collection getCar();
  public void addCar(Car object);
  public void removeCar(Car object);
} // Option

// Style.java
package car;

import com.ibm.xmi.framework.*;
import java.util.*;

public interface Style extends XMIObject {
  public String getMake();
  public void setMake(String value);

  public String getModel();
  public void setModel(String value);

  public int getYear();
  public void setYear(int value);
} // Style
```

As you can see, these interfaces enable Dave to create the objects he will put in XMI files. The XMI Framework maps the *int* and *float* UML datatypes to Java types *int* and *float*, respectively. It also maps the *String* UML datatype to the Java class *java.lang.String*. It maps the UML enumeration *Status* to the Java class *java.lang.String* as well as the UML datatypes *Date* and *Time*. A more sophisticated code generator would respect the multiplicities in the model and would enable users to map the UML *Date* datatype to the Java class *java.util.Date*. Note that all the interfaces were generated in a *car* Java package that was specified as an option to the XMI Framework code generator. From this example, you should now have an idea of how the XMI Framework generates code. We provide a detailed description of the code generated by the XMI Framework in Chapter 8.

Implementing the System

With the definition, design, and code generation steps complete, Dave and Bob can now complete the implementation of their parts of the car purchasing application. Since Dave is using XMI software, he does not need to implement as much functionality as Bob does. Both of them need to implement code that is unique to their parts of the application. For example, Dave may need to implement code to work with the car dealer's inventory system. However, since the XMI files are clearly defined and conform to a standard specification, neither Dave nor Bob needs to worry about misinterpreting the contents of the XMI files. If either Dave or Bob needs to make his XMI files more complicated to satisfy new requirements for his part of the application, he can do so without interfering with the other parts of the application. If they want to expand the system in the future by including more dealers or brokers, they can do so, and the additional dealers and brokers can understand the XMI files by looking at the UML model Dave and Bob produced.

Summary

The XMI specification does not require you to employ a particular process for your XMI projects; however, by following the process outlined in this chapter, you can take advantage of the benefits that XMI provides. The XMI process described here consists of five steps: creating a UML model that defines your objects, creating an XMI schema, designing your files by considering which XMI features are beneficial for your application, generating code from the model, and implementing the system. It is not necessary to generate a schema or generate code from your model, but you can do so if you wish. Doing so can help you implement your applications more quickly and ensure that your applications are correctly aligned with your model. We saw how using the XMI process can help Dave and Bob implement their system. Additionally, by basing their data representation on a standard like XMI, they also gain the benefit of being able to more easily integrate their application with other systems that use XMI in the future.

Now that you understand the entire process, you can begin to focus on each step of the process in more detail. The next chapter explains details about creating UML models for use with XMI and reverse engineering UML models from XML documents, DTDs, and schemas.

Creating Models
for XMI

As discussed in Chapter 4, the first step in using XML Metadata Interchange (XMI) is to create a Unified Modeling Language (UML) model for your objects. This chapter provides information that will help you create UML models to use with XMI.

UML enables you to create models without considering how they will be implemented. Since XMI creates Extensible Markup Language (XML) representations for UML models though, you may need to modify your models so XMI can create legal XML representations for them. You may need to provide legal XML element names for the constructs in your model, for example. Although modeling tools help you create models, some of them have features that you need to use with care to achieve the results you expect. The first part of this chapter helps you create models for use with XMI, and it contains advice for effectively using modeling tools.

You can create new models for use with XMI. However, you may want to create models based on existing XML. Doing so allows you to use the power of UML and XMI while building on your existing XML work. The second part of this chapter describes how you can reverse engineer models from XML documents, Document Type Definitions (DTDs), and schemas. You can revise these models to suit your needs. It can be quicker and more accurate to reverse engineer and modify models than to create UML models manually.

UML Modeling Issues

UML models can be created without considering how they will be implemented, so you may need to revise your UML models to make them suitable for use with XMI. These revisions may include providing additional information. Software that supports XMI may provide useful defaults for required information that is not specified in UML models, but if the XMI software you are using does not provide defaults, you may need to supplement your models with additional information.

The parts of UML that are used with XMI are classes, packages, datatypes, attributes, association ends, and tagged values. XMI ignores other parts of UML.

Several modeling tools exist that can help you create UML models. Some of these tools have features that should be used with care. You should be aware of two issues when you use modeling tools:

- Some modeling tools do not completely implement the UML specification.

- Some modeling tools provide the capability for UML constructs to exist without being displayed in UML diagrams. Software that supports XMI uses the model constructs rather than the diagrams. If your tool has this capability, you should be careful that when you delete a construct, the construct is deleted from the model rather than deleted only from a diagram.

The rest of this section discusses how to use UML modeling tools to create UML models for use with XMI.

Names

XMI uses the names of UML classes as XML element names. XMI also uses the names of UML attributes and UML association ends as either XML attribute names or XML element names. This means that the names in the model need to be legal XML element and attribute names. Fortunately, legal XML element names are also legal XML attribute names.

A legal XML element name or attribute name consists of letters, digits, and the period (.), hyphen (-), underscore (_), and colon (:) characters. The first character must be a letter, a _, or a :. We recommend that you avoid using the : character in your names because that character is used with XML namespaces. In general, punctuation marks are not allowed in names, and space characters are also not allowed. There are three ways to make illegal XML element names legal. The first way is to convert illegal characters to legal ones; the second way is to remove illegal characters from names. The third way is to provide a substitute name. For example, the name *My Class* is not a legal XML element name because of the space character. It can be transformed into a legal name by replacing the space character with _ to get the legal name *My_Class*. It can also be changed to a legal name by removing the space character to get the legal name *MyClass*.

If the name of a UML construct is not specified in your model, or a name is not a legal XML element name, you can provide a legal name by using a tagged value. The name of the tag is *org.omg.xmi.xmiName*, and the value is a legal XML element name. XMI software will use the value of the tag rather than the name of the construct. By using a tagged value, you do not need to modify the names of the constructs.

Another issue to consider with model names is that UML requires the names in your model to be unique within a namespace or scope. For example, the names of attributes and association ends that belong to a class must be unique, and they must be unique for all inherited attributes and association ends as well. The presence of duplicate names in a model may cause errors when generating code from the model or when creating an XMI schema from the model.

Multiplicities

UML specifies that multiplicities consist of a lower bound and an upper bound, with the lower bound greater than or equal to 0 and the upper bound greater than or equal to the lower bound. The upper bound may be unbounded, which can be specified by -1 or *. A modeling tool may also store the multiplicities in a form that is not defined by UML. You need to make sure that the multiplicities in the model are legal for XMI, even if your modeling tool enables you to specify illegal multiplicities. You also need to make sure that the XMI software you are using can use the multiplicities from the modeling tool.

Attributes

As discussed, the names of attributes must be legal XML element names, and the multiplicities of attributes need to be legal UML multiplicities. You may also need to overcome the limitations of some modeling tools in specifying multiplicities for attributes and be careful when setting the types of attributes.

Some modeling tools do not support multiplicities for attributes, although the UML specification says that attributes have multiplicities. If your tool does not support them, consider specifying the multiplicity of an attribute using a UML stereotype. For example, if the multiplicity of an attribute *a* for class *C* is *, you can set the stereotype of the attribute to *, which is shown as <<*>> in Figure 5.1. Of course, this representation of attribute multiplicities is not

Figure 5.1 Attribute multiplicity specified using a UML stereotype.

standard, so you may not be able to share your UML models with other tools without modifying them. This technique may help you specify attribute multiplicities if you need to use a modeling tool that does not support them. You can then transform the stereotypes representing attribute multiplicities to attribute multiplicities in a form that other tools understand.

We recommend that you specify a type for each attribute in your models and that the type be a class or datatype defined in the model. The advantages of including datatypes are explained in the next section. Also, when specifying attribute types, take care that you specify the correct type if there are classes or datatypes with the same name in different packages in your model. A modeling tool should enable you to distinguish them, but it may make it difficult to do so. If you believe an attribute type is referring to one class but it is referring to another of the same name in a different package, your DTDs, schemas, and generated code will not match your intentions. Therefore, you should be careful when you set the types of the attributes in your models if there are multiple classes or datatypes with the same name.

Datatypes

We recommend that you include datatypes in your models, even if your modeling tool automatically interprets names as concrete datatypes such as Java datatypes or XML datatypes. There are several reasons for this recommendation. Including the datatypes allows you to document any particular restrictions or requirements you need for the datatype. For example, you might need an integer that can be represented using 32 or 64 bits, or you may require that a string be composed of Unicode characters. Even if the modeling tool you are using maps datatypes to particular programming language datatypes, if you try to use the same model with another modeling tool, the other tool may not handle the datatypes in your models in the same way. If you include the datatypes in the model, you may be able to use tagged values to explicitly map them to XML datatypes. To change the mapping of the datatypes in your UML models to XML datatypes, you can modify the datatype mappings in your models without changing the rest of your models.

Association Ends

When working with association ends, you need to provide a legal XML element name for each association end in your model that is navigable. You also need to specify a legal multiplicity for each navigable association end and to consider the setting of navigability and aggregation properties for them.

Most software will give default names to association ends based on the name of the class they are attached to. If an association end is not navigable, most software that generates code from your model probably ignores the end, and XMI software will not include the association end in XMI DTDs or XMI schemas created from the model.

It is possible to delete constructs like associations from a UML diagram without removing the association from your model using some modeling tools. This can be a useful feature if you use it carefully, because you can then put the construct into another diagram without re-creating the construct. However, if you are not careful, you may end up with more constructs than you intend. This is especially true for associations; if you think you delete one from a model, but instead only delete it from a diagram and then create another association, there will be too many associations and association ends in your UML model. If you are using XMI software and you discover that your schemas have more declarations than they should, there might be constructs in your model that are not displayed in UML diagrams.

You should also consider how the aggregation property is specified using your modeling tool. Some modeling tools enable you to specify the aggregation property in more than one way. Depending on the way you specify the aggregation property, the tool may or may not modify the way the association is displayed in class diagrams, so you may not be able to determine how the aggregation property is set for an association end by examining only the class diagrams.

Reverse Engineering Models from XML

You can create new UML models at the beginning of your XMI projects. However, it may be more efficient to revise UML models that are created for you. One source of UML models is to reverse engineer models from existing XML. For example, you can reverse engineer UML models from XML documents, DTDs, and schemas. You can create more useful UML models from XMI DTDs and XMI schemas than you can create from XML DTDs and schemas that do not conform to the XMI specification. This is because you can identify which XML element declarations correspond to classes and which correspond to parts of classes (attributes and association ends) in XMI DTDs and XMI schemas. You cannot reliably make that determination for arbitrary XML DTDs and schemas.

Many companies have invested considerable resources to create XML DTDs and schemas that define the format for data interchange in their systems. Often, they want to leverage this investment to provide more capabilities. Moving from XML to UML is a simple way to begin to unlock the value in their XML and start to use a model-driven architecture, as explained in Chapter 1. The benefits of reverse engineering UML models from XML include:

- Documenting the implicit models in the XML

- Upgrading your development process to use a model-driven architecture

- Starting from models that you can modify rather than creating whole models yourself

You can write software that creates UML models from XML documents, DTDs, and schemas; however, UML is a more expressive language than XML, so the process of reverse engineering results in incomplete UML models. You can refine the models by using additional information about the problem domain that is outside the XML representation. You can supply this information to software performing the reverse engineering, or you can use it to manually refine the models after they have been created by software.

For example, it is not possible to determine the types of XML attributes by examining XML documents only. If you create UML attributes from XML attributes, you need to decide how to set the types of the UML attributes. You can decide to not set the types, you can set the types to a default type, or you can set the types based on knowledge of the problem domain. Although XML DTDs and schemas specify some type information for each XML attribute, they do not have all of the information that is needed to create complete UML models.

Reverse engineering UML models from XML can be done using one of two general approaches. You can create UML classes and UML attributes based on XML elements and XML attributes in XML documents, or you can create them based on element declarations and attribute declarations in XML DTDs and schemas. The names of the UML classes that are created are based on the XML elements' tag names, while the names of the UML attributes are based on the XML attributes' names. If an XML element has an XML attribute, the UML attribute corresponding to the XML attribute is added to the UML class corresponding to the XML element. The nesting of XML elements within other XML elements is represented either by UML attributes or by UML associations. Finally, you can create UML attributes that enable you to store text in XML elements. Table 5.1 summarizes this mapping.

Table 5.1   XML to UML

XML CONSTRUCT OR DECLARATION	UML CONSTRUCT
Element	UML class
Attribute	UML attribute
Nested element	UML association or UML attribute
Text	UML attribute

We recommend that you use the simplest approach to reverse engineering UML models from XML that meets your needs.[1] We describe fairly simple techniques, but we also suggest how to apply more complicated techniques to create more useful UML models. We also recommend that you use software to automate the reverse engineering as much as possible, and the algorithms and techniques we describe in this section are meant to help you implement software to perform the reverse engineering.

XML Documents to UML

To create a UML model from an XML document, examine each XML element in the document and create the corresponding UML constructs if they have not already been created. When examining each XML element, consider the XML attributes for the element, the XML element that contains the XML element being examined, and the text in the content of the XML element.

Perform the following steps for each XML element:

1. Create a class with a name that is based on the tag name of the XML element. If the tag name begins with a lower-case letter, begin the name of the class with the corresponding upper-case letter. For example, if the tag name is *blah*, set the name of the class to *Blah*. If the XML attribute *xsi:type* or *xmi:type* exists for the XML element, use the value of that attribute as the name of the UML class instead.

2. Create a UML attribute for each XML attribute belonging to the XML element. Add each UML attribute to the class corresponding to the XML element. For each UML attribute that is created, set its name to a name based on the XML attribute name. If the name of the XML attribute begins with an upper-case letter, begin the UML attribute name with the corresponding lower-case letter. Set the UML attribute's multiplicity to *0..1*, and set its type to a default type, such as *String*. This datatype represents string values. You can also use another default type if you wish.

3. If there is text in the content of the XML element, create a UML attribute, set its name to *value*, set its type to *String*, and set its multiplicity to *0..1*. Add the UML attribute to the class corresponding to the XML element.

4. If this XML element is contained in another XML element, you can create a UML attribute to represent the containment or create a UML association, as described in step 5. Add the UML attribute to the class corresponding to the XML element that contains this XML element. Set the name of the UML attribute to a name based on this XML element's tag name, set the type of the UML attribute to the class corresponding to this XML element, and set the multiplicity of the UML attribute to *0..**. If the tag name begins with an upper-case letter, begin the UML attribute name with the corresponding lower-case letter.

5. If this XML element is contained in another XML element, you can create a UML association to represent the containment if you do not create a UML attribute to represent the containment.

Here are the steps for creating a UML association to represent containment (these steps are an expansion of step 5 above):

A. Create a UML association and connect its association ends to the classes corresponding to the XML elements.

B. Set the name of each association end to the name of the class it is attached to, making the first letter lower case.

C. For the association end attached to the class corresponding to the container XML element, set its multiplicity to *0..1*, its navigability property to *false*, and its aggregation property to *composition*.

D. For the association end attached to the class corresponding to the contained XML element, set its multiplicity to * and its navigability property to *true*.

Do not create duplicate UML constructs. For example, if there are two XML elements in a document with the same tag name, reuse the UML class instead of creating a new one. Also, do not create a UML attribute for a UML class if a UML attribute with the same name already exists for the class.

Using this algorithm for creating a UML model from an XML document results in a UML model that contains classes that do not inherit from each other, UML attributes with types that are set to a default type, and association ends with names that are based on the names of the classes they are attached to. You can apply knowledge of the problem domain to determine inheritance among the classes, to set the UML attributes to a more specific type than the default type, and to assign the association ends names that describe their roles. It is easy to extend the appropriate steps of the algorithm to take advantage of this information if it is available. For example, you can modify step 2 to set the type of a created UML attribute to a user-specified type, rather than setting the type to a default type. You can also add a step for creating inheritance links between classes as specified by a user.

The following is an example of how to create a model from an XML element nested within another XML element. Consider an XML element *Beta* in an XML element *Alpha*:

```
<Alpha>
  <Beta/>
</Alpha>
```

Using this reverse engineering process, the model corresponding to these two elements contains classes *Alpha* and *Beta*. You can create a UML attribute to represent the containment or a UML association. If you decide to create a UML attribute, add the attribute to UML class *Alpha*. Set the name of the attribute to *beta*, since the tag name of the contained XML element is *Beta*, but a UML attribute name should begin with a lower-case letter. Then set the type of the attribute to *Beta* and the multiplicity to *0..**. Figure 5.2 shows the UML model for this case.

Rather than creating a UML attribute to represent the containment, you can create an association. If you take this approach, connect the association ends of the association to the classes *Alpha* and *Beta*. Set the name of the association end attached to class *Alpha* to *alpha*, set its multiplicity to *1*, set its navigability property to *false*, and set its aggregation property to *composition*. Also set the name of the association end connected to class *Beta* to *beta*, set its multiplicity to ***, and set its navigability property to *true*. The corresponding UML model is illustrated in Figure 5.3.

Now let's consider text in the content of an XML element. Here's an example:

```
<D>Some text</D>
```

The corresponding model contains class *D*. You can create a UML attribute called *value* with *String* as its type to represent the text. Figure 5.4 contains the model corresponding to XML element *D*. Note that we have also created a class called *String*, and its stereotype has been set to indicate that it is functioning as a datatype in this model.

Figure 5.2   A UML attribute corresponding to a nested XML element.

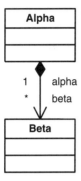

Figure 5.3   A UML association corresponding to a nested XML element.

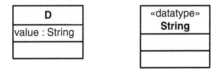

Figure 5.4   A UML attribute corresponding to text in an XML document.

One refinement to the approach described here involves setting the multiplicities of UML attributes based on the number of occurrences of XML attributes in a document, rather than always setting the multiplicities to *0..1*. Consider the following XML elements:

```
<F attrib="value"/>
<F/>
```

When the first element *F* is encountered, you can set the multiplicity of the UML attribute corresponding to XML attribute *attrib* to *1*. Then, when the second element *F* is encountered, you can set the multiplicity to *0..1*, since the XML attribute *attrib* does not appear in this element.

You can use a similar approach to set the multiplicities of association ends in UML models based on the number of nested elements that occur in a document.

XML DTDs to UML

You can reverse engineer UML models from XML DTDs as well as from XML documents. XML DTDs contain XML element declarations and XML attribute declarations that provide more information than can be obtained from examining XML elements and attributes in XML documents. For example, the types of XML attributes are declared in DTDs, but the types of XML attributes cannot be determined by examining XML documents. The multiplicities of attributes and of nested XML elements can only be inferred from XML documents, but they are specified in DTDs.

Since DTDs contain more information than XML documents, the UML models that you can reverse engineer from DTDs are more complete than the models created from XML documents. However, the models may still be incomplete, and knowledge of the problem domain may be required to complete them. As was the case for reverse engineering models from documents, you can provide this additional knowledge to software that performs the reverse engineering, or you can apply the knowledge by manually revising the models that are created. We recommend that you use the former approach, if possible.

Perform the following steps to create a UML model from an XML DTD:

1. Create a class for each XML element declaration. Set the name of the class to a name based on the XML element declaration name. If the name begins with a lower-case letter, begin the name of the class with the corresponding upper-case letter.

2. Create a UML attribute for each XML attribute declaration and add the UML attribute to the class corresponding to the XML element declaration. Then set the name of the UML attribute to a name based on the XML attribute name. If the XML attribute name begins with an upper-case letter, begin the name of the UML attribute with the corresponding lower-case letter. Set the type of the UML attribute to a default type like *String*, and set its multiplicity to *0..1*. The UML datatype *String* represents string values. You can use another default datatype if you wish.

3. If #PCDATA appears in the declaration of the XML element content, create a UML attribute called *value* and add it to the class corresponding to the element declaration. Set its type to *String* and its multiplicity to *0..1*.

4. For each XML element that appears in the declaration of this XML element's content, you can create a UML attribute to represent the containment or a UML association, as described in step 5. Add the UML attribute to the class corresponding to this element declaration. Set the name of the attribute to a name based on the name of the element in the content. If the name begins with an upper-case letter, begin the name of the UML attribute with the corresponding lower-case letter. Set the type of the attribute to the class corresponding to the element declaration for the element in the content, and set the multiplicity of the attribute to *0..**.

5. If you do not create a UML attribute for each XML element that appears in the content of an element declaration, follow these steps to create a UML association for the containment.

A. Create a UML association and connect its association ends to the classes corresponding to the element declaration and the element in the content of the element declaration.

B. Set the name of each association end to the name of the class it is attached to, making the first letter lower case.

C. For the association end attached to the class corresponding to the element declaration, set its multiplicity to *0..1*, set its navigability property to *false*, and set its aggregation property to *composition*.

D. For the association end attached to the class corresponding to the element in the content of the element declaration, set its multiplicity to * and its navigability property to *true*.

Follow steps 4 and 5 described previously for each element in the content of the element declaration. Ignore whether sequences of XML elements or choices of XML elements are specified in the content of the XML element. For example, treat the following declarations of XML element *H* the same when performing this step:

```
<!ELEMENT H (I | J | K) >
<!ELEMENT H (I, J, K) >
<!ELEMENT H ( (I | J), K) >
```

Since there can only be one XML element declaration for an XML element in a DTD, you do not need to be concerned about creating duplicate UML classes. Also, since there can only be one XML attribute declaration for the same attribute within an XML element declaration, you do not need to worry about creating duplicate UML attributes either.

The algorithm in the previous section creates models that can be refined using knowledge of the problem domain; this algorithm does also. Using this algorithm for reverse engineering results in UML models that contain classes that do not inherit from each other, UML attributes with types that are set to a default type, and association ends with names that are based on the names of the classes they are attached to. You can apply knowledge of the problem domain to determine inheritance among the classes, to set the UML attributes to a more reasonable type than the default type, and to name the association ends with names that describe their roles. It is easy to extend the appropriate steps of the algorithm to take advantage of this information if it is available. For example, you can modify step 2 to set the type of a created UML attribute to a user-specified type, rather than setting the type to a default type. You can also add a step for creating inheritance links between classes as specified by a user.

You can also refine this algorithm by using other information in the DTD. For example, you can refine step 2, the creation of UML attributes from XML attribute declarations, based on the information in the attribute declarations. Rather than always setting the multiplicity of the UML attributes to *0..1*, you can set it based on some of the keywords in the XML attribute declaration. If the #FIXED or #REQUIRED keywords appear in the XML attribute declaration, set the multiplicity of the corresponding UML attribute to *1*. If the #IMPLIED keyword appears in an XML attribute declaration, set the multiplicity of the corresponding UML attribute to *0..1*.

You can use the type in an XML attribute declaration to create a more complete model also. If the type is *CDATA* or *ID*, create a UML attribute with *String* as its type, as described in step 2. If the type of the XML attribute is an XML enumeration, create a UML enumeration from the XML enumeration. If the type is *IDREF* or *IDREFS*, you can use knowledge of the problem domain to create a more complete model.

If the type of the XML attribute is an XML enumeration, create a UML attribute as well as a UML enumeration if one does not already exist with the same enumeration literals. Create the attribute according to step 2 of the algorithm, except for the setting of the attribute type. Rather than setting the attribute type to a default type, set the attribute type to a UML enumeration. Perform the following steps to create the UML enumeration:

1. Create a UML class and add an *<<enumeration>>* stereotype to it. Set the name of the class to the name of the XML attribute, with the first letter of the name in upper case, followed by the letters *Enum*.

2. For each enumeration literal in the XML enumeration, create a corresponding enumeration literal for the UML enumeration. To do this, create a UML attribute that has the literal as its name, and add it to the UML class.

Consider the following XML element and XML attribute declaration:

```
<!ELEMENT G EMPTY>
<!ATTLIST G a (v1 | v2 | v3) #IMPLIED>
```

Figure 5.5 contains the corresponding UML model. It consists of UML class *G* that has attribute *a*, which has *AEnum* as its type. *AEnum* is a UML enumeration and its literals are *v1*, *v2*, and *v3*.

Figure 5.5 A UML enumeration corresponding to an XML enumeration.

If an XML attribute has an XML enumeration with literals *true* and *false*, consider creating a UML datatype called *Boolean,* rather than a UML enumeration for the XML enumeration. For example, for the following declaration:

```
<!ELEMENT H EMPTY>
<!ATTLIST H b (true | false) #IMPLIED>
```

you can set the type of the UML attribute corresponding to the XML attribute *b* to a UML datatype called *Boolean,* rather setting the type to a UML enumeration called *BEnum* with literals *true* and *false*.

For each XML attribute with type *ID*, you should create a UML attribute with type *String*. These attributes may be declared as a result of implementing a model in XML, rather than being intrinsic to a particular problem domain. The only way to determine whether this is the case is to apply domain knowledge to the UML model to determine whether the UML attributes are necessary. If they are not necessary for the problem domain, you can delete them.

XML does not restrict the XML elements that can be referred to in an XML attribute with the type *IDREF* or *IDREFS*. XML enables you to put a reference to any XML element in an XML document in such an attribute. For example, consider the following element declarations:

```
<!ELEMENT Person EMPTY>
<!ATTLIST Person id ID #REQUIRED>

<!ELEMENT Car EMPTY>
<!ATTLIST Car owner IDREFS #IMPLIED>
```

The XML identifiers of *Person* XML elements can be put in the XML attribute *owner*; however, the identifiers of any other XML elements in the XML document can be put in the *owner* attribute as well.

Because of this feature of XML, you cannot determine which XML elements are going to be referenced in XML attributes that have *IDREF* or *IDREFS* types based on information in the DTD itself. If you use knowledge of the problem domain, you can create UML associations between the UML classes corresponding to the XML elements.

For example, in the *Person* and *Car* element declarations, it is likely that the XML elements referenced in the XML attribute *owner* will be *Person* elements, since persons own cars. Based on that assumption, you can create a UML association between the UML classes *Person* and *Car* in the UML model corresponding to these element declarations. Set the name of the association end attached to the *Car* class to *owner* and set its navigability property to *true*; then set the navigability property of the other association end to *false*. Since the type of XML attribute *owner* is *IDREFS*, set the multiplicity of the association end *owner* to *. If the type had been *IDREF* instead, you would set the multiplicity to *1*. Figure 5.6 illustrates this model.

Figure 5.6   A UML association corresponding to an XML attribute of type IDREFS.

In the last example, it was prudent to create a unidirectional association from the UML class *Car* to the UML class *Person*, since there were no XML attributes in *Person* that referred to *Car* XML elements. If you always create a unidirectional association for each XML attribute with a type of *IDREF* or *IDREFS*, you may create too many associations. Consider the following declarations:

```
<!ELEMENT Person EMPTY>
<!ATTLIST Person id ID #IMPLIED
                car IDREFS #IMPLIED>

<!ELEMENT Car EMPTY>
<!ATTLIST Car owner IDREFS #IMPLIED
             id ID #IMPLIED>
```

The simple approach results in the model displayed in Figure 5.7, which contains two unidirectional associations between the UML classes *Person* and *Car*. However, both of these associations represent the fact that persons own cars, so you can combine these two associations into one bidirectional association using knowledge of the problem domain.

You can refine the treatment of contained elements as well as XML attributes. Since multiplicities are specified for XML elements that appear in the content of XML element declarations, you can set the multiplicities of UML attributes and UML association ends that represent containment based on the actual multiplicities, rather than always setting them to *. If you decide to base the multiplicities in your UML models on the multiplicities appearing in the declaration of XML elements' content, you can use the mapping in Table 5.2.

XMI DTDs to UML

XMI DTDs are XML DTDs, so you can use the techniques described in the previous section to reverse engineer UML models from them. However, because they conform to the XMI 1.0, XMI 1.1, or XMI 1.2 specifications, you can create more realistic UML models from them. Those specifications describe in detail how to create XMI DTDs from UML models, so you should consult those specifications for more details about XMI DTDs if you are interested in creating the most useful UML models possible from XMI DTDs. Reverse engineering UML

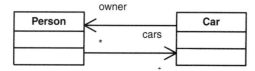

owner

| Person | | | Car |

cars
*

Figure 5.7   Two unidirectional associations between the *Person* and *Car* classes.

Table 5.2   XML Multiplicities to UML Multiplicities

XML MULTIPLICITY	UML MULTIPLICITY
Exactly 1	1
0 or 1 (?)	0..1
0 or more (*)	0..* or *
1 or more (+)	1..*

models from XMI DTDs is not included in the XMI specification, but we include it here to help you create UML models from XMI DTDs if you need to do so.

Before you begin to reverse engineer a UML model using techniques that apply to XMI DTDs rather than XML DTDs, you need to determine whether an XML DTD is an XMI DTD. An XML DTD is an XMI DTD if it contains certain element declarations that every XMI DTD is required to have. Each XMI DTD declares an XML element called *XMI* that has an XML attribute declaration for an attribute called *xmi.version*. The fixed value of the attribute is the version of the XMI specification. For example, if the fixed value is *1.1*, the XMI DTD conforms to the XMI 1.1 specification.

When reverse engineering UML models from XML DTDs, you create a UML class for each element declaration. However, XMI DTDs contain element declarations representing UML classes, UML packages, UML attributes, and UML association ends. They also contain element declarations defined by the XMI specification.

We include a set of rules for converting declarations in an XMI DTD to the corresponding UML constructs. Following these rules, we work through some examples showing their applications so you can see how to apply them to your own XMI DTDs. Here are the rules:

- If an element is declared with a name that begins with the letters *XMI*, it is an element declaration that is defined by the XMI specification rather than representing a part of a UML model, so it does not go into your model. However, you can use the *XMI* XML element declaration to determine the version of XMI that was used to create the DTD, as explained previously.

- If an element is declared and its content contains the keyword #PCDATA, create a UML attribute that has a UML datatype as its type. You can determine the class that the UML attribute belongs to by examining the element name. The name of the element is the name of the class followed by . and the name of the UML attribute. Set the type to a default datatype like *String* or a datatype based on knowledge of the problem domain.

- If an empty element is declared, create a UML attribute that has as its type either a UML datatype representing *Boolean* values or a UML enumeration. Each empty element declaration contains the declaration of an XML attribute called *xmi.value*. This XML attribute's declaration contains the XML enumeration that corresponds to the UML enumeration you should use for the new UML attribute's type. You can determine the class the UML attribute belongs to by examining the element name. The name of the element is the name of the class followed by . and the name of the UML attribute. If the literals of the XML enumeration are *true* and *false*, set the type of the UML attribute to a *Boolean* datatype; otherwise, create a UML enumeration from the XML enumeration and set the type to the UML enumeration (the *XML DTDs to UML* section describes how to create UML enumerations).

- If the content of the element declaration contains *XMI.extension*, create either a class or a package. To determine what to create, examine the content of each element that appears in the content of the declaration. If the content of any element contains *XMI.extension*, create a package; otherwise, create a class.

- If none of the previous rules apply to the element declaration, the element represents an association end. You can determine the name of the class the association end belongs to by examining the element name. The name of the element is the name of the class followed by . and the name of the association end. You can determine if the aggregation property of the association end should be set to *composition* by examining the element declaration for the class the association end belongs to. If there is an XML attribute declared with the same name as the association end in that element declaration, do not set the aggregation property of the end to *composition*. Otherwise, you can do so. The content of the element declaration for the association end lists XML elements that represent classes; the classes are the class the association end is attached to and its subclasses. The subclasses are not required to be listed in XMI 1.1.

Here are some examples of element declarations in XMI DTDs. Consider the following element declaration:

```
<!ELEMENT C.a EMPTY >
<!ATTLIST C.a
          xmi.value (v1 | v2 | v3) #REQUIRED
>
```

Since the content is EMPTY, this declaration represents a UML attribute that has a UML enumeration as its type. This corresponds to the situation described previously in the third rule. Since the name of the element is *C.a*, the name of the attribute is *a*, and the name of the class it belongs to is *C*. The type of the UML attribute is a UML enumeration with the literals *v1*, *v2*, and *v3*.

The following element declarations represent either classes or packages, since their content contains *XMI.extension*:

```
<!ELEMENT C1 (XMI.extension)* >
<!ATTLIST C1
                  %XMI.element.att;
                  %XMI.link.att;
>


<!ELEMENT P (C1 | XMI.extension)* >
<!ATTLIST P
                  %XMI.element.att;
                  %XMI.link.att;
>
```

The two entities *XMI.element.att* and *XMI.link.att* represent the required XMI attribute declarations for classes and packages. Does element *P* represent a class or a package? To answer this question, look at the declaration of *C1*, which is in the content of *P*. Since *C1* also contains *XMI.extension*, *P* represents a package. However, since *C1* only contains *XMI.extension*, we cannot determine whether *C1* represents a class or a package. Following the fourth rule, we create a class *C1*.

Now consider the element declaration *C2.a1*:

```
<!ELEMENT C2.a1 (C3 | C4 | C5)* >

<!ELEMENT C2 (XMI.extension | C2.a1)* >
<!ATTLIST C2
            a1 IDREFS #IMPLIED
            %XMI.element.att;
            %XMI.link.att;
>
```

C2.a1 represents a UML association end. To determine whether the aggregation property should be set to composition, examine the attributes declared for element *C2*, the element declaration corresponding to the class the association end belongs to. Since there is an attribute declaration for an attribute named *a1* in element *C2*, do not set the aggregation property of the end to *composition*. Since the content of *C2.a1* contains *C3*, *C4*, and *C5*, the end is attached to one of the classes *C3*, *C4*, or *C5*, and the other classes are subclasses of the class the end is attached to.

The names of XML elements differ, depending on the version of XMI that is used. The names of classes and packages are fully qualified in XMI 1.0 DTDs. For example, if a class *C6* is in a package called *p1*, which is in package *p2*, the name of the XML element for this class in an XMI 1.0 DTD is *p2.p1.C6*. The name of the element for this class in XMI 1.1 or XMI 1.2 is simply *C6*, or *n:C6*, where *n* is an XML namespace prefix. The name of the XML element corresponding to a UML attribute *attrib* for class *C6* is *p2.p1.C6.attrib* in XMI 1.0 DTDs, and *C6.attrib* or *n:C6.attrib* in XMI 1.1 or XMI 1.2 DTDs.

When you reverse engineer models from XML DTDs, you cannot create inheritance links between the classes you create unless you apply knowledge of the problem domain. However, you can create inheritance links for classes you create from an XMI DTD. To do so, examine the content of an element declaration for a class. The content contains the XML elements representing the UML attributes and UML association ends for the class, as well as its inherited attributes and association ends. Since the names of the XML elements for UML attributes and UML association ends contain the name of the class they belong to, it is possible to determine which classes are superclasses for a given class. By examining each of the element declarations for those classes, you can determine which superclasses are direct superclasses of a given class and which superclasses inherit from other superclasses. For example, consider the following part of an element declaration for a class *M* in an XMI 1.1 DTD:

```
<!ELEMENT M (O.p1 | N.p2 | M.p3 | XMI.extension)* >
```

Its content contains XML elements *O.p1*, *N.p2*, and *M.p3*. These XML elements correspond to either attributes or association ends belonging to classes *O*, *N*, and *M* Therefore, classes *O* and *N* are superclasses of class *M*. By examining the XML element declarations for classes *O* and *N*, we can determine whether class *M* inherits from them directly or indirectly. Consider the element declarations for *O* and *N*:

```
<!ELEMENT O (O.p1 | XMI.extension)* >
<!ELEMENT N (O.p1 | N.p2 | XMI.extension)* >
```

Class *N* must inherit from class *O* because it contains XML element *O.p1*. Using this knowledge, class *M* must inherit from class *N*. Figure 5.8 shows the class hierarchy for classes *O*, *M*, and *N*.

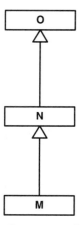

Figure 5.8   The class hierarchy for classes *O*, *M*, and *N*.

Of course, if a class has no attributes or association ends, you cannot determine which classes inherit from it by using this technique.

XML Schemas to UML

Like XML DTDs, XML schemas contain XML element declarations and XML attribute declarations. This means that you can use the same algorithm for reverse engineering UML models from XML schemas as you can use for reverse engineering UML models from XML DTDs. For each element declaration, you can create a class. For each attribute declaration, you can create a UML attribute. Nested declarations can be handled the same as nested declarations in DTDs. However, XML schemas are more powerful than XML DTDs, so you can use more advanced techniques to reverse engineer models from them, based on the features of schemas that are not in DTDs.

XML schemas enable you to declare types as well as XML elements, and you can specify that types are extensions or restrictions of other types. You can create classes from type declarations, and each class you create can inherit from the class corresponding to the type that was the base type for the extension or restriction. XML schemas also distinguish between simple types and complex types, and you can map simple types in schemas to UML datatypes and complex types in schemas to classes.

For example, consider the following type declaration in an XML schema:

```
<simpleType name="Little">
    <restriction base="int">
        <enumeration value="1"/>
```

```
            <enumeration value="2"/>
        </restriction>
    </simpleType>
```

This declaration defines a simple type called *Little* that restricts the built-in datatype *int* to have two legal values, *1* and *2*. Since this type is a simple type, and it is derived by restriction from the built-in simple type *int*, you can create a UML datatype called *Little* and make that datatype inherit from a UML datatype called *int*.

Consider the following type declarations:

```
<complexType name="SuperType"/>

<complexType name="SubType">
    <complexContent>
        <extension base="SuperType">
            <sequence>
                <element name="something" type="string"/>
            </sequence>
        </extension>
    </complexContent>
</complexType>
```

These declarations define two complex types, *SuperType* and *SubType*. *SubType* extends *SuperType* by including the element *something* in its content. You can create two UML classes from these declarations, called *SuperType* and *SubType*, and make the UML class *SubType* inherit from the UML class *SuperType*. (In this example, the *SubType* class would include a UML attribute called *something* of type *String*.)

Multiplicities in schemas map well to UML multiplicities because multiplicities in schemas are expressed by the values of *minOccurs* and *maxOccurs* XML attributes. The values of *minOccurs* and *maxOccurs* can be used to set the UML multiplicity. The value of *minOccurs* can be used for the lower limit of the UML multiplicity, and the value of *maxOccurs* can be used for the upper limit of the UML multiplicity. If the value of *maxOccurs* is *unbounded*, set the upper limit of the UML multiplicity to *. For example, if *minOccurs* has a value of *0* and *maxOccurs* has a value of *unbounded*, the corresponding UML multiplicity is *0..**.

XMI Schemas to UML

The reverse engineering from XMI schemas to UML models can be done following the suggestions in the previous section. Chapter 3 describes the rules for generating XMI schemas from UML models in detail. You may want to review the rules to help you to reverse engineer UML models from XMI schemas effectively.

Summary

You need to be aware of several issues when creating UML models for use with XMI. You need to ensure that the names in the models are legal XML tag and attribute names, that you provide names for each construct used by XMI, and that you carefully consider the datatypes you are using in your models, among other issues. You also need to be aware of certain features of some modeling tools that may cause your UML models to differ from what you want when you use the UML models with XMI software. You can create new UML models when you use XMI, or you can reverse engineer UML models from existing XML documents, DTDs, and schemas. You can use simple or advanced techniques to reverse engineer UML models. We recommend you use the simplest technique that suits your purposes, and use the guidelines we have outlined in this chapter to automate as much of the reverse engineering as possible.

Creating and Reading Simple XMI Documents with Standard XML APIs

Since every XML Metadata Interchange (XMI) document is an Extensible Markup Language (XML) document, you can use any standard XML Application Programming Interface (API) to work with XMI documents. Two common APIs that we cover in this chapter are the Document Object Model (DOM) and the Simple API for XML (SAX). The only drawback to using these APIs with XMI documents is that you need to ensure that the documents you produce are valid XMI documents, and you need to know about the format of XMI documents in order to get the data from them. In this chapter, we provide examples of how to use DOM to create an XMI document and then read it, printing data about the objects that were written in the XMI document. Then we demonstrate how to use SAX to read an XMI document and use the data it contains to create corresponding instances of Java classes and set their fields.

In the first section of this chapter, we introduce a problem domain and model that we will use in this and the next three chapters. Therefore, you should read the following *Car Rental Agency Application* section. If you are not interested in learning about the DOM or SAX APIs, you do not need to read the *Using DOM* and *Using SAX* sections of this chapter. Readers who do read these sections, however, can compare using DOM and SAX to using software that directly supports XMI that we introduce in the next chapter.

Car Rental Agency Application

The programming examples in this chapter and the next three chapters are based on an application for a car rental agency. The purpose of the application is to report information about each car that the agency owns. The information includes the style of the car (make, model, and year), the options the car has, the car's vehicle identification number, and whether the car is available to be rented or not. If a car has been rented, the application reports the name and license number of each person that will drive the car. Although a real car rental agency needs to track more information about its cars and the people that have rented them, we are using a simplified car rental agency model so the examples in this book are easy to understand.

We can model the required information in the following four classes:

- *Car*
- *Style*
- *Option*
- *Person*

The *Car* class has the vehicle identification number (vin) of the car and a flag to indicate whether the car is available to be rented. For our purposes, the flag is *false* if the car has already been rented or it does not run because of mechanical problems; the flag is *true* when the car is available for a customer to rent. The *Car* class also has an *option* attribute, and its multiplicity is *0..**. The type of the *option* attribute is the class *Option*. This attribute is used to hold the options that a *Car* object can have. The *Style* class holds the make, model, and year of one or more cars. The *Option* class contains the name of an option the car has. As you would expect, each car can have multiple options, but only one style. The *Person* class has the name of a person and that person's driver's license number. Figure 6.1 illustrates the classes, their attributes, and their relationships in Unified Modeling Language (UML) notation.

We will next show you how to write an instance of each class in the car rental agency model to an XMI document. To begin with, we create an object model having an instance of each class in the car rental agency model. In this chapter and the next two chapters, we show how to write an instance of each class in the car rental agency model to an XMI document. We use the same objects in all three chapters. The UML object diagram for these four objects is shown in Figure 6.2.

As you look at the figure, note that only the *Option* object has been given a name. This name, *option1*, appears in the top pane of the object, followed by a colon, and the class name *Option*. As you will see, we use this name to assign this object to the *option* attribute value in the *Car* object. Since this is the only

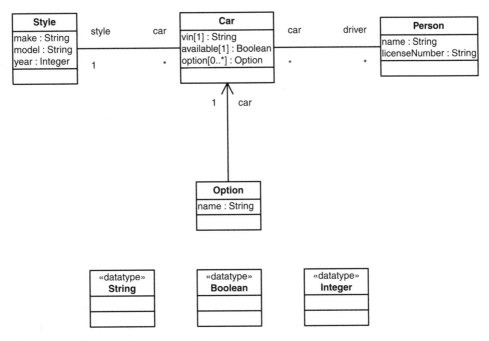

Figure 6.1 Car rental agency model.

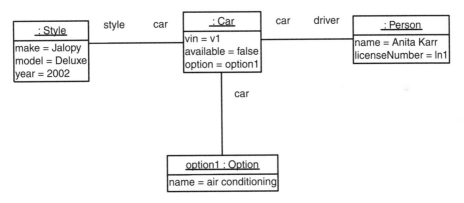

Figure 6.2 Car rental agency objects.

object value, this is the only object we need to name. We use this name only for the figure; it is not used by XMI. For the other objects, the top pane has a colon followed by the class name of the object.

In this example, the instance of the *Car* class has already been rented, so its *available* attribute is set to *false*. The *vin* attribute has the value *v1*. Examining the *Style* object, we see that it has a *make* of *Jalopy*, a *model* of *Deluxe*, and its *year* is *2002*. The *Option* object, which designates the single option in the *Car* instance, has its *name* attribute set to *air conditioning*. Note that the name of the object, *option1*, has been assigned to the *option* attribute in the *Car* object. This indicates that the *Car* object is equipped with air conditioning. Recall that object attributes have composition semantics. Therefore, *option1* is contained in the *Car* object. If another *Car* object had air conditioning, another *Option* object would be required for that *Car* object. The *Person* object, which designates the person who has rented the car, has its *name* attribute set to *Anita Karr* and its *licenseNumber* attribute set to *ln1*. Now that we have established the model we will work with, let's see how we can use a couple of standard XML APIs to work with this model in XMI.

Using Standard XML APIs

You can use standard XML APIs to create and read XMI documents. Working in our problem domain, we will now examine some sample programs that show how to use DOM and SAX, two standard APIs supported by XML parsers, to work with XMI. We will not explain all the details of either API, but we will explain enough about them so you can understand the programs in this chapter. You can find additional information on DOM and SAX in the references we include with this book.

Using DOM

DOM represents XML files (and therefore XMI files) as trees of nodes. XML parsers enable you to write a DOM tree to an XMI file and to get a DOM tree from an XMI file. You need to understand XML to use DOM. If you want to use DOM to create XMI files and read them, you also need to know about XMI. Specifically, you need to know how to create a DOM tree that represents an XMI file from your objects, and you need to know how to get your object data from a DOM tree that represents an XMI file. You can write your own code based on DOM to support XMI files, but this section uses DOM to explain the issues you face when using a standard XML API to work with XMI. DOM has been developed as a series of specification phases or *levels* for the World Wide Web Consortium (W3C). The examples presented in this chapter are based on *DOM Level 2*.

Before we explain how to create a DOM tree that represents an XMI file, we need to present some basic information about DOM trees and nodes. Each node in a DOM tree implements the *Node* interface in the Java package *org.w3c.dom*. The *Node* interface contains methods to get the node's:

- Type
- Name
- Parent node
- Sibling nodes
- Child nodes

It also contains methods to add and remove child nodes.

The top node of a DOM tree is a *Document node*. A Document node has a *Document element*, which is the root XML element for the document. The Document node also serves as a factory for making the other node types and enables you to get *Element nodes* based on their tag names or XML IDs. An Element node represents an XML element in an XML document. Each Element node has attributes corresponding to the XML element's XML attributes. There is an *Attr node* for each XML attribute. The child nodes of an Element node represent the element's content. For our purposes, the child nodes of an Element node are either Element nodes or *Text nodes*. A Text node represents character data in the content of an XML element that are not in an XML CDATA section. The Text nodes in a DOM tree may represent XML ignorable whitespace unless you tell your XML parser to ignore it.

There are more types of DOM nodes, but we will not be using them in our examples in this chapter. For more information, consult the DOM specification or a book that explains DOM.

The DOM tree corresponding to the following simple XML document is shown in Figure 6.3:

```
<?xml version="1.0"?>
<root a1="v1"><child>Child text</child>Root text</root>
```

The DOM tree for this document consists of a Document node with a Document element that is an Element node named *root*. The *root* Element node has one Attr node with *a1* as its name and *v1* as its value. The *root* Element node has two child (Element and Text) nodes: an Element node named *child* and a Text node with the value *Root text*. The Element node named *child* has a child node of its own that is a Text node and its value is *Child text*.

Now that you know the basics of DOM, we can explain how to create a DOM tree that represents an XMI 2.0 file. We first present a step-by-step overview of this process and then include a more detailed algorithm that expands the last step outlined in the overview. Both of these algorithms are then mapped into a Java programming example that creates an XMI document. The best way to understand these algorithms is to first read them through and then examine the example Java program in Source Code 6.1 that

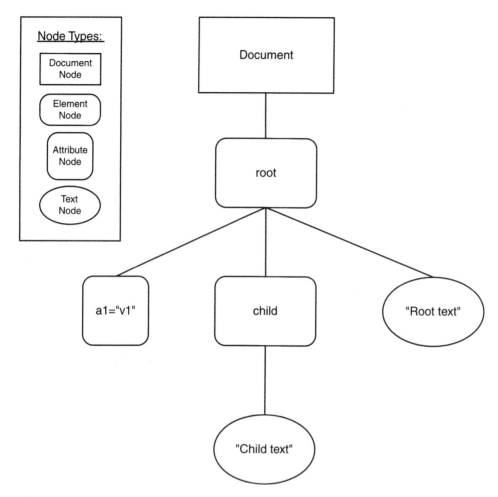

Figure 6.3   A simple DOM tree.

shows how the steps of the algorithms are implemented for our car rental agency application. To make this easier, we've provided comments in the example that link sections of the code back to the steps in the algorithms.

Overview Algorithm

Here is an overview algorithm for creating a DOM tree for an XMI 2.0 document:

1. Create a Document node.
2. Create an Element node for the XMI XML element. Include an attribute declaring the XMI namespace prefix. By convention, *xmi* is typically

used for the prefix, and this is what we will use in this book. Set this attribute equal to the XMI namespace URI (*http://www.omg.org/XMI*). Name this element node *xmi:XMI*. Also include an attribute for the XMI version (*xmi:version*) and set its value to *2.0*. Include additional attributes that declare any other namespaces that are used in the XMI document. Make this node a child of the Document node created in step 1.

3. If you want your document to include documentation information such as the name and version of the tool that created the document, create an Element node named *xmi:Documentation* and make it a child of the XMI Element node created in step 2. Then create Element and Text nodes to represent the XMI documentation information you want in the XMI document. Make these Element nodes descendants of the Element node created for documentation information.

4. For each object you want to put in the XMI document, create an Element node that is named with the XMI name for the object's class. Then set the node's attributes and create its descendant Element nodes based on the object's attribute values and references.

Many details are not described in the previous steps, and some optional steps have been omitted entirely. For example, you may want to use extensions or, if you are working with differences between XMI documents, you may want to include *xmi:Add*, *xmi:Delete*, and *xmi:Replace* XML elements. However, the previous four steps are sufficient for the DOM example we use in this book.

Step 4, creating the part of the DOM tree that represents your objects, is the most important step in the overview algorithm. You need to handle the objects' identities, their attribute values, and their references (object extensions are covered in Chapter 8). For attribute values and references, you need to know whether to represent them as XML attributes or XML elements. The following section is a detailed algorithm for step 4. It explains how to create DOM nodes for your objects to be saved in an XMI 2.0 document (for details about previous versions of XMI, please consult the appropriate specifications.)

As you may recall from our earlier discussion on terminology in Chapter 2, we define a *reference* to be an instance of an association end. Because we use attributes to represent composition rather than association ends, association ends and references in this book do not have composition semantics. We define a *data value* to be a value of an attribute with a datatype as its type (such as *5*, *3.141*, or *Hello*). We define an *object value* to be a value of an attribute with a class as its type (such as *option1* in the car rental agency object model). A data value corresponds to a *data attribute*, and an object value corresponds to an *object attribute*.

Object Algorithm

The following steps provide a detailed algorithm for step 4 in the *Overview Algorithm* section:

1. Create an Element node for the object, as explained in step 4 in the *Overview Algorithm* section.

2. Set the *xmi:id*, *xmi:uuid*, and *xmi:label* attributes of the Element node as appropriate for your application. Although all these attributes are optional, we recommend setting the *xmi:id* attribute for each object to clearly indicate the XML elements in the XMI document that are objects. Another strong reason for recommending this practice is to enable other XML elements in the same document or in other documents to refer to this element.

3. For each data attribute that has a single data value, set an XML attribute for the Element node. For the XML attribute's name, use the name of the data attribute and set its value to a *String* representing the data value. (Note: When discussing Java programs in this book, we use *String* to refer to the *java.lang.String* class. The Java APIs for DOM use a *java.lang.String* to represent an XML attribute value.)

4. For all the references of an association end, set an XML attribute for the Element node. The XML attribute's name is the name of the association end, and its value is a *String* containing the value of the *xmi:id* of each referenced object. (Recall that the reference belonging to the object will appear *across from* the object, *not* adjacent to it, in a UML object diagram.) If there is more than one *xmi:id* value (because there are multiple references), separate them by spaces.

5. For a data attribute that has *multiple* data values, do the following: For *every* data value, make an Element node. Set the name of this node to the name of the data attribute. Next, make a Text node and set its value to the data value. Make this Text node a child of the Element node for the data value. Finally, make the Element node for the data value a child of the Element node for the object created in step 1.

6. For each object value for an attribute, do the following: Create an Element node that is named with the object attribute's name. Then follow steps 2 through 6 of this algorithm for the object value. Finally, make the Element node for the object value a child of the Element node for the object created in step 1.

7. Make the Element node for the object created in step 1 of this algorithm a child of the *xmi:XMI* Element node created in step 2 of the *Overview Algorithm* section.

Once you make the DOM tree, you can write the tree to an XML document. IBM's XML4J parser has a nice interface for doing that.

Source Code 6.1 is an example of creating an XMI file containing the instances of the *Car*, *Person*, *Style*, and *Option* classes described in the *Car Rental Agency Application* section. You may want to go back to that section to remind yourself what the model is and what the objects to be saved are. To keep the example simple, all the data to be saved is specified as *Strings*; we do not recommend that you adopt this approach in your programs (unless you are writing a book, too). Also, rather than handling exceptions that may occur during the program, the program stops immediately after they are thrown. In an actual application program, we probably need to handle the exceptions ourselves.

As you read this example, notice how the steps for creating an XMI document and creating DOM nodes for each object are implemented using DOM interfaces. We have included comments to help you link the following Java implementation with the steps in the overview and object algorithms we have presented in this chapter.

```java
// DOMWrite.java
import org.apache.xerces.dom.*;
import org.apache.xml.serialize.*;
import org.w3c.dom.*;
import java.util.*;
import java.io.*;

// This program writes the Car, Option, Style, and Person objects
// described in the Car Rental Agency Application section to an XMI
// 2.0 document using the steps described in the Using DOM section
// in this chapter.
public class DOMWrite {

public static void main(String[] args) throws Exception {

  // Overview step 1.
  Document doc = new DocumentImpl();

  // Overview step 2. Create the XMI Element node.
  Element xmi = doc.createElement("xmi:XMI");
  xmi.setAttribute("xmi:version", "2.0");
  xmi.setAttribute("xmlns:xmi", "http://www.omg.org/XMI");
  doc.appendChild(xmi);

  // Overview step 3. Create the XMI Documentation element, specifying
```

Source Code 6.1 *DOMWrite* program–creating a DOM tree.

```
// the program that produced the file (the exporter) and its version.
Element documentation = doc.createElement("xmi:Documentation");

Element exporter = doc.createElement("exporter");
Text exporterText = doc.createTextNode("XMI DOM Serialize Example");
exporter.appendChild(exporterText);

Element version  = doc.createElement("exporterVersion");
Text versionText = doc.createTextNode("0.5");
version.appendChild(versionText);

documentation.appendChild(exporter);
documentation.appendChild(version);
xmi.appendChild(documentation);

// Overview step 4. Write the objects.

// Object step 1 for the Car object.
Element car = doc.createElement("Car");

// Object step 2.
car.setAttribute("xmi:id", "_1");

// Object step 3. Since available and vin are data attributes
// with one value, put the values in XML attributes.
car.setAttribute("available", "false");
car.setAttribute("vin", "v1");

// Object step 4. Because style and driver are references,
// put the xmi:id of the referenced object in an XML attribute.
car.setAttribute("style", "_2");
car.setAttribute("driver", "_3");

// Object step 6. Since option is an object attribute
// of the Car object indicating a contained Option object, make
// an Element node for the contained object as a descendant of the
// car Element node.
Element option = doc.createElement("option");

// Object step 2 for the Option object.
option.setAttribute("xmi:id", "_1.1");

// Object step 3.
option.setAttribute("name", "air conditioning");

// Object step 4.
```

Source Code 6.1 *DOMWrite* program–creating a DOM tree. (*Continued*)

```
        option.setAttribute("car", "_1");

        // Last part of Object step 6.
        car.appendChild(option);

        // Object step 7 for the Car object.
        xmi.appendChild(car);

        // Object step 1 for the Style object.
        Element style = doc.createElement("Style");

        // Object step 2.
        style.setAttribute("xmi:id", "_2");

        // Object step 3.
        style.setAttribute("make", "Jalopy");
        style.setAttribute("model", "Deluxe");
        style.setAttribute("year", "2002");

        // Object step 4.
        style.setAttribute("car", "_1");

        // Object step 7.
        xmi.appendChild(style);

        // Object steps 1-4 and 7 for the Person object.
        Element person = doc.createElement("Person");
        person.setAttribute("xmi:id", "_3");
        person.setAttribute("name", "Anita Karr");
        person.setAttribute("licenseNumber", "ln1");
        person.setAttribute("car", "_1");
        xmi.appendChild(person);

        // Create the XMI document from the parse tree. See the XML4J
        // parser documentation for more details.
        OutputFormat format  = new OutputFormat(doc, "UTF-8", true);
        FileWriter file = new FileWriter("DOMWrite.xmi");
        XMLSerializer serial = new XMLSerializer(file, format);
        serial.asDOMSerializer();

        serial.serialize(doc.getDocumentElement());
        file.close();
    }
}
```

Source Code 6.1 *DOMWrite* program—creating a DOM tree. (*Continued*)

The program produces the following XMI 2.0 file as output:

```
<?xml version="1.0" encoding="UTF-8"?>
<xmi:XMI xmi:version="2.0" xmlns:xmi="http://www.omg.org/XMI">
    <xmi:Documentation>
        <exporter>XMI DOM Serialize Example</exporter>
        <exporterVersion>0.5</exporterVersion>
    </xmi:Documentation>
    <Car available="false" driver="_3" style="_2" vin="v1"
        xmi:id="_1">
        <option car="_1" name="air conditioning" xmi:id="_1.1"/>
    </Car>
    <Style car="_1" make="Jalopy" model="Deluxe" xmi:id="_2"
        year="2002"/>
    <Person car="_1" licenseNumber="ln1" name="Anita Karr"
        xmi:id="_3"/>
</xmi:XMI>
```

As you can see from this example, it takes some work to use the DOM API to create an XMI document. You need to know many details about XMI, and you need to faithfully implement each step or you will not get an XML document that conforms to the XMI specification. It is possible to make it easier to use DOM to create XMI documents, of course. One approach is to create an *XMIDocument* class that implements the DOM Document interface. The *XMIDocument* class could contain methods that provide an interface for setting documentation information easily. Clients of the *XMIDocument* class would not need to know the details of which DOM nodes were created to put that information into an XMI file. If you make a generic representation of objects, their attribute values, and their references, or use Java reflection, the *XMIDocument* class could create the appropriate DOM nodes to represent a user's objects. We don't provide an *XMIDocument* class for you, but in the next chapter we explain code that you can use to make XMI documents without knowing too much about XMI. Additionally, you should consider the issues discussed in Chapter 4 to help you decide which parts of XMI to use or support in your software.

Reading an XMI document using the DOM API also requires you to know many of the details of XMI so that you know how to handle the nodes in a DOM tree from an XMI document. However, depending on what you want to do with the contents of the XMI document, you may not need to know all the details, especially when using some of the advanced features of DOM. For example, DOM now includes *NodeIterators* that will iterate through the nodes of a DOM tree, filtering the nodes according to a *NodeFilter* that you can provide. This makes it easy to get all the Element nodes that represent objects from the XMI document produced by *DOMWrite*. The program in Source Code 6.2 creates a DOM tree from the file written by the previous DOM application,

DOMWrite.xmi. It uses a *NodeFilter* to print the name of each Element node representing an object and the XML attributes for each of these Element nodes.

```java
// DOMRead.java
import org.apache.xerces.parsers.*;
import org.w3c.dom.*;
import org.w3c.dom.traversal.*;
import org.xml.sax.*;
import java.util.*;
import java.io.*;

// This program creates a DOM tree for the file specified as a command
// line option and demonstrates the use of a NodeFilter to obtain the
// Element nodes corresponding to objects in an XMI document.
public class DOMRead {

  // Return the nodes that represent objects; the "xmi:id" attribute
  // is optional, and XMI extension elements may have "xmi:id"
  // attributes too, so this filter will not work for every XMI
  // file, but it is good enough for the DOM example in this chapter.
  private static class ObjectFilter implements NodeFilter {

    public short acceptNode(Node n) {
      if (n.getNodeType() == Node.ELEMENT_NODE) {
        Element e = (Element) n;

        if (e.getAttributeNode("xmi:id") != null)
          return NodeFilter.FILTER_ACCEPT;
      }

      return NodeFilter.FILTER_REJECT;
    }
  }

public static void main(String[] args) throws Exception {
  if (args.length != 1) {
    System.out.println("Enter the name of the file to parse.");
    return;
  }

  DOMParser parser = new DOMParser();
  parser.parse(args[0]);

  Document d = parser.getDocument();
  DocumentTraversal dt = (DocumentTraversal) d;
```

Source Code 6.2 *DOMRead* program—reading an XMI document using DOM.

```
  //Create the NodeIterator with the filter created above. The
  //NodeIterator will apply the filter before returning the next node.
  NodeIterator it = dt.createNodeIterator(d.getDocumentElement(),
                                          NodeFilter.SHOW_ALL,
                                          new ObjectFilter(),
                                          true);


  Node n =  it.nextNode();

  while (n != null) {
    writeObject(n);
    n = it.nextNode();
  }
}


// Write the name of the Element node and the XML attributes and
// their values.
public static void writeObject(Node object) {
  System.out.println(object.getNodeName() + ":");
  System.out.println("  attributes:");
  NamedNodeMap attribs = object.getAttributes();

  for (int j = 0; j < attribs.getLength(); ++j)
    System.out.println("    " + attribs.item(j).getNodeName() +
                       ": '" + attribs.item(j).getNodeValue() + "'");
}
}
```

Source Code 6.2   *DOMRead* program—reading an XMI document using DOM. (*Continued*)

The following is the output from running this program on the file produced by *DOMWrite*. Note that since the *option* object attribute of the *Car* object is represented by an XML element, it is not included in the list of the XML attributes for the *Car* object.

```
Car:
  attributes:
    available: 'false'
    driver: '_3'
    style: '_2'
    vin: 'v1'
    xmi:id: '_1'
option:
  attributes:
    car: '_1'
```

```
        name: 'air conditioning'
        xmi:id: '_1.1'
Style:
  attributes:
    car: '_1'
    make: 'Jalopy'
    model: 'Deluxe'
    xmi:id: '_2'
    year: '2002'
Person:
  attributes:
    car: '_1'
    licenseNumber: 'ln1'
    name: 'Anita Karr'
    xmi:id: '_3'
```

We realize that in a real application you will want to do much more than simply print the XML attributes of the XML elements that represent objects in an XMI document. You may want to do something based on the XMI documentation information, for example. Most likely, you will want to create objects from the XML elements. The next section demonstrates how to do that using SAX. The same techniques we explain in the next section can be used to create objects from Element nodes in a DOM tree as well.

The *DOMRead* program assumes that every XML element in an XMI document that has an attribute called *xmi:id* represents an object, and that you can determine all the objects in an XMI document by looking for such elements. This is not true in all cases for several reasons. Some of the predefined XML elements in the XMI namespace, such as *xmi:Extension*, also have *xmi:id* attributes, so you need to be sure to exclude these elements if you only want elements that represent your objects to be processed. The *xmi:id* attribute is optional, so an XML element representing an object does not need to have it. Also, XMI enables you to rename the attribute holding an XML ID, so it may be named something else in a particular document. Finally, you can choose a namespace prefix other than *xmi*.

You can usually determine which elements correspond to your objects, except in the unlikely event that objects have no attributes or references. You know that an XML element represents one of your objects if any of the following conditions are true:

- The XML element has an *xmi:id*, *xmi:uuid*, *xmi:label*, *xmi:idref*, or *href* XML attribute and is not one of the elements defined by XMI.

- The XML element has an *xmi:version* XML attribute and it is not one of the elements defined by XMI.

- The XML element is directly contained in the *xmi:XMI* XML element and is not one of the elements defined by XMI.

- The XML element is directly contained in an XML element representing an object and it has attributes not defined by XMI.

- The XML element is directly contained in an XML element representing an object and it has XML elements inside it.

The fact that you can usually determine which XML elements represent objects in an XMI document makes it easier to restore objects from XMI documents than from XML documents that do not conform to the XMI specification.

Using SAX

As the previous section explains, once you parse an XML file with a DOM-based parser, all the information in the XML file is in the DOM tree the parser creates. Since all the information is in memory, a DOM tree can take up quite a bit of memory for large XML files. The SAX interface does not have this limitation. Because the interface lets you access information from an XML file while it is being parsed, the information is not automatically put in a data structure. Instead, you must do this yourself. If you use SAX, you decide whether the data from the XML file will be put into a data structure in memory or not. Therefore, your applications that read XML files may use less memory if you use SAX than if you use DOM.

The main interfaces in SAX are called *handlers,* and they consist of callback methods that an XML parser invokes when it is reading an XML file. We will use SAX version 2.0 (SAX2) in this book, since version 2.0 is the most recent version. The handler that we will explain the most is the *ContentHandler.* The callback methods in the *ContentHandler* enable your code to be informed when any of the following occurs:

- An XML file begins or ends.

- An XML element begins or ends.

- Character data in an XML file are parsed.

The *ErrorHandler* interface enables an application to determine whether an error has occurred in the XML file and whether the error is a severe one or not. For more information about SAX, please see the references we include with this book.

Although you can use SAX to produce XMI documents by implementing SAX handlers that create output, we will not focus on that in this section. The issues you face when creating XMI documents using SAX are almost the same ones you face when you create an XMI document using DOM; the only differences are a result of the different nature of the two interfaces. If you are interested in using SAX to produce XMI documents after we have introduced the

SAX API, refer to the *Using DOM* section for information that will help you when creating XMI documents using SAX.

To use SAX to read an XML document, you need to do the following:

1. Implement one or more handlers.

2. Register your handlers with an object that implements the *XMLReader* interface.

3. Invoke the *parse()* method of the object implementing the *XMLReader* interface.

To help you implement a handler, you can extend from the *DefaultHandler* class in the *org.xml.sax.helpers* package. That class implements all the methods in the *ContentHandler* and *ErrorHandler* interfaces; almost all the methods in the *DefaultHandler* class do nothing. The only exception is the *fatalError()* method, which throws an exception if a fatal error occurs. Most of the time that is what you want to do with fatal errors, since you might not get meaningful data from the parser if you continue parsing after getting a fatal error.

To help you learn the methods in the *ContentHandler* interface that we will be using in this section, we present a simple SAX handler that will print messages as an XML file is being parsed. The handler implements the methods the XML parser invokes when the parser encounters the beginning and end of the XML file, the beginnings and ends of XML elements, and character data in the content of XML elements. Our handler inherits from the *DefaultHandler* class, so we do not need to implement all the methods in the *ContentHandler* interface. The implementation of our handler is shown in Source Code 6.3:

```
// SAXPrintHandler.java
import org.xml.sax.helpers.DefaultHandler;
import org.xml.sax.Attributes;

// This SAX2 handler prints a message when the parser encounters the
// beginning and ending of the XML file, the beginnings and endings
// of XML elements, and character data in the content of
// XML elements.
public class SAXPrintHandler extends DefaultHandler {

// Print a message for the beginning of the XML file.
public void startDocument() {
   System.out.println("XML file begins . . . ");
}

// Print a message for the ending of the XML file.
```

Source Code 6.3 SAXPrintHandler—a simple SAX handler.

```
public void endDocument() {
    System.out.println("XML file ends . . . ");
}

// Print the name of the element and the element's attributes,
// if any.
public void startElement(String uri, String name, String qName,
                         Attributes atts) {
    System.out.println("start element: " + name);

    if (atts.getLength() > 0) {
        System.out.println("  attributes:");
        String attribs = "    ";

        for (int attrib = 0; attrib < atts.getLength(); ++attrib)
            attribs += atts.getLocalName(attrib) + ": '" +
                       atts.getValue(attrib) + "' ";

        System.out.println(attribs);
    }
    else
        System.out.println("  no attributes");
}

// Print a message for the end of the XML element.
public void endElement(String uri, String name, String qName) {
    System.out.println("end Element: " + name);
}

// Print character data. This method may be called more times than you
// expect, and the data may include whitespace. For the examples in
// the book, it is okay to remove leading and trailing whitespace, as
// we do here with the trim() method.
public void characters(char ch[], int start, int length) {
    String chars = new String(ch, start, length);
    System.out.println("  characters: '" + chars.trim() + "'");
}
}
```

Source Code 6.3 SAXPrintHandler—a simple SAX handler. (*Continued*)

By reading the code for the handler, you can learn how to get the names of the XML elements and their XML attributes. The only slightly complicated part of the handler is in dealing with character data that is whitespace; we can ignore leading and trailing whitespace in the contents of XML elements for the example in this section. It might be important for you to preserve that whitespace for your applications, though.

Now we are ready to implement the program that creates an instance of our handler, registers the handler with an *XMLReader,* and parses an XML file. The program gets the name of the XML file to parse from the command line. The program is shown in Source Code 6.4.

Recall from the DOM section of this chapter that we created an XMI file that contained a car of a particular style (a 2002 Jalopy Deluxe), and that it was equipped with one option (air conditioning) and had one driver (Anita Karr). The XMI file was called *DOMWrite.xmi.* Here is the output from *SAXPrint* when it is invoked by specifying *DOMWrite.xmi* as the file to parse:

```
XML file begins...
start element: XMI
  attributes:
    version: '2.0'
  characters: ''
start element: Documentation
  no attributes
```

```
// SAXPrint.java
import org.xml.sax.XMLReader;
import org.xml.sax.InputSource;
import org.apache.xerces.parsers.SAXParser;
import java.io.FileReader;

// Create a SAX parser, parse the file indicated on the command line,
// and print basic information as the file is being parsed.
public class SAXPrint {
  public static void main(String[] args) throws Exception {
    if (args.length != 1) {
      System.out.println("Enter the name of the file to parse.");
      return;
    }

    XMLReader xmlReader      = new SAXParser();
    SAXPrintHandler handler = new SAXPrintHandler();

    xmlReader.setContentHandler(handler);
    xmlReader.setErrorHandler(handler);

    FileReader reader = new FileReader(args[0]);
    xmlReader.parse(new InputSource(reader));
  }
}
```

Source Code 6.4 *SAXPrint* program parsing an XML file using SAX.

```
      characters: ''
start element: exporter
  no attributes
  characters: 'XMI DOM Serialize Example'
end Element: exporter
  characters: ''
start element: exporterVersion
  no attributes
  characters: '0.5'
end Element: exporterVersion
  characters: ''
end Element: Documentation
  characters: ''
start element: Car
  attributes:
    available: 'false' driver: '_3' style: '_2' vin: 'v1' id: '_1'
  characters: ''
start element: option
  attributes:
    car: '_1' name: 'air conditioning' id: '_1.1'
end Element: option
  characters: ''
end Element: Car
  characters: ''
start element: Style
  attributes:
    car: '_1' make: 'Jalopy' model: 'Deluxe' id: '_2' year: '2002'
end Element: Style
  characters: ''
start element: Person
  attributes:
    car: '_1' licenseNumber: 'ln1' name: 'Anita Karr' id: '_3'
end Element: Person
  characters: ''
end Element: XMI
XML file ends...
```

If you compare this output to the *DOMWrite.xmi* file in the DOM section, you can see that all the XML element names and attributes are included, and that all the character data in the content of the XML elements is included also. This output also includes numerous empty strings, since the contained XML elements in the file that was read were indented by four spaces, and each XML element begins on a new line. *SAXPrint* removes this whitespace when it prints character data.

Now that you know how to implement a simple SAX handler and register it with an *XMLReader*, we can begin to implement more complicated handlers. In the rest of this chapter, we present a series of four increasingly sophisticated handlers that create instances of some Java classes that implement the car rental agency model described in the first section of this chapter.

Our implementation of the car rental agency model is straightforward. For each of the four classes in the model, we create a corresponding Java class. Each UML attribute in the model with a multiplicity of *1* is implemented as a private field of a Java class that also has *get* and *set* accessor methods to get and set the value. (For readability, *boolean* attributes have *is* and *set* accessor methods.) Each association end in the UML model is implemented as a private field also. For association ends with multiplicities greater than 1, we have used a field name that ends in s. For example, we use *cars* instead of *car*. If the multiplicity of the association end is *1*, the type of the field is the Java class corresponding to the UML class attached to the association end. As with the other fields, the Java class the field belongs to has the appropriate accessor methods. If the multiplicity of an association end or attribute is more than *1*, the corresponding field has a type of *ArrayList*. In this case, the Java class that has the field has three accessor methods: one returns a collection of the associated objects, one adds an object to the list, and one removes an object from the list. This pattern should become clearer as we explain each Java class. Each Java class also implements the *toString()* method, enabling us to print instances of the class to determine what the values of the fields are.

The first Java class we present is the *Style* class. According to the car rental agency UML model, there are three attributes: *make* and *model* of type *String*, and *year* of type *Integer*. Correspondingly, the Java *Style* class has *make* and *model* fields of type *String*, and a *year* field of type *int*. It also contains accessor methods to get and set each field. The *Style* class in the model has one association end called *cars* attached to the *Car* class; the *cars* association end has a multiplicity of *. The Java *Style* class has a *cars* field that has an *ArrayList* as its type; the three accessor methods for the association end have the following signatures:

```
public Collection getCars();
public void add(Car car);
public void remove(Car car);
```

In other applications it might be important to be able to order the cars, but these three methods are sufficient for our needs.

Source Code 6.5 is the code for the Java *Style* class. Note that the class is in the *cars* Java package.

We can implement the other classes in the car rental agency model following a similar process. The source code for the other three Java classes is shown in Source Code 6.6, Source Code 6.7, and Source Code 6.8.

```
// Style.java
package cars;
import java.util.*;

// The Style class holds the make, model, and year, and
// it contains a list of the cars it is related to.
public class Style {
   private String make, model;
   private int year;
   private ArrayList cars;

public Style() { cars = new ArrayList(); }

public String getMake() { return make; }
public void   setMake(String m) { make = m; }

public String getModel() { return model; }
public void setModel(String m) { model = m; }

public int getYear() { return year; }
public void setYear(int y) { year = y; }

public Collection getCars() { return cars; }
public void add(Car car) { cars.add(car); }
public void remove(Car car) { cars.remove(car); }

public String toString() {
   String s = "Style make: " + make + " model: " + model +
             " year: " + year;

   if (cars.size() > 0) {
      s += " cars:";
      Iterator c = cars.iterator();

      while (c.hasNext())
         s += " " + ((Car) c.next()).getVIN();
   }

   return s;
}
}
```

Source Code 6.5 The *Style* class.

```java
// Person.java
package cars;
import java.util.*;

// The Person class holds the name and licenseNumber of a person,
// as well as a list of the cars the person drives.
public class Person {
  private String name, licenseNumber;
  private ArrayList cars;

public Person() { cars = new ArrayList(); }

public String getName() { return name; }
public void setName(String n) { name = n; }

public String getLicenseNumber() { return licenseNumber; }
public void setLicenseNumber(String l) { licenseNumber = l; }

public Collection getCars() { return cars; }
public void add(Car car) { cars.add(car); }
public void remove(Car car) { cars.remove(car); }

public String toString() {
   String s = "Person name: " + name + " licenseNumber: " +
             licenseNumber;

   if (cars.size() > 0) {
      s += " cars:";
      Iterator c = cars.iterator();

      while (c.hasNext())
        s += " " + ((Car) c.next()).getVIN();
   }

   return s;
}
}
```

Source Code 6.6   The *Person* class.

```
// Car.java
package cars;
import java.util.*;

// The Car class holds the vehicle identification number, the
// style, and the available flag; it contains a list of the
// options the car has and the drivers of the car.
public class Car {
  private String vin;
  private boolean available;
  private ArrayList options, drivers;
  private Style style;

public Car() {
  options = new ArrayList();
  drivers = new ArrayList();
}

public String getVIN() { return vin; }
public void setVIN(String v) { vin = v; }

public boolean isAvailable() { return available; }
public void setAvailable (boolean v) { available = v; }

public Collection getOptions() { return options; }
public void add(Option o) { options.add(o); }
public void remove(Option o) { options.remove(o); }

public Collection getDrivers() { return drivers; }
public void add(Person p) { drivers.add(p); }
public void remove(Person p) { drivers.remove(p); }

public Style getStyle() { return style; }
public void setStyle(Style s) { style = s; }

public String toString() {
  String s = "Car vin: " + vin + " available: " + available;

  if (style != null)
    s += " make: " + style.getMake() + " model: " +
         style.getModel() + " year: " + style.getYear();

  if (options.size() > 0) {
    s += "\n  Options: ";
    Iterator o = options.iterator();

    while (o.hasNext())
      s += "\n    " + ((Option) o.next()).getName();
```

Source Code 6.7 The *Car* class.

```
    }

    if (drivers.size() > 0) {
        s += "\n  Drivers: ";
        Iterator d = drivers.iterator();

        while (d.hasNext())
            s += "\n    " + ((Person) d.next()).getName();
    }

    return s;
    }
}
```

Source Code 6.7 The *Car* class. (*Continued*)

```
// Option.java
package cars;
import java.util.*;

// The Option class contains the name of the option and the car
// the option belongs to.
public class Option {
  private String name;
  private Car car;

public String getName() { return name; }
public void setName(String n) { name = n; }

public Car getCar() { return car; }
public void setCar(Car c) { car = c; }

public String toString() {
    String s = "Option: " + name;

    if (car != null)
        s += " car: " + car.getVIN();

    return s;
    }
}
```

Source Code 6.8 The *Option* class.

Some of the handlers we implement make instances of the Java classes in the *cars* package. We need to be able to get the objects the handlers make. We accomplish this by creating an interface for our handlers to implement. Since our handlers deal with the car rental agency model, we call the interface they will implement *CRAHandler* (for Car Rental Agency Handler). The *CRAHandler* interface extends the standard SAX handler interfaces and contains a method to let us get the objects our handlers make. The interface is as follows:

```
// CRAHandler.java
import org.xml.sax.*;
import java.util.Collection;


// Each of our SAX2 handlers implements this interface. The
// getObjects() method lets us get the objects the handlers make.
// The interfaces this interface extends are the four standard SAX2
// handler interfaces.
public interface CRAHandler extends EntityResolver, DTDHandler,
                                    ContentHandler, ErrorHandler {

// Returns the objects created by the handler.
public Collection getObjects();
}
```

Now that we know the interface that each of our handlers will implement, we can write a program to enable us to parse the *DOMWrite.xmi* file with *any* of the handlers we develop. Let's call this program *SAXRead*. This program uses two command-line arguments: the name of the file to parse and the name of the handler class. Since our handlers will contain a no argument constructor, we can invoke the *newInstance()* method of *java.lang.Class* to make instances of them. We can get the correct *java.lang.Class* object by invoking the static method *forName()* in *java.lang.Class*. Once *SAXRead* creates an instance of one of our handlers, it registers the handler instance with an *XMLReader*, parses the XMI document, calls the *getObjects()* method of the *CRAHandler*, and finally prints each object. The *SAXRead* program is shown in Source Code 6.9.

CRAHandler1: Accessing and Printing Data in the XMI File

Now that we have implemented the car rental agency model in Java, created an interface for our handlers, and written a program that will parse a document with the handlers we write, it is time to implement our first handler. The first handler is a simple one that prints the *exporter* and *exporterVersion* from the *xmi:Documentation* element of an XMI document. It demonstrates how to accumulate character data that is in the content of an XML element using a *StringBuffer*. When an XML element begins, a new *StringBuffer* is created so the

```
// SAXRead.java
import org.xml.sax.XMLReader;
import org.xml.sax.InputSource;
import org.apache.xerces.parsers.SAXParser;
import java.util.Collection;
import java.util.Iterator;
import java.io.FileReader;

// Parse the file that has the name of the first command-line
// argument using the car rental agency handler that has the class
// name of the second command-line argument. After the file is parsed,
// print the objects made by the handler.
public class SAXRead {
   public static void main(String[] args) throws Exception {
     if (args.length != 2) {
       System.out.println("Enter file name and handler class name.");
       return;
     }

     XMLReader xr = new SAXParser();

     java.lang.Class cls = java.lang.Class.forName(args[1]);
     CRAHandler handler = (CRAHandler) cls.newInstance();

     if (handler != null) {
       xr.setContentHandler(handler);
       xr.setErrorHandler(handler);

       FileReader reader = new FileReader(args[0]);
       xr.parse(new InputSource(reader));

       Collection objects = handler.getObjects();
       Iterator o = objects.iterator();

       while (o.hasNext())
         System.out.println(o.next());
     }
   }
}
```

Source Code 6.9   *SAXRead* program.

buffer does not contain characters from the content of a previous XML element. Then, when the parser invokes the *characters()* method of the handler, the character data is appended to the *StringBuffer*. Finally, when an XML element ends, if the name of the element is *exporter* or *exporterVersion*, the *StringBuffer* is printed. This technique can be used to get the values of attributes if the values are in the content of an XML element. It can also be used to get other information in the *xmi:Documentation* element. This handler implements the *CRAHandler* interface and extends the *DefaultHandler* class, so we don't need to implement all the methods in the SAX2 handler interfaces ourselves. Our first car rental agency handler is shown in Source Code 6.10.

When we run the *SAXRead* program with *DOMWrite.xmi* and *CRAHandler1* as the command-line arguments, it creates the following output:

```
exporter: XMI DOM Serialize Example
exporter version: 0.5
```

CRAHandler2: Making Java Instances of the XMI Document Objects

Now let's try something more interesting. The next handler makes instances of the *Car*, *Person*, *Style*, and *Option* classes in the *cars* package using the same Java technique we used to make an instance of a *CRAHandler* in the *SAXRead* program. In the *DOMWrite.xmi* file, the elements that represent the objects have tag names of *Car*, *Person*, *Style*, and *Option,* while the classes to instantiate are *cars.Car*, *cars.Person*, *cars.Style*, and *cars.Option*.[1] We need to implement a method that takes a tag name, uses that name to determine the class name, and then makes an instance of the class. We will put the method in a class called *CRAFactory* to make the handler easier to understand. The *CRAFactory* class contains a *HashMap* that maps from tag names to class names. It has a *newInstance()* method that takes a tag name as a parameter and returns an instance of the appropriate class. The *CRAFactory* program is shown in Source Code 6.11.

The handler that uses the *CRAFactory* to make instances stores each new instance in a list so they can be obtained using the *getObjects()* method. This handler inherits from the previous handler, so it invokes *CRAHandler1*'s *startElement()* method and constructor. The next two handlers will need access to the most recent instance made by this handler, so the *newObject* field is protected to let subclasses access it, and it is set to each new instance. Our second handler is shown in Source Code 6.12.

Does this work? When we use this handler with *SAXRead* on the same file as before, this is the output:

```
exporter: XMI DOM Serialize Example
exporter version: 0.5
Car vin: null available: false
Option: null
Style make: null model: null year: 0
Person name: null licenseNumber: null
```

As expected, the objects were created, but none of their fields were restored. Also, this handler prints the *exporter* and *exporterVersion*, just like the first handler.

```java
// CRAHandler1.java
import org.xml.sax.helpers.DefaultHandler;
import org.xml.sax.Attributes;
import java.util.Collection;
import java.util.Collections;

// This handler prints the exporter and exporter version in the
// XMI Documentation element.
public class CRAHandler1 extends DefaultHandler implements CRAHandler {
  private StringBuffer buffer;

  // This flag is true if processing the xmi:Documentation element.
  private boolean inXMIDocumentation=false;

// Create a new buffer, since we don't want the buffer to contain
// characters from previous XML elements.
public void startElement(String uri, String name, String qName,
                         Attributes atts) {
   buffer = new StringBuffer();
   if (qName.equals("xmi:Documentation"))
     inXMIDocumentation=true;
}


// Print the exporter and exporter version.
public void endElement(String uri, String name, String qName) {
   if (inXMIDocumentation) // Ensure these are exporter and
                           // exporterVersion in the XMI model.
     if (name.equals("exporter"))
        System.out.println("exporter: " + buffer);
     else if (name.equals("exporterVersion"))
       System.out.println("exporter version: " + buffer);

   if (qName.equals("xmi:Documentation"))
     inXMIDocumentation=false;
}

// Append characters to the buffer as the parser encounters them.
public void characters(char ch[], int start, int length) {
   buffer.append(ch, start, length);
}

// Since no objects are created, return an empty list.
public Collection getObjects() {
   return Collections.EMPTY_LIST;
}
}
```

Source Code 6.10 CRAHandler1.

```
// CRAFactory.java
import java.util.HashMap;
import cars.*;

// This class makes instances of the classes in the cars package
// given tag names of XML elements in an XMI file.
public class CRAFactory {
  private HashMap tagNamesToClassNames;

// Initialize tagNamesToClassNames for the car rental agency.
public CRAFactory() {
  tagNamesToClassNames = new HashMap();

  // In the HashMap, we map the tag name of the element
  // for an object to the Java class name. Note that there are two
  // entries that map to cars.Option. Since the object attribute for
  // the Car object's options is called "option", this is the tag name
  // for the element for the Option object in the XMI file we wrote.
  // Since there could also be an Option object with an XML element tag
  // name of "Option" in another file, we include both "option" and
  // "Option" in the Hashmap for completeness.

  tagNamesToClassNames.put("Style",  "cars.Style");
  tagNamesToClassNames.put("Car",    "cars.Car");
  tagNamesToClassNames.put("Option", "cars.Option");
  tagNamesToClassNames.put("option", "cars.Option");
  tagNamesToClassNames.put("Person", "cars.Person");
}

// Make an instance of the correct class given the tag name of an XML
// element from an XMI file. Throw an exception if unsuccessful.
public Object newInstance(String tagName) throws Exception {
    String clsName = (String) tagNamesToClassNames.get(tagName);
    java.lang.Class cls = java.lang.Class.forName(clsName);
    return cls.newInstance();
  }
}
```

Source Code 6.11 CRAFactory.

```java
// CRAHandler2.java
import org.xml.sax.Attributes;
import java.util.ArrayList;
import java.util.Collection;

// This handler makes instances of the classes in the cars package
// using the CRAFactory.  Each instance is added to the objects list.
// The newObject is set to each instance when it is created, so
// handlers that subclass this class can access the new object.
public class CRAHandler2 extends CRAHandler1 {
  private ArrayList objects;

  protected static final String XMI_ID = "xmi:id";

  protected CRAFactory factory;
  protected Object newObject;

// Initialize the objects list and the factory.
public CRAHandler2() {
   super();
   factory = new CRAFactory();
   objects = new ArrayList();
}

// Make a new instance if the XML element represents an object. In
// this application, every XML element that represents an object has
// an xmi:id attribute, which is not true for every XMI file.
public void startElement(String uri, String name, String qName,
                          Attributes atts) {
   super.startElement(uri, name, qName, atts);

   if (atts.getValue(XMI_ID) != null)
     try {
       newObject = factory.newInstance(name);
       objects.add(newObject);
     }
     catch (Exception e) {
       e.printStackTrace();
     }
}

// Return the objects that were created.
public Collection getObjects() {
   return objects;
}
}
```

Source Code 6.12   CRAHandler2.

CRAHandler3: Setting the Fields of the Java Instances

Now it's time to begin restoring the objects' fields. The next handler sets the fields of the object that correspond to UML data attributes from the car rental agency model.[2] Each of these attributes is represented by an XML attribute. To make the handler easier to understand, we add some methods to the *CRAFactory* class. The first method returns the names of the XML attributes that correspond to UML data attributes in the CRA model. The second method sets the value of an object's field given the object, the name of the field, and the field's value. Since the attribute values will be read in as Java *String*s, note that we have included code to handle the cases where we are setting a field with a value that is a Java *int* or *boolean*. The methods that we add to the *CRAFactory* are shown in Source Code 6.13.

```
// New methods for CRAFactory.java

// Return the names of the XML attributes that correspond to UML
// attributes.
public String[] getAttributeNames(Object object) {
    if (object instanceof Car)
        return new String[] { "vin", "available" };
    else if (object instanceof Option)
        return new String[] { "name" };
    else if (object instanceof Person)
        return new String [] { "name", "licenseNumber" };
    else if (object instanceof Style)
        return new String [] { "make", "model", "year" };
    else
        return new String[0];
}

// Call the appropriate method based on the type of the object.
public void setAttribute(Object object, String attribName,
                         String value) {
  if (object instanceof Car)
    setAttribute((Car) object, attribName, value);
  else if (object instanceof Option)
    setAttribute((Option) object, attribName, value);
  else if (object instanceof Style)
    setAttribute((Style) object, attribName, value);
  else if (object instanceof Person)
    setAttribute((Person) object, attribName, value);
}
```

Source Code 6.13 New methods for the CRAFactory.

```
// Set the vin or available field of the Car object.
private void setAttribute(Car c, String attribName, String value) {
  if (attribName.equals("vin"))
    c.setVIN(value);
  else if (attribName.equals("available") && value != null) {
    if (value.equals("true"))
      c.setAvailable(true);
    else if (value.equals("false"))
      c.setAvailable(false);
  }
}


// Set the name of the Option object.
private void setAttribute(Option o, String attribName, String value) {
  if (attribName.equals("name"))
    o.setName(value);
}


// Set the name and license number of the Person object.
private void setAttribute(Person p, String attribName, String value) {
  if (attribName.equals("name"))
    p.setName(value);
  else if (attribName.equals("licenseNumber"))
    p.setLicenseNumber(value);
}


// Set the make, model, and year of the Style object.
private void setAttribute(Style s, String attribName, String value) {
  if (attribName.equals("make"))
    s.setMake(value);
  else if (attribName.equals("model"))
    s.setModel(value);
  else if (attribName.equals("year")) {
    int year = -1;

    try {
      if (value != null)
        year = Integer.parseInt(value);
    }
    catch (Exception e) {
      e.printStackTrace();
    }

    if (year != -1)
      s.setYear(year);
  }
}
```

Source Code 6.13   New methods for the CRAFactory. (*Continued*)

With this capability implemented in *CRAFactory*, for each XML element that represents an object we need to get the XML attribute names from the *CRAFactory*, get the values of the attributes, and then call the *setAttribute()* method in the *CRAFactory* for each XML attribute that does not have *null* as its value. We can get the new instance by using the *newObject* field in *CRAHandler2*. Our third handler is shown in Source Code 6.14.

The output from *SAXRead* using this handler and the file produced by *DOMWrite* looks like this:

```java
// CRAHandler3.java
import org.xml.sax.Attributes;

// This handler sets the fields of the objects in the cars package that
// correspond to UML data attributes in the car rental agency model.
// It uses the CRAFactory to set the fields.
public class CRAHandler3 extends CRAHandler2 {

// If the XML element has an xmi:id XML attribute, then newObject is
// the instance made by CRAHandler2. Call the setAttribute() method
// of the CRAFactory from CRAHandler3 to restore the fields of the
// Java classes that correspond to UML data attributes.
public void startElement(String uri, String name, String qName,
                         Attributes atts) {
  super.startElement(uri, name, qName, atts);

  if (atts.getValue(XMI_ID) != null)
    setAttributes(newObject, atts);
}

// Set the fields of the objects that correspond to UML data
// attributes.
private void setAttributes(Object object, Attributes atts) {
   String [] attribNames = factory.getAttributeNames(object);

   for (int name = 0; name < attribNames.length; ++name) {
     String value = atts.getValue(attribNames[name]);

     if (value != null)
       factory.setAttribute(object, attribNames[name], value);
   }
 }
}
```

Source Code 6.14 CRAHandler3.

```
exporter: XMI DOM Serialize Example
exporter version: 0.5
Car vin: v1 available: false
Option: air conditioning
Style make: Jalopy model: Deluxe year: 2002
Person name: Anita Karr licenseNumber: ln1
```

This handler works for the *DOMWrite.xmi* document, but it will not handle attributes in all XMI documents, since it does not handle attributes with multiple values or attributes that have a class as their type instead of a datatype (object attributes). Those kinds of attributes are represented by XML elements rather than XML attributes. The handler also does not handle references.

CRAHandler4: Dealing with References

Now we need to set the fields of the objects that represent references and object values in the UML model. If you look at *DOMWrite.xmi*, references are represented by XML attributes with values that are XML IDs. For example, the *Car* object's *style* is represented as an XML attribute with a value of _2, which is the XML ID for the *Style* XML element. (The value of the *Style* element's XML ID is stored in its *xmi:id* attribute.) Also, notice that when you are processing an object having references, the referenced objects may not have been loaded yet. In our first example, the *Style* XML element comes after the *Car* XML element in the file, so it is not available when the *Car* element is parsed. This means that we need to store forward references when parsing the file and set them when the file has been completely parsed. The *option* object attribute is handled differently from how we handle references. Since *option* is an object value in the *Car* object, the XML element corresponding to the object value is written *inside* the XML element corresponding to the *Car* object.

Once again, to make the handler easier to understand, we add several methods to the *CRAFactory* class that will call the appropriate methods on the Java classes in the *cars* package to set the references and the object attribute as we parse the file. The next handler also needs to know the names of the references that are represented by XML attributes. The new methods for the *CRAFactory* are shown in Source Code 6.15.

Now that those methods are implemented, we can implement the last handler. For each XML element in the document that represents an object, the handler asks the *CRAFactory* for the names of the references represented by XML attributes. Then the handler gets the XML ID of the object that is the value of the reference. If the object was already created, it can be looked up and the reference can be set; otherwise, a *ForwardLink* object is created so the reference can be set when the end of the file is reached. In *DOMWrite.xmi*, the XML attributes that represent references have only one XML ID for their values, but there can be more than one XML ID in general. That is why we parse the value of the

```
//New methods for CRAFactory.java

// Returns the names of the references represented by XML attributes
// for the given type of object.
public String[] getXMLAttributeReferences(Object object) {
  if (object instanceof Car)
    return new String[] { "driver", "style" };
  else if (object instanceof Person ||
          object instanceof Style    ||
          object instanceof Option)
    return new String[] { "car" };
  else
    return new String[0];
}


// Calls the appropriate method to set the reference based on the type
// of the object.
public void setReference(Object object, String referenceName,
                      Object value){
  if (object instanceof Car)
    setReference((Car) object,    referenceName, value);
  else if (object instanceof Option)
    setReference((Option) object, referenceName, value);
  else if (object instanceof Style)
    setReference((Style) object,  referenceName, value);
  else if (object instanceof Person)
    setReference((Person) object, referenceName, value);
}

// Set the driver or style references on a Car object.
private void setReference(Car c, String referenceName, Object value) {
  if (referenceName.equals("driver") && (value instanceof Person))
    c.add((Person) value);
  else if (referenceName.equals("style") && (value instanceof Style))
    c.setStyle((Style) value);
}

// Set the car reference from an Option object to a Car object.
private void setReference(Option o, String referenceName,
                      Object value) {
  if (referenceName.equals("car") && (value instanceof Car))
    o.setCar((Car) value);
}

// Set the car reference from a Style object to a Car object.
private void setReference(Style s, String referenceName,
                      Object value) {
  if (referenceName.equals("car") && (value instanceof Car))
```

Source Code 6.15 New methods for the CRAFactory.

```
        s.add((Car) value);
}

// Set the car reference from a Person object to a Car object.
private void setReference(Person p, String referenceName,
                          Object value) {
  if (referenceName.equals("car") && (value instanceof Car))
    p.add((Car) value);
}
```

Source Code 6.15 New methods for the CRAFactory. (*Continued*)

XML attributes with a *StringTokenizer*, although it is not necessary to do so for this example. Finally, we set the *option* object attribute of the *Car* object when the *Option* object is created, since that object attribute is not represented by an XML attribute. *CRAHandler4* is shown in Source Code 6.16.

The output from the *SAXRead* program when this handler is used with the XMI document created by *DOMWrite* is as follows:

```
exporter: XMI DOM Serialize Example
exporter version: 0.5
Car vin: v1 available: false make: Jalopy model: Deluxe year: 2002
  Options:
    air conditioning
  Drivers:
    Anita Karr
Option: air conditioning car: v1
Style make: Jalopy model: Deluxe year: 2002 cars: v1
Person name: Anita Karr licenseNumber: ln1 cars: v1
```

As you can see, the objects are now fully restored.

If you want to implement SAX handlers that will work for any XMI document, you need to address many issues beyond those we covered in the previous handlers. These include:

- Data attributes with multiple values need to be handled.

- Objects may be nested in other objects to any depth. To correctly restore attributes with object values, you may need to implement a stack of objects that have been created and then pop the stack after finishing an object. The handlers we presented used a *newObject* field rather than a stack of new objects.

- If the XMI documents will be in different problem domains, you need to implement a generic mechanism for restoring the objects' attribute values and references. You may also need to implement a scheme for

```
// CRAHandler4.java
import org.xml.sax.*;
import java.util.*;
import cars.Option;
import cars.Car;

// This handler sets the fields that correspond to references
// in the car rental agency model. It handles references to objects
// that have not been parsed yet using the ForwardLink class.
public class CRAHandler4 extends CRAHandler3 {
    private HashMap IDsToObjects;
    private ArrayList forwardLinks;
    private Object lastObject;

    // This class stores the object, the name of the reference, and the
    // XML ID so the reference can be set when the entire file has been
    // parsed.
    private static class ForwardLink {
      private Object object;
      private String name, ID;

      ForwardLink(Object object, String name, String ID) {
        this.object = object;
        this.name = name;
        this.ID = ID;
      }

      Object getObject() { return object; }
      String getName()   { return name;   }
      Object getID()     { return ID;     }
    }

// Initialize IDsToObjects and forwardLinks.
public CRAHandler4() {
    super();
    IDsToObjects = new HashMap();
    forwardLinks = new ArrayList();
}

// If the XML element has an xmi:id XML attribute, then newObject is
// the instance made by CRAHandler2. Call the setReferences method to
// set the references represented by XML attributes. Set the option
// object attribute of the Car explicitly, since that object attribute
// has its own XML element.
public void startElement(String uri, String name, String qName,
                         Attributes atts) {
  lastObject = newObject;
```

Source Code 6.16 CRAHandler4.

```
    super.startElement(uri, name, qName, atts);
    String ID = atts.getValue(XMI_ID);

    if (ID != null) {
      IDsToObjects.put(ID, newObject);
      setReferences(newObject, atts);

      // Handle the option object attribute for the car.
      if ((newObject instanceof Option) && (lastObject instanceof Car))
        ((Car)(lastObject)).add((Option)newObject);
    }
  }

// Get the names of the references represented by XML attributes for
// the given object. Next, for each reference, get the XML ID that is
// the value of the XML attribute representing the reference.
// Then try to get the object with the ID. If the object was
// already created, set the reference; otherwise, create a
// ForwardLink so the reference can be set at the end of the file.
private void setReferences(Object obj, Attributes atts) {
  String [] referenceNames = factory.getXMLAttributeReferences(obj);

  for (int reference = 0; reference < referenceNames.length;
       ++reference) {
    String IDs = atts.getValue("", referenceNames[reference]);

    if (IDs != null) {
      StringTokenizer t = new StringTokenizer(IDs);

      while (t.hasMoreTokens()) {
        String ID = t.nextToken();
        java.lang.Object value = IDsToObjects.get(ID);

        if (value == null)
          forwardLinks.add(new ForwardLink(obj,
                           referenceNames[reference], ID));
        else
          factory.setReference(obj, referenceNames[reference],
                               value);
      } // while (t.hasMoreTokens())
    } // if (IDs != null)
  } // for (int reference = 0  . . .
}

// Resolve the forward links; the IDsToObjects HashMap should have
// all of the objects in it because the end of the document has been
// reached.
```

Source Code 6.16   CRAHandler4. (*Continued*)

```
public void endDocument() {
  for (int i = 0; i < forwardLinks.size(); ++i) {
    ForwardLink link = (ForwardLink) forwardLinks.get(i);
    Object value    = IDsToObjects.get(link.getID());
    factory.setReference(link.getObject(), link.getName(), value);
  }
}
}
```

Source Code 6.16   CRAHandler4. (*Continued*)

determining whether an XML attribute in an XMI document represents an attribute or a reference for an object, as well as implementing a factory that makes objects.

■ Other XMI features that the simple handlers here do not cover need to be handled. One example is XMI extensions, which we explain in Chapter 8.

Summary

Since XMI is built on top of XML, you can use standard XML APIs such as DOM and SAX both to create and read XMI documents. Also, if there are generic advances in XML—such as new techniques for creating XML documents and reading them—you can take advantage of those techniques with XMI documents. Although these APIs provide the flexibility to deal with generic XML documents, using them with XMI documents requires that you understand how XMI documents are structured. It is much easier to use APIs that have been designed specifically to support XMI, however, as we will see in the next chapter.

CHAPTER

7

Creating and Reading Simple XMI Documents with the XMI Framework

In the last chapter, we looked at how the standard Extensible Markup Language (XML) Application Programming Interfaces (APIs) Document Object Model (DOM) and Simple API for XML (SAX) could be used to work with XML Metadata Interchange (XMI) documents. Although those APIs are not designed particularly for XMI documents, in this chapter we look at APIs that are designed specifically for XMI. One example of such an API is the Java Object Bridge (JOB), which enables you to store any Java objects in an XMI document and restore them from an XMI document. In the beginning of this chapter, we will look at how to use JOB to do this.

Another API that supports XMI is the XMI Framework. The Framework provides a generic representation of objects and their states in a simple object model. It enables you to create XMI documents from generic objects and to make generic objects when reading XMI documents. You can also use your own Java objects rather than generic versions of them by writing code that connects your Java classes with the Framework. We explain how to use the Framework with generic objects and with instances of Java classes that are not part of the Framework. We also examine how the Framework may interpret the data in XMI documents differently depending on whether or not it knows the model that defines the data in the documents.

You should read this chapter before reading Chapters 8 and 9, since both chapters contain code examples that are based on the examples in this chapter. This chapter covers basic issues you need to deal with when you write programs that work with XMI documents. Chapter 8 covers more advanced issues such as XML namespaces, identifying your models, XMI extensions, ZIP files, and cross-file references. Chapter 9 explains how to use the Framework to generate schemas. This chapter contains the information you need to know to fully understand the issues presented in Chapters 8 and 9.

The examples we use throughout this chapter are based on the car rental agency model that we introduced in Chapter 6. Although you do not need to have read all of Chapter 6 to understand this chapter, you will need to be familiar with the car rental agency model presented in the beginning of Chapter 6 to understand the examples presented in this chapter.

Using the Java Object Bridge (JOB)

After reading the previous chapter, you might think that creating and reading XMI documents is very complicated. The reason the previous examples were complicated is because they used interfaces that were designed to handle *any* XML document. Neither DOM nor SAX was designed to support the power of XMI. Starting with this section, we present interfaces that are explicitly designed to support XMI. These interfaces make it much easier to work with XMI documents than DOM and SAX.

Creating an XMI Document

The minimum amount of work necessary to create an XMI document is to make your objects and then invoke a method with a collection of those objects and the name of the XMI document to create. JOB provides this minimal interface. It uses Java reflection to get the data for each object and the XMI Framework (discussed in the next section) to read and write XMI documents.

JOB's purpose is to serialize and deserialize Java objects using XMI. JOB does not work with UML models; it works with Java objects and classes. For this reason, there are differences between the XMI files that JOB creates based on a Java implementation of a model and XMI files that are created based on knowledge of the model. We explain these differences later in this section.

JOB ENHANCEMENTS

An enhanced version of JOB that uses code generation would run more efficiently. The reflection would be done once at code generation time to decide which class-specific calls to make. Also, if JOB knew about the model, it would be able to write Java objects in a way that matches the model. The internals of the XMI utilities in Websphere Studio Application Developer (included in the accompanying CD-ROM) have these capabilities.

Before we use JOB to create an XMI document, let's write code to create the objects we will put in an XMI document. In the first section of Chapter 6, we described the car rental agency model and four objects that are instances of classes in the model. We implemented the car rental agency model using four classes in the *cars* package: *Car*, *Option*, *Style*, and *Person*. Those four classes are displayed for your convenience in Source Code 7.1, Source Code 7.2, Source Code 7.3, and Source Code 7.4, respectively.

```java
// Car.java
package cars;
import java.util.*;

// The Car class holds the vehicle identification number, the
// style, and the available flag; it contains a list of the
// options the car has and the drivers of the car.
public class Car {
  private String vin;
  private boolean available;
  private ArrayList options, drivers;
  private Style style;

public Car() {
  options = new ArrayList();
  drivers = new ArrayList();
}

public String getVIN() { return vin; }
public void setVIN(String v) { vin = v; }

public boolean isAvailable() { return available; }
public void setAvailable (boolean v) { available = v; }

public Collection getOptions() { return options; }
public void add(Option o) { options.add(o); }
public void remove(Option o) { options.remove(o); }

public Collection getDrivers() { return drivers; }
public void add(Person p) { drivers.add(p); }
public void remove(Person p) { drivers.remove(p); }

public Style getStyle() { return style; }
public void setStyle(Style s) { style = s; }

public String toString() {
   String s = "Car vin: " + vin + " available: " + available;

   if (style != null)
```

Source Code 7.1 The *Car* class.

```
        s += " make: " + style.getMake() + " model: " +
            style.getModel() + " year: " + style.getYear();

    if (options.size() > 0) {
        s += "\n  Options: ";
        Iterator o = options.iterator();

        while (o.hasNext())
            s += "\n      " + ((Option) o.next()).getName();
    }

    if (drivers.size() > 0) {
        s += "\n  Drivers: ";
        Iterator d = drivers.iterator();

        while (d.hasNext())
            s += "\n      " + ((Person) d.next()).getName();
    }

    return s;
    }
    }
```

Source Code 7.1   The *Car* class. *(Continued)*

Now we can use these classes to make the objects to put in an XMI document. We add a new method to the *CRAFactory* class that we developed in the last chapter. This method, *makeExample()*, makes the objects we'll put into an XMI document using the classes in the *cars* package. The objects returned by the *makeExample()* method correspond to the objects we described in Chapter 6. Source Code 7.5 contains the *makeExample()* method. The rest of the *CRAFactory* class is not shown here since we only use the *makeExample()* method.

A program that uses JOB to produce an XMI document with the example objects is very simple and is displayed in Source Code 7.6. Although the *makeExample()* method returns three objects, you could pass any one of them to JOB, because they reference each other directly or indirectly. JOB writes all objects that are referenced from the objects you give it. It ensures that it does not write objects multiple times. For more information about the options for using JOB, please see the documentation for JOB on the CD-ROM.

The file created by *JOBWrite, job.xmi,* is as follows (some of the longer lines have been split to accommodate the page width of the book and your results may vary due to differences among Java virtual machines in the order that data is returned using Java reflection):[1]

```java
// Option.java
package cars;
import java.util.*;

// The Option class contains the name of the option and the car
// the option belongs to.
public class Option {
  private String name;
  private Car car;

public String getName() { return name; }
public void setName(String n) { name = n; }

public Car getCar() { return car; }
public void setCar(Car c) { car = c; }

public String toString() {
   String s = "Option: " + name;

   if (car != null)
     s += " car: " + car.getVIN();

   return s;
}
}
```

Source Code 7.2   The *Option* class.

```xml
<?xml version="1.0" encoding="UTF-8"?>
<xmi:XMI xmi:version="2.0" xmlns:xmi="http://www.omg.org/XMI"
                     xmlns:job="http://www.ibm.com/xmi/job"
                     xmlns:p1="Java:cars"
                     xmlns:p2="Java:java.util">
   <xmi:Documentation>
     <exporter>Java Object Bridge (JOB)</exporter>
     <exporterVersion>0.95</exporterVersion>
   </xmi:Documentation>
  <p1:Car xmi:id="_1" available="false" vin="v1" job:top="true"
        style="_2" drivers="_1.2" options="_1.3"/>
  <p1:Style xmi:id="_2" year="2002" model="Deluxe" make="Jalopy"
          job:top="true" cars="_2.1"/>
  <p1:Person xmi:id="_3" licenseNumber="ln1" job:top="true"
           cars="_3.1">
   <name>Anita Karr</name>
  </p1:Person>
  <p2:ArrayList xmi:id="_1.2" items="_3"/>
```

```
// Style.java
package cars;
import java.util.*;

// The Style class holds the make, model, and year, and
// it contains a list of the cars it is related to.
public class Style {
   private String make, model;
   private int year;
   private ArrayList cars;

public Style() { cars = new ArrayList(); }

public String getMake() { return make; }
public void    setMake(String m) { make = m; }

public String getModel() { return model; }
public void setModel(String m) { model = m; }

public int getYear() { return year; }
public void setYear(int y) { year = y; }

public Collection getCars() { return cars; }
public void add(Car car) { cars.add(car); }
public void remove(Car car) { cars.remove(car); }

public String toString() {
   String s = "Style make: " + make + " model: " + model +
              " year: " + year;

   if (cars.size() > 0) {
      s += " cars:";
      Iterator c = cars.iterator();

      while (c.hasNext())
         s += " " + ((Car) c.next()).getVIN();
   }

   return s;
}
}
```

Source Code 7.3   The *Style* class.

```
// Person.java
package cars;
import java.util.*;

// The Person class holds the name and licenseNumber of a person,
// as well as a list of the cars the person drives.
public class Person {
  private String name, licenseNumber;
  private ArrayList cars;

public Person() { cars = new ArrayList(); }

public String getName() { return name; }
public void setName(String n) { name = n; }

public String getLicenseNumber() { return licenseNumber; }
public void setLicenseNumber(String l) { licenseNumber = l; }

public Collection getCars() { return cars; }
public void add(Car car) { cars.add(car); }
public void remove(Car car) { cars.remove(car); }

public String toString() {
   String s = "Person name: " + name + " licenseNumber: " +
            licenseNumber;

   if (cars.size() > 0) {
      s += " cars:";
      Iterator c = cars.iterator();

      while (c.hasNext())
        s += " " + ((Car) c.next()).getVIN();
   }

   return s;
}
}
}
```

Source Code 7.4 The *Person* class.

```
// The makeExample() method in the CRAFactory class.

// Make the example objects using the classes in the cars package.
public ArrayList makeExample() {
    Car    c = new Car();
    Option o = new Option();
    Style  s = new Style();
    Person p = new Person();

    c.setAvailable(false);
    c.setVIN("v1");
    c.add(p);
    c.add(o);
    c.setStyle(s);

    o.setName("air conditioning");
    o.setCar(c);

    s.setMake("Jalopy");
    s.setModel("Deluxe");
    s.setYear(2002);
    s.add(c);

    p.setLicenseNumber("ln1");
    p.setName("Anita Karr");
    p.add(c);

    // The Option object does not need to be added to the ArrayList
    // of returned objects, since it is already contained in the Car
    // object.
    ArrayList l = new ArrayList();
    l.add(c);
    l.add(s);
    l.add(p);

    return l;
}
```

Source Code 7.5 The *makeExample()* method in the *CRAFactory* class.

```
// JOBWrite.java
import com.ibm.xmi.job.Job;
import java.util.ArrayList;

// Use the CRAFactory to make the example objects to save, then
// write them to an XMI document called job.xmi.
public class JOBWrite {
   public static void main(String[] args) throws Exception {
      CRAFactory factory = new CRAFactory();
      ArrayList objects = factory.makeExample();
      Job.writeObjects(objects, "job.xmi");
   }
}
```

Source Code 7.6 The *JOBWrite* program.

```
   <p2:ArrayList xmi:id="_1.3" items="_1.3.1"/>
   <p1:Option xmi:id="_1.3.1" car="_1">
     <name>air conditioning</name>
   </p1:Option>
   <p2:ArrayList xmi:id="_2.1" items="_1"/>
   <p2:ArrayList xmi:id="_3.1" items="_1"/>
</xmi:XMI>
```

As you can see, you do not need to be an XMI expert to use JOB to create an XMI document.

If you examine the previous output, you will notice that it is different than the XMI document we saw in the last chapter. The document from the last chapter, *DOMWrite.xmi*, is as follows:

```
<?xml version="1.0" encoding="UTF-8"?>
<xmi:XMI xmi:version="2.0" xmlns:xmi="http://www.omg.org/XMI">
    <xmi:Documentation>
        <exporter>XMI DOM Serialize Example</exporter>
        <exporterVersion>0.5</exporterVersion>
    </xmi:Documentation>
    <Car available="false" driver="_3" style="_2" vin="v1"
        xmi:id="_1">
        <option car="_1" name="air conditioning" xmi:id="_1.1"/>
    </Car>
    <Style car="_1" make="Jalopy" model="Deluxe" xmi:id="_2"
          year="2002"/>
    <Person car="_1" licenseNumber="ln1" name="Anita Karr"
          xmi:id="_3"/>
</xmi:XMI>
```

Notice that the *exporter* and *exporterVersion* are different, reflecting the programs that created each file. There are differences in the representation of the objects as well.

The reason for the differences in the two files is that the document from the last chapter was created by following the XMI serialization rules based on knowledge of the car rental agency model. JOB does not know about the car rental agency model. It obtains the information it needs to serialize objects using Java reflection. The file created by JOB is based on the Java classes that implement the car rental agency model, not the car rental agency model itself.

Using the Java classes rather than the model results in different tag names and attribute names in the XMI documents. For example, the XML element for the *Car* object has a tag name of *Car* in *DOMWrite.xmi*, since the name of the corresponding class in the model is *Car*. In *job.xmi*, the XML element has a tag name of *p1:Car*, because JOB creates an XML namespace for each Java package and uses the namespace prefix when it serializes instances of classes in the package. In *job.xmi*, an XML attribute called *cars* is used in the elements for the *Style* object and the *Person* object. In *DOMWrite.xmi*, those XML attributes are called *car*. There is an association end named *car* in the model, so *DOMWrite.xmi* uses that name in the corresponding XML attributes. JOB uses the names of the Java fields in *Style.java* and *Person.java* that implement the association ends; those fields are called *cars*.

The file *job.xmi* represents the *Option* object using an XML element called *p1:Option*. The *p1:Car* XML element refers to this element through an XML element representing a Java *ArrayList*. The value of the *options* attribute in the *p1:Car* element, *_1.3*, matches the *xmi:id* of the second *p2:ArrayList* element in the file. In turn, the value of the *items* attribute of that *p2:ArrayList* element, *_1.3.1*, matches the *xmi:id* of the *p1:Option* element. If this is not clear, you may want to take a minute to study the *job.xmi* file and trace this example through to see how it is done.

Unlike the *job.xmi* file, the file *DOMWrite.xmi* represents the *Option* object as an XML element called *option* that is inside the *Car* XML element. The reason for this difference is that an object attribute in Unified Modeling Language (UML), an attribute with a class as its type, has composition semantics, so the program that wrote *DOMWrite.xmi* considered the *Option* object to be an object value of the *Car* object. This means that the *Option* object has a composition relationship with the *Car* object. However, Java fields do not have composition semantics. As a result, JOB treats the values of Java fields that are objects as references (references are instances of association ends that do not have composition semantics). Finally, notice that *job.xmi* includes all the *ArrayList* objects that are values of the Java fields of type *ArrayList* in the Java classes. Since these objects are part of the implementation of the model rather than the model itself, the *DOMWrite.xmi* file does not include these objects.

If you run *JOBWrite* at the command prompt, you will notice that in addition to writing the file *job.xmi*, the following output appears in the command prompt window:

```
--> 8 objects saved into job.xmi
```

This indicates that eight objects (the four from the car rental agency model plus the four *ArrayList* objects) were saved into *job.xmi*.

Reading an XMI Document

How difficult is it to use JOB to read an XMI document and get the objects from it? Source Code 7.7 shows that this is also very simple.

The output of *JOBRead* indicates that the objects were correctly restored. Here is the output:

```
Car vin: v1 available: false make: Jalopy model: Deluxe year: 2002
  Options:
    air conditioning
  Drivers:
    Anita Karr
Style make: Jalopy model: Deluxe year: 2002 cars: v1
Person name: Anita Karr licenseNumber: ln1 cars: v1
```

```java
// JOBRead.java
import com.ibm.xmi.job.Job;
import java.util.Collection;
import java.util.Iterator;

// This class reads the job.xmi document and prints the objects so we
// can tell if they were restored correctly.
public class JOBRead {
  public static void main(String[] args) throws Exception {
    Collection objects = Job.readObjects("job.xmi");
    Iterator objs = objects.iterator();

    while (objs.hasNext()) {
      System.out.println(objs.next());
    }
  }
}
```

Source Code 7.7 The *JOBRead* program.

If you run *JOBRead* at the command prompt, you will notice that in addition to the output shown previously, the following output appears in the command prompt window:

```
--> 8 objects loaded from job.xmi
```

JOB reports that eight objects were loaded from the *job.xmi* file. This includes the three top-level objects that were written by *JOBWrite*, the *Option* object, and the four *ArrayList* objects discussed previously that implement the object values and references in the objects (the *style* reference in the *Car* object was not implemented as an *ArrayList* since its multiplicity is *1*).

We do not think it is possible for an interface to be simpler than the JOB interface for creating and reading XMI documents. Another advantage of using JOB is that it works for any Java object, as long as the Java *SecurityManager* enables Java reflection to get the private and protected fields of that Java object. JOB also demonstrates that it is feasible to use XMI for Java object serialization. Finally, JOB works by using the XMI Framework, the subject of the next section. The source code for JOB is included on the accompanying CD-ROM, so you will be able to examine it to learn how JOB works with the XMI Framework to serialize and deserialize Java objects. You should read the next section before looking at the code, since it explains Framework concepts you need to know to understand how JOB works.

Using the XMI Framework

Just like JOB, the XMI Framework provides interfaces that enable you to work with XMI documents. The Framework is more complicated than JOB though, because it provides more sophisticated capabilities. The Framework enables you to tailor the XMI documents you create by providing a class, *XMIFile*, that enables you to easily set information that goes in *xmi:Documentation*, *xmi:Model*, and *xmi:MetaModel* elements. When you use the Framework to read an XMI document, you can easily get information from those elements. The Framework also lets you work with XMI extensions and make XMI schemas, as we explain in Chapters 8 and 9, respectively.

The purpose of the XMI Framework is to help you learn about XMI and begin to use XMI without being an XMI expert. As you learn more about XMI, you can use the more sophisticated capabilities of the Framework. In this section, we introduce what you need to know to use the Framework as we take you through some sample programs. We first present two programs that use the Framework to create an XMI document for the car rental agency application. After that, we'll look at three programs that use the Framework to read the document.

We do not provide a comprehensive description of the Framework's capabilities in this chapter or the next several chapters. We explain the parts of the Framework we use, rather than describing all the parts of the Framework. You may want to consult the Framework documentation for more details about the Framework itself, or Appendix A, which contains detailed information on the Framework's capabilities.

Creating an XMI Document

There are two ways to use the Framework to create an XMI document. The first, and easier, way is to use the Framework's object model to represent your data and then create the document using the *XMIFile* class. The second way involves implementing a *writer adapter* so that the Framework can write instances of your own Java classes to an XMI document. To use this approach, you need to register the writer adapter you implement with the Framework and then give the *XMIFile* class the instances of your classes to write. The first two programs we will look at demonstrate both of these ways of creating an XMI document using the Framework.

Using the Framework Object Model

The Framework object model provides a generic representation of objects, their attribute values, and their references.[2] The model is simpler than the Meta Object Facility (MOF), the OMG data representation standard on which XMI is based. However, it can also hold information about objects from an XMI document. For example, each object in the object model has an *id*, *uuid*, and *label*, the three pieces of information that enable you to specify an object's identity using XMI. We will first explain the parts of the Framework object model that you need to know to represent the car rental agency objects; other parts of the object model will be introduced as we go along.

A UML object is represented in the Framework object model by the *XMIObject* interface. Every *XMIObject* has an XMI name, which is the tag name for the XML element that represents the object in an XMI document. As mentioned before, each Framework object also has an *id*, *uuid*, and *label*, which identify the object in XMI documents.

The *Value* interface is used for an object's values. These values are either attribute values or references. The *AttributeValue* interface in the Framework lets you work with attribute values. Each *AttributeValue* object consists of the XMI name for the attribute, one or more values, and the type (the kind of Framework value). Each *AttributeValue* object represents either the single value of an attribute in an object, or it represents multiple values for an attribute in an object.[3]

The *Reference* interface in the Framework lets you work with references. A *Reference* object has an XMI name, one or more values, and a type (the kind of Framework value). Each value is an *XMIObject* that has a relationship with the *XMIObject* that has the *Reference*. The relationship is not a composition relationship. Each *Reference* object represents all the instances of a given association end in an object.

The *XMIObject*, *AttributeValue*, and *Reference* interfaces all inherit from the *Data* interface. The *Data* interface represents everything that each part of the object model has in common. For example, each part of the object model has an XMI name, so the methods to get and set it are provided by the *Data* interface. Figure 7.1 illustrates how the *Data*, *XMIObject*, *Value*, *AttributeValue*, and *Reference* interfaces are related.

The concepts from the Framework object model map to the UML object model. A Framework object corresponds to a UML object, an *AttributeValue* of a Framework object corresponds to one or more UML attribute values, and a *Reference* of a Framework object corresponds to one or more instances of a UML association end. Note that if a UML object has several values for the same attribute, a single Framework *AttributeValue* represents all those attribute values. Similarly, a single Framework *Reference* corresponds to all instances of a particular association end in an object. The Framework was designed to include the concepts in UML and MOF that are required for XMI so that you can easily create XMI documents without being an expert in either UML or MOF.

As we mentioned earlier, the *AttributeValue* interface is used for an object's attribute values. There are three kinds of *AttributeValues* in the Framework, but we only use two of them in this book. The *DataValue* interface represents one or more data values in an object. A data value is the value of a data attribute, a UML attribute with a type that is a UML datatype. The *DataValue* interface uses a Java *String* to hold the value of a primitive type like a Java *int* or a *float*. The *ObjectValue* interface represents one or more object values in an object. An object value is the value of an object attribute, a UML attribute with a class as its type. Each object value is an *XMIObject*. Also, each object value has a composition relationship with the object that has the value. Figure 7.2 shows the relationship between the *AttributeValue*, *DataValue*, and *ObjectValue* interfaces.

Table 7.1 summarizes the representation of attribute values and references in the Framework as well as the terminology that we will use to refer to them.

The Framework provides default implementations of the interfaces in the Framework object model. The name of an interface's corresponding implementation class is the name of the interface with the suffix *Impl*. For example, the default implementation of the *XMIObject* interface is *XMIObjectImpl*. We make instances of the implementation classes to represent objects, their attribute values, and their references using the Framework object model.

There are more parts to the Framework object model, but we know enough already to represent the car rental agency objects using the object model. Each

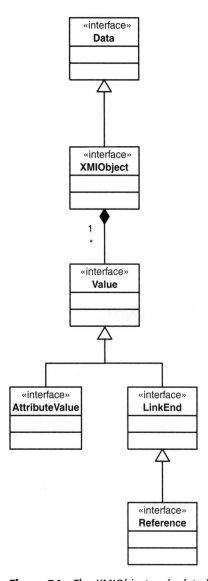

Figure 7.1 The *XMIObject* and related interfaces.

of the objects is represented in the Framework by an *XMIObject*. The Framework objects have attribute values and references.

Looking first at just the attribute values of the objects we want to create, we see that there is one object value and the rest of the attribute values are data values. The *Option* object is an object value for the *option* attribute in the *Car* object. All the other values are data values, because the types of the other UML attributes in the car rental agency model are the UML datatypes *String*, *Boolean*, and *Integer*.

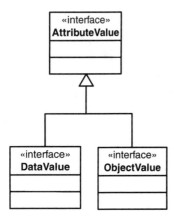

Figure 7.2 Kinds of *AttributeValues*.

Table 7.1 Framework Values

INTERFACE	VALUE'S TYPE	EXAMPLES OF VALUES	ALSO CALLED
DataValue	A datatype	*5, 3.141, Hello*	A data value
ObjectValue	A class	An *Option* instance	An object value
Reference	A class	The *style* reference in a *Car* object	A reference

Now looking at the references, we see that each object has at least one reference. The *Style, Person,* and *Option* objects each have a *car* reference. The *Car* object has two references, *style* and *driver.*

We add a method to the *CRAFactory* class, *makeFOMExample()*, to create the Framework object model representation of our car rental agency objects. Then we can reuse that method in later examples. As you read through *make-FOMExample()*, notice that the method to add an attribute value to an object, a*ddXMIValue()*, lets you specify:

- The XMI name of the attribute value or reference
- The value of the attribute value or reference
- The kind of *Value* it is in the Framework (such as *Value.DATA* or *Value.REFERENCE*)

Each attribute value or reference is then added to the Framework object that the *addXMIValue()* method is invoked on. For example, to represent the attribute value for the *name* attribute of the *Person* object, a data value is created; its XMI name is *name* and its value is *Anita Karr.* We indicate that this attribute value is a data value by specifying *Value.DATA* as the third parameter to the *addXMIValue()* method. The method invocation to do this appears as follows:

```
person.addXMIValue("name","Anita Karr",Value.DATA);
```

This adds a data value to the *XMIObject* representing an instance of the *Person* class. Table 7.2 summarizes how the behavior of the *addXMIValue()* method varies with the different values that can be used for the third parameter.

Since the *makeFOMExample()* method uses classes in the Framework, we add the following import statement to the top of the *CRAFactory.java* file:

```
import com.ibm.xmi.framework.*;
```

The *makeFOMExample()* method is displayed in Source Code 7.8.

Now we can use the *XMIFile* class in the Framework to write the objects to an XMI document. By default, an *XMIFile* is for an XMI 2.0 document. We will use the *write()* method of the *XMIFile* class to create the XMI document. This method takes an iterator for the collection of objects to write to the XMI document and a writing option. For our purposes, we can use *XMIFile.DEFAULT* as the option. See the Framework documentation for a description of the other options if you are interested. The program is displayed in Source Code 7.9.

This program produces the following XMI file. It is basically the same as the *DOMWrite.xmi* file we saw in Chapter 6 except for a few minor differences. First, the *exporter* and *exporterVersion* elements reflect that the Framework created the document. Second, the order of the XML attributes differs, but in XML the attribute order does not matter, so this difference does not change the meaning of the file. Finally, in this output the *option* element includes an *xmi:type* attribute. The reason that this is included is because the Framework does not know the car rental agency model, so it serializes object values with an *xmi:type* attribute to indicate the actual type of the object. We will see how to relate an *XMIObject* and its values to parts of models that define them later in this chapter. As before, we have split lines that are too long for the page width into two lines.

Table 7.2   *addXMIValue()* Behavior

THIRD PARAMETER	CORRESPONDING FRAMEWORK INTERFACE
Value.DATA	*DataValue*
Value.OBJECT	*ObjectValue*
Value.REFERENCE	*Reference*

```
// The makeFOMExample() method in the CRAFactory class.

// Make the Framework object model representation of the car rental
// agency objects to write to an XMI document.
public ArrayList makeFOMExample() {
  XMIObject car     = new XMIObjectImpl("Car");
  XMIObject option  = new XMIObjectImpl("Option");
  XMIObject style   = new XMIObjectImpl("Style");
  XMIObject person  = new XMIObjectImpl("Person");

  // Set the values for the Car object.
  car.addXMIValue("available", "false", Value.DATA);
  car.addXMIValue("vin",       "v1",    Value.DATA);
  car.addXMIValue("driver",     person, Value.REFERENCE);
  car.addXMIValue("style",      style,  Value.REFERENCE);
  car.addXMIValue("option",     option, Value.OBJECT);

  // Set the values for the Option object.
  option.addXMIValue("name", "air conditioning", Value.DATA);
  option.addXMIValue("car",   car,                Value.REFERENCE);

  // Set the values for the Style object.
  style.addXMIValue("make",  "Jalopy", Value.DATA);
  style.addXMIValue("model", "Deluxe", Value.DATA);
  style.addXMIValue("year",  "2002",   Value.DATA);
  style.addXMIValue("car",    car,     Value.REFERENCE);

  // Set the values for the Person object.
  person.addXMIValue("licenseNumber", "ln1",       Value.DATA);
  person.addXMIValue("name",          "Anita Karr", Value.DATA);
  person.addXMIValue("car",            car,          Value.REFERENCE);

  ArrayList xmiObjects = new ArrayList();
  xmiObjects.add(car);
  xmiObjects.add(style);
  xmiObjects.add(person);

  return xmiObjects;
}
```

Source Code 7.8 The *makeFOMExample()* method in the *CRAFactory* class.

```
<?xml version="1.0" encoding="UTF-8"?>
<xmi:XMI xmi:version="2.0" xmlns:xmi="http://www.omg.org/XMI">
   <xmi:Documentation>
     <exporter>XMI Framework</exporter>
     <exporterVersion>1.2</exporterVersion>
   </xmi:Documentation>
  <Car xmi:id="_1" available="false" vin="v1" driver="_3"
```

```
// FrameWrite.java
import com.ibm.xmi.framework.XMIFile;
import java.util.ArrayList;

// Use the CRAFactory class to make the Framework object model
// representation of the car rental agency objects, then write them
// to an XMI document using the XMIFile class in the XMI Framework.
public class FrameWrite {
  public static void main(String[] args) throws Exception {
    CRAFactory factory  = new CRAFactory();
    ArrayList xmiObjects = factory.makeFOMExample();

    XMIFile file = new XMIFile("frame1.xmi");

    file.write(xmiObjects.iterator(), XMIFile.DEFAULT);
  }
}
```

Source Code 7.9   The *FrameWrite* program writing XMIObjects in an XMI document.

```
        style="_2">
    <option xmi:id="_1.1" xmi:type="Option" name="air conditioning"
            car="_1"/>
  </Car>
  <Style xmi:id="_2" make="Jalopy" model="Deluxe" year="2002"
         car="_1"/>
  <Person xmi:id="_3" licenseNumber="ln1" name="Anita Karr"
          car="_1"/>
</xmi:XMI>
```

Using Your Own Java Classes

To use the Framework object model, you need to copy all your data to instances of Framework classes. If you have a lot of data, the memory requirements may be too much for your application. Alternatively, you can use the Framework to write instances of *your* Java classes to an XMI document by implementing an *object writer adapter*. Then you can pass an iterator for a collection of your objects to the *write()* method of the *XMIFile* class, rather than passing an iterator for a collection of Framework *XMIObject*s. Figure 7.3 shows the relationship among the writer adapter, the Framework, and your objects.

NOTE IBM's WebSphere Studio Application Developer, included on the CD-ROM, uses an advanced XMI reader and writer based on the principles described in this chapter.

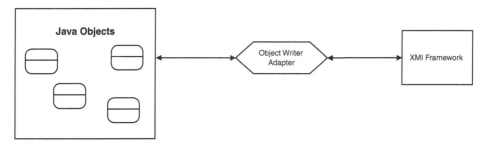

Figure 7.3 Using an object writer adapter with the Framework.

The Framework invokes methods in the *ObjectWriterAdapter* interface to get the data it needs for each object as it writes an XMI document. There are many methods in that interface, but each method is relatively simple. To help focus on the methods we need to implement for this application, we provide a *Default-ObjectWriterAdapter* class in the Framework that implements many of the methods of the *ObjectWriterAdapter* interface. Each method of the *DefaultObject-WriterAdapter* for which there is an implementation returns either *null* or an empty collection, as appropriate, or has no return value. The methods for which you need to provide an implementation in your object writer adapter have been declared *abstract*. Since the adapter that we implement to handle the car rental agency application inherits from the *DefaultObjectWriterAdapter*, we can ignore the methods that we don't need to implement. The *DefaultObjectWriterAdapter* is similar in principle to the *DefaultHandler* in SAX, which we used in the SAX section of Chapter 6 to simplify the SAX handlers we implemented.

What information does the Framework need for the car rental agency objects to write them to an XMI document? For each object, it needs to determine the tag name of the XML element that will represent the object in the XMI file it writes. It uses the *getXMIName()* method with the object as a parameter to get the tag name to use for that object. It also needs the XMI *id* (to use as the value of the *xmi:id* XML attribute) for the object. It invokes the *getId()* method with the object as a parameter of the method. If that method returns *null*, the Framework creates an *id* for the object and calls the *setId()* method to inform the adapter of the new *id*. The Framework expects the *id* it creates to be returned in subsequent calls of the *getId()* method.

Once the Framework knows the tag name for the object and its XMI *id*, it needs to know the attribute values and references for the object. It invokes the *getValues()* method to obtain this data. The object being queried is a parameter for this method. The method returns a collection of objects, and each object in the collection represents either an attribute value or a reference. The Framework then uses those objects as parameters to the *getXMIName()*, *getType()*, *get-*

Value(), and *getOwner()* methods to get the information about each attribute value or reference so it can write it to the XMI document. The *getType()* method returns one of the Framework constants for the kind of the attribute value or reference. For the car rental agency objects, the method returns *Value.DATA*, *Value.OBJECT*, or *Value.REFERENCE*. The *getValue()* method returns the value for the attribute or reference.

The *DefaultObjectWriterAdapter* already provides implementations for the *getId()* and *setId()* methods that utilize a *HashMap*. It puts the *ids* and objects in the *HashMap* in the *setId()* method. The *getId()* method gets the *id* from the *HashMap*. The first time the Framework invokes that method for an object, it will return *null*, so the Framework makes an XMI *id* for the object and calls the *setId()* method. Later, when the Framework calls *getId()* again, the object and *id* are in the *HashMap*.

There are six abstract methods in the *DefaultObjectWriterAdapter* that we will need to implement in our adapter. Although the *getNamespace()* method requires an implementation, because we are not using namespaces, we can simply return *null* in the method body. The remaining methods in the *Default-ObjectWriterAdapter* that we need to provide implementations for are the following:

- *getOwner()*
- *getType()*
- *getXMIName()*
- *getValue()*
- *getValues()*

To implement these, it is useful to create a class that holds the relevant information about each value of a Framework object in our application. As described previously, this information is the name, type, value, and owner. We name this class *ValueWriteData*, since it contains the information the Framework needs to write a value of an object. In the *getValues()* method of the writer adapter, we create instances of this class and return them. When the Framework invokes a method with a *ValueWriteData* object as a parameter, we will easily be able to get the information the Framework needs for the corresponding attribute value or reference. Source Code 7.10 contains the *ValueWriteData* class.

Source Code 7.11 contains the code for the car rental agency object writer adapter, which shows how we utilize instances of the *ValueWriteData* class.

How do we get the Framework to use our writer adapter rather than the one it would normally use? We implement a Framework *adapter factory* that returns an instance of our writer adapter, and then we register one of our adapter

```
// ValueWriteData.java

// This class holds the information the Framework needs to write
// an object's value to an XMI file. We use one of the following
// Framework constants to identify the kind of Value for the car
// rental agency example (the constant is used in the getType()
// and setType() methods):
//
//  Value.DATA
//  Value.OBJECT
//  Value.REFERENCE
//
public class ValueWriteData {
   private String xmiName;
   private Object value;
   private int    type;
   private Object owner;

   ValueWriteData(String name, Object value, int type, Object owner) {
      xmiName    = name;
      this.value = value;
      this.type  = type;
      this.owner = owner;
   }

   String getName()  { return xmiName; }
   Object getValue() { return value; }
   Object getOwner() { return owner; }
   int    getType()  { return type; }

   void setName (String name)  { xmiName = name; }
   void setValue(Object value) { this.value = value; }
   void setOwner(Object owner) { this.owner = owner; }
   void setType (int type)     { this.type = type; }
}
```

Source Code 7.10   The *ValueWriteData* class.

factories with the Framework before writing an *XMIFile*. The adapter factory that makes our writer adapter is displayed in Source Code 7.12.

Now we can implement the program that will use the Framework to write instances of the classes in the *cars* package to an XMI document. We use the *makeExample()* method of the *CRAFactory* to make the instances to write. The program is displayed in Source Code 7.13.

FrameWrite2 creates the following XMI document, which is identical to the previous XMI document we created with the Framework, except for the order

```java
// CRAObjectWriterAdapter.java
import com.ibm.xmi.framework.*;
import java.util.*;
import cars.*;

public class CRAObjectWriterAdapter extends DefaultObjectWriterAdapter
{
public Namespace getNamespace(Object data) {
    return null;
}

public Object getOwner(Object data) {
// getOwner() is declared abstract in the DefaultObjectWriterAdapter,
// so you must provide an implementation when you subclass it.
// However, for XMI 2.0, you could simply have this method return null.
// Since the Framework is compatible with XMI 1.0 and XMI 1.1, we
// include a complete implementation here.
   if (data instanceof ValueWriteData)
       return ((ValueWriteData) data).getOwner();
   else
       return null;
}

public int getType(Object data) {
   if (data instanceof ValueWriteData)
       return ((ValueWriteData) data).getType();
   else
       return -1;
}

public String getXMIName(Object data) {
   if (data instanceof ValueWriteData)
       return ((ValueWriteData) data).getName();
   else if (data instanceof Car)
       return "Car";
   else if (data instanceof Style)
       return "Style";
   else if (data instanceof Person)
       return "Person";
   else if (data instanceof Option)
       return "Option";
   else
       return null;
}

public Object getValue(Object value) {
   return ((ValueWriteData) value).getValue();
```

Source Code 7.11   The *CRAObjectWriterAdapter* class.

```
}

public Collection getValues(Object object) {
   ArrayList values = new ArrayList();
   if (object instanceof Car) {
      values.add(new ValueWriteData("vin",
                           ((Car) object).getVIN(),
                           Value.DATA, object));
      values.add(new ValueWriteData("available",
                           "" + ((Car) object).isAvailable(),
                           Value.DATA, object));
      values.add(new ValueWriteData("driver",
                           ((Car) object).getDrivers(),
                           Value.REFERENCE, object));
      values.add(new ValueWriteData("style",
                           ((Car) object).getStyle(),
                           Value.REFERENCE, object));
      values.add(new ValueWriteData("option",
                           ((Car) object).getOptions(),
                           Value.OBJECT, object));

   }
   if (object instanceof Style) {
      values.add(new ValueWriteData("make",
                           ((Style) object).getMake(),
                           Value.DATA, object));
      values.add(new ValueWriteData("model",
                           ((Style) object).getModel(),
                           Value.DATA, object));
      values.add(new ValueWriteData("year", "" +
                           ((Style) object).getYear(),
                           Value.DATA, object));
      values.add(new ValueWriteData("car",
                           ((Style) object).getCars(),
                           Value.REFERENCE, object));

   }
   if (object instanceof Option) {
      values.add(new ValueWriteData("name",
                           ((Option) object).getName(),
                           Value.DATA, object));
      values.add(new ValueWriteData("car",
                           ((Option) object).getCar(),
                           Value.REFERENCE, object));

   }
   if (object instanceof Person) {
```

Source Code 7.11 The *CRAObjectWriterAdapter* class. (*Continued*)

```
        values.add(new ValueWriteData("name",
                             ((Person) object).getName(),
                             Value.DATA, object));
        values.add(new ValueWriteData("licenseNumber",
                             ((Person) object).getLicenseNumber(),
                             Value.DATA, object));
        values.add(new ValueWriteData("car",
                             ((Person) object).getCars(),
                             Value.REFERENCE, object));


    }

    return values;
    }
}
```

Source Code 7.11   The *CRAObjectWriterAdapter* class. (*Continued*)

```
// CRAAdapterFactory.java
import com.ibm.xmi.framework.*;

// This class is the adapter factory for the car rental
// agency problem domain.
public class CRAAdapterFactory extends AdapterFactory {
// Return the CRAObjectWriterAdapter. This method is called
// automatically by the Framework.
public ObjectWriterAdapter createObjectWriterAdapter() {
    return new CRAObjectWriterAdapter();
}
}
```

Source Code 7.12   The *CRAAdapterFactory* class.

of the XML attributes. As before, we have split lines that are too wide for the width of this page:

```
<?xml version="1.0" encoding="UTF-8"?>
<xmi:XMI xmi:version="2.0" xmlns:xmi="http://www.omg.org/XMI">
    <xmi:Documentation>
      <exporter>XMI Framework</exporter>
      <exporterVersion>1.2</exporterVersion>
    </xmi:Documentation>
  <Car xmi:id="_1" vin="v1" available="false" driver="_3"
      style="_2">
    <option xmi:id="_1.1" xmi:type="Option" name="air conditioning"
            car="_1"/>
```

```
// FrameWrite2.java
import com.ibm.xmi.framework.*;
import java.util.ArrayList;
import java.util.Iterator;

// Use the CRAFactory to make the instances of the cars package to
// write, register the CRAAdapterFactory with the Framework, and then
// write the objects using an XMIFile.
public class FrameWrite2 {
    public static void main(String[] args) throws Exception {
        CRAFactory factory = new CRAFactory();
        ArrayList objects = factory.makeExample();

        AdapterFactoryRegister.registerAdapterFactory(
                        new CRAAdapterFactory());

        XMIFile file = new XMIFile("frame2.xmi");
        file.write(objects.iterator(), XMIFile.DEFAULT);
    }
}
```

Source Code 7.13 The *FrameWrite2* program.

```
    </Car>
    <Style xmi:id="_2" make="Jalopy" model="Deluxe" year="2002"
        car="_1"/>
    <Person xmi:id="_3" name="Anita Karr" licenseNumber="ln1"
        car="_1"/>
</xmi:XMI>
```

Reading an XMI Document

Now that you know two ways of saving the car rental agency objects in an XMI file using the Framework, you are probably wondering how to read the XMI documents we created with the Framework. There are several ways to do this. We start with the easiest way. There is a *load()* method in the *XMIFile* class we can use that takes the following three parameters:

- The name of an XMI document

- A load option (which is always *XMIFile.DEFAULT* for our purposes)

- A *boolean* flag that indicates whether to use XML validation when parsing the XMI document

In this chapter and the next one, we do not validate the documents, so we will set the validation flag to *false*. (We discuss validation in Chapter 9.) The *load()* method returns an *XMIFile*. You can get the objects that the Framework made as it read the XMI document from the *XMIFile*. Unless you implement a *reader adapter*, as explained later in this chapter, the Framework makes *XMIObjects* with *AttributeValues* from the Framework object model when it loads an XMI document.

The Framework enables you to put *XMIObjects* in an *XMIContainer*. The *XMIContainer* class implements the *toString()* method so that all the objects directly in the *XMIContainer* and contained in those objects can be printed. We can use that method to print the *XMIObjects* that the Framework makes when parsing an XMI document. Source Code 7.14 displays a program that uses the Framework to parse an XMI document, puts the *XMIObjects* made by the Framework in an *XMIContainer,* and finally prints them.

If you run this program and specify the name of either of the XMI documents created by the *FrameWrite* or *FrameWrite2* programs, the output shows each *XMIObject* that the Framework creates when parsing the XMI document. The output from this program is formatted somewhat differently than what we have seen before. Information about each *XMIObject*, along with its *Values*, appears between dashed lines. The first line of each entry starts with *Object:*, followed by the XMI name of the object, then by *id:*, and finally the value of the *xmi:id* for the object. Under *Values:* are listed the Framework values that belong to the object. The name of each *Value* is followed by a keyword enclosed between the < and > symbols that specifies its type, such as *<DATA>*. The value (or values) for each *Value* object appears last. Table 7.3 summarizes the meanings of the type specifiers you will see in the output included in this book.

```
// FrameRead.java
import com.ibm.xmi.framework.XMIFile;
import com.ibm.xmi.framework.XMIContainer;

// This class parses an XMI document, and then puts the XMIObjects the
// Framework made into an XMIContainer so they can be printed.
public class FrameRead {
    public static void main(String[] args) throws Exception {
        if (args.length != 1) {
            System.out.println("Enter the name of an XMI document.");
            return;
        }

        XMIFile file = XMIFile.load(args[0], XMIFile.DEFAULT, false);
        XMIContainer c = new XMIContainer(file.getObjects().iterator());
        System.out.println(c);
    }
}
```

Source Code 7.14 The *FrameRead* program.

Table 7.3 *FrameRead* Output Key

TYPE SPECIFIER	MEANING
<DATA>	Data value
<OBJ>	Object value
<REF>	Reference

Here is the output of running *FrameRead* on the *frame1.xmi* file with the irrelevant parts of the output omitted:

```
--------------------------------
Object: Car id: _1
  Values:
    available <DATA> 'false'
    vin <DATA> 'v1'
    driver <DATA> '_3'
    style <DATA> '_2'
    option <OBJ> [XMIObject Option _1.1]
End object: Car
--------------------------------
Object: Option id: _1.1
  Values:
    name <DATA> 'air conditioning'
    car <DATA> '_1'
End object: Option
--------------------------------
Object: Style id: _2
  Values:
    make <DATA> 'Jalopy'
    model <DATA> 'Deluxe'
    year <DATA> '2002'
    car <DATA> '_1'
End object: Style
--------------------------------
Object: Person id: _3
  Values:
    licenseNumber <DATA> 'ln1'
    name <DATA> 'Anita Karr'
    car <DATA> '_1'
End object: Person
--------------------------------
```

If you compare the *XMIObjects* that the Framework created with the *XMIObjects* that were saved in the *FrameWrite* program, you may notice that they are not the same. For example, the original *Car XMIObject* had a reference called *driver*, but the restored *Car XMIObject* has a data value (indicated by *<DATA>*

next to the value's name) called *driver*. What is going on? It turns out that in XMI 2.0 data values and references are written as XML attributes. It is not possible to distinguish them with the syntax of an XMI 2.0 document without being aware of the model that the data corresponds to. Therefore, in this case the Framework assumes that XML attributes represent data values. As we shall see, by providing the Framework with information about the model for the data in an XMI file, the Framework has the capability to correctly distinguish different types of data, even when they have a similar format in an XMI file.

Notice that no information was lost when reading the XMI document; it was just not interpreted in terms of the car rental agency model. For example, the original *driver* reference that had the *Person* object as its value was not lost; it was restored as a data value set to _3, the XMI *id* of the *Person* object. In fact, if you create another XMI document by writing the restored *XMIObject*s that have only data values and object values, that document would be equivalent to the original document.

To correctly restore the references, the Framework needs to know the car rental agency model since that model defines the objects in the XMI document. Not surprisingly, there is a *Model* class in the Framework that represents models. A model consists of *packages* and *classes*. A package is represented in the Framework by the *Package* interface, and a class is represented by the *XMIClass* interface. The *XMIClass* interface inherits from the *Classifier* interface, as does the *Datatype* interface. A package contains either packages or classes, and a class has *features*, which include attributes and association ends. As you might expect, a feature is represented in the Framework with the *Feature* interface, an attribute is represented with the *Attribute* interface, and an association end is represented with the *AssociationEnd* interface. Figure 7.4 shows the relationships among these interfaces as well as the ones we saw before when we looked at the *XMIObject* interface. For completeness, the entire Framework object model is included, although we do not use all of it in this book.

The difference between an *XMIClass* and an *XMIObject* is that the attributes and association ends of an *XMIClass* define the legal Framework *Values* for an *XMIObject* that is an instance of that *XMIClass*. Thus, the relationship between an *XMIClass* and an *XMIObject* is similar to that between a class and an object in Java.

To represent the car rental agency model in the Framework, we need to make an *XMIClass* for each UML class in the model and then add features to each *XMIClass*. After we have created an *XMIClass* for each class in our model, we add the *XMIClass* objects to a *Model* instance. Source Code 7.15 displays the *CRAModel* program that creates the car rental agency model. Although we use the *Feature* interface throughout, we could have used the *Attribute* and *AssociationEnd* interfaces as well to create the features for a given *XMIClass*.

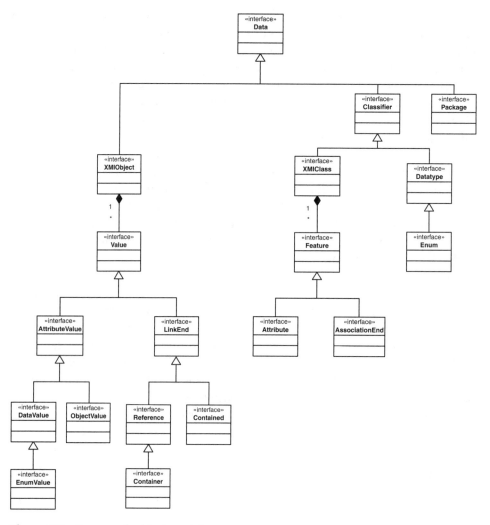

Figure 7.4   Framework object model.

```
// CRAModel.java
import com.ibm.xmi.framework.*;
import java.util.*;

// This class creates an XMI Framework model for the car rental agency
// problem domain.  This model can be added to a workspace so the
// Framework will correctly restore XMI objects from an XMI document.
public class CRAModel {
public static Model makeCRAModel() throws Exception {
```

Source Code 7.15   The *CRAModel* program.

```
ArrayList classes = new ArrayList();
XMIClass car     = new XMIClassImpl("Car");
XMIClass style   = new XMIClassImpl("Style");
XMIClass person  = new XMIClassImpl("Person");
XMIClass option  = new XMIClassImpl("Option");

classes.add(car);
classes.add(style);
classes.add(person);
classes.add(option);

// Car class
Feature vin = new FeatureImpl("vin");
vin.setXMIValueType(Value.DATA);
car.add(vin);

Feature available = new FeatureImpl("available");
available.setXMIValueType(Value.DATA);
car.add(available);

Feature carStyle = new FeatureImpl("style");
carStyle.setXMIValueType(Value.REFERENCE);
carStyle.setXMIType(style);
car.add(carStyle);

Feature driver = new FeatureImpl("driver");
driver.setXMIValueType(Value.REFERENCE);
driver.setXMIType(person);
car.add(driver);

Feature carOption = new FeatureImpl("option");
carOption.setXMIValueType(Value.OBJECT);
carOption.setXMIType(option);
car.add(carOption);

// Option class
Feature optionName = new FeatureImpl("name");
optionName.setXMIValueType(Value.DATA);
option.add(optionName);

Feature optionCar = new FeatureImpl("car");
optionCar.setXMIValueType(Value.REFERENCE);
optionCar.setXMIType(car);
option.add(optionCar);

// Style class
Feature make = new FeatureImpl("make");
make.setXMIValueType(Value.DATA);
```

Source Code 7.15   The *CRAModel* program. (*Continued*)

```
        style.add(make);

        Feature model = new FeatureImpl("model");
        model.setXMIValueType(Value.DATA);
        style.add(model);

        Feature year = new FeatureImpl("year");
        year.setXMIValueType(Value.DATA);
        style.add(year);

        Feature styleCar = new FeatureImpl("car");
        styleCar.setXMIValueType(Value.REFERENCE);
        styleCar.setXMIType(car);
        style.add(styleCar);

        // Person class
        Feature personName = new FeatureImpl("name");
        personName.setXMIValueType(Value.DATA);
        person.add(personName);

        Feature licenseNumber = new FeatureImpl("licenseNumber");
        licenseNumber.setXMIValueType(Value.DATA);
        person.add(licenseNumber);

        Feature personCar = new FeatureImpl("car");
        personCar.setXMIValueType(Value.REFERENCE);
        personCar.setXMIType(car);
        person.add(personCar);

        Model m = new Model("Car Rental Agency", classes.iterator());

        return m;
    }

    // Print the model to determine if it is correct.
    public static void main(String[] args) throws Exception {
        Model m = makeCRAModel();
        System.out.println(m);
    }
    }
```

Source Code 7.15   The *CRAModel* program. (*Continued*)

Note in the program that if we set the *XMIValueType* of a *Feature* to *Value.DATA* we do not need to set an *XMIType* that is a Framework *Datatype* for that *Feature* (although it is possible to do that). This makes it a little easier to work with this kind of feature in the Framework. All the other kinds of features have both their *XMIValueType* and *XMIType* set.

Just like the *XMIContainer* class, the *Model* class implements a *toString()* method that lets you print the contents of the model it represents. You can run the *CRAModel* program if you want to verify that the model was created correctly. We explain the format of the output and the symbols that appear in it immediately after the output of the *CRAModel* program itself:

```
Model:
name: Car Rental Agency version: null file: null
XMIClass Car
   Features:
      vin <DATA> owner: [XMIClass Car]
      available <DATA> owner: [XMIClass Car]
      style <REF> type: [XMIClass Style] owner: [XMIClass Car]
      driver <REF> type: [XMIClass Person] owner: [XMIClass Car]
      option <OBJ> type: [XMIClass Option] owner: [XMIClass Car]
XMIClass Style
   Features:
      make <DATA> owner: [XMIClass Style]
      model <DATA> owner: [XMIClass Style]
      year <DATA> owner: [XMIClass Style]
      car <REF> type: [XMIClass Car] owner: [XMIClass Style]
XMIClass Person
   Features:
      name <DATA> owner: [XMIClass Person]
      licenseNumber <DATA> owner: [XMIClass Person]
      car <REF> type: [XMIClass Car] owner: [XMIClass Person]
XMIClass Option
   Features:
      name <DATA> owner: [XMIClass Option]
      car <REF> type: [XMIClass Car] owner: [XMIClass Option]
```

The *CRAModel* program output includes information about each of the four classes in the car rental agency model that we have represented in the Frame-work with an *XMIClass*. Following the name of the class is a list of each *Feature* that belongs to that class. For each *Feature*, the following information is included:

- The name of the *Feature*
- The Framework *Value* type for the values of the *Feature*, such as *<DATA>*
- The type for the *Feature*, if specified
- The owner of the *Feature*, which is the class the *Feature* belongs to

Table 7.4 explains the symbols used to show the Framework *Value* type for the values of a *Feature* in the *CRAModel* program. It also shows how features in an *XMIClass* map to values in an *XMIObject*.

Now that we know how to use the Framework to create the car rental agency model, we need to make the model available to the Framework. By

Table 7.4 Output Symbols and Value Types

OUTPUT SYMBOL	FEATURE INTERFACE	VALUE TYPE	VALUE IS CALLED
<DATA>	*Attribute*	*Value.DATA*	Data value
<OBJ>	*Attribute*	*Value.OBJECT*	Object value
<REF>	*AssociationEnd*	*Value.REFERENCE*	Reference

doing this, the Framework can use the model to determine whether a Framework object's *Value* is an *AttributeValue* or a *Reference*. We can do this using the *Workspace* class. A *Workspace* is a set of models and files. It works with another Framework class, *XMIFiles*, which represents a set of related XMI documents. There are *load()* methods in the *XMIFiles* class that work the same way as the *load()* methods in the *XMIFile* class. If you add an *XMIFiles* instance to a *Workspace* and then call a *load()* method on the instance, the Framework can find models that were added to the *Workspace* when it parses an XMI document. The Framework matches the data in the XMI document with the model or models in the *Workspace*. If it finds a match, the Framework makes the correct type of values. For example, if an XML attribute name in the XMI document matches a feature of a class in a model in the *Workspace,* and that feature's *XMI-ValueType* is *Value.REFERENCE*, the Framework makes a reference rather than a data value in the corresponding *XMIObject*. Source Code 7.16 shows the *FrameRead2* program that loads an XMI document using a *Workspace* that contains the car rental agency model.

When you run this program and specify the name of either of the XMI documents we created with the Framework, what you will see is similar to the output shown here from a run of *FrameRead2* using the *frame1.xmi* file (irrelevant parts of the output have been omitted, and some minor formatting has been done to accommodate the page width):

```
   --------------------------------
Object: Car id: _1
  definer: XMIClass Car
  Values:
    available <DATA> 'false'  definer: [available <DATA> owner:
        [XMIClass Car]]
    vin <DATA> 'v1'  definer: [vin <DATA> owner: [XMIClass Car]]
    driver <REF> [XMIObject Person _3]  definer: [driver <REF> type:
        [XMIClass Person] owner: [XMIClass Car]]
    style <REF> [XMIObject Style _2]  definer: [style <REF> type:
        [XMIClass Style] owner: [XMIClass Car]]
    option <OBJ> [XMIObject Option _1.1]  definer: [option <OBJ> type:
        [XMIClass Option] owner: [XMIClass Car]]
```

```
// FrameRead2.java
import com.ibm.xmi.framework.*;

// This class demonstrates that the Framework matches data in an XMI
// document with models that define the data when a Workspace is used.
// Using a Workspace enables the Framework to create the appropriate
// kind of attribute values and references for the XMIObjects that are
// restored.
public class FrameRead2 {
    public static void main(String[] args) throws Exception {
        if (args.length != 1) {
            System.out.println("Enter the name of an XMI document.");
            return;
        }

        Workspace w = new Workspace();
        Model craModel = CRAModel.makeCRAModel();
        w.add(craModel);
        XMIFiles files = new XMIFiles();
        w.add(files);
        XMIFile file = files.load(args[0], XMIFile.DEFAULT, false);
        XMIContainer c = new XMIContainer(file.getObjects().iterator());
        System.out.println(c);
    }
}
```

Source Code 7.16   The *FrameRead2* program.

```
End object: Car
---------------------------------
Object: Option id: _1.1
  definer: XMIClass Option
  Values:
    name <DATA> 'air conditioning'  definer: [name <DATA> owner:
        [XMIClass Option]]
    car <REF> [XMIObject Car _1]  definer: [car <REF> type:
        [XMIClass Car] owner: [XMIClass Option]]
End object: Option
---------------------------------
Object: Style id: _2
  definer: XMIClass Style
  Values:
    make <DATA> 'Jalopy'  definer: [make <DATA> owner:
        [XMIClass Style]]
    model <DATA> 'Deluxe'  definer: [model <DATA> owner:
        [XMIClass Style]]
    year <DATA> '2002'  definer: [year <DATA> owner: [XMIClass Style]]
    car <REF> [XMIObject Car _1]  definer: [car <REF> type:
        [XMIClass Car] owner: [XMIClass Style]]
```

```
End object: Style
---------------------------------
Object: Person id: _3
  definer: XMIClass Person
  Values:
    licenseNumber <DATA> 'ln1'  definer: [licenseNumber <DATA> owner:
        [XMIClass Person]]
    name <DATA> 'Anita Karr'  definer: [name <DATA> owner:
        [XMIClass Person]]
    car <REF> [XMIObject Car _1]  definer: [car <REF> type:
        [XMIClass Car] owner: [XMIClass Person]]
End object: Person
---------------------------------
```

As you can see, the attribute values and references of the Framework objects are now correctly restored. To enable semantic checking of objects, the Framework's object model specifies a *definer* for objects and values. The definer of an object is its class, and the definer of a value belonging to the object is the corresponding feature in the class. The previous output shows that when the Framework loaded the *frame1.xmi* file, it was able to connect objects and their values to their corresponding definers in the model we created. You can see that each *XMIObject* has been matched to the *XMIClass* in the model that defines its structure. Also, each attribute value has been matched with its corresponding attribute in the model, and each reference has been matched with its corresponding association end in the model.

Now that you know how to get Framework objects from an XMI document, you may want to know how to get instances of your own classes from an XMI document. To do this for our example, we need to implement a *reader adapter* and register it with the Framework. This is similar to when we implemented an object writer adapter and registered it with the Framework to enable the Framework to write instances of our classes to an XMI document, rather than writing *XMIObjects*.

A Framework reader adapter is similar to a SAX content handler. The Framework converts SAX events to object events. For example, rather than calling a method each time the beginning of an XML element is encountered, the Framework invokes a *createObject()* method when an XML element that represents an object is encountered and a *setValue()* method when an object's value is encountered in an XMI document.

There is also a *getType()* method that the Framework invokes when encountering an XML attribute. The Framework expects one of the value types— *Value.DATA, Value.OBJECT,* or *Value.REFERENCE*—to be returned. If the type is *Value.OBJECT* or *Value.REFERENCE,* the Framework treats the value of the XML attribute as an object; otherwise, it treats the value as a *String*. For example, when the XML attribute *driver* that has a value of _3 is encountered in one of the XMI documents we created with the Framework, if *Value.DATA* is

THE *XMI:TYPE* ATTRIBUTE AND A VALUE'S DEFINER

When we looked at the output of the *FrameWrite* program earlier in the chapter, we noted that the *option* element included an *xmi:type* attribute. Now that you have seen what a definer is, we can explain the reason that this attribute was included. When an *XMIFile* is written, the Framework determines whether to write the *xmi:type* attribute when it serializes an object value. It does this by comparing the actual type of the value with the type of the feature that is the value's definer. If there is a definer, and the type in the definer matches the type of the value, no *xmi:type* attribute needs to be written because the Framework will use the type in the definer when it loads the file. In the *FrameWrite* program, there was no definer set for the *option* object value, so the Framework included the *xmi:type* attribute when it serialized the *option* object value.

returned as the type, the Framework invokes *setValue()* and sets the value to _3. However, if *Value.REFERENCE* is returned as the type, the Framework attempts to get the object with an XMI *id* of _3 and then invokes *setValue()*. The value is then treated as a reference to an object rather than a *String*. How does the Framework handle references to objects that it hasn't seen yet? After parsing the complete document, the Framework invokes the *resolveValue()* method to set the values that could not be set previously because the values were forward references to objects that appear later in the XMI document.

Now that we know the names and behaviors of the methods involved, let's look at the overall flow of things. The general flow of control proceeds as follows: The Framework begins parsing an XMI file. For each XML element that represents an object, it invokes *createObject()*. For each value in the object, the Framework first invokes the *getType()* method and then it invokes the *setValue()* method.

Before we show you the implementation of our reader adapter, we need to explain the *ObjectInfo* class and the *ValueInfo* class. An *ObjectInfo* instance is passed as a parameter when the Framework invokes the *createObject()* method. An *ObjectInfo* instance contains the information you need to correctly create one of your objects. An *ObjectInfo* contains the tag name of the XML element representing the object; the object's XMI *id*, *uuid*, and *label*; and other information that we do not need for this application, such as the *namespace*, *idref*, and *href*. A *ValueInfo* instance is passed as a parameter when the Framework invokes the *setValue()* method and the *getType()* method. A *ValueInfo* instance contains the information you need to correctly set a value for an object that you have created in the *createObject()* method. A *ValueInfo* contains the object the value belongs to, the name of the value, and the value itself. As explained previously, the value is a *String* if the type of the value is *Value.DATA*; otherwise, the value is an object. The value is *null* if it is a forward reference to an object that occurs later in the XMI document.

One more detail of the *setValue()* method needs to be explained. If the value passed in to be set is not *null*, the reader adapter can set it and then return to the caller of the method. In this case, it returns the value *null* itself to indicate that the value has been set. However, if the value passed in to be set is *null*, it means that the value is an object that occurs later in the file. Therefore, the value cannot be set until later. In this case, the reader adapter needs to return an object that represents this so the Framework will remember to set it later. That object will then be passed to the reader adapter when the Framework invokes the second *setValue()* method, and it will serve to identify the value to be set. For our purposes, all that we need to know is the name of the value, so we can simply return the name of the value in a Java *String* object in this case. Table 7.5 summarizes this behavior.

We can use the functionality of the *CRAFactory* class to help us implement the reader adapter. We have added a couple new methods to the *CRAFactory* class in this chapter, although most of it was developed in Chapter 6. The methods that were developed in Chapter 6 that we need are included in Source Code 7.17. The *newInstance()* method creates an instance of the appropriate class from the *cars* package given an XML tag name. We can use this method to implement the *createObject()* method of the reader adapter. The *setAttribute()* and *setReference()* methods call the appropriate methods of the classes in the *cars* package to set the attributes and references. We can use those methods to implement the *setValue()* method of the reader adapter.

We have provided a *DefaultReaderAdapter* in the Framework with default implementations of some of the methods in the *ReaderAdapter* interface to make it easier to implement your own reader adapter. The methods that you must implement are marked as *abstract*. Our *CRAReaderAdapter*, shown in Source Code 7.18, inherits from the *DefaultReaderAdapter*, so we can ignore the methods that we do not need to implement.

If you modify the *CRAAdapterFactory* by implementing the *createReader-Adapter()* method, it can be used to register the *CRAReaderAdapter* with the Framework. The complete *CRAAdapterFactory* class is shown in Source Code 7.19.

Table 7.5   Behavior of *setValue()*

VALUE PASSED IN	ACTION TAKEN	VALUE RETURNED	FRAMEWORK INTERPRETATION
Non-*null* value	Value is set.	*null*	Value has been set.
Null	Value is not set.	*String* with the value's name	Value is set later using *setValue()*.

```
// Methods in the CRAFactory class created in Chapter 6.  We
// include the constructor so you can see how the
// tagNamesToClassNames HashMap is initialized.

// Initialize tagNamesToClassNames for the car rental agency.
public CRAFactory() {
  tagNamesToClassNames = new HashMap();

  // In the HashMap, we map the tag name of the element
  // for an object to the Java class name. Note that there are two
  // entries that map to cars.Option. Since the object attribute for
  // the Car object's options is called "option", this is the tag name
  // for the element for the Option object in the XMI file we wrote.
  // Since there could also be an Option object with an XML element tag
  // name of "Option" in another file, we include both "option" and
  // "Option" in the Hashmap for completeness.

  tagNamesToClassNames.put("Style",  "cars.Style");
  tagNamesToClassNames.put("Car",    "cars.Car");
  tagNamesToClassNames.put("Option", "cars.Option");
  tagNamesToClassNames.put("option", "cars.Option");
  tagNamesToClassNames.put("Person", "cars.Person");
}

// Make an instance of the correct class given the tag name of an XML
// element from an XMI file. Throw an exception if unsuccessful.
public Object newInstance(String tagName) throws Exception {
  String clsName = (String) tagNamesToClassNames.get(tagName);
  java.lang.Class cls = java.lang.Class.forName(clsName);
  return cls.newInstance();
}
}

// Call the appropriate method based on the type of the object.
public void setAttribute(Object object, String attribName,
                         String value) {
  if (object instanceof Car)
    setAttribute((Car) object, attribName, value);
  else if (object instanceof Option)
    setAttribute((Option) object, attribName, value);
  else if (object instanceof Style)
    setAttribute((Style) object, attribName, value);
  else if (object instanceof Person)
    setAttribute((Person) object, attribName, value);
}

// Set the vin or available field of the Car object.
```

Source Code 7.17 *CRAFactory* methods used by *CRAReaderAdapter*.

```
private void setAttribute(Car c, String attribName, String value) {
  if (attribName.equals("vin"))
    c.setVIN(value);
  else if (attribName.equals("available") && value != null) {
    if (value.equals("true"))
      c.setAvailable(true);
    else if (value.equals("false"))
      c.setAvailable(false);
  }
}

// Set the name of the Option object.
private void setAttribute(Option o, String attribName, String value) {
  if (attribName.equals("name"))
    o.setName(value);
}

// Set the name and license number of the Person object.
private void setAttribute(Person p, String attribName, String value) {
  if (attribName.equals("name"))
    p.setName(value);
  else if (attribName.equals("licenseNumber"))
    p.setLicenseNumber(value);
}

// Set the make, model, and year of the Style object.
private void setAttribute(Style s, String attribName, String value) {
  if (attribName.equals("make"))
    s.setMake(value);
  else if (attribName.equals("model"))
    s.setModel(value);
  else if (attribName.equals("year")) {
    int year = -1;

    try {
      if (value != null)
        year = Integer.parseInt(value);
    }
    catch (Exception e) {
      e.printStackTrace();
    }

    if (year != -1)
      s.setYear(year);
  }
```

Source Code 7.17   *CRAFactory* methods used by *CRAReaderAdapter.* *(Continued)*

```
}

// Calls the appropriate method to set the reference based on the type
// of the object.
public void setReference(Object object, String referenceName,
                         Object value){
  if (object instanceof Car)
    setReference((Car) object,    referenceName, value);
  else if (object instanceof Option)
    setReference((Option) object, referenceName, value);
  else if (object instanceof Style)
    setReference((Style) object,  referenceName, value);
  else if (object instanceof Person)
    setReference((Person) object, referenceName, value);
}

// Set the driver or style references on a Car object.
private void setReference(Car c, String referenceName, Object value) {
  if (referenceName.equals("driver") && (value instanceof Person))
    c.add((Person) value);
  else if (referenceName.equals("style") && (value instanceof Style))
    c.setStyle((Style) value);
}

// Set the car reference from an Option object to a Car object.
private void setReference(Option o, String referenceName,
                          Object value) {
  if (referenceName.equals("car") && (value instanceof Car))
    o.setCar((Car) value);
}

// Set the car reference from a Style object to a Car object.
private void setReference(Style s, String referenceName,
                          Object value) {
  if (referenceName.equals("car") && (value instanceof Car))
    s.add((Car) value);
}

// Set the car reference from a Person object to a Car object.
private void setReference(Person p, String referenceName,
                          Object value) {
  if (referenceName.equals("car") && (value instanceof Car))
    p.add((Car) value);
}
```

Source Code 7.17   *CRAFactory* methods used by *CRAReaderAdapter. (Continued)*

```
// CRAReaderAdapter.java
import com.ibm.xmi.framework.*;
import cars.Car;
import cars.Option;

// This class implements a Framework reader adapter to restore
// instances of the classes in the cars package.
public class CRAReaderAdapter extends DefaultReaderAdapter {
  private CRAFactory factory;

// Initialize the factory.
public CRAReaderAdapter() {
  factory = new CRAFactory();
}

// Create an object, given the tag name.
public java.lang.Object createObject(ObjectInfo info) {
  Object newObject = null;

  try {
    if (info.getXMIName() != null)
      newObject = factory.newInstance(info.getXMIName());
  }
  catch (Exception e) {
    e.printStackTrace();
  }

  return newObject;
}

// If the value is a String, call setAttribute(); if the value is not
// a String (and not null), call setReference(); if the value is null,
// return the name of the object value. The setReference() method does
// not handle the option reference for Car objects, so it needs to
// be set here.
public java.lang.Object setValue(ValueInfo info) {
  if (info.getValue() instanceof String)
    factory.setAttribute(info.getObject(), info.getXMIName(),
                         (String) info.getValue());
```

Source Code 7.18 The *CRAReaderAdapter* class.

```
      else if (info.getValue() != null &&
              info.getXMIName().equals("option"))
        ((Car) info.getObject()).add((Option) info.getValue());
      else if (info.getValue() != null)
        factory.setReference(info.getObject(), info.getXMIName(),
                        info.getValue());

    if (info.getValue() == null)
      return info.getXMIName();
    else
      return null;
}


// Returns Value.DATA for data values, Value.OBJECT for object
// values, and Value.REFERENCE for references.
public int getType(ValueInfo info) {
    if (info.getXMIName().equals("option"))
        return Value.OBJECT;
    else if (info.getXMIName().equals("style") ||
            info.getXMIName().equals("driver") ||
            info.getXMIName().equals("car"))
      return Value.REFERENCE;
    else
      return Value.DATA;
}


public int getType(ObjectInfo info) {
    return -1;
}


// This method is called to set the value of references that could not
// be set when setValue() was called because the object that is
// the value occurred later in the file.
public void setValue(java.lang.Object object,
                     java.lang.Object reference,
                     java.lang.Object value) {
  factory.setReference(object, (String) reference, value);
}
}
```

Source Code 7.18 The *CRAReaderAdapter* class. (*Continued*)

```
// CRAAdapterFactory.java
import com.ibm.xmi.framework.*;

// This class is the adapter factory for the car rental
// agency problem domain.
public class CRAAdapterFactory extends AdapterFactory {

  // Return the CRAObjectWriterAdapter. This method is called
  // automatically by the Framework.
  public ObjectWriterAdapter createObjectWriterAdapter() {
    return new CRAObjectWriterAdapter();
  }

  // Return the CRAReaderAdapter. This method is called
  // automatically by the Framework.
  public ReaderAdapter createReaderAdapter() {
    return new CRAReaderAdapter();
  }
}
```

Source Code 7.19   The completed *CRAAdapterFactory* class.

Finally, the program *FrameRead3*, displayed in Source Code 7.20, reads the *frame1.xmi* file, registering the *CRAReaderAdapter* (by registering the *CRAAdapterFactory*) with the Framework first.

Here is the output of the *FrameRead3* program:

```
Car vin: v1 available: false make: Jalopy model: Deluxe year: 2002
  Options:
    air conditioning
  Drivers:
    Anita Karr
Style make: Jalopy model: Deluxe year: 2002 cars: v1
Person name: Anita Karr licenseNumber: ln1 cars: v1
```

This output indicates that instances of the Java classes in the cars package were created, and the fields of those objects have been correctly restored.

Summary

It is much easier to use APIs that have been designed specifically to support XMI than to use APIs that have been designed for XML. JOB lets you create and restore XMI documents that contain your Java objects, with a minimum of effort on your part. The XMI Framework lets you explore many of the issues

```
// FrameRead3.java
import com.ibm.xmi.framework.*;
import cars.*;
import java.util.*;

// Use the CRAReaderAdapter when reading the file.
public class FrameRead3 {
  public static void main(String[] args) throws Exception {
    AdapterFactory af = new CRAAdapterFactory();
    AdapterFactoryRegister.registerAdapterFactory(af);
    XMIFile file = XMIFile.load("frame1.xmi", XMIFile.DEFAULT,
                                 false);
    Iterator obj = file.getObjects().iterator();

    while (obj.hasNext())
      System.out.println(obj.next());
  }
}
```

Source Code 7.20   The *FrameRead3* program.

that are involved with creating and reading XMI documents, including matching the data in XMI documents to models that you define. You can use the
Framework to work with generic representations of objects and their attribute
values and references, or you can work with your own objects by implementing adapters and registering them with the Framework. You should select the
techniques that make the most sense for your application. Now that you know
the basic concepts of the XMI Framework, you are ready to learn about
advanced Framework capabilities.

CHAPTER 8

Creating and Reading Advanced XMI Documents with the XMI Framework

Chapter 7 describes how to use the XMI Framework to read and write XMI documents. This chapter explains the advanced functionality the Framework provides. It builds on the material presented in Chapter 7, so you should read that chapter before reading this one.

Although we strongly recommend that you specify namespaces in your models, the programs in Chapter 7 do not deal with namespaces. We explain in this chapter how to use Extensible Markup Language (XML) namespaces with the XML Metadata Interchange (XMI) Framework. Other topics that we explain in this chapter include how the Framework supports information describing your XMI documents, using XMI extensions, compressing XMI documents, handling cross-file references, and generating Java code. By learning how the XMI Framework supports this functionality, you can gain an understanding of what XMI software can do for you.

We continue to use the car rental agency model and objects that were explained in detail in the first section of Chapter 6. You may want to refer to that section to review the details of the car rental agency model and the objects we use.

We present a brief review of the basic concepts of the XMI Framework before explaining how the Framework supports advanced functionality. You can skip this section if you remember the Framework concepts explained in Chapter 7. Since this chapter builds on Chapter 7's Framework concepts, you need to know them to understand this chapter. This chapter also uses the software presented in Chapter 7, so we review that as well before discussing advanced XMI functionality.

A Quick Review

The XMI Framework was introduced in Chapter 7. That chapter explained how the XMI Framework represents your objects using the *XMIObject* interface. Each *XMIObject* has an XMI *name, id, uuid, label,* and possibly *Value* objects. The *Value* interface contains the information needed to serialize one or more attribute values or references belonging to an object using XMI. Each *Value* object has an XMI name, a type, and the actual value, which is a *String,* an *XMIObject,* a *Collection* of *Strings,* or a *Collection* of *XMIObjects*. One *Value* object is used to represent all the values of an attribute for an object. One *Value* object is used to represent all references that are instances of a particular association end for an object. We use three kinds of Framework values: data values, object values, and references.

The *XMIFile* class in the Framework represents an XMI document. You create an XMI document by creating an instance of the *XMIFile* class and then invoking the *write()* method. The *write()* method has a parameter that is an *Iterator* for a *Collection* containing the objects to write to the document; it also has a parameter for a write option. For our purposes, we always use the default write option, *XMIFile.DEFAULT*.

There are two approaches for using the XMI Framework to write an XMI document. You create an *XMIFile* and invoke the *write()* method for both approaches. The difference between the approaches is in the objects you use. The first approach involves representing your objects using the Framework implementations of the *XMIObject* and *Value* interfaces. The second approach involves using your own Java classes and implementing an object writer adapter so the Framework can obtain the information it needs to write your objects to an XMI document.

We saw both approaches in Chapter 7. We created a method called *make-FOMExample()* in the *CRAFactory* class that creates *XMIObjects* and *Values* representing the car rental agency objects; we then used that method in the *FrameWrite* program to create the objects to put in an XMI document. To demonstrate the second approach, we created a *makeExample()* method in the *CRAFactory* class that creates instances of the four classes *Style, Option, Car,* and *Person* in the *cars* package. Then we created an object writer adapter called *CRAObjectWriterAdapter* that enables the Framework to get the information it needs to write the objects. We also created an adapter factory called *CRAAdapterFactory* that creates an instance of *CRAObjectWriterAdapter*. The *FrameWrite2* program registered the adapter factory with the Framework and then used instances of the classes in the *cars* package from the *makeExample()* method, rather than *XMIObjects*.

We also saw that the Framework creates an *XMIFile* object whenever it loads an XMI document. You can use the *getObjects()* method to obtain the top-level objects from the XMI document. The Framework correctly interprets XMI documents when it knows the model that defines the data in a document. The *Workspace* class enables you to register models with the Framework. We also saw that you can implement a reader adapter to create instances of your own classes rather than *XMIObjects* when the Framework loads an XMI document. The three programs *FrameRead*, *FrameRead2*, and *FrameRead3* in Chapter 7 demonstrate three ways of loading an XMI document using the Framework.

Namespaces

You can use the XMI Framework to read and write XMI documents that contain XML namespaces. We explain how to do this after we review what XML namespaces are and how to specify them in your models.

We saw in Chapter 2 that XML namespaces specify the context for a particular XML element or XML attribute. Each XML namespace consists of a namespace Uniform Resource Identifier (URI) that uniquely identifies the namespace and a namespace prefix that is used in a particular XML document to identify the namespace.

We saw in Chapter 3 that you can specify the XML namespaces to use for your models by specifying values for the *nsURI* and *nsPrefix* tags (remember that XMI tags begin with the prefix *org.omg.xmi.*, which is omitted in this chapter for clarity). If you provide values for those tags in your model, XMI specifies that the corresponding schema has a target namespace with the value of the *nsURI* tag as its URI and with the value of the *nsPrefix* tag as its prefix. There are several advantages to doing this. First, you can avoid name collisions in XML documents if data from your model is mixed with data from different models. Second, you can avoid name collisions between classes in different packages in the same model by assigning an XML namespace to each package. In our opinion, the advantages of specifying namespaces outweigh the additional work required and the slight increase in the complexity of XMI documents.

To use a namespace with the car rental agency problem domain, we need to decide what the URI is for the namespace and which namespace prefix to use. We decide that the URI is *http://mycompany.com/CarRentalAgency*, and we will use the namespace prefix *CRA* (for car rental agency) in our XMI documents.

The Framework has a *Namespace* class that you use to specify a namespace. You specify the namespace prefix and the namespace URI when you create a *Namespace* object. You use the *setXMINamespace()* method to set the namespace for any of the constructs in the Framework object model. In particular, you can set the namespace for an *XMIObject*. The Framework uses the namespace for an *XMIObject* when it serializes the object in an XMI document.

Recall from Chapter 3 that XMI enables you to control the use of namespaces in XMI documents by using the *form* tag. If that tag has the value *qualified*, then the *form* XML attribute of the declarations for attributes and association ends is set to *qualified*, requiring the use of namespaces. The Framework always serializes values without using namespace prefixes, though. It is possible that a future version of the Framework will enable namespace prefixes to be used when serializing values when the *form* tag is set to *qualified*.

The car rental agency model does not use the *form* tag. This means that the declarations for the attributes and association ends are local ones, so a namespace should not be used when attribute values and references are serialized in an XMI document. If we set the namespace for the objects themselves rather than the values of the objects, the Framework will serialize them correctly.

We can serialize the car rental agency objects by creating an *XMIObject* for each of them, setting the values of each *XMIObject*, setting the namespace for each *XMIObject*, and then using the *XMIFile* class. We can also serialize instances of the Java classes in the *cars* package by modifying the *CRAObjectWriterAdapter* to support the namespace we have chosen, registering the *CRAAdapterFactory* with the Framework, and then using the *XMIFile* class. We explain both approaches.

The *makeFOMExample()* method of the *CRAFactory* class makes an *XMIObject* for each object to save and sets the values for each *XMIObject*. It returns the created objects in an *ArrayList*. We need to set the namespace for each *XMIObject*. We can set the namespace for the objects by implementing a new method in the *CRAFactory* class. The new method is called *assignNamespace()*, and it takes two arguments: a *Namespace* and a *Collection* of objects. It invokes a helper method to set the namespace for each object in the *Collection* and each object value. The two methods we add to the *CRAFactory* class are displayed in Source Code 8.1. Note that we need to add import statements for the *java.util.Collection* and *java.util.Iterator* classes to *CRAFactory.java*; those import statements are not shown in Source Code 8.1.

The *NamespaceWrite* program writes the objects to an XMI document using the namespace. It is shown in Source Code 8.2.

The document produced by *NamespaceWrite* is as follows (we split the lines that were too long to fit the page width of this book):[1]

```
<?xml version="1.0" encoding="UTF-8"?>
<xmi:XMI xmi:version="2.0" xmlns:xmi="http://www.omg.org/XMI"
       xmlns:CRA="http://mycompany.com/CarRentalAgency">
   <xmi:Documentation>
     <exporter>XMI Framework</exporter>
     <exporterVersion>1.2</exporterVersion>
   </xmi:Documentation>
  <CRA:Car xmi:id="_1" available="false" vin="v1" driver="_3"
         style="_2">
```

```
// New methods in CRAFactory to assign a Framework namespace to
// a collection of XMIObjects.

// Assign a namespace to each object in the Collection as well
// as to the object values for each object.
public void assignNamespace(Namespace n, Collection objects) {
   Iterator objs = objects.iterator();

   while (objs.hasNext())
      assignNamespace(n, (XMIObject) objs.next());
}

// Assign the namespace to the given object and each object
// value the object has.
public void assignNamespace(Namespace n, XMIObject obj) {
   obj.setXMINamespace(n);
   Iterator values = obj.getXMIValues().iterator();

   while (values.hasNext()) {
      Value v = (Value) values.next();

      // Object values have the type Value.OBJECT.
      if (v.getXMIType() == Value.OBJECT) {
         Object value = v.getXMIValue();

         if (value instanceof Collection) {
            Iterator objs = ((Collection) value).iterator();

               while (objs.hasNext())
                  assignNamespace(n, (XMIObject) objs.next());
         }
         else if (value instanceof XMIObject)
            assignNamespace(n, (XMIObject) value);
      }
   }
}
```

Source Code 8.1 Methods in *CRAFactory* to assign a Framework namespace to a *Collection* of *XMIObjects*.

```
    <option xmi:id="_1.1" xmi:type="CRA:Option" name="air conditioning"
            car="_1"/>
  </CRA:Car>
  <CRA:Style xmi:id="_2" make="Jalopy" model="Deluxe" year="2002"
            car="_1"/>
  <CRA:Person xmi:id="_3" licenseNumber="ln1" name="Anita Karr"
            car="_1"/>
</xmi:XMI>
```

```
// NamespaceWrite.java
import com.ibm.xmi.framework.*;
import java.util.ArrayList;

// This class uses the CRAFactory to create XMIObjects and Values,
// sets the namespace for the objects, and then saves them in an XMI
// document.
public class NamespaceWrite {
  public static void main(String[] args) throws Exception {
    CRAFactory f = new CRAFactory();
    Namespace n = new Namespace("CRA",
                        "http://mycompany.com/CarRentalAgency");

    ArrayList l = f.makeFOMExample();
    f.assignNamespace(n, l);

    XMIFile file = new XMIFile("namespace.xmi");
    file.write(l.iterator(), XMIFile.DEFAULT);
  }
}
```

Source Code 8.2 The *NamespaceWrite* program.

Notice that the Framework automatically put the namespace declaration for the car rental agency namespace in the XMI document for us. The *option* XML element does not use the namespace prefix *CRA* because XMI does not use namespaces for attribute values and references unless the *form* tag is set to *qualified*.

Now consider how to write instances of the classes *Style*, *Person*, *Car*, and *Option* in the *cars* package. We will modify the *CRAObjectWriterAdapter* we implemented in Chapter 7 to provide the namespace information the Framework needs to write the namespaces to the document. Recall from Chapter 7 that the *getNamespace()* method of the *CRAObjectWriterAdapter* always returns *null*, because we did not use namespaces in Chapter 7.

The Framework calls the *getNamespace()* method for each object and value it writes to an XMI document. We add the following declaration to the *CRAObjectWriterAdapter* to avoid making a *Namespace* object each time the *getNamespace()* method returns the namespace:

```
private static Namespace namespace = new Namespace("CRA",
                "http://mycompany.com/CarRentalAgency");
```

Since we need the namespace for the objects themselves, not the values, we implement the *getNamespace()* method as follows:

```
public Namespace getNamespace(Object data) {
   if (data instanceof ValueWriteData)
      return null;
```

```
    else
        return namespace;
}
```

Remember from Chapter 7 that we use the *ValueWriteData* class to represent the data needed to write each value of an object. The *getNamespace()* method returns *null* for *ValueWriteData* objects because a namespace is not required for an object's values for this example.

We also need to modify the *getXMIName()* method of the *CRAObjectWriter-Adapter*. The Framework expects the XMI name to include the namespace prefix in the name, if there is one. We implement an *addNamespace()* method that takes a name and an object. It checks if the object has a namespace and adds the namespace prefix to the object's name if there is a namespace for the object and the prefix is not the empty string (the prefix is the empty string for the default namespace). Then we call the *addNamespace()* method in *getXMIName()* for instances of the *Car*, *Style*, *Person*, and *Option* classes. Both methods appear in Source Code 8.3.

```
// New addNamespace() method and updated getXMIName() method for the
// CRAObjectWriterAdapter class.

// Add the namespace prefix if there is one for the given object to
// the given name.
private String addNamespace(String name, Object object) {
    Namespace n = getNamespace(object);

    if (n != null && n.getPrefix() != null && !n.getPrefix().equals(""))
        return n.getPrefix() + ":" + name;
    else
        return name;
}


public String getXMIName(Object data) {
    if (data instanceof ValueWriteData)
        return ((ValueWriteData) data).getName();
    else if (data instanceof Car)
        return addNamespace("Car", data);
    else if (data instanceof Style)
        return addNamespace("Style", data);
    else if (data instanceof Person)
        return addNamespace("Person", data);
    else if (data instanceof Option)
        return addNamespace("Option", data);
    else
        return null;
}
```

Source Code 8.3 A new and updated method in *CRAObjectWriterAdapter* for namespaces.

Now that we have modified the *CRAObjectWriterAdapter* to handle namespaces for our application, we can use the *CRAAdapterFactory* class from Chapter 7 to register our object writer adapter with the Framework. We can also use the *makeExample()* method of the *CRAFactory* class to make instances of the classes in the *cars* package. The *NamespaceWrite2* program in Source Code 8.4 is identical to the *FrameWrite2* program in Chapter 7, except that the name of the XMI document it creates is *namespace2.xmi*.

The *NamespaceWrite2* program produces the file *namespace2.xmi*, which is equivalent to *namespace.xmi*. The only differences in the files occur because some of the XML attributes appear in a different order (this difference does not affect the semantics of the XML document, though). The contents of *namespace2.xmi* are as follows (some lines have been split to fit the page width):

```xml
<?xml version="1.0" encoding="UTF-8"?>
<xmi:XMI xmi:version="2.0" xmlns:xmi="http://www.omg.org/XMI"
        xmlns:CRA="http://mycompany.com/CarRentalAgency">
    <xmi:Documentation>
      <exporter>XMI Framework</exporter>
      <exporterVersion>1.2</exporterVersion>
    </xmi:Documentation>
  <CRA:Car xmi:id="_1" vin="v1" available="false" driver="_3"
          style="_2">
    <option xmi:id="_1.1" xmi:type="CRA:Option" name="air conditioning"
```

```java
// NamespaceWrite2.java
import com.ibm.xmi.framework.*;
import java.util.ArrayList;
import java.util.Iterator;

// Use the CRAFactory to make the instances of the cars package to
// write, register the CRAAdapterFactory with the Framework, and then
// write the objects using an XMIFile.
public class NamespaceWrite2 {
   public static void main(String[] args) throws Exception {
      CRAFactory factory = new CRAFactory();
      ArrayList objects = factory.makeExample();

      AdapterFactoryRegister.registerAdapterFactory(
                        new CRAAdapterFactory());

      XMIFile file = new XMIFile("namespace2.xmi");
      file.write(objects.iterator(), XMIFile.DEFAULT);
   }
}
```

Source Code 8.4   The *NamespaceWrite2* program.

```
                car="_1"/>
   </CRA:Car>
   <CRA:Style xmi:id="_2" make="Jalopy" model="Deluxe" year="2002"
              car="_1"/>
   <CRA:Person xmi:id="_3" name="Anita Karr" licenseNumber="ln1"
                  car="_1"/>
 </xmi:XMI>
```

The Framework creates instances of the *Namespace* class and sets the namespaces for objects and values when it loads an XMI document that contains XML namespaces. You can use the *getNamespaces()* method of the *XMIFile* class to obtain the *Namespace* objects from an XMI document.

Recall from Chapter 7 that the *XMIContainer* class in the Framework can be used to print *XMIObjects* and their values. The namespaces of the objects and values are printed if they are set. We presented a simple program in Chapter 7 called *FrameRead* that reads an XMI document, puts the objects in an *XMIContainer*, and prints the container. For convenience, we include the program in Source Code 8.5.

When this program is run with *namespace.xmi*, the following output is printed:

```
--------------------------------
Object: CRA:Car id: _1
  isProxy: false
```

```java
// FrameRead.java
import com.ibm.xmi.framework.XMIFile;
import com.ibm.xmi.framework.XMIContainer;



// This class parses an XMI document, and then puts the XMIObjects the
// Framework made into an XMIContainer so they can be printed.
public class FrameRead {
   public static void main(String[] args) throws Exception {
      if (args.length != 1) {
         System.out.println("Enter the name of an XMI document.");
         return;
      }

      XMIFile file = XMIFile.load(args[0], XMIFile.DEFAULT, false);
      XMIContainer c = new XMIContainer(file.getObjects().iterator());
      System.out.println(c);
   }
}
```

Source Code 8.5 The *FrameRead* program.

```
        namespace: 'CRA',http://mycompany.com/CarRentalAgency
        Values:
          available <DATA> 'false'
          vin <DATA> 'v1'
          driver <DATA> '_3'
          style <DATA> '_2'
          option <OBJ> [XMIObject CRA:Option _1.1]
      End object: CRA:Car
      -------------------------------
      Object: CRA:Option id: _1.1
        isProxy: false
        namespace: 'CRA',http://mycompany.com/CarRentalAgency
        Values:
          name <DATA> 'air conditioning'
          car <DATA> '_1'
      End object: CRA:Option
      -------------------------------
      Object: CRA:Style id: _2
        isProxy: false
        namespace: 'CRA',http://mycompany.com/CarRentalAgency
        Values:
          make <DATA> 'Jalopy'
          model <DATA> 'Deluxe'
          year <DATA> '2002'
          car <DATA> '_1'
      End object: CRA:Style
      -------------------------------
      Object: CRA:Person id: _3
        isProxy: false
        namespace: 'CRA',http://mycompany.com/CarRentalAgency
        Values:
          licenseNumber <DATA> 'ln1'
          name <DATA> 'Anita Karr'
          car <DATA> '_1'
      End object: CRA:Person
      -------------------------------
```

We describe proxies later in this chapter. Note that the namespace has been set for the objects. Notice also that even though the *option* XML element does not include a namespace prefix in its tag name, the *Option* object has its namespace correctly set. This happens because the value of the *xmi:type* attribute of the *option* XML element includes the namespace prefix *CRA*. Also, as explained in Chapter 7, since the car rental agency model was not registered with the Framework before loading the file, the references in the file have been restored as data values. You may want to review Chapter 7 if you do not understand why this occurs.

Describing Your Documents

XMI enables you to specify information that describes XMI documents. For example, you can identify the tool (its name and version number) that created the document. You can also save the physical location of the model that defines your objects.

Chapter 3 described the information that XMI enables you to put in your documents to describe them. The additional information appears in a *Documentation* XML element, a *Model* XML element, and other elements. We saw examples of the use of the *Documentation* XML element in the XMI documents created by the Framework because the Framework identifies itself as the exporter of an XMI document unless you change the exporter. We explain how the Framework supports the *Documentation* XML element so you can put your information into it. We also explain how to put a *Model* XML element into your XMI documents that enables you to specify a physical location for a model identified with a URI. We use the information in the *Model* XML element to create an application that loads a model if it is needed.

Documentation Information

As explained in Chapter 3, XMI enables you to put a variety of information that describes a document into a *Documentation* XML element. The Framework enables you to specify this information by using methods on the *XMIFile* class. The Framework puts the information into a *Documentation* element for you when it writes objects to an XMI document. When the Framework loads an XMI document, it saves the information in the *Documentation* XML element in an *XMIFile* object, and you can get the information using accessor methods in the *XMIFile* class.

If you do not set any of this information, the Framework specifies *XMI Framework* for the exporter and *1.2* for the exporter version. You can provide your own values for the exporter and exporter version rather than the default ones.

For each kind of information in the *Documentation* element, there are two accessor methods in the *XMIFile* class. For example, to specify the exporter, you use the *setExporter()* method. To get the exporter, you use the *getExporter()* method. One limitation of the Framework is that you can only specify one value for each kind of information, whereas the XMI specification says that you can specify multiple values. For example, you should be able to put two contacts in an XMI document.

Consider how to specify that your tool, which is called *MyTool* version *0.5*, is the exporter of XMI documents. Consider also how to put a short comment into an XMI document that says *Excellent Stuff*. You can use the *setExporter()* method, the *setExporterVersion()* method, and the *setShortDescription()* method of the *XMIFile* class to provide this information; then use the *write()* method to serialize your objects. We serialize a *Car* object by creating an *XMIObject* to represent it. The *DocumentationWrite* program can be found in Source Code 8.6.

The contents of *documentation.xmi* are as follows:

```
<?xml version="1.0" encoding="UTF-8"?>
<xmi:XMI xmi:version="2.0" xmlns:xmi="http://www.omg.org/XMI">
    <xmi:Documentation>
      <exporter>MyTool</exporter>
      <exporterVersion>0.5</exporterVersion>
      <shortDescription>Excellent Stuff</shortDescription>
    </xmi:Documentation>
  <Car xmi:id="_1"/>
</xmi:XMI>
```

Notice that the information we provided to the *XMIFile* class is inside the *Documentation* XML element.

We can obtain *Documentation* information from an XMI document by using the *XMIFile* object created when the Framework loads the XMI document. To do so, we use the accessor methods on the *XMIFile* class. The *DocumentationRead* program prints the exporter, exporter version, and a short description after loading the *documentation.xmi* XMI document. It is shown in Source Code 8.7.

```
// DocumentationWrite.java
import com.ibm.xmi.framework.*;
import java.util.ArrayList;

// This class demonstrates how to set documentation information for an
// XMI document using the Framework.
public class DocumentationWrite {
  public static void main(String[] args) throws Exception {
    XMIObject obj = new XMIObjectImpl("Car");
    ArrayList l = new ArrayList();
    l.add(obj);

    XMIFile file = new XMIFile("documentation.xmi");
    file.setExporter("MyTool");
    file.setExporterVersion("0.5");
    file.setShortDescription("Excellent Stuff");
    file.write(l.iterator(), XMIFile.DEFAULT);
  }
}
```

Source Code 8.6 The *DocumentationWrite* program.

```
// DocumentationRead.java
import com.ibm.xmi.framework.*;
import java.util.ArrayList;

// This class demonstrates how to get documentation information for an
// XMI document after loading it using the Framework.
public class DocumentationRead {
  public static void main(String[] args) throws Exception {
    XMIFile f = XMIFile.load("documentation.xmi", XMIFile.DEFAULT,
                             false);
    System.out.println("exporter: " + f.getExporter());
    System.out.println("exporter version: " + f.getExporterVersion());
    System.out.println("short description: " +
                       f.getShortDescription());
  }
}
```

Source Code 8.7   The *DocumentationRead* program.

The output of the *DocumentationRead* program is as follows:

```
exporter: MyTool
exporter version: 0.5
short description: Excellent Stuff
```

To improve the Framework application programming interfaces (APIs), a *Documentation* class could be provided that would enable you to get and set multiple values for each attribute in the *Documentation* class in the XMI model. Then you could provide the *Documentation* object along with your other objects when serializing a file, and the *Documentation* object could be handled the same way as other objects being serialized. This may be added in a future version of the Framework.

Model Information

By specifying a value for the *nsURI* tag, you can provide a URI for a model that identifies your model unambiguously. However, a namespace URI does not necessarily provide the location of a file containing the model. You can provide the name of a file that contains a model using the *Model* XML element defined by XMI.

Recall from Chapter 3 that XMI enables you to specify a *name*, a *version*, and an *href* for a *Model* XML element. By setting the *name* of the *Model* element to a namespace prefix in an XMI document, you can associate the *Model* element with a particular XML namespace; the namespace URI of the XML namespace is the URI for the model. The *version* attribute of the *Model* XML element can be used to specify the version of the model (you can put the version in the URI for the model as well). You can set the *href* attribute of the *Model* XML element to point to a file that contains the model. This way XMI software can load the model from the physical location specified in the *href* attribute if the URI of the model does not provide the location.

The XMI Framework enables you to put one or more *Model* XML elements in an XMI document and access the information in them after loading an XMI document. The *XMIFile.Model* class in the Framework, which is an inner class of the *XMIFile* class in the Framework, enables you to set the *name, version,* and *href* for a *Model* XML element in an XMI document. You can create an instance of the *XMIFile.Model* class, and then use the *add()* method of the *XMIFile* class to add the *XMIFile.Model* instance to the *XMIFile*. The Framework creates a *Model* element for each *XMIFile.Model* instance when it writes objects to an XMI document. The Framework creates an instance of the *XMIFile.Model* class for each *Model* element in an XMI document when it loads the XMI document. You can access the *Model* element information by using the *getModels()* method of the *XMIFile* class.

We saw in the *Namespaces* section of this chapter how to use the namespace with a URI of *http://mycompany.com/CarRentalAgency* and a prefix of *CRA* in the car rental agency application. We can indicate that the car rental agency model is saved in the file *cramodel.xmi* by writing a *Model* XML element in an XMI document. The *Model* XML element has its *href* attribute set to *cramodel.xmi*, its *version* attribute set to *1.0*, and its *name* attribute set to *CRA* (to match the namespace prefix). The *NamespaceWrite* program in the *Namespaces* section of this chapter created the car rental agency objects and set the namespace of each object. We can do the same thing: Create an instance of the *XMIFile.Model* class, add the instance to an *XMIFile*, and then invoke the *write()* method of the *XMI-File* to create the same document as the *NamespaceWrite* program did, except for the inclusion of the *Model* XML element. The *ModelWrite* program does all this and saves the information in an XMI document called *model.xmi*. This program is shown in Source Code 8.8.

As you can see from the following output, a *Model* element is in *model.xmi* (we split some lines that were too long for the page width):

```
<?xml version="1.0" encoding="UTF-8"?>
<xmi:XMI xmi:version="2.0" xmlns:xmi="http://www.omg.org/XMI"
         xmlns:CRA="http://mycompany.com/CarRentalAgency">
    <xmi:Documentation>
      <exporter>XMI Framework</exporter>
      <exporterVersion>1.2</exporterVersion>
    </xmi:Documentation>
    <xmi:Model name="CRA" version="1.0" href="cramodel.xmi"/>
  <CRA:Car xmi:id="_1" available="false" vin="v1" driver="_3"
           style="_2">
    <option xmi:id="_1.1" xmi:type="CRA:Option" name="air conditioning"
            car="_1"/>
```

```
// ModelWrite.java
import com.ibm.xmi.framework.*;
import java.util.ArrayList;

// This class demonstrates how to add model information to an XMI
// document using the Framework.
public class ModelWrite {
  public static void main(String[] args) throws Exception {
    CRAFactory f = new CRAFactory();
    Namespace n = new Namespace("CRA",
                        "http://mycompany.com/CarRentalAgency");

    ArrayList l = f.makeFOMExample();
    f.assignNamespace(n, l);

    XMIFile file = new XMIFile("model.xmi");
    file.add(new XMIFile.Model("CRA", "1.0", "cramodel.xmi"));
    file.write(l.iterator(), XMIFile.DEFAULT);
  }
}
```

Source Code 8.8 The *ModelWrite* program.

```
  </CRA:Car>
  <CRA:Style xmi:id="_2" make="Jalopy" model="Deluxe" year="2002"
          car="_1"/>
  <CRA:Person xmi:id="_3" licenseNumber="ln1" name="Anita Karr"
          car="_1"/>
</xmi:XMI>
```

After loading an XMI document that has *Model* elements in it, you can access the information in them by using the *getModels()* method of the *XMIFile* class. The *PrintModel* program shown in Source Code 8.9 demonstrates the use of this method.

The output of the program is as follows:

```
name:    CRA
version: 1.0
href:    cramodel.xmi
```

Now that we know how to put a *Model* XML element into an XMI document and obtain the information from it, we can put that information to use. So far in this book, we have presented simple programs that only work with XMI documents that contain objects from the car rental agency model. You can write more sophisticated applications, of course. We show you how to write an application that loads a model from a file when it reads an XMI document that

```
// PrintModel.java
import com.ibm.xmi.framework.*;
import java.util.Iterator;

// This class demonstrates how to get model information from an
// XMI document after loading it using the Framework.
public class PrintModel {
  public static void main(String[] args) throws Exception {
     XMIFile f = XMIFile.load("model.xmi", XMIFile.DEFAULT, false);
     Iterator models = f.getModels().iterator();

     while(models.hasNext()) {
        XMIFile.Model m = (XMIFile.Model) models.next();
        System.out.println("name:    " + m.getName());
        System.out.println("version: " + m.getVersion());
        System.out.println("href:    " + m.getHref());
     }
  }
}
```

Source Code 8.9 The *PrintModel* program.

contains a *Model* XML element. In fact, the application will load a model from the file identified in the *href* attribute of the *Model* XML element.

Why is it desirable to do this? The Framework correctly interprets an XMI document if you provide it with the model that defines the objects in the document. To do this, you can use the Framework classes *Workspace, Model,* and *XMI-Files.* The *Workspace* class is a collection of models that the Framework uses to match objects in a file to their definers in models. Each instance of the *Model* class represents a Framework model; this class is different than the *XMIFile.Model* class we explained previously that contains the information for a *Model* XML element in an XMI document. The *XMIFiles* class represents a collection of related XMI documents. To provide the Framework with a model so that it correctly interprets an XMI document when it is loaded, perform the following actions:

1. Make an instance of the *Workspace* class.

2. Make an instance of the *Model* class and add Framework declarations to represent your model (you may want to review Chapter 7 for a more complete explanation).

3. Add the *Model* instance to the *Workspace* instance.

4. Make an instance of the *XMIFiles* class.

5. Add the *XMIFiles* instance to the *Workspace* instance.

6. Use the *load()* method in the *XMIFiles* class to load the XMI document.

You can add the *XMIFiles* instance to the *Workspace* instance before you add the *Model* instance, if you want. You can also add more than one *Model* instance to a *Workspace* instance. However, you must add a *Model* instance to the *Workspace* instance before you load the XMI document to make the *Model* available to the Framework.

Chapter 7 explained how to create a Framework model using Framework classes. You can also make a Framework model by loading an XMI document that represents a model, as we explain later. Since you may forget to provide the model to the Framework before loading an XMI document, it is better for the Framework to load the model from a file and add the model to a *Workspace*, so you do not need to remember to do it.

We implement this functionality by creating the *Repository*, *LoadModelAdapter*, and *LMAdapterFactory* classes, and the *LoadModel* program. The *Repository* class loads an XMI document containing a model and makes a Framework model. The *LoadModelAdapter* class is a reader adapter that obtains the *XMIFile.Model* instance from an *XMIFile*; it gets the *href* that identifies the file containing the model and uses a *Repository* instance to load the file and create a Framework model. The *LoadModelAdapter* class adds the Framework model to a *Workspace* instance. The *LMAdapterFactory* creates a *LoadModelAdapter*. The *LoadModel* program registers the *LMAdapterFactory*, creates a *Workspace*, adds an *XMIFiles* object to it, and loads an XMI document using the *XMIFiles* object. Because the *LoadModelAdapter* adds a Framework model to the *Workspace*, the *LoadModel* program does not need to do so. We explain the *Repository* first, and then the *LoadModelAdapter*, the *LMAdapterFactory*, and the *LoadModel* program.

The *Repository* class loads an XMI document and creates a Framework model from the objects in it. The *DeclarationFactory* class in the Framework creates a Framework model from the objects in an XMI document. (Currently, the *DeclarationFactory* requires an XMI 1.0 document rather than an XMI 2.0 document, but a future version of the Framework may work with XMI 2.0 documents as well.) The CD-ROM for the book includes the *cramodel.xmi* XMI 1.0 document that contains the car rental agency model. The parts of a Framework model are called *declarations*, so the class that makes them is called *DeclarationFactory*.

The Framework enables you to specify the namespace prefix and namespace URI to use in a model when you create a *DeclarationFactory* object. When you specify a URI and a prefix, the *DeclarationFactory* class creates a *Namespace* object and sets the namespace of each part of the model to that *Namespace* object. In the *Namespaces* section, we set the namespace for the objects, but not for the values of the objects. The *LoadModel* program works if the namespace is set for the attributes and association ends in the Framework representation of the car rental agency model as well as the classes. The *Repository* class is shown in Source Code 8.10.

```
// Repository.java
import com.ibm.xmi.framework.*;
import java.util.Iterator;

// This class loads a model with the given filename, and then assigns
// a namespace with the given prefix and the given URI to the
// model.
public class Repository {
    public Model load(String prefix, String uri, String filename)
                throws Exception {
        XMIFile f = XMIFile.load(filename, XMIFile.DEFAULT, false);
        DeclarationFactory df = new DeclarationFactory(prefix, uri);
        Iterator decls =
                df.makeDeclarations(f.getObjects().iterator()).iterator();
        Model m = new Model("", decls);
        m.setURI(uri);
        return m;
    }
}
```

Source Code 8.10 The *Repository* class.

The default implementation of the *ReaderAdapter* interface is *ReaderAdapter-Impl*. We implement the *LoadModelAdapter* by inheriting from *ReaderAdapter-Impl* so the *LoadModelAdapter* inherits the functionality of creating *XMIObjects* and *Values* when reading an XMI document.

We can load the file containing a model by implementing the *setXMIFile()* method in the *LoadModelAdapter*. The Framework invokes the *setXMIFile()* method after processing any *Documentation* or *Model* XML elements in an XMI document, but before XML elements for user objects are processed. The *XMI-File* object the Framework creates when it loads an XMI document is a parameter in the *setXMIFile()* method. This enables us to access the *Model* information from the *XMIFile*, determine which file to load, and load the file. We can obtain the URI for the model by getting the XML namespace that has the same prefix as the name of the model. We can obtain the *Workspace* indirectly by accessing the *XMIFiles* object from the *XMIFile* object and then getting the *Workspace* from the *XMIFiles* object. Then we use the *Repository* class to load the model and add the model to the *Workspace*. The *LoadModelAdapter* class is shown in Source Code 8.11.

The *LMAdapterFactory*, which is shown in Source Code 8.12, creates a *Load-ModelAdapter*. The *LoadModel* program is shown in Source Code 8.13. Notice that no model is added to the *Workspace* before an XMI document is loaded.

```java
// LoadModelAdapter.java
import com.ibm.xmi.framework.*;
import java.util.Iterator;

// This class implements a reader adapter that loads a model based on
// the model information in an XMI document.
public class LoadModelAdapter extends ReaderAdapterImpl {

// The Framework invokes this method after loading any documentation
// or model information, but before your objects are loaded.
public void setXMIFile(XMIFile file) {
   super.setXMIFile(file);
   Workspace w = null;

   if (file.getXMIFiles() != null)
      w = file.getXMIFiles().getWorkspace();

   if (w != null) {
      Iterator models = file.getModels().iterator();
      Repository r = new Repository();

      while (models.hasNext()) {
         XMIFile.Model m = (XMIFile.Model) models.next();
         Namespace n = file.getNamespace(m.getName());
         Model frameworkModel = null;

         try {
            frameworkModel = r.load(n.getPrefix(), n.getURI(),
                                    m.getHref());
         }
         catch (Exception e) {
            e.printStackTrace();
         }

         if (frameworkModel != null)
            w.add(frameworkModel);
      }
   }
}
}
```

Source Code 8.11   The *LoadModelAdapter* class.

```
// LMAdapterFactory.java
import com.ibm.xmi.framework.*;

// This class is the adapter factory for the
// LoadModelAdapter.
public class LMAdapterFactory extends AdapterFactory {

// Return the LoadModelAdapter. This method is called
// automatically by the Framework.
public ReaderAdapter createReaderAdapter() {
   return new LoadModelAdapter();
}
}
```

Source Code 8.12   The *LMAdapterFactory* class.

```
// LoadModel.java
import com.ibm.xmi.framework.*;

// This class demonstrates that the LoadModelAdapter actually loads a
// model from a file if you don't add it to the Workspace yourself.
public class LoadModel {
   public static void main(String[] args) throws Exception {
      if (args.length != 1) {
         System.out.println("Enter the name of the file to load...");
         return;
      }

      AdapterFactoryRegister.registerAdapterFactory(
                                       new LMAdapterFactory());
      Workspace w = new Workspace();
      XMIFiles files = new XMIFiles();
      w.add(files);
      XMIFile file = files.load(args[0], XMIFile.DEFAULT, false);
      XMIContainer c = new XMIContainer(file.getObjects().iterator());
      System.out.println(c);
   }
}
```

Source Code 8.13   The *LoadModel* program.

When we run *LoadModel* with *model.xmi*, the *LoadModelAdapter* determines that the car rental agency model can be found in *cramodel.xmi* and loads it before loading the car rental agency objects in *model.xmi*. The following is the output of *LoadModel* when *model.xmi* is loaded:

```
--------------------------------

Object: CRA:Car id: _1
  definer: XMIClass CRA:Car
  isProxy: false
  namespace: 'CRA',http://mycompany.com/CarRentalAgency
  Values:
    CRA:available <ENUM> 'false'  definer: [CRA:available <ENUM> type:
        [Enumeration boolean true false] owner: [XMIClass CRA:Car]
        namespace: 'CRA',http://mycompany.com/CarRentalAgency]
        namespace: 'CRA',http://mycompany.com/CarRentalAgency
    CRA:vin <DATA> 'v1'  definer: [CRA:vin <DATA> type: [String] owner:
        [XMIClass CRA:Car] namespace:
        'CRA',http://mycompany.com/CarRentalAgency] namespace:
        'CRA',http://mycompany.com/CarRentalAgency
    CRA:driver <REF> [XMIObject CRA:Person _3]  definer: [CRA:driver
        <REF> type: [XMIClass CRA:Person] owner: [XMIClass CRA:Car]
        multiplicity: '0..n' namespace:
        'CRA',http://mycompany.com/CarRentalAgency] namespace:
        'CRA',http://mycompany.com/CarRentalAgency
    CRA:style <REF> [XMIObject CRA:Style _2]  definer: [CRA:style <REF>
        type: [XMIClass CRA:Style] owner: [XMIClass CRA:Car]
        multiplicity: '1' namespace:
        'CRA',http://mycompany.com/CarRentalAgency] namespace:
        'CRA',http://mycompany.com/CarRentalAgency

    CRA:option <OBJ> [XMIObject CRA:Option _1.1]  definer: [CRA:option
        <OBJ> type: [XMIClass CRA:Option] owner: [XMIClass CRA:Car]
        multiplicity: '0..*' namespace:
        'CRA',http://mycompany.com/CarRentalAgency] namespace:
        'CRA',http://mycompany.com/CarRentalAgency
End object: CRA:Car
--------------------------------
Object: CRA:Option id: _1.1
  definer: XMIClass CRA:Option
  isProxy: false
  namespace: 'CRA',http://mycompany.com/CarRentalAgency
  Values:
    CRA:name <DATA> 'air conditioning'  definer: [CRA:name <DATA> type:
        [String] owner: [XMIClass CRA:Option] namespace:
        'CRA',http://mycompany.com/CarRentalAgency] namespace:
        'CRA',http://mycompany.com/CarRentalAgency
    CRA:car <REF> [XMIObject CRA:Car _1]  definer: [CRA:car <REF> type:
        [XMIClass CRA:Car] owner: [XMIClass CRA:Option] multiplicity:
        '1' namespace: 'CRA',http://mycompany.com/CarRentalAgency]
        namespace: 'CRA',http://mycompany.com/CarRentalAgency
End object: CRA:Option
--------------------------------
Object: CRA:Style id: _2
  definer: XMIClass CRA:Style
  isProxy: false
```

```
            namespace: 'CRA',http://mycompany.com/CarRentalAgency
            Values:
              CRA:make <DATA> 'Jalopy'  definer: [CRA:make <DATA> type: [String]
                    owner: [XMIClass CRA:Style] namespace:
                    'CRA',http://mycompany.com/CarRentalAgency] namespace:
                    'CRA',http://mycompany.com/CarRentalAgency
              CRA:model <DATA> 'Deluxe'  definer: [CRA:model <DATA> type: [String]
                    owner: [XMIClass CRA:Style] namespace:
                    'CRA',http://mycompany.com/CarRentalAgency] namespace:
                    'CRA',http://mycompany.com/CarRentalAgency
              CRA:year <DATA> '2002'  definer: [CRA:year <DATA> type: [int] owner:
                    [XMIClass CRA:Style] namespace:
                    'CRA',http://mycompany.com/CarRentalAgency] namespace:
                    'CRA',http://mycompany.com/CarRentalAgency
              CRA:car <REF> [XMIObject CRA:Car _1]  definer: [CRA:car <REF> type:
                    [XMIClass CRA:Car] owner: [XMIClass CRA:Style] multiplicity:
                    '0..n' namespace: 'CRA',http://mycompany.com/CarRentalAgency]
                    namespace: 'CRA',http://mycompany.com/CarRentalAgency
        End object: CRA:Style
        -------------------------------
        Object: CRA:Person id: _3
          definer: XMIClass CRA:Person
          isProxy: false
          namespace: 'CRA',http://mycompany.com/CarRentalAgency
          Values:
              CRA:licenseNumber <DATA> 'ln1'  definer: [CRA:licenseNumber <DATA>
                    type: [String] owner: [XMIClass CRA:Person] namespace:
                    'CRA',http://mycompany.com/CarRentalAgency] namespace:
                    'CRA',http://mycompany.com/CarRentalAgency
              CRA:name <DATA> 'Anita Karr'  definer: [CRA:name <DATA> type:
                    [String] owner: [XMIClass CRA:Person] namespace:
                    'CRA',http://mycompany.com/CarRentalAgency] namespace:
                    'CRA',http://mycompany.com/CarRentalAgency
              CRA:car <REF> [XMIObject CRA:Car _1]  definer: [CRA:car <REF> type:
                    [XMIClass CRA:Car] owner: [XMIClass CRA:Person] multiplicity:
                    '0..n' namespace: 'CRA',http://mycompany.com/CarRentalAgency]
                    namespace: 'CRA',http://mycompany.com/CarRentalAgency
        End object: CRA:Person
        -------------------------------
```

This output indicates that the objects in *model.xmi* were correctly restored and attached to their definers, which were created from the contents of *cramodel.xmi*. This output is similar to the output of the *FrameRead2* program in Chapter 7. Please see that chapter for more details about the content. You may notice that the *available* attribute value for the *Car* object is marked not as *<DATA>*, which indicates a data value, but as *<ENUM>*. This occurs because the *DeclarationFactory* makes a Framework *enumeration* for the *Boolean* datatype in the model to support previous versions of XMI. XMI 2.0 does not require this behavior, so a future version of the Framework may not do this.

XMI Extensions

So far in this chapter, we have discussed how to use the Framework to create XMI documents that contain XML namespaces and information describing the documents. Using those capabilities of XMI helps create XMI documents that can be interpreted correctly. This section explains how to put data into an XMI document that is not to be shared with other applications. As explained in Chapter 3, XMI defines an *Extension* XML element that can be put in either an XML element that represents an object or in an *XMI* XML element.

The Framework can be used to create XMI extensions. There are two ways to do so. The Framework creates XMI extensions for you if you specify sets of tag values for an object. You can also use the *Extension* class in the Framework to create advanced extensions.

Tag values in the Framework consist of a tag and a value, each represented by a *String*. The tag identifies the value. They are similar to UML tagged values. Unlike UML tagged values, they can be grouped into sets, where each set is identified by a *String*. You can create tag values for any *XMIObject*; the tag values for one *XMIObject* are independent of the tag values that belong to other *XMIObjects*. You can use a set to distinguish tag values for your application from tag values for other applications if you use the name of your application as the name of the set.

Consider a program used by the car rental agency that tracks the last time a car was washed and the location of the car in the agency's parking lot if the car has not been rented. This information is not defined by the car rental agency model. If other programs for the car rental agency need access to this data, it should be added to the model so it can be reliably exchanged. However, no other program for the car rental agency needs this information. Because it is information that is specific to a particular program, we can put the information in an XMI extension.

To use Framework tag values, we decide that the tag *lastWashed* has a value that is the date when the car was last washed. The tag *location* has a value that is the number of the space in the parking lot where the car is parked. The program that uses this information is called *Program1*, so we put the tag values in a set called *Program1*.

The following program creates an XMI document that contains a *Car* object that has an *Extension* in it. The method *setXMITagValue()* has a set, a tag, and a value as its parameters. It sets the value for the tag and puts the tag in the given set. If the set does not exist, *setXMITagValue()* creates it. If the set already exists, the tag is added to the existing set. The program is shown in Source Code 8.14.

The following is the output from the *Extension1* program:

```
<?xml version="1.0" encoding="UTF-8"?>
<xmi:XMI xmi:version="2.0" xmlns:xmi="http://www.omg.org/XMI">
```

```
// Extension1.java
import com.ibm.xmi.framework.*;
import java.util.ArrayList;

// This program demonstrates how to set tag values for XMI objects.
public class Extension1 {
    public static void main(String[] args) throws Exception {
        XMIObject car = new XMIObjectImpl("Car");

        // Sets the "lastWashed" tag to the value "July 1, 2001".  A
        // set called "Program1" is created since it does not exist.
        // The "lastWashed" tag is added to the "Program1" set.
        car.setXMITagValue("Program1", "lastWashed", "July 1, 2001");

        // Sets the "location" tag to the value "E23" and adds it to
        // the "Program1" set.
        car.setXMITagValue("Program1", "location", "E23");

        ArrayList l = new ArrayList(1);
        l.add(car);

        XMIFile file = new XMIFile("extension1.xmi");
        file.write(l.iterator(), XMIFile.DEFAULT);
    }
}
```

Source Code 8.14   The *Extension1* program.

```
  <xmi:Documentation>
    <exporter>XMI Framework</exporter>
    <exporterVersion>1.2</exporterVersion>
  </xmi:Documentation>
<Car xmi:id="_1">
  <xmi:Extension extender="IXAF TVS" extenderID="">
    <ixafs n="Program1">
      <ixaftv t="location" v="E23"/>
      <ixaftv t="lastWashed" v="July 1, 2001"/>
    </ixafs>
  </xmi:Extension>
</Car>
</xmi:XMI>
```

Notice that the tag values were stored in an XMI extension and its *extender* attribute is *IXAF TVS* (which stands for IBM XMI Application Framework Tag Value Sets). The *Program1* set is represented by an *ixafs* XML element. Each tag value is represented by an *ixaftv* XML element.

When you use the Framework to load this document, it will restore the sets of tag values based on the contents of the extension. You can use the *getXMISets()*, *getXMITags()*, and *getXMITagValue()* methods to access the sets of tag values.

If you use the *FrameRead* program from Chapter 7 to load *extension1.xmi*, the output appears as follows:

```
--------------------------------
Object: Car id: _1
  isProxy: false
  Tag values:
    set: 'Program1' tag: 'location' value: 'E23'
    set: 'Program1' tag: 'lastWashed' value: 'July 1, 2001'
End object: Car
--------------------------------
```

This output indicates that the tag values were correctly restored.

You can create advanced extensions using the *Extension* and *XMLElement* interfaces. The *Extension* interface lets you specify the values of the *extender* and *extenderID* XML attributes for the extension, as well as the content of the extension. You can add *XMIObjects* or *XMLElements* to an extension. For each XML element, you can specify its tag name, XML attributes, and content. You can add text or an XML element to the content of an XML element using the *XMLElement* interface.

For example, consider a program called *Program2* that displays information about cars using a graphical user interface. This program needs to store the user interface data for each car, which consists of the location of the car icon on the screen, the size of the icon, its color, and the font used to label it. This information can be represented by an extension that has *Program2UIInfo* as its *extender*. The extension contains three XML elements. The first XML element has the tag name *coordinates* and has the XML attributes *x*, *y*, *width*, and *height,* which specify the location of the upper-left corner of the icon, the width of the icon, and the height. The second XML element has the tag name *color*; its content specifies the color. The third XML element has the tag name *font* and two XML attributes called *name* and *size*, which describe the font.

The *Extension2* program shown in Source Code 8.15 creates the extension and XML elements.

The output of the *Extension2* program is as follows:

```
<?xml version="1.0" encoding="UTF-8"?>
<xmi:XMI xmi:version="2.0" xmlns:xmi="http://www.omg.org/XMI">
    <xmi:Documentation>
      <exporter>XMI Framework</exporter>
      <exporterVersion>1.2</exporterVersion>
    </xmi:Documentation>
  <Car xmi:id="_1">
    <xmi:Extension extender="Program2UIInfo" extenderID="">
      <coordinates x="100" y="200" width="20" height="40"/>
```

```
// Extension2.java
import com.ibm.xmi.framework.*;
import java.util.ArrayList;

// This program demonstrates how to use the Framework to create an
// extension and add XML elements to it.
public class Extension2 {
   public static void main(String[] args) throws Exception {
      XMIObject car = new XMIObjectImpl("Car");

      // Create an extension with "Program2UIInfo" extender
      // and  "" extenderID.
      Extension ext = new ExtensionImpl("Program2UIInfo", "");
      car.add(ext);

      // Create an XML element with "coordinates" tag name.
      XMLElement coordinates = new XMLElementImpl("coordinates");
      ext.add(coordinates);

      // Set the XML attributes for the coordinates XML element
      coordinates.add("x", "100");
      coordinates.add("y", "200");
      coordinates.add("width", "20");
      coordinates.add("height", "40");

      XMLElement color = new XMLElementImpl("color");
      ext.add(color);

      // Set the contents of the color XML element to "red"
      // String.
      color.add("red");

      XMLElement font = new XMLElementImpl("font");
      ext.add(font);
      font.add("name", "Times New Roman");
      font.add("size", "10");

      ArrayList l = new ArrayList(1);
      l.add(car);

      XMIFile file = new XMIFile("extension2.xmi");
      file.write(l.iterator(), XMIFile.DEFAULT);
   }
}
```

Source Code 8.15   The *Extension2* program.

```
      <color>red</color>
      <font name="Times New Roman" size="10"/>
    </xmi:Extension>
  </Car>
</xmi:XMI>
```

If *extension2.xmi* is loaded using the *FrameRead* program, the output is as follows:

```
--------------------------------
Object: Car id: _1
  isProxy: false
  Extensions:
    extender: 'Program2UIInfo' extenderID: ''
      contents:
        XML element tag: coordinates
          attribs: [x,"100" y,"200" width,"20" height,"40"]
        XML element tag: color
          attribs: []
          contents:
            'red'
          end contents:
        XML element tag: font
          attribs: [name,"Times New Roman" size,"10"]
      end contents:
End object: Car
--------------------------------
```

This output shows that the Framework restored the extension and the XML elements inside it. You can use the *Extension* and *XMLElement* interfaces to obtain each XML element from the extension, the values of the XML attributes for each XML element, and the content of each XML element.

Using Framework tag values to create extensions is easier than using the *Extension* and *XMLElement* interfaces to create extensions. We recommend that you use tag values to create extensions if possible. If you need to make more advanced extensions, use the *Extension* interface to do so.

ZIP Files

The XMI documents we create in this book are very small; however, you might want to save many objects in an XMI document. XMI 2.0 files are smaller than the equivalent XMI 1.1 files. Nevertheless, it is still useful to reduce the size of XMI 2.0 documents by using ZIP files.

The Framework enables XMI documents to be written to an output stream that you create, and XMI documents to be read from an input stream that you create. The streams can be associated with ZIP files, ordinary files, or network connections.

It is not hard to write an XMI document to a *ZipOutputStream*. You are responsible for creating the output stream and closing it; the Framework makes an entry in the output stream, writes the document, and then closes the entry. The *XMIFile* class has a constructor that takes a *ZipOutputStream* and the name of an entry. The *ZipOut* program shown in Source Code 8.16 creates a ZIP file called *my.zip* that has an entry *c.xmi,* which is an XMI document containing a *Car* object.

You can also put multiple XMI documents in one ZIP file. You can do this because the Framework does not close the *ZipOutputStream* after it writes an XMI document. You can create as many *XMIFile* objects as you want with the same *ZipOutputStream*; in this case, an entry is created in the same ZIP file each time the Framework creates an XMI document. You are responsible for closing the *ZipOutputStream* after the last XMI document is written to the ZIP file.

```java
// ZipOut.java
import com.ibm.xmi.framework.*;
import java.util.zip.*;
import java.util.*;
import java.io.*;

// This demonstrates how to write an XMI document to a ZIP file.
public class ZipOut {
    public static void main(String[] args) throws Exception {
        XMIObject o = new XMIObjectImpl("Car");

        File zip = new File("my.zip");
        FileOutputStream fos = new FileOutputStream(zip);
        ZipOutputStream zos = new ZipOutputStream(fos);

        ArrayList l = new ArrayList();
        l.add(o);

        XMIFile f = new XMIFile(zos, "c.xmi");
        f.write(l.iterator(), XMIFile.DEFAULT);

        zos.close();
    }
}
```

Source Code 8.16 The *ZipOut* program.

There are two ways to load an XMI document from a ZIP file. The first way is to create an *InputStream* for the entry of a ZIP file to be loaded and use that *InputStream* when loading. The other way is to set the file path for an *XMIFiles* object that contains the location of a ZIP file, and then specify the entry name in the *load()* method of the *XMIFiles* object. We explain both ways.

One of the load methods in the *XMIFile* class enables the Framework to read an XMI document from an *InputStream*. To use that capability with ZIP files, you need to create an input stream for the entry in the ZIP file. The *ZipIn* program shown in Source Code 8.17 reads *c.xmi* from the *my.zip* file created by the *ZipOut* program.

The output of the *ZipIn* program, which indicates that the XMI file was successfully loaded, is as follows:

```
---------------------------------
Object: Car id: _1
  isProxy: false
End object: Car
---------------------------------
```

The second way to load from a ZIP file involves setting the file path of an *XMIFiles* object. A file path consists of a sequence of directories or ZIP files separated by semicolons. When you invoke a *load()* method for the *XMIFiles* object, the Framework searches the directories and ZIP files in the file path

```java
// ZipIn.java
import com.ibm.xmi.framework.*;
import java.util.zip.*;
import java.io.InputStream;


// This demonstrates how to read an XMIFile from a ZIP file.
public class ZipIn {
    public static void main(String[] args) throws Exception {
        ZipFile zf = new ZipFile("my.zip");
        ZipEntry ze = zf.getEntry("c.xmi");
        InputStream is = zf.getInputStream(ze);

        XMIFile f = XMIFile.load("c.xmi", is, XMIFile.DEFAULT, false);
        XMIContainer c = new XMIContainer(f.getObjects().iterator());
        System.out.println(c);

        zf.close();
    }
}
```

Source Code 8.17   The *ZipIn* program.

until the file is found. By setting the file path to a ZIP file, you can avoid creating an *InputStream* for the particular entry you want to load. The Framework will load the correct entry from the ZIP file and close the input streams that it opens.

The *ZipIn2* program shown in Source Code 8.18 sets the file path to the ZIP file *my.zip* and then loads *c.xmi*.

The output of the *ZipIn2* program is the same as the output of the *ZipIn* program.

Cross-File References

So far, the programs in this book have saved objects in a single XMI file. However, XMI enables objects to be saved in multiple XMI files. If an object in a file has a value that is an object in another file, the file contains a cross-file reference to the object in the other file. Each cross-file reference created by the Framework is similar to a simple XLink. Although XMI lets you use all of the capabilities of XLinks described in the XLink specification, the Framework does not support XLinks. This section explains how to use the Framework to create XMI files with cross-file references and how to load XMI files with cross-file references.

There are advantages and disadvantages of using this capability. Some of the disadvantages are that it adds complexity to your applications and slows the loading of files. One advantage of splitting your objects into multiple XMI files is that it gives you the opportunity to process a subset of your objects

```java
// ZipIn2.java
import com.ibm.xmi.framework.*;

// This demonstrates how to read an XMI document from a ZIP file
// by setting a file path.
public class ZipIn2 {
    public static void main(String[] args) throws Exception {
        XMIFiles files = new XMIFiles();
        files.setFilepath("my.zip");
        XMIFile f = files.load("c.xmi", XMIFile.DEFAULT, false);

        XMIContainer c = new XMIContainer(f.getObjects().iterator());
        System.out.println(c);
    }
}
```

Source Code 8.18   The *ZipIn2* program.

without loading all of them. For more discussion of the pros and cons of this approach, please see the *Cross-File References* section in Chapter 4.

When you create an *XMIFile* object, you specify the name of the XMI file that will be created when you write objects using the *XMIFile* object. Each object that is written is put in that file unless you specify a particular Framework tag value for the object. If the value part of the tag value is different than the name of the XMI file being written, the object that has the tag value is not written to the file; instead, the Framework creates a cross-file reference to the object.

Recall that a Framework tag value consists of a tag and a value, each represented by a *String*. Framework tag values are grouped in named sets. The particular tag value that determines whether an object is put in the document being written or whether a cross-file reference is created for the object has the tag name *xmiFile*. It is put in the set that has the empty *String* ("") as its name. For example, the following line of code sets the *xmiFile* tag to the value *car.xmi* for *XMIObject car1*:

```
car1.setXMITagValue("", "xmiFile", "car1.xmi");
```

The *xmiFile* tag applies to the *XMIObject* that has the tag and its contained objects, which are related to the object via composition relationships. Recall that an object value (an attribute value that is an object) has a composition relationship to the *XMIObject* that has the value. The *xmiFile* tag applies to the directly contained objects, and the contained objects in the directly contained objects, to any depth.

When the Framework creates a cross-file reference, it does not create the file that is being referred to. For example, consider what happens if the Framework writes file *file.xmi*, and it creates a cross-file reference to an object in file *file2.xmi*. At the end of writing *file.xmi*, the Framework has created *file.xmi* only; it has not created *file2.xmi* as a result of creating the cross-file reference. You can create an *XMIFile* object for *file2.xmi* and write objects to it. In fact, you should write the object in *file2.xmi* that is referenced in *file.xmi* so the cross-file reference in *file.xmi* is valid.

If the value of the *xmiFile* tag for an object matches the name of the file currently being written, a cross-file reference is not created; the object that has the tag is written to the file. For example, if an *XMIFile* object is created for file *file1.xmi* and an object has the value *file1.xmi* for its *xmiFile* tag, the object is written in *file1.xmi*.

Each cross-file reference that the Framework produces uses the object's identifier (the value of the attribute of type *ID*) and the file's name to create a URI that is put in an XML attribute named *href*. For example, if an object of class *C* is saved in a file called *f.xmi* and its identifier is *id*, a cross-file reference to this object appears as follows:

```
<C href="f.xmi#id"/>
```

In our favorite example so far in this chapter, and in the last chapter, we saved a *Car* object, a *Style* object, an *Option* object, and a *Person* object in a single XMI file. Imagine that the car rental agency needs to save information about its customers separately from information about its cars. To do so, we will save the *Person* object in a separate file from the other objects.

Because we are not saving all of our objects in the same file, we need to set the *xmiFile* tags for the objects. We name the files to be saved so we know the values to set for the *xmiFile* tags. There are two ways to set the tags. We first describe the two ways in general terms here and then explain an example using each way. The first way involves analyzing which relationships among the objects cross files and then setting the *xmiFile* tags for the objects that have such relationships. The second way is to set the *xmiFile* tag for each top-level object in each file. The cross-file references are created correctly regardless of which way you choose.

Let's look at an example of the first way using the car rental agency objects. We determine how to set the *xmiFile* tags for the objects by first naming the files to be saved and deciding which objects will go in which files. Next we examine the relationships among the objects to see which ones, if any, cross files. For this example, let's save the *Car*, *Option*, and *Style* objects in file *car.xmi* and the *Person* object in file *person.xmi*. The *Car* object is related to the *Person* object through the *driver* reference, and the two objects are to be saved in different files. To create a cross-file reference to the *Person* object when *car.xmi* is written, we need to set the *Person* object's *xmiFile* tag to *person.xmi*. Note that the *Person* object is related to the *Car* object through the *car* reference. To create a cross-file reference to the *Car* object when *person.xmi* is written, we need to set the *xmiFile* tag of the *Car* object to *car.xmi*. Since neither the *Style* object nor the *Option* object participates in a cross-file relationship, their *xmiFile* tags do not need to be set.

Now let's look at an example of the second way using the car rental agency objects. As in the previous example, let's suppose we have decided to save the *Car*, *Option*, and *Style* objects in file *car.xmi* and the *Person* object in file *person.xmi*. The *Car* and *Style* objects will be at the top level in file *car.xmi*, so we assign the value *car.xmi* to the *xmiFile* tags for the *Car* and *Style* objects. Since the *Option* object is contained in the *Car* object, and the *xmiFile* tag is set for the *Car* object, we do not need to set the *xmiFile* tag for the *Option* object. If we do set the *xmiFile* tag for the *Option* object to *car.xmi*, the Framework will still write the *Car*, *Option*, and *Style* objects to the *car.xmi* file. Since the *Person* object will be at the top level in file *person.xmi*, we assign the value *person.xmi* to the *xmiFile* tag for the *Person* object. Notice that we did not need to determine which relationships crossed files, as we did previously. Instead, we determined which objects would be at the top level in each file and set the *xmiFile* tags for each of these objects to the corresponding filename.

Now we can write a program to save the objects in the two XMI files. The program needs to set the *xmiFile* tags for the objects. We create a class *Cross-*

FileHelper that has a method that sets the tags. Using this class makes the program to save the objects less cluttered, and we can add methods to the *Cross-FileHelper* class that makes the other programs in this section less cluttered as well. The *CrossFileHelper* class is shown in Source Code 8.19.

Note that the method assigns the minimum number of *xmiFile* tags based on the analysis of the objects' relationships that cross files presented previously.

The *CrossWrite* program uses the *CRAFactory* class to make the *XMIObjects* for the *Car*, *Option*, *Style*, and *Person* objects; invokes the *assignXMIFileTags()* method to set the tag values; and then writes the *Car*, *Option*, and *Style* objects to file *car.xmi* and the *Person* object to file *person.xmi*. The program is not generic since it relies on the order of the objects in the *ArrayList* returned by the *makeFOMExample()* method that gets the *Car*, *Style*, and *Person* objects. The *CrossWrite* program is shown in Source Code 8.20.

The file *car.xmi* appears as follows (with some lines split to fit the page width). Note that this file does not contain the *Person* object. It refers to the *Person* object in the *person.xmi* file:

```
<?xml version="1.0" encoding="UTF-8"?>
<xmi:XMI xmi:version="2.0" xmlns:xmi="http://www.omg.org/XMI">
    <xmi:Documentation>
       <exporter>XMI Framework</exporter>
```

```java
// CrossFileHelper.java
import com.ibm.xmi.framework.XMIObject;
import java.util.ArrayList;
import java.util.Iterator;


// This class contains methods that make the programs to save and
// load XMI files with cross-file references less cluttered.
public class CrossFileHelper {
    // Assign car.xmi to the xmiFile tag for the Car object.
    // Assign person.xmi to the xmiFile tag for the Person object.
    public static void assignXMIFileTags(ArrayList objects) {
        Iterator i = objects.iterator();
        while (i.hasNext()) {
            XMIObject obj = (XMIObject) i.next();
            if (obj.getXMIName().equals("Car"))
                obj.setXMITagValue("", "xmiFile", "car.xmi");
            else if (obj.getXMIName().equals("Person"))
                obj.setXMITagValue("", "xmiFile", "person.xmi");
        }
    }
}
```

Source Code 8.19 The *CrossFileHelper* class.

```
// CrossWrite.java
import com.ibm.xmi.framework.*;
import java.util.*;

// This program writes the Car, Option, and Style objects to file
// car.xmi, and the Person object to person.xmi.
public class CrossWrite {
    public static void main(String[] args) throws Exception {
        ArrayList objs = new CRAFactory().makeFOMExample();
        CrossFileHelper.assignXMIFileTags(objs);

        ArrayList carObjs = new ArrayList();
        carObjs.add(objs.get(0));    // Car object
        carObjs.add(objs.get(1));    // Style object

        XMIFile f = new XMIFile("car.xmi");
        f.write(carObjs.iterator(), XMIFile.DEFAULT);

        ArrayList personObjs = new ArrayList();
        personObjs.add(objs.get(2));        // Person object

        XMIFile f2 = new XMIFile("person.xmi");
        f2.write(personObjs.iterator(), XMIFile.DEFAULT);
    }
}
```

Source Code 8.20   The *CrossWrite* program.

```
        <exporterVersion>1.2</exporterVersion>
    </xmi:Documentation>
  <Car xmi:id="_1" available="false" vin="v1" style="_2">
      <option xmi:id="_1.1" xmi:type="Option" name="air conditioning"
              car="_1"/>
      <xmi:Extension extender="IXAF TVS" extenderID="">
        <ixafs n="">
          <ixaftv t="xmiFile" v="car.xmi"/>
        </ixafs>
      </xmi:Extension>
      <driver href="person.xmi#_1.2E"/>
  </Car>
  <Style xmi:id="_2" make="Jalopy" model="Deluxe" year="2002"
         car="_1"/>
</xmi:XMI>
```

The file *person.xmi* appears as follows. Note the cross-file reference to the *Car* object in *car.xmi*:

```
<?xml version="1.0" encoding="UTF-8"?>
<xmi:XMI xmi:version="2.0" xmlns:xmi="http://www.omg.org/XMI">
```

```
      <xmi:Documentation>
        <exporter>XMI Framework</exporter>
        <exporterVersion>1.2</exporterVersion>
      </xmi:Documentation>
    <Person xmi:id="_1.2E" licenseNumber="ln1" name="Anita Karr">
      <xmi:Extension extender="IXAF TVS" extenderID="">
        <ixafs n="">
          <ixaftv t="xmiFile" v="person.xmi"/>
        </ixafs>
      </xmi:Extension>
      <car href="car.xmi#_1"/>
    </Person>
  </xmi:XMI>
```

To use the Framework to load files with cross-file references, you need to understand how the Framework handles cross-file references when a file is loaded. A cross-file reference to an object that has not been loaded yet is represented by the Framework as a *proxy object*. It is called a proxy object because it represents a reference to the actual object, but it is not the actual object referenced. When the actual object is loaded, the Framework resolves the proxy object by setting the values for the proxy object based on the values for the actual object and changing the proxy object to a normal *XMIObject*.

To resolve proxy objects, the Framework needs to track the objects that have been loaded. The *XMIFiles* class does this. By using the load methods in the *XMIFiles* class, you enable the Framework to resolve proxy objects. When the actual object is loaded from a file, a proxy object representing the actual object is resolved. There is only a single proxy object for each actual object, even if there are multiple cross-file references to the actual object. This feature ensures that if you have a reference to a proxy object, you can use the same reference to obtain the actual object after the proxy has been resolved.

When you load a file containing a cross-file reference using the *XMIFiles* class, the Framework takes one of the following actions when it loads the cross-file reference depending on the circumstances:

- The Framework creates a proxy object if the actual object has not been loaded and a proxy object has not been created yet.
- The Framework obtains the proxy object from the *XMIFiles* object if a proxy object exists, so there will only be one proxy object for an actual object.
- The Framework obtains the actual object from the *XMIFiles* object and uses it.

There are two ways to load the XMI file containing the actual object that a proxy object represents. The first way is to invoke a load method in the *XMIFiles* class for the correct file. The other way involves using a Framework feature called *demand loading*. Demand loading will load a file containing an actual object if you ask a proxy object for information that can only be obtained from the actual object. For example, if you ask a proxy object for the values of the actual object, the actual object needs to be loaded. The Framework will load the file containing the actual object, resolving the proxy by changing it to the actual object, and then return the values of the actual object. Using demand loading, your application will load files only when it is necessary, and you do not need to load the files yourself.

This proxy-handling scheme is very simple; there are many more advanced mechanisms for handling proxies. The proxy-handling scheme in the Framework enables you to experiment with cross-file references and demand loading. (IBM's Websphere Studio Application Developer software on the CD-ROM uses an advanced demand loading algorithm.)

We present three programs that demonstrate how the Framework handles cross-file references when loading files. Each program prints all the objects from the file *car.xmi* using the Framework *XMIContainer* class. If the *Car* and *Style* objects are added to an *XMIContainer* and the container is printed, the *Option* object is also printed because it is contained by the *Car* object through a composition relationship. However, the *Person* object is not printed because it is not contained in the *Car* object. To print all the objects using the Framework, it is necessary to obtain the *Person* object through its relationship with the *Car* object; put the *Car*, *Style*, and *Person* objects in the *XMIContainer*; and then print the container. Since each program needs to obtain the *Person* object from the *Car* object, we add the *getPerson()* method to the *CrossFileHelper* class. This method is shown in Source Code 8.21.

```
// The getPerson() method of the CrossFileHelper class.

// Iterate through the list of objects, and, when a Car object
// is found, obtain the Person object that is a driver for the Car.
// This method assumes that there is only one driver; however, the
// CRA model supports multiple drivers, so it won't work for
// all Car objects.
public static XMIObject getPerson(ArrayList objs) {
   Iterator i = objs.iterator();
   while (i.hasNext()) {
      XMIObject obj = (XMIObject) i.next();
      if (obj.getXMIName().equals("Car"))
         return (XMIObject) obj.getXMIValueOfValue("driver");
   }
   return null;
}
```

Source Code 8.21 The *getPerson()* method in the *CrossFileHelper* class.

The parameter to this method is a collection of objects that are the top-level objects from *car.xmi* (the *Car* and *Style* objects).

To ensure that the values of the objects in *car.xmi* are restored correctly, we need to use a *Workspace* and add the car rental agency model to it. We can obtain the model by using the *CRAModel* class from Chapter 7. The *CrossRead* program loads *car.xmi* and prints all the objects in it; the program is shown in Source Code 8.22.

```java
// CrossRead.java
import com.ibm.xmi.framework.*;
import java.util.*;

// This class demonstrates that a proxy object is created when a
// cross-file reference is loaded and the actual object has not been
// loaded yet.
public class CrossRead {
    public static void main(String[] args) throws Exception {
        // Add the CRA model to the workspace, so the values
        // can be restored correctly.
        Workspace w = new Workspace();
        Model craModel = CRAModel.makeCRAModel();
        w.add(craModel);

        // Add XMIFiles object to the workspace.
        XMIFiles files = new XMIFiles();
        w.add(files);

        XMIFile file = files.load("car.xmi", XMIFile.DEFAULT, false);

        // Since the collection returned by getObjects() is not
        // modifiable, copy the top-level objects to a list.
        ArrayList objs = new ArrayList();
        objs.addAll(file.getObjects());

        // Add the Person object to the list.
        XMIObject p = CrossFileHelper.getPerson(objs);
        if (p != null)
            objs.add(p);

        // Print the objects.
        XMIContainer c = new XMIContainer(objs.iterator());
        System.out.println(c);
    }
}
```

Source Code 8.22 The *CrossRead* program.

The following is the output of the *CrossRead* program, formatted to fit the width of the page. Note that the *Person* object is a proxy because the actual *Person* object in *person.xmi* was not loaded.

```
-------------------------------
Object: Car id: _1
  definer: XMIClass Car
  isProxy: false
  Tag values:
    set: '' tag: 'xmiFile' value: 'car.xmi'
  Values:
    available <DATA> 'false'
         definer: [available <DATA> owner: [XMIClass Car]]
    vin <DATA> 'v1'  definer: [vin <DATA> owner: [XMIClass Car]]
    style <REF> [XMIObject Style _2]
         definer: [style <REF> type: [XMIClass Style]
         owner: [XMIClass Car]]
    option <OBJ> [XMIObject Option _1.1]
         definer: [option <OBJ> type: [XMIClass Option]
         owner: [XMIClass Car]]
    driver <REF> [XMIObject Person _1.2E]
         definer: [driver <REF> type: [XMIClass Person]
         owner: [XMIClass Car]]
End object: Car
-------------------------------
Object: Option id: _1.1
  definer: XMIClass Option
  isProxy: false
  Values:
    name <DATA> 'air conditioning'
         definer: [name <DATA> owner: [XMIClass Option]]
    car <REF> [XMIObject Car _1]
         definer: [car <REF> type: [XMIClass Car]
         owner: [XMIClass Option]]
End object: Option
-------------------------------
Object: Style id: _2
  definer: XMIClass Style
  isProxy: false
  Values:
    make <DATA> 'Jalopy'  definer: [make <DATA>
         owner: [XMIClass Style]]
    model <DATA> 'Deluxe'
         definer: [model <DATA> owner: [XMIClass Style]]
    year <DATA> '2002'  definer: [year <DATA>
         owner: [XMIClass Style]]
    car <REF> [XMIObject Car _1]
         definer: [car <REF> type: [XMIClass Car]
         owner: [XMIClass Style]]
```

```
End object: Style
---------------------------------
Object: Person id: _1.2E
  href:    person.xmi#_1.2E
  definer: XMIClass Person
  isProxy: true
End object: Person
---------------------------------
```

Since the *Person* object is a proxy object, it does not have the values for the actual object.

If both the *car.xmi* and *person.xmi* files are loaded using the same *XMIFiles* object, the *Person* object that is a proxy object is resolved to the actual *Person* object. The *CrossRead2* program shown in Source Code 8.23 demonstrates this.

The output of the *CrossRead2* program shows that the *Person* object is no longer a proxy object; its values have been filled in (since the *Car*, *Style*, and *Option* objects are identical to the output of the *CrossRead* program, they have been omitted):

```
---------------------------------
Object: Person id: _1.2E
  href:    person.xmi#_1.2E
  definer: XMIClass Person
  isProxy: false
  Tag values:
    set: '' tag: 'xmiFile' value: 'person.xmi'
  Values:
    licenseNumber <DATA> 'ln1'
      definer: [licenseNumber <DATA> owner: [XMIClass Person]]
    name <DATA> 'Anita Karr'
      definer: [name <DATA> owner: [XMIClass Person]]
    car <REF> [XMIObject Car _1]
      definer: [car <REF> type: [XMIClass Car] owner: [XMIClass Person]]
End object: Person
---------------------------------
```

Rather than explicitly loading *person.xmi*, we can invoke a method on the *Person* proxy object that will cause the Framework to load *person.xmi* to obtain the actual object. The *CrossRead3* program invokes the *getXMIValues()* method on the proxy object to cause demand loading to occur. The *CrossRead3* program appears in Source Code 8.24.

The output of the *CrossRead3* program is identical to the output of the *CrossRead2* program. You can run the *CrossRead3* program yourself to verify this.

If you do not want demand loading to occur, you can turn it off for a particular *XMIFiles* object.

```
// CrossRead2.java
import com.ibm.xmi.framework.*;
import java.util.*;

// This class demonstrates that the Framework resolves a proxy object
// if the file containing the actual object is explicitly loaded.
public class CrossRead2 {
    public static void main(String[] args) throws Exception {
        // Add the CRA model to the workspace so the values can be
        // restored correctly.
        Workspace w = new Workspace();
        Model craModel = CRAModel.makeCRAModel();
        w.add(craModel);

        // Add the XMIFiles object to the workspace.
        XMIFiles files = new XMIFiles();
        w.add(files);

        // Load both car.xmi and person.xmi
        XMIFile file1 = files.load("car.xmi", XMIFile.DEFAULT, false);
        XMIFile file2 = files.load("person.xmi", XMIFile.DEFAULT, false);

        // Obtain the top-level objects from car.xmi and add it to a
        // list
        ArrayList objs = new ArrayList();
        objs.addAll(file1.getObjects());

        // Obtain the Person object and add it to the list.
        XMIObject p = CrossFileHelper.getPerson(objs);
        if (p != null)
            objs.add(p);

        // Print the objects.
        XMIContainer c = new XMIContainer(objs.iterator());
        System.out.println(c);
    }
}
```

Source Code 8.23 The *CrossRead2* program.

Code Generation

As mentioned in Chapter 4, the Framework generates Java code from a UML model. This capability is useful because it enables you to create objects with simple interfaces derived from your model, rather than using the more abstract *XMIObject* and *Value* interfaces. The generated code creates a Framework model from the UML model. Using the generated code requires you to

```java
// CrossRead3.java
import com.ibm.xmi.framework.*;
import java.util.*;

// This class demonstrates that the Framework resolves a proxy when
// it loads the file containing the actual object during demand
// loading.
public class CrossRead3 {
   public static void main(String[] args) throws Exception {
      // Add the CRA model to the workspace so the values can
      // be restored correctly.
      Workspace w = new Workspace();
      Model craModel = CRAModel.makeCRAModel();
      w.add(craModel);

      // Add the XMIFiles object to the workspace.
      XMIFiles files = new XMIFiles();
      w.add(files);

      XMIFile file = files.load("car.xmi", XMIFile.DEFAULT, false);

      // Put the top-level objects from car.xmi in a list.
      ArrayList objs = new ArrayList();
      objs.addAll(file.getObjects());

      // Obtain the Person object and add it to the list; trigger
      // demand loading by invoking getXMIValues() for the Person
      // object.
      XMIObject p = CrossFileHelper.getPerson(objs);
      if (p != null) {
         p.getXMIValues(); // Triggers demand load
         objs.add(p);
      }

      // Print the objects.
      XMIContainer c = new XMIContainer(objs.iterator());
      System.out.println(c);
   }
}
```

Source Code 8.24 The *CrossRead3* program.

know less about the Framework interfaces than using the Framework interfaces directly.

We explain how to generate code from the Framework, and then we explain the interfaces and highlight the implementations of those interfaces that result from code generation. It is not our intention to describe all aspects of Framework code generation here, but we hope to give you an overview of the code you get. This will help you understand some of the issues you face when using generated code created by XMI software or when you implement your own code generation software.

To generate Java code from the Framework, you need to have a UML model in XMI format. The *UML2Java* program enables you to run the code generation from the command line. We will generate code for the car rental agency model that is stored in *cramodel.xmi*. We put the code in Java package *cra* (car rental agency). Then we explain how to use the generated code to load and save the car rental agency objects. After we do that, we explain some details about the implementation of the generated interfaces.

How to Generate Java Code

The Framework generates code from an XMI representation of a UML model. There are numerous options you can use when generating code. We will not explain all of them here, but we will explain the options that we use to generate the code from the car rental agency model. You can run the *UML2Java* program from the command line with no arguments to get a complete list of all the code generation options along with a brief description of each one.

We use the following code generation options when we run *UML2Java* from the command line:

-package cra.   This option tells the Framework to put the generated code in the given Java package.

-namespaceName CRA.   This option tells the Framework to use this namespace prefix.

-namespaceURI http://mycompany.com/CarRentalAgency.   This option tells the Framework to use this namespace URI.

-interfaces.   This option tells the Framework to generate a Java interface and a Java class for each class in the model (if this option is not specified, the Framework creates a Java class for each class in the model).

-oneConstructor.   This option tells the Framework to generate a single no argument constructor for the generated Java class.

We also need to tell the Framework which file contains the model. In our case, the model is in *cramodel.xmi*. We use the *-model* option to indicate the file that contains the model. The following is the complete command-line invocation of the *UML2Java* program:

```
java com.ibm.xmi.framework.UML2Java
        -model cramodel.xmi
        -package cra
        -namespaceName CRA
```

```
-namespaceURI http://mycompany.com/CarRentalAgency
-interfaces
-oneConstructor
```

The Framework creates a *cra* directory in the directory where *UML2Java* is invoked, and it places the generated Java code in that directory. You can then compile the generated code. Now that you know how to generate the code, let's see how to use it.

The Generated Interfaces

If you look at the generated code, you will observe that there is an interface for each class in the car rental agency model. The interfaces are located in files *Car.java*, *Option.java*, *Person.java*, and *Style.java*. There are three methods in each interface for each association end. There are either two or three methods for each attribute, depending on the attribute's multiplicity. If the maximum multiplicity is *1*, there are two methods. If the maximum multiplicity is greater than *1*, there are three methods. We explain in detail the generated methods for attributes and association ends in this section.

We start by explaining the three methods that are generated for each association end. The three methods enable you to add a referenced object, get the referenced objects, and delete a referenced object for a particular object. For example, the *Person* class in the car rental agency model has a *car* association end. The following are the method signatures for the three methods in the *Person* interface that correspond to the *car* association end:

```
public Collection getCar();
public void addCar(Car object);
public void removeCar(Car object);
```

The *getCar()* method enables you to get all the *Car* objects that are referenced objects for a *Person* object via the *Person* object's *car* reference. If there are no such objects, an empty *Collection* is returned. The *addCar()* method makes a *Car* object a referenced object for a *Person* object via the *Person* object's *car* reference. The *removeCar()* method removes a *Car* object from being a referenced object for a *Person* object via the *Person* object's *car* reference.

A current limitation of the Framework is that it generates these three methods regardless of the multiplicity of the association end. If the maximum multiplicity of the association end is *1*, it would suffice to generate get and set methods to get and set the one referenced object. This would prevent multiple referenced objects from being specified. It is possible that a later version of the Framework will have this enhancement.

For object attributes with a maximum multiplicity greater than *1*, three methods are generated just like the three methods that are generated for an association end. For example, the *Car* class has an *option* object attribute with a multiplicity of *0..**. The three methods in the *Car* interface for the *option* object attribute are as follows:

```
public Collection getOption();
public void addOption(Option object);
public void removeOption(Option object);
```

For each attribute with a maximum multiplicity of *1*, the Framework creates two accessor methods: a get method that returns the attribute value and a set method that sets the attribute value. We show examples of these two methods for some of the data attributes in the car rental agency model.

The Framework maps *integer*, *float*, and *boolean* datatypes in a model to the Java datatypes *int*, *float*, and *boolean*, respectively, regardless of the capitalization of the names in the model. The Framework maps all other datatypes in a model to the Java class *java.lang.String*. Table 8.1 summarizes this mapping.

Consider the *make* data attribute for the *Style* UML class in the car rental agency model. The Framework generates the following two methods in the *Style* interface:

```
public String getMake();
public void setMake(String value);
```

If the Framework maps the type of a data attribute to the Java *boolean* type, the get accessor method name does not begin with *get*; it begins with *is* instead to follow Java coding conventions. For example, the *available* data attribute in the *Car* class in the car rental agency model has type *Boolean*, so the Framework generates the following two methods for the *Car* interface corresponding to the *available* data attribute:

```
public boolean isAvailable();
public void setAvailable(boolean value);
```

For each generated interface, the Framework creates a Java class that implements the interface. The name of the class is the name of the interface followed

Table 8.1   Framework Datatype Mapping

MODEL DATATYPE NAME (CAPITALIZATION IGNORED)	GENERATED JAVA TYPE
int, integer	int
float	float
boolean	boolean

by *Impl*. For example, the *OptionImpl* class implements the *Option* interface.

The Framework also generates a *UserFactory* class. We explain this class in the next section.

Now that we know what the generated interfaces are for the car rental agency model, we can use them to work with XMI documents.

Using the Generated Code

In this section, we explain how to use the generated code to work with XMI documents. You can use the generated interfaces to create objects without using the *XMIObject* and *Value* interfaces directly. You can use the factory generated by the Framework to create a Framework model, and then register that model with the Framework. This causes the Framework to create instances of the generated classes when loading an XMI document rather than generic *XMIObjects*.

Consider how to use the generated code to make the car rental agency objects and save them in an XMI document. We can accomplish this task by using the generated interfaces and classes to create the objects, and then by passing those objects to an *XMIFile* object. The *GeneratedWrite* program in Source Code 8.25 accomplishes this task.

Notice that the only Framework class you need to use is *XMIFile*.

The *generated.xmi* file has the following contents (we split lines that were too long for the page width):

```
<?xml version="1.0" encoding="UTF-8"?>
<xmi:XMI xmi:version="2.0" xmlns:xmi="http://www.omg.org/XMI"
        xmlns:CRA="http://mycompany.com/CarRentalAgency">
    <xmi:Documentation>
      <exporter>XMI Framework</exporter>
      <exporterVersion>1.2</exporterVersion>
    </xmi:Documentation>
  <CRA:Car xmi:id="_1" available="false" vin="v1" style="_2"
          driver="_3">
    <option xmi:id="_1.1" name="air conditioning" car="_1"/>
  </CRA:Car>
  <CRA:Style xmi:id="_2" make="Jalopy" model="Deluxe" year="2002"
          car="_1"/>
  <CRA:Person xmi:id="_3" name="Anita Karr" licenseNumber="ln1"
          car="_1"/>
</xmi:XMI>
```

Although we did not create Framework namespaces and assign them before writing the objects, the namespace we specified during code generation is used correctly. That is one advantage of using the generated code.

You may have noticed that a *UserFactory* class is created when the Framework generates code from a UML model. This class is an instance of the

```
//GeneratedWrite.java
import cra.*;
import com.ibm.xmi.framework.XMIFile;
import java.util.ArrayList;


// This program demonstrates how to use generated code to create
// objects to be written to an XMI document.
public class GeneratedWrite {
   public static void main(String[] args) throws Exception {
      Car car = new CarImpl();
      Option option = new OptionImpl();
      Person person = new PersonImpl();
      Style style = new StyleImpl();

      car.setAvailable(false);
      car.setVin("v1");
      car.addStyle(style);
      car.addDriver(person);
      car.addOption(option);

      option.setName("air conditioning");
      option.addCar(car);

      person.setName("Anita Karr");
      person.setLicenseNumber("ln1");
      person.addCar(car);

      style.setMake("Jalopy");
      style.setModel("Deluxe");
      style.setYear(2002);
      style.addCar(car);

      ArrayList objs = new ArrayList();
      objs.add(car);
      objs.add(style);
      objs.add(person);

      XMIFile f = new XMIFile("generated.xmi");
      f.write(objs.iterator(), XMIFile.DEFAULT);
   }
}
```

Source Code 8.25 The *GeneratedWrite* program.

Framework *Factory* class. It is shown in Source Code 8.26. When you make an instance of this class, it registers itself with the Framework. That way, when the Framework loads an XMI document, it creates instances of the generated classes rather than the *XMIObjectImpl* class.

The *UserFactory* class creates instances of the generated classes when the *makeXMIObject()* methods are invoked. The first *makeXMIObject()* method uses a *HashMap* called *ixafntc*, which relates XMI names to Java *Class* objects. If there is no entry in that *HashMap*, the method looks up the correct class name from an XMI name using the *HashMap* called *ixafntcn*, and then invokes *Class.for-Name()* to obtain the Java Class object. If the class is found, it creates an entry in the *HashMap* called *ixafntc,* so the *Class.forName()* method does not need to be invoked multiple times for the same class. The *HashMap* called *ixafntcn* is initialized in the *init()* method. That method is invoked by the first *makeXMIObject()* method if it needs to use the *HashMap* called *ixafntcn* and it has not been initialized yet; that is why the *init()* method is not invoked in the constructor of the *UserFactory* class.

```
package cra;

import com.ibm.xmi.framework.*;
import com.ibm.xmi.framework.Package;
import java.util.*;

public class UserFactory extends FactoryAdapter {
   static private Model ixafm;

   static private HashMap ixafntc, ixafntcn;

   public UserFactory() {
     FactoryRegister.registerFactory(this);
   }

   private void init() {
     ixafntcn = new HashMap();
     ixafntcn.put("CRA:Car", "cra.CarImpl");
     ixafntcn.put("Car", "cra.CarImpl");
     ixafntcn.put("CRA:Person", "cra.PersonImpl");
     ixafntcn.put("Person", "cra.PersonImpl");
     ixafntcn.put("CRA:Style", "cra.StyleImpl");
     ixafntcn.put("Style", "cra.StyleImpl");
     ixafntcn.put("CRA:Option", "cra.OptionImpl");
     ixafntcn.put("Option", "cra.OptionImpl");
   }

   public XMIObject makeXMIObject(String xmiName) {
     if (ixafntc == null)
       ixafntc = new HashMap();
```

Source Code 8.26   A generated *UserFactory* class.

```
    java.lang.Class cls = (java.lang.Class) ixafntc.get(xmiName);

  if (cls == null) {
    if (ixafntcn == null)
      init();

    String name = (String) ixafntcn.get(xmiName);

    try {
      if (name != null)
        cls = java.lang.Class.forName(name);
    }
    catch (ClassNotFoundException e) {}

    if (cls != null)
      ixafntc.put(xmiName, cls);
  }

  if (cls == null)
    return super.makeXMIObject(xmiName);
  else {
    java.lang.Object o = null;

    try {
      o = cls.newInstance();
    }
    catch (Exception e) {}

    return (XMIObject) o;
  }
}

public XMIObject makeXMIObject(String xmiName,
                        com.ibm.xmi.framework.Namespace n) {
  if (n.getPrefix() == null || n.getPrefix().equals(""))
    return makeXMIObject(xmiName);
  else
    return makeXMIObject(n.getPrefix() + ":" + xmiName);
}

public Model getModel() {
  if (ixafm != null)
    return ixafm;

  ixafm = new Model("cramodel");

  try {
```

Source Code 8.26 A generated *UserFactory* class. (*Continued*)

```
com.ibm.xmi.framework.Namespace ixafn1 = new
            com.ibm.xmi.framework.Namespace("CRA",
                "http://mycompany.com/CarRentalAgency");
XMIClass CRA_Car = makeXMIClass(null, "Car");
CRA_Car.setXMINamespace(ixafn1);
XMIClass CRA_Person = makeXMIClass(null, "Person");
CRA_Person.setXMINamespace(ixafn1);
XMIClass CRA_Style = makeXMIClass(null, "Style");
CRA_Style.setXMINamespace(ixafn1);
XMIClass CRA_Option = makeXMIClass(null, "Option");
CRA_Option.setXMINamespace(ixafn1);


com.ibm.xmi.framework.Feature ixaff;
ixaff = makeFeature(CRA_Car, "vin", null, Value.DATA,
                null);
ixaff.setXMINamespace(ixafn1);
ixaff = makeFeature(CRA_Car, "available", null,
                Value.ENUM, null);
ixaff.setXMINamespace(ixafn1);
ixaff = makeFeature(CRA_Car, "option", CRA_Option,
                Value.OBJECT, null);
ixaff.setXMINamespace(ixafn1);
ixaff = makeFeature(CRA_Car, "driver", CRA_Person,
                Value.REFERENCE, null);
ixaff.setXMINamespace(ixafn1);
ixaff = makeFeature(CRA_Car, "style", CRA_Style,
                Value.REFERENCE, null);
ixaff.setXMINamespace(ixafn1);


ixaff = makeFeature(CRA_Person, "name", null, Value.DATA,
                null);
ixaff.setXMINamespace(ixafn1);
ixaff = makeFeature(CRA_Person, "licenseNumber", null,
                Value.DATA, null);
ixaff.setXMINamespace(ixafn1);
ixaff = makeFeature(CRA_Person, "car", CRA_Car,
                Value.REFERENCE, null);
ixaff.setXMINamespace(ixafn1);


ixaff = makeFeature(CRA_Style, "make", null, Value.DATA,
                null);
ixaff.setXMINamespace(ixafn1);
ixaff = makeFeature(CRA_Style, "model", null, Value.DATA,
                null);
ixaff.setXMINamespace(ixafn1);
ixaff = makeFeature(CRA_Style, "year", null, Value.DATA,
                null);
```

Source Code 8.26 A generated *UserFactory* class. (*Continued*)

```
        ixaff.setXMINamespace(ixafn1);
        ixaff = makeFeature(CRA_Style, "car", CRA_Car,
                        Value.REFERENCE, null);
        ixaff.setXMINamespace(ixafn1);

        ixaff = makeFeature(CRA_Option, "name", null, Value.DATA, null);
        ixaff.setXMINamespace(ixafn1);
        ixaff = makeFeature(CRA_Option, "car", CRA_Car, Value.REFERENCE,
                        null);
        ixaff.setXMINamespace(ixafn1);

        ixafm.add(CRA_Car);
        ixafm.add(CRA_Person);
        ixafm.add(CRA_Style);
        ixafm.add(CRA_Option);

    } catch(XMIException e) {
      e.printStackTrace();
    }
    return ixafm;
  }

} // UserFactory
```

Source Code 8.26   A generated *UserFactory* class. (*Continued*)

The *getModel()* method of the *UserFactory* class returns the Framework model corresponding to the UML model. It creates the model once and reuses the existing model when *getModel()* is invoked again. The *getModel()* method returns the model if it has already been created. Otherwise, it creates the classes, sets their namespaces, and then creates the features of the classes and sets their namespace. Note that the *makeFeature()* method adds the new feature to the given class. Then the *getModel()* method adds the created classes to the model. The *getModel()* method creates a variable for each created class based on the name of the class and the namespace prefix, if there is one. To avoid potential name collisions, the other variables in the *UserFactory* class begin with a prefix of *ixaf*.

You can use the *UserFactory* class to create a model to register with a *Workspace* before loading an XMI document. The *GeneratedRead* program shown in Source Code 8.27 demonstrates the use of the generated *UserFactory* class.

You can run this program yourself to verify that the output is correct. Notice that you do not need to make a Framework model yourself; the generated *UserFactory* makes a Framework model for you.

```
// GeneratedRead.java
import cra.*;
import com.ibm.xmi.framework.*;
import java.util.*;

// This program demonstrates the use of a generated UserFactory
// class when an XMI document is loaded.
public class GeneratedRead {
    public static void main(String[] args) throws Exception {
        Workspace w = new Workspace();
        UserFactory f = new UserFactory();
        w.add(f.getModel());

        XMIFiles files = new XMIFiles();
        w.add(files);

        XMIFile file = files.load("generated.xmi", XMIFile.DEFAULT,
                                   false);

        XMIContainer c = new XMIContainer(file.getObjects().iterator());
        System.out.println(c);
    }
}
```

Source Code 8.27   The *GeneratedRead* program.

Understanding the Implementation Classes

Now that you have seen how to use the generated code, we make some general observations about the Framework's implementation of the generated interfaces and the *UserFactory* class. It is not our intention to describe all aspects of the implementations, but we will make some observations about the general way that the code works. We also explain alternative strategies that you might employ for your own generated code. You can skip this section if you are not interested in the details of the generated code.

Each interface the Framework makes inherits from the *XMIObject* Framework interface, and each implementation class inherits from *XMIObjectImpl*. The constructor for each implementation class sets the XMI name appropriately, sets the namespace for the object if necessary, and sets the definer of the class. This ensures that the Framework will serialize the object correctly.

The implementations of the accessor methods work with Framework *Value* objects. They use the *XMIObject* interface methods to add, set, and delete

Framework *Value* objects. They also set the definer for newly created *Value* objects so the Framework serializes the *Value* objects correctly. One advantage of this approach is that the user does not need to be aware of the creation of *Value* objects. Source Code 8.28 shows the generated implementation class for the *Style* interface.

```
package cra;

import com.ibm.xmi.framework.*;
import java.util.*;
import cra.UserFactory;

public class StyleImpl extends XMIObjectImpl implements Style {
  private com.ibm.xmi.framework.Model getXMIModel() {
    cra.UserFactory f;

    if (FactoryRegister.getFactory() instanceof cra.UserFactory)
      f = (cra.UserFactory) FactoryRegister.getFactory();
    else
      f = new cra.UserFactory();

    return f.getModel();
  }

  public StyleImpl() {
    super();
    try { setXMIName("Style"); } catch (XMIException e) {}
    com.ibm.xmi.framework.Model m = getXMIModel();
    com.ibm.xmi.framework.Namespace n = new
                  com.ibm.xmi.framework.Namespace("CRA",
                  "http://mycompany.com/CarRentalAgency");
    com.ibm.xmi.framework.Data definer = m.getDeclaration(n,
                  WriterAdapter.CLASS, "Style", false);
    try { setXMIDefiner(definer); } catch (XMIException e) {};
  }

  public String getMake() {
    return (String) getXMIValueOfValue("CRA:make");
  }

  public void setMake(String value) {
    com.ibm.xmi.framework.Value p = setXMIValue("CRA:make", value,
                                          Value.DATA);
```

Source Code 8.28 A generated implementation class for the *Style* interface.

```
   if (p.getXMIDefiner() == null) {
     com.ibm.xmi.framework.Model m = getXMIModel();
     com.ibm.xmi.framework.Namespace n = new
            com.ibm.xmi.framework.Namespace("CRA",
            "http://mycompany.com/CarRentalAgency");
     com.ibm.xmi.framework.Data definer = m.getDeclaration(n,
            getXMIDefiner(), "make", false);
     try { p.setXMIDefiner(definer); } catch (XMIException e) {};
   }
}

public String getModel() {
  return (String) getXMIValueOfValue("CRA:model");
}

public void setModel(String value) {
  com.ibm.xmi.framework.Value p = setXMIValue("CRA:model", value,
                                              Value.DATA);

  if (p.getXMIDefiner() == null) {
    com.ibm.xmi.framework.Model m = getXMIModel();
    com.ibm.xmi.framework.Namespace n = new
           com.ibm.xmi.framework.Namespace("CRA",
           "http://mycompany.com/CarRentalAgency");
    com.ibm.xmi.framework.Data definer = m.getDeclaration(n,
           getXMIDefiner(), "model", false);
    try { p.setXMIDefiner(definer); } catch (XMIException e) {};
  }
}

public int getYear() {
  return Integer.valueOf((String)
           getXMIValueOfValue("CRA:year")).intValue();
}

public void setYear(int value) {
  com.ibm.xmi.framework.Value p = setXMIValue("CRA:year",
                          String.valueOf(value), Value.DATA);

  if (p.getXMIDefiner() == null) {
    com.ibm.xmi.framework.Model m = getXMIModel();
    com.ibm.xmi.framework.Namespace n = new
           com.ibm.xmi.framework.Namespace("CRA",
           "http://mycompany.com/CarRentalAgency");
    com.ibm.xmi.framework.Data definer = m.getDeclaration(n,
           getXMIDefiner(), "year", false);
    try { p.setXMIDefiner(definer); } catch (XMIException e) {};
```

Source Code 8.28 A generated implementation class for the *Style* interface. (*Continued*)

```
    }
  }

  public Collection getCar() {
    java.lang.Object v = getXMIValueOfValue("car");
    if (v instanceof java.util.Collection)
      return (Collection) v;
    ArrayList l = new ArrayList(1);
    if (v instanceof XMIObject)
      l.add(v);
    return l;
  }

  public void addCar(Car object) {
    com.ibm.xmi.framework.Value l = addXMIValue("car", object,
                                          Value.REFERENCE);

    if (l.getXMIDefiner() == null) {
      com.ibm.xmi.framework.Model m = getXMIModel();
      com.ibm.xmi.framework.Namespace n = new
                com.ibm.xmi.framework.Namespace("CRA",
                "http://mycompany.com/CarRentalAgency");
      com.ibm.xmi.framework.Data definer = m.getDeclaration(n,
                getXMIDefiner(), "car", false);
      try { l.setXMIDefiner(definer); } catch (XMIException e) {};
    }
  }

  public void removeCar(Car object) {
    java.lang.Object v = getXMIValueOfValue("car");
    if (v == object)
      try { delete(getXMIValue("car")); } catch (XMIException e) {};
    if (v instanceof Collection) {
      ((Collection) v).remove(object);
      if (((Collection) v).size() == 0)
        try { delete(getXMIValue("car")); } catch (XMIException e) {};
    }
  }

} // StyleImpl
```

Source Code 8.28 A generated implementation class for the *Style* interface. (*Continued*)

A drawback to this approach is that getting and setting values is not as efficient as it could be because it requires the creation and setting of *Value* objects. The *Value* objects are actually only required when the Framework serializes objects. A more efficient approach would be for the implementation of the accessor methods to be simpler, using a field in each implementation class to store the values. Then each implementation class could implement the *getXMIValues()* method of the *XMIObject* interface and create the *Value* objects in the implementation of that method. This approach makes getting and setting values efficient, and the serialization of the objects slightly less efficient. It also makes loading an XMI document more complicated, but that extra complication may be worth the price for greater efficiency in setting and getting object values.

Summary

Now you know how to use the Framework to work with XMI files that contain namespaces, information describing your documents, extensions, and cross-file references. You also know how to put XMI documents in ZIP files and load them from ZIP files using the Framework, as well as how to generate Java code using the Framework. Although the Framework functionality is simple, using it can help you to understand the kinds of services that XMI software can provide for you. Now that you know how to use the Framework to work with XMI documents, you are ready to learn how to use the Framework to create schemas.

XMI Schemas

The previous three chapters explain how to work with XML Metadata Interchange (XMI) documents. This chapter explains how to create XMI schemas using the XMI Framework so that Extensible Markup Language (XML) parsers can perform XML validation on your XMI documents. This chapter also explains how to perform XML validation when you load an XMI document with the Framework.

Although Chapter 3 describes in detail how to create XMI schemas, it doesn't describe the kinds of errors that can be detected by using validation with schemas or how your choices to tailor the schemas affect validation. This chapter gives you more insight into whether validation is useful in your applications and whether tailoring the default schemas to detect more errors is necessary.

This chapter uses the XMI Framework. The capabilities of the XMI Framework are described in Chapter 7 and Chapter 8. This chapter also uses software from those chapters, so you should refer to those chapters for more information about the Framework. Additional information on the Framework is provided in Appendix A.

Creating XMI Schemas

The Framework creates XMI schemas, but it does not support the XMI tags that enable you to tailor the schemas you create. At this time, you can use the Framework to create default XMI schemas. You can also supply a namespace Uniform Resource Identifier (URI) and a namespace prefix by adding a Framework namespace to the Framework representation of a model; if the Framework supports the XMI tags in the future, you will also be able to specify a namespace by using the *nsURI* and *nsPrefix* tags (remember that XMI tags have the prefix *org.omg.xmi*, which we are omitting for brevity).

In this chapter, we examine how to create a schema for the car rental agency model using the Framework. Then we discuss how to use the generated schema to validate an XMI document when loading the document with the Framework. We demonstrate that validation occurs by loading an XMI document that is a well-formed XML document, but that also contains data that is not defined by the car rental agency model and therefore not defined by the schema generated from the model. Unless XML validation is done when the document is loaded, the parser does not report an error.

Creating an XMI Schema with the *XMISchema* Framework Class

The *XMISchema* class in the Framework represents an XMI schema. You specify a filename when you create an *XMISchema* object, and then you invoke the *write()* method to create a schema. The parameter for the *write()* method is an *Iterator* for the declarations in the model (classes, features, and packages in a model are called declarations in the Framework). If you create a schema with a target namespace, you must set the target namespace (using the *setTargetNamespace()* method) before invoking the *write()* method.

Recall from Chapter 7 that the Framework represents packages and classes in a model using the *Package* and *XMIClass* interfaces. The attributes and association ends of a class are represented by interfaces that inherit from the *Feature* interface. Chapter 7 includes a Java class called *CRAModel* that has a method that uses the Framework interfaces to create a Framework representation for the car rental agency model.

In this chapter, we modify the *CRAModel* class by adding a method that assigns a namespace to the declarations in a Framework model. Then we use that method to create the Framework declarations to put in the schema.

As in Chapter 8, we use a namespace with a namespace URI of *http://mycompany.com/CarRentalAgency* and a namespace prefix of *CRA*.

The *addNamespace()* method that we add to the *CRAModel* class assigns the given namespace to each declaration in the given model:

```
// Method added to CRAModel.java

// Adds the given Namespace to the declarations in the given Model.
public static void addNamespace(Namespace n, Model m)
     throws Exception {
   Iterator decls = m.getDeclarations().iterator();

   while (decls.hasNext()) {
      Data decl = (Data) decls.next();
      decl.setXMINamespace(n);
   }
}
```

We can use that method in the following *CRASchema* program to create a default XMI schema for the car rental agency model:

```
// CRASchema.java
import com.ibm.xmi.framework.*;
import java.util.*;

// This program demonstrates how to create a schema from the
// Framework representation of a model.
public class CRASchema {
    public static void main(String[] args) throws Exception {
        Model m = CRAModel.makeCRAModel();
        Namespace n = new Namespace("CRA",
                       "http://mycompany.com/CarRentalAgency");
        CRAModel.addNamespace(n, m);

        XMISchema schema = new XMISchema("cra.xsd");
        schema.setTargetNamespace(n);
        schema.write(m.getDeclarations().iterator());
    }
}
```

Notice that the target namespace of the *XMISchema* is set before writing the schema because the current version of the Framework requires it to be set. The content of the file *cra.xsd* is as follows:

```
<?xml version="1.0" encoding="UTF-8"?>
<xsd:schema xmlns:xsd="http://www.w3.org/2001/XMLSchema"
            xmlns:xmi="http://www.omg.org/XMI"
            xmlns="http://mycompany.com/CarRentalAgency"
            targetNamespace="http://mycompany.com/CarRentalAgency">

<xsd:import namespace="http://www.omg.org/XMI"
            schemaLocation="xmi20.xsd"/>

<xsd:annotation>
```

```
      <xsd:documentation>CLASS: Car</xsd:documentation>
  </xsd:annotation>

  <xsd:complexType name="Car">
    <xsd:choice minOccurs="0" maxOccurs="unbounded">
      <xsd:element name="vin" type="xsd:string" nillable="true"/>
      <xsd:element name="available" type="xsd:string" nillable="true"/>
      <xsd:element name="option" type="xmi:Any"/>
      <xsd:element name="style" type="xmi:Any"/>
      <xsd:element name="driver" type="xmi:Any"/>
      <xsd:element ref="xmi:Extension"/>
    </xsd:choice>
    <xsd:attribute ref="xmi:id"/>
    <xsd:attributeGroup ref="xmi:ObjectAttribs"/>
    <xsd:attribute name="vin" type="xsd:string" use="optional"/>
    <xsd:attribute name="available" type="xsd:string" use="optional"/>
    <xsd:attribute name="style" type="xsd:IDREFS" use="optional"/>
    <xsd:attribute name="driver" type="xsd:IDREFS" use="optional"/>
  </xsd:complexType>

  <xsd:element name="Car" type="Car"/>

  <xsd:annotation>
    <xsd:documentation>CLASS: Style</xsd:documentation>
  </xsd:annotation>

  <xsd:complexType name="Style">
    <xsd:choice minOccurs="0" maxOccurs="unbounded">
      <xsd:element name="make" type="xsd:string" nillable="true"/>
      <xsd:element name="model" type="xsd:string" nillable="true"/>
      <xsd:element name="year" type="xsd:string" nillable="true"/>
      <xsd:element name="car" type="xmi:Any"/>
      <xsd:element ref="xmi:Extension"/>
    </xsd:choice>
    <xsd:attribute ref="xmi:id"/>
    <xsd:attributeGroup ref="xmi:ObjectAttribs"/>
    <xsd:attribute name="make" type="xsd:string" use="optional"/>
    <xsd:attribute name="model" type="xsd:string" use="optional"/>
    <xsd:attribute name="year" type="xsd:string" use="optional"/>
    <xsd:attribute name="car" type="xsd:IDREFS" use="optional"/>
  </xsd:complexType>

  <xsd:element name="Style" type="Style"/>

  <xsd:annotation>
    <xsd:documentation>CLASS: Person</xsd:documentation>
  </xsd:annotation>

  <xsd:complexType name="Person">
    <xsd:choice minOccurs="0" maxOccurs="unbounded">
      <xsd:element name="name" type="xsd:string" nillable="true"/>
```

```
        <xsd:element name="licenseNumber" type="xsd:string"
                     nillable="true"/>
        <xsd:element name="car" type="xmi:Any"/>
        <xsd:element ref="xmi:Extension"/>
    </xsd:choice>
    <xsd:attribute ref="xmi:id"/>
    <xsd:attributeGroup ref="xmi:ObjectAttribs"/>
    <xsd:attribute name="name" type="xsd:string" use="optional"/>
    <xsd:attribute name="licenseNumber" type="xsd:string"
                   use="optional"/>
    <xsd:attribute name="car" type="xsd:IDREFS" use="optional"/>
</xsd:complexType>

<xsd:element name="Person" type="Person"/>

<xsd:annotation>
  <xsd:documentation>CLASS: Option</xsd:documentation>
</xsd:annotation>

<xsd:complexType name="Option">
  <xsd:choice minOccurs="0" maxOccurs="unbounded">
    <xsd:element name="name" type="xsd:string" nillable="true"/>
    <xsd:element name="car" type="xmi:Any"/>
    <xsd:element ref="xmi:Extension"/>
  </xsd:choice>
  <xsd:attribute ref="xmi:id"/>
  <xsd:attributeGroup ref="xmi:ObjectAttribs"/>
  <xsd:attribute name="name" type="xsd:string" use="optional"/>
  <xsd:attribute name="car" type="xsd:IDREFS" use="optional"/>
</xsd:complexType>

<xsd:element name="Option" type="Option"/>

</xsd:schema>
```

If you do not set the Framework datatype for an attribute, the Framework uses the schema *string* datatype. Notice also that the Framework set the default namespace for the schema to the target namespace rather than using the namespace prefix *CRA*. If there are aspects of this schema that you do not understand, please read the *Generating Schemas from Models* section in Chapter 3, which explains XMI schemas in detail, or read the *Schemas* section in Chapter 2, which explains XML schemas.

Validating Documents with the Framework

Now that we have an XMI schema, we can use it to validate an XMI document when we load one with the Framework. To do this, we need to specify the schema location for the car rental agency namespace and the XMI namespace in the XMI document so that the parser can locate the schemas that will be used. In Chapter 8, we discuss a program called *NamespaceWrite* that creates an XMI document called *namespace.xmi*, which has the following content:

```
<?xml version="1.0" encoding="UTF-8"?>
<xmi:XMI xmi:version="2.0" xmlns:xmi="http://www.omg.org/XMI"
        xmlns:CRA="http://mycompany.com/CarRentalAgency">
    <xmi:Documentation>
      <exporter>XMI Framework</exporter>
      <exporterVersion>1.2</exporterVersion>
    </xmi:Documentation>
  <CRA:Car xmi:id="_1" available="false" vin="v1" driver="_3"
          style="_2">
    <option xmi:id="_1.1" xmi:type="CRA:Option" name="air conditioning"
          car="_1"/>
  </CRA:Car>
  <CRA:Style xmi:id="_2" make="Jalopy" model="Deluxe" year="2002"
          car="_1"/>
  <CRA:Person xmi:id="_3" licenseNumber="ln1" name="Anita Karr"
          car="_1"/>
</xmi:XMI>
```

We need to add the schema location for the car rental agency namespace and the XMI namespace so that the XML parser can locate the schemas that will be used when validating the file. We can use the *schemaLocation* attribute to do this. The value of that attribute consists of pairs of information; each pair consists of a namespace URI and the file that contains the namespace. We include the schema *xmi20.xsd* on the CD-ROM; the target namespace of that schema is the XMI namespace. We created the schema *cra.xsd* with the CRASchema program. The updated content appears as follows (some lines have been split to fit the page):[1]

```
<?xml version="1.0" encoding="UTF-8"?>
<xmi:XMI xmi:version="2.0" xmlns:xmi="http://www.omg.org/XMI"
        xmlns:CRA="http://mycompany.com/CarRentalAgency"
        xmlns:xsi="http://www.w3.org/2001/XMLSchema-instance"
        xsi:schemaLocation="http://www.omg.org/XMI xmi20.xsd
                    http://mycompany.com/CarRentalAgency cra.xsd">
    <xmi:Documentation>
      <exporter>XMI Framework</exporter>
      <exporterVersion>1.2</exporterVersion>
    </xmi:Documentation>
  <CRA:Car xmi:id="_1" available="false" vin="v1" driver="_3"
          style="_2">
    <option xmi:id="_1.1" xmi:type="CRA:Option" name="air conditioning"
          car="_1"/>
  </CRA:Car>
  <CRA:Style xmi:id="_2" make="Jalopy" model="Deluxe" year="2002"
```

```
                car="_1"/>
  <CRA:Person xmi:id="_3" licenseNumber="ln1" name="Anita Karr"
                car="_1"/>
</xmi:XMI>
```

Notice that the *schemaLocation* attribute is declared in the schema instance namespace, so we declare that namespace as well. We put this updated content in the file *valid.xmi* to avoid confusion with the *namespace.xmi* file from Chapter 8.

Once this is done, we can load *valid.xmi* using the Framework and instruct the Framework to perform validation when the document is loaded. In Chapters 7 and 8, we use the program *FrameRead*, which loads a document, puts the objects in a Framework container, and prints the container. In this chapter, we modify that program to create the program *ValidateRead*, which performs schema validation. The only change we need to make to *FrameRead* to perform validation is to set the validation parameter of the *load()* method of the *XMIFile* class to *true*. To run *ValidateRead*, the XMI document and all the schemas need to be in the directory where *ValidateRead* is run. The following is the source code for *ValidateRead*:

```java
// ValidateRead.java
import com.ibm.xmi.framework.XMIFile;
import com.ibm.xmi.framework.XMIContainer;

// This class parses an XMI document and then puts the XMIObjects the
// Framework made into an XMIContainer so they can be printed. It
// performs XML validation on the XMI document.
public class ValidateRead {
    public static void main(String[] args) throws Exception {
        if (args.length != 1) {
            System.out.println("Enter the name of an XMI document.");
            return;
        }

        XMIFile file = XMIFile.load(args[0], XMIFile.DEFAULT, true);
        XMIContainer c = new XMIContainer(file.getObjects().iterator());
        System.out.println(c);
    }
}
```

Running *ValidateRead* with *valid.xmi* results in the expected output—the document is loaded and each *XMIObject* and *Value* created by the Framework is printed. You can verify this yourself by running the program.

The file *valid.xmi* validates correctly with the generated schema. Let's create an XMI document that is well-formed, but does not validate. To do so, we add an XML attribute called *invalid* to the *Car* XML element in *valid.xmi*. We give *invalid* a value called *anything*. Then we put this content in a file called *invalid.xmi* (as before, some lines have been split to fit the page):

```
<?xml version="1.0" encoding="UTF-8"?>
<xmi:XMI xmi:version="2.0" xmlns:xmi="http://www.omg.org/XMI"
        xmlns:CRA="http://mycompany.com/CarRentalAgency"
        xmlns:xsi="http://www.w3.org/2001/XMLSchema-instance"
        xsi:schemaLocation="http://www.omg.org/XMI xmi20.xsd
                    http://mycompany.com/CarRentalAgency cra.xsd">
    <xmi:Documentation>
      <exporter>XMI Framework</exporter>
      <exporterVersion>1.2</exporterVersion>
    </xmi:Documentation>
  <CRA:Car xmi:id="_1" available="false" vin="v1" driver="_3"
          style="_2" invalid="anything">
    <option xmi:id="_1.3" xmi:type="CRA:Option" name="air conditioning"
          car="_1"/>
  </CRA:Car>
  <CRA:Style xmi:id="_2" make="Jalopy" model="Deluxe" year="2002"
            car="_1"/>
  <CRA:Person xmi:id="_3" licenseNumber="ln1" name="Anita Karr"
            car="_1"/>
</xmi:XMI>
```

When *ValidateRead* loads *invalid.xmi*, it reports the following error:

```
org.xml.sax.SAXParseException: Attribute "invalid" must be
declared for element type "CRA:Car".
```

This demonstrates that *ValidateRead* is performing validation. If *FrameRead*, which does not perform validation, loads *invalid.xmi*, the document loads without a parser error.

Validating with XMI Schemas

As we demonstrated in the last section, XMI schemas can be used to perform XML validation with XMI documents, although you are not required to do so. However, XML validation cannot perform semantic checking; it can only perform syntactic checking. This section explains the types of errors that XML validation with XMI schemas detects, so you can decide whether to use XML validation.

XML Validation

Before discussing which types of checking can be done by XMI schemas, it is useful to review which types of checking can be done by XML schemas. There are three kinds of checking that can be done for any XML document:

Well-formed document checking. Is the XML document well formed according to the XML 1.0 specification? For example, do all begin tags have corresponding end tags? All XML parsers are required to perform this level of checking.

Syntactic checking. Does the syntax of an XML document conform to a schema? For example, are the correct number and type of XML elements nested inside other XML elements? XML parsers that perform validation do this checking.

Semantic checking. Does the XML document reflect the semantics of the data being represented? To accomplish this checking, the minimum necessary processing is to match the data in an XML document with a definition of the data and determine whether the data conforms to the semantics expressed in the definition. For XMI, the objects in a model are compared to a model that defines the objects, enabling semantic checking.

Schemas enable more powerful syntactic checking than Document Type Definitions (DTDs), but they do not enable semantic checking. More semantic checking can be done by matching objects in an XML document with a Unified Modeling Language (UML) model. This is because there is a loss of information when creating a schema from a model. For example, if there is multiple inheritance in the model, it cannot be directly mapped to schemas by using schema extension because a schema type can extend only one other type. As a result, you cannot determine all of the superclasses of a class by examining the corresponding type declaration in a schema.

XML parsers that perform XML validation with XML schemas can detect the following kinds of errors:

- Incorrectly nested XML elements
- An incorrect number of nested XML elements
- XML elements that appear in an incorrect order
- XML elements that are in the document, but are not declared in the schema
- XML attributes that are not declared
- XML attributes with values that are not legal

Some of these errors are reported only if strict validation is performed, rather than lax or skip validation. For example, if lax validation is performed for an XML element, a validating parser does not report an error for XML attributes and nested XML elements that are not declared in a schema. If a declaration exists for them and they do not match the declaration, then a validating parser reports an error with lax validation.

Errors Detected by Default XMI Schemas

XMI schemas specify that the *XMI* XML element is validated using strict validation. The XML elements corresponding to object values and references are validated using skip validation by default. In terms of the objects and values that are written in an XMI document and the models that define them, default XMI schemas detect the following kinds of errors when used with XML validation:

- Top-level objects that are not defined by a model
- XML attributes and elements that do not correspond to UML attributes or association ends in a model
- Incorrect references to objects within an XMI document
- Incorrect XML attributes specified for the XML elements defined by XMI

We already saw an example of the second type of error from this list in a previous section. In that example, we started with a document named *valid.xmi* and added an XML attribute named *invalid* to an XML element representing a *Car* object. This resulted in a parser validation error because the attribute did not correspond to a UML attribute or association end in the *Car* class from the car rental agency model. Note that in contrast to this situation, XMI specifies that lax validation is performed for *Extension* XML elements, so you can put additional information in them that is not defined in a model without causing a parser error during validation.

We'll now look at examples of some of the other kinds of errors in the list by creating variations of the *valid.xmi* document we used before. We'll also see the error messages that arise when these variations are loaded with the *Validate-Read* program.

Consider the XMI document *error1.xmi*:

```
<?xml version="1.0" encoding="UTF-8"?>
<xmi:XMI xmi:version="2.0" xmlns:xmi="http://www.omg.org/XMI"
         xmlns:CRA="http://mycompany.com/CarRentalAgency"
         xmlns:xsi="http://www.w3.org/2001/XMLSchema-instance"
         xsi:schemaLocation="http://www.omg.org/XMI xmi20.xsd
                     http://mycompany.com/CarRentalAgency cra.xsd">
    <xmi:Documentation>
      <exporter>XMI Framework</exporter>
      <exporterVersion>1.2</exporterVersion>
    </xmi:Documentation>
  <CRA:NoClass xmi:id="_1"/>
</xmi:XMI>
```

The *NoClass* XML element should correspond to an object that is an instance of a class from the car rental agency model. However, there is not a class in that model called *NoClass*. This is an example of a top-level object that is not defined by a model. *ValidateRead* reports the following error when it loads *error1.xmi*:

```
org.xml.sax.SAXParseException: Element type "CRA:NoClass"
must be declared.
```

Consider *error2.xmi*, which contains a *Car* element that has a *driver* attribute that is supposed to have the value _2, the value of the *xmi:id* attribute of the *Person* element. The value is incorrectly specified without the leading under-score as 2:

```
<?xml version="1.0" encoding="UTF-8"?>
<xmi:XMI xmi:version="2.0" xmlns:xmi="http://www.omg.org/XMI"
         xmlns:CRA="http://mycompany.com/CarRentalAgency"
         xmlns:xsi="http://www.w3.org/2001/XMLSchema-instance"
         xsi:schemaLocation="http://www.omg.org/XMI xmi20.xsd
                        http://mycompany.com/CarRentalAgency cra.xsd">
    <xmi:Documentation>
      <exporter>XMI Framework</exporter>
      <exporterVersion>1.2</exporterVersion>
    </xmi:Documentation>
  <CRA:Car xmi:id="_1" driver="2"/>
  <CRA:Person xmi:id="_2" car="_1"/>
</xmi:XMI>
```

Since 2 is not a valid XML identifier (XML identifiers cannot begin with a number), *ValidateRead* reports the following error when *error2.xmi* is loaded:

```
org.xml.sax.SAXParseException: Datatype error: Value '2' is
not a valid IDREF.
```

Errors Detected by Tailored XMI Schemas

You can tailor XMI schemas so that parsers detect the following errors that they do not detect when using default XMI schemas:

- Incorrect object values
- Incorrect numbers of values and references
- Incorrect data values

Use the *useSchemaExtensions* tag to detect the first kind of error, the *enforceMinimumMultiplicity* and *enforceMaximumMultiplicity* tags to detect the second kind of error, and the *schemaType* tag to detect the third kind of error.

To show you how to tailor schemas to detect these errors, we present two simple models and the default XMI schemas for those models, and explain how to tailor the schemas to detect these three kinds of errors. We cannot use the Framework to create the tailored schemas because it does not currently handle XMI tags. However, we can use the *ValidateRead* program to load XMI documents that use the tailored schemas to verify that they detect these errors.

Consider the *Car1* model in Figure 9.1. It consists of a *Car* class with a *wheel* object attribute that has the class *Wheel* as its type. The multiplicity of the *wheel* attribute is *4..4*. *FancyWheel* is a subclass of *Wheel*. For XMI documents containing instances of the classes in Figure 9.1, we can use a namespace URI of *http://Car1* and a namespace prefix of *CAR1*.

We can create the Framework model for the *Car1* UML model and generate the default XMI schema for it, placing the schema in the file *car1.xsd* as follows:

```
<?xml version="1.0" encoding="UTF-8"?>
<xsd:schema xmlns:xsd="http://www.w3.org/2001/XMLSchema"
            xmlns:xmi="http://www.omg.org/XMI"
            xmlns="http://Car1"
            targetNamespace="http://Car1">

<xsd:import namespace="http://www.omg.org/XMI"
            schemaLocation="xmi20.xsd"/>

<xsd:annotation>
  <xsd:documentation>CLASS: Car</xsd:documentation>
</xsd:annotation>

<xsd:complexType name="Car">
  <xsd:choice minOccurs="0" maxOccurs="unbounded">
    <xsd:element name="wheel" type="xmi:Any"/>
    <xsd:element ref="xmi:Extension"/>
  </xsd:choice>
```

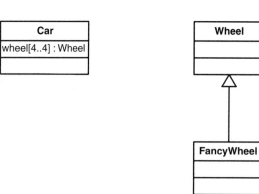

Figure 9.1 The *Car1* model.

```
      <xsd:attribute ref="xmi:id"/>
      <xsd:attributeGroup ref="xmi:ObjectAttribs"/>
    </xsd:complexType>


    <xsd:element name="Car" type="Car"/>


    <xsd:annotation>
      <xsd:documentation>CLASS: Wheel</xsd:documentation>
    </xsd:annotation>


    <xsd:complexType name="Wheel">
      <xsd:choice minOccurs="0" maxOccurs="unbounded">
        <xsd:element ref="xmi:Extension"/>
      </xsd:choice>
      <xsd:attribute ref="xmi:id"/>
      <xsd:attributeGroup ref="xmi:ObjectAttribs"/>
    </xsd:complexType>


    <xsd:element name="Wheel" type="Wheel"/>


    <xsd:annotation>
      <xsd:documentation>CLASS: FancyWheel</xsd:documentation>
    </xsd:annotation>


    <xsd:complexType name="FancyWheel">
      <xsd:choice minOccurs="0" maxOccurs="unbounded">
        <xsd:element ref="xmi:Extension"/>
      </xsd:choice>
      <xsd:attribute ref="xmi:id"/>
      <xsd:attributeGroup ref="xmi:ObjectAttribs"/>
    </xsd:complexType>


    <xsd:element name="FancyWheel" type="FancyWheel"/>


    </xsd:schema>
```

We do not include the program that creates this schema because it is similar to the *CRASchema* program we presented in the first section of this chapter. We do include the schemas and XMI documents covered in this section on the CD-ROM.

Consider the XMI document *car1A.xmi* that contains a *Car* object and a *Wheel* object:

```
<?xml version="1.0" encoding="UTF-8"?>
<xmi:XMI xmi:version="2.0" xmlns:xmi="http://www.omg.org/XMI"
         xmlns:CAR1="http://Car1"
         xmlns:xsi="http://www.w3.org/2001/XMLSchema-instance"
         xsi:schemaLocation="http://www.omg.org/XMI xmi20.xsd
                             http://Car1 car1.xsd">
    <CAR1:Car>
```

```
      <wheel/>
    </CAR1:Car>
  </xmi:XMI>
```

When *ValidateRead* loads *car1A.xmi*, no parser error is reported even though there is only one wheel because default XMI schemas do not enforce multiplicities.

Now consider the XMI document *car1B.xmi* that contains a *Car* object with the correct number of values for the *wheel* attribute; however, the last value is a *Car* object rather than a *Wheel* object:

```
<?xml version="1.0" encoding="UTF-8"?>
<xmi:XMI xmi:version="2.0" xmlns:xmi="http://www.omg.org/XMI"
         xmlns:CAR1="http://Car1"
         xmlns:xsi="http://www.w3.org/2001/XMLSchema-instance"
         xsi:schemaLocation="http://www.omg.org/XMI xmi20.xsd
                             http://Car1 car1.xsd">
  <CAR1:Car>
    <wheel/>
    <wheel/>
    <wheel/>
    <wheel xmi:type="CAR1:Car"/>
  </CAR1:Car>
</xmi:XMI>
```

When *ValidateRead* loads *car1B.xmi*, no parser error is reported because the parser cannot detect an incorrect value for the *type* attribute in the XMI namespace. If the *xsi:type* attribute is used instead, a parser error is detected because the parser can determine from the schema that the *Car* complex type is not related to the *Wheel* complex type by schema extension.

We can create a schema that detects both kinds of errors. To do so, we set the *enforceMinimumMultiplicity* and *enforceMaximumMultiplicity* tags to *true* for the *Car* class in the *Car1* UML model. We also set the *useSchemaExtensions* tag to *true* for the *Wheel* class and *FancyWheel* class. The XMI schema that results, *car1_strict.xsd*, is as follows:

```
<?xml version="1.0" encoding="UTF-8"?>
<xsd:schema xmlns:xsd="http://www.w3.org/2001/XMLSchema"
            xmlns:xmi="http://www.omg.org/XMI"
            xmlns="http://Car1"
            targetNamespace="http://Car1">

<xsd:import namespace="http://www.omg.org/XMI"
            schemaLocation="xmi20.xsd"/>

<xsd:annotation>
  <xsd:documentation>CLASS: Car</xsd:documentation>
</xsd:annotation>
```

```
<xsd:complexType name="Car">
  <xsd:sequence>
    <xsd:element name="wheel" minOccurs="4" maxOccurs="4"
                 type="Wheel"/>
    <xsd:element ref="xmi:Extension" minOccurs="0"
                 maxOccurs="unbounded"/>
  </xsd:sequence>
  <xsd:attribute ref="xmi:id"/>
  <xsd:attributeGroup ref="xmi:ObjectAttribs"/>
</xsd:complexType>

<xsd:element name="Car" type="Car"/>

<xsd:annotation>
  <xsd:documentation>CLASS: Wheel</xsd:documentation>
</xsd:annotation>

<xsd:complexType name="Wheel">
  <xsd:choice minOccurs="0" maxOccurs="unbounded">
    <xsd:element ref="xmi:Extension"/>
  </xsd:choice>
  <xsd:attribute ref="xmi:id"/>
  <xsd:attributeGroup ref="xmi:ObjectAttribs"/>
</xsd:complexType>

<xsd:element name="Wheel" type="Wheel"/>

<xsd:annotation>
  <xsd:documentation>CLASS: FancyWheel</xsd:documentation>
</xsd:annotation>

<xsd:complexType name="FancyWheel">
  <xsd:complexContent>
    <xsd:extension base="Wheel"/>
  </xsd:complexContent>
</xsd:complexType>

<xsd:element name="FancyWheel" type="FancyWheel"/>

</xsd:schema>
```

Notice that the *FancyWheel* type declaration extends the *Wheel* type declaration.

We create a new XMI document called *car1A_strict.xmi* that is the same as *car1A.xmi* except that *car1_strict.xsd* is specified in the *schemaLocation* attribute. The file *car1A_strict.xmi* is as follows:

```
<?xml version="1.0" encoding="UTF-8"?>
<xmi:XMI xmi:version="2.0" xmlns:xmi="http://www.omg.org/XMI"
```

```
                  xmlns:CAR1="http://Car1"
                  xmlns:xsi="http://www.w3.org/2001/XMLSchema-instance"
                  xsi:schemaLocation="http://www.omg.org/XMI xmi20.xsd
                                      http://Car1 car1_strict.xsd">
    <CAR1:Car>
      <wheel/>
    </CAR1:Car>
  </xmi:XMI>
```

When *ValidateRead* loads *car1A_strict.xmi*, it reports the following error:

```
org.xml.sax.SAXParseException: The content of element type "CAR1:Car"
is incomplete, it must match "(wheel,wheel,wheel,wheel,Extension*)".
```

This demonstrates that the tailored schema is correctly enforcing multiplicities.

We create the XMI document *car1B_strict.xmi* with the same contents as *car1B.xmi* except that it specifies the *car1_strict.xsd* schema in the *schemaLocation* attribute. Also, rather than using the *xmi:type* attribute, the *xsi:type* attribute is used because extension is used. The file *car1B_strict.xmi* appears as follows:

```
<?xml version="1.0" encoding="UTF-8"?>
<xmi:XMI xmi:version="2.0" xmlns:xmi="http://www.omg.org/XMI"
         xmlns:CAR1="http://Car1"
         xmlns:xsi="http://www.w3.org/2001/XMLSchema-instance"
         xsi:schemaLocation="http://www.omg.org/XMI xmi20.xsd
                             http://Car1 car1_strict.xsd">
  <CAR1:Car>
    <wheel/>
    <wheel/>
    <wheel/>
    <wheel xsi:type="CAR1:Car"/>
  </CAR1:Car>
</xmi:XMI>
```

When *ValidateRead* loads *car1B_strict.xmi*, it reports the following error:

```
org.xml.sax.SAXParseException: General Schema Error: Type :
http://Car1,Car does not derive from the type http://Car1,Wheel.
```

This demonstrates that the tailored schema can detect incorrect values for an object attribute.

We included the *FancyWheel* class in the *Car1* model, so you can verify that *car1_strict.xsd* allows a *FancyWheel* object to be a value for the wheel attribute. The file *car1C_strict.xmi* is identical to *car1B_strict.xmi* except that the value of the *xsi:type* attribute of the last *wheel* attribute is *CAR1:FancyWheel*:

```
<?xml version="1.0" encoding="UTF-8"?>
<xmi:XMI xmi:version="2.0" xmlns:xmi="http://www.omg.org/XMI"
```

```
              xmlns:CAR1="http://Car1"
              xmlns:xsi="http://www.w3.org/2001/XMLSchema-instance"
              xsi:schemaLocation="http://www.omg.org/XMI xmi20.xsd
                                  http://Car1 car1_strict.xsd">
    <CAR1:Car>
      <wheel/>
      <wheel/>
      <wheel/>
      <wheel xsi:type="CAR1:FancyWheel"/>
    </CAR1:Car>
  </xmi:XMI>
```

When *car1C_strict.xmi* is loaded with *ValidateRead,* no parser error occurs, indicating that *car1_strict.xsd* allows a *FancyWheel* object to be the value of the *wheel* attribute.

To demonstrate how tailoring a schema can detect an illegal attribute value, consider the model *Car2* shown in Figure 9.2. It has a *Car* class with one attribute, *year,* which has *Integer* as its type. We use the namespace URI *http://Car2* for this model. The Framework creates the following default XMI schema for this model in file *car2.xsd*:

```
<?xml version="1.0" encoding="UTF-8"?>
<xsd:schema xmlns:xsd="http://www.w3.org/2001/XMLSchema"
            xmlns:xmi="http://www.omg.org/XMI"
            xmlns="http://Car2"
            targetNamespace="http://Car2">

<xsd:import namespace="http://www.omg.org/XMI"
            schemaLocation="xmi20.xsd"/>

<xsd:annotation>
  <xsd:documentation>CLASS: Car</xsd:documentation>
</xsd:annotation>

<xsd:complexType name="Car">
  <xsd:choice minOccurs="0" maxOccurs="unbounded">
    <xsd:element name="year" type="xsd:string" nillable="true"/>
    <xsd:element ref="xmi:Extension"/>
  </xsd:choice>
  <xsd:attribute ref="xmi:id"/>
  <xsd:attributeGroup ref="xmi:ObjectAttribs"/>
```

Figure 9.2 The *Car2* model.

```
    <xsd:attribute name="year" type="xsd:string" use="optional"/>
</xsd:complexType>

<xsd:element name="Car" type="Car"/>

</xsd:schema>
```

Notice that the type for *year* is the schema *string* datatype rather than the schema *int* datatype because the Framework maps datatypes in a model to the schema *string* datatype. Now consider the file *car2.xmi*, where the *year* attribute is given the illegal value *this year*:

```
<?xml version="1.0" encoding="UTF-8"?>
<xmi:XMI xmi:version="2.0" xmlns:xmi="http://www.omg.org/XMI"
        xmlns:CAR2="http://Car2"
        xmlns:xsi="http://www.w3.org/2001/XMLSchema-instance"
        xsi:schemaLocation="http://www.omg.org/XMI xmi20.xsd
                            http://Car2 car2.xsd">
  <CAR2:Car year="this year"/>
</xmi:XMI>
```

When *ValidateRead* loads *car2.xmi*, no parser error is reported.

If the *schemaType* tag is set to *int* for the *Integer* datatype in the *Car2* model, XMI specifies the XMI schema *car2_strict.xsd*:

```
<?xml version="1.0" encoding="UTF-8"?>
<xsd:schema xmlns:xsd="http://www.w3.org/2001/XMLSchema"
            xmlns:xmi="http://www.omg.org/XMI"
            xmlns="http://Car2"
            targetNamespace="http://Car2">

<xsd:import namespace="http://www.omg.org/XMI"
            schemaLocation="xmi20.xsd"/>

<xsd:annotation>
  <xsd:documentation>CLASS: Car</xsd:documentation>
</xsd:annotation>

<xsd:complexType name="Car">
  <xsd:choice minOccurs="0" maxOccurs="unbounded">
    <xsd:element name="year" type="xsd:int" nillable="true"/>
    <xsd:element ref="xmi:Extension"/>
  </xsd:choice>
  <xsd:attribute ref="xmi:id"/>
  <xsd:attributeGroup ref="xmi:ObjectAttribs"/>
  <xsd:attribute name="year" type="xsd:int" use="optional"/>
```

```
</xsd:complexType>

<xsd:element name="Car" type="Car"/>

</xsd:schema>
```

Notice that the type of the XML element and the XML attribute corresponding to the *year* attribute is now *xsd:int*.

The file *car2_strict.xmi* is the same as *car2.xmi* except that *car2_strict.xsd* is specified in the *schemaLocation* attribute so that schema is used by the parser when it performs XML validation:

```
<?xml version="1.0" encoding="UTF-8"?>
<xmi:XMI xmi:version="2.0" xmlns:xmi="http://www.omg.org/XMI"
         xmlns:CAR2="http://Car2"
         xmlns:xsi="http://www.w3.org/2001/XMLSchema-instance"
         xsi:schemaLocation="http://www.omg.org/XMI xmi20.xsd
                             http://Car2 car2_strict.xsd">
  <CAR2:Car year="this year"/>
</xmi:XMI>
```

When *ValidateRead* loads *car2_strict.xmi*, the following parser error is reported:

```
org.xml.sax.SAXParseException: Datatype error: 'this year' is not a
decimal.
```

This demonstrates that you can tailor a schema to detect illegal attribute values by using the *schemaType* tag.

Summary

You can use the XMI Framework to produce XMI schemas by representing your models using Framework interfaces and classes like *XMIClass*, *Model*, and *Package*. You can validate an XMI document when you load it with the Framework. The default schemas specified by XMI can be used to perform some checking, but more checking can be performed if you tailor the schemas.

The last four chapters have provided a variety of examples that describe the kinds of programs you can write that work with XMI. The next chapter explains how XMI fits into a broad strategy for using models in software development and how XMI can be used with models that are not UML models.

Model Driven Architecture (MDA) and XMI

In this chapter, we examine the role that XML Metadata Interchange (XMI) plays in the Model Driven Architecture (MDA), a new software development approach that leverages the open standards that have been developed by the Object Management Group (OMG), the World Wide Web Consortium (W3C), and others. After introducing MDA, we examine the advantages it has over more traditional software development techniques. As an example of the many types of modeling that fall under the MDA approach, we introduce the Flow Composition Model (FCM) and examine how it can be used by software developers to describe the data and control flows among application components in a software system. Finally, we develop an FCM model for an extension of the car broker domain example that we introduced in Chapter 4. By doing this, we show how a new application can be built that leverages an existing legacy application—in this case, an application that manages the inventory for a car dealer. The integration points of this example utilize XMI. If you have not read Chapter 4, the introduction that we give to the car broker example in this chapter is sufficient to understand how we extend the example here.

Compared to most of the earlier chapters in this book, this chapter is written at a higher, more conceptual level. Although understanding the technical details presented in the earlier chapters will enhance your understanding of the material we present in this chapter, you can still get a general understanding of MDA and the role XMI plays in it without having read all of the preceding chapters. We recommend, however, that you do read Chapter 1 prior to reading this chapter so that you have a basic introduction to XMI. Also, if you have no prior experience with software modeling, you may want to read the sections of Chapter 2 that describe the Unified Modeling Language (UML). Since we show XMI files in this chapter, if you do read this chapter without having read all of the earlier material, you may want to selectively read parts of it again after learning more about XMI, as this may enhance your understanding of the topics we present.

What Is the Model Driven Architecture?

Since its founding in 1990, the focus of the OMG has been on the development of open standards that facilitate the integration of multivendor and multilanguage software systems. To this end, the OMG successfully developed interoperability standards for the Object Management Architecture (OMA). Building upon this, and recognizing the introduction of new technologies like Java and XML, the scope of the OMG has more recently expanded.

Beginning in 1997, the OMG issued several new specifications, including the following:

- UML, which we introduced in Chapter 2.
- The Meta Object Facility (MOF), which provides a universal way of describing modeling constructs (known as *metamodels*).
- XMI, a standard for the representation, sharing, and interchange of data and meta data.
- The Common Warehouse Metamodel (CWM), which includes a metamodel for relational data modeling.
- The Enterprise Distributed Object Computing (EDOC) Profile, which includes a model for FCM, Java, and Enterprise JavaBeans (EJB).
- The Enterprise Application Integration (EAI) specification. The EAI specification defines models for messages, C, C++, and COBOL, and provides datatype mappings between mixed languages, facilitating access to enterprise applications.

In addition to these, the Java Metadata Interface (JMI), an upcoming standard from the Java Community Process, provides standard Java interfaces for software models.

To effectively define the relationships among these new standards (and those yet to come) and provide a roadmap for how they can be used in a coordinated fashion, the OMG has expanded its original vision of the OMA. This new architecture is what is known as MDA.

The MDA approach is based on using abstraction techniques to effectively manage the high level of complexity that arises in software development. As its name suggests, MDA achieves this by utilizing *modeling*. In Chapter 2, we provide a basic introduction to UML, and throughout the book, we present examples of how modeling can serve as a useful way to provide an abstraction for a problem domain. Since the models we have seen have been depicted in UML class and object diagrams, you might wonder if *any* pictorial representation of a problem can serve as a model for the purpose of MDA. If not, what restrictions apply?

As defined by the OMG, a model is a formal specification of the structure or function of a system. A pictorial representation can be used to provide a visual embodiment of a model. The model follows the rules of MOF, which we cover later in this chapter, whereas the visual representation is based on the diagrammatic rules defined for the type of model that it represents. Under this definition, a specification that is not based on some rigorously defined notation is not considered a model. Thus, the kinds of models that can serve as abstractions of systems being developed using the MDA approach must follow the rigorous guidelines of standards like UML and MOF. Picture diagrams that are not backed by strict semantic guidelines that ensure uniformity of representation and a standard understanding of their content are not considered representations of models under MDA.

Benefits of Modeling

If you have been developing software for a while in your organization, you probably have a process that you follow. Whatever process you use, you probably progress through the following steps in going from the initial idea for an application to a working implementation of that application that is in use by your customers:

1. Design
2. Development
3. Test
4. Delivery
5. Maintenance and support

These steps are not necessarily done only one time in the application life cycle or only in the order shown. Often, there are repeated iterations of these steps, with feedback from one iteration serving as input into the next. However, all of these activities need to take place at some time in the application life cycle. Additionally, although these steps usually require participation by the development team, at some point members of other groups in the organization, such as marketing or technical writing, will become involved in the development, sale, or delivery of the application. Finally, current or potential customers may participate in focus groups or have interactions with the development team, thereby providing valuable input into the design of the application.

There are a number of ways that you can go about creating the design for an application. Modeling, as a design approach, has a number of advantages over more traditional ways of creating and documenting a product design. In some cases, software teams create technical documents that detail the design of the application that they are developing. Although these documents provide a way to record and share ideas with other team members, it takes time to write, review, and then update the documents as the design changes. Even with the best intentions of keeping the design documents up-to-date, as the developers become involved in translating the design into a working application, the documents often become out-of-date, especially when time becomes scarce. In fact, it is often during those times when the design needs to change to accommodate a new requirement or correct a defect that members of the development team have the least amount of time to update the design specifications. At that point, the only real embodiment of the design is the software itself. This creates a problem: Once the software becomes the only accurate reflection of the design, there is no easy way to share the design with others, since reading the code provides too much detail to quickly understand the structure and interfaces of the application.

An alternative to working with design documents is to utilize modeling as a way to record the design. Modeling does not preclude the use of textual annotations to provide detailed descriptions of the components of the model, but because the model is expressed graphically, it does provide a pictorial representation of the application that is easy to share with others. In some cases, it may be the only way to effectively share the design with people who are not programmers themselves. Because this representation is an abstraction of the application, it is easier—and faster—for people to understand. Additionally, with the proper tools, a model can be used to generate some of the initial application code itself. Tools that support reverse engineering enable the development team to easily update the model as the application code evolves, thereby keeping the model synchronized with the application over time. Finally, because the model provides a visual representation of the problem domain, it can be helpful in enabling programmers to visualize and clarify relationships in the application that may be less apparent from examining the actual code itself.

Beyond the benefits of documenting and enabling the sharing of the design among those involved in the development of the application, using a model can be helpful in spanning the organizational boundaries within a company. Because the model surfaces the interfaces of the application, programming teams working in different areas of the same company can see the possible integration points that exist between two designs more easily. Also, reorganizations within the company, or even mergers with another company, can be more effectively managed because the interfaces to the differing groups' software can be seen more readily. Finally, when new people join the organization, they may be able to become contributors to the team faster because an up-to-date model enables them to learn the structure of an application more quickly.

There are other advantages to using modeling that can help you to develop better products—and build them faster. Because a model can be shared more easily with others than a written design specification, you're more likely to get early feedback from people within your own group and from other groups that have dependencies on the software that you're going to deliver. It is much easier to make changes to the model (and application code) during the early stages of development than if you wait until the implementation has been completed and you find out that it doesn't meet the requirements of the other groups that depend on it. By helping to surface the application interfaces, intra- and intergroup dependencies can be analyzed early in the product development cycle when it's easier to correct problems.

Finally, modeling is helpful to the management team because it helps to ensure that the organization doesn't allow the big picture to become obscured by the details of the implementation. As Harvard University professor Theodore Levitt explained in his landmark paper "Marketing Myopia" (Levitt, 1960), businesses that define themselves too narrowly are less able to adapt to change. The railroad industry experienced trouble because they thought they were in the railroad business, instead of the transportation business. With the advent of television, the Hollywood film industry experienced trouble because they thought they were in the movie business, instead of the entertainment business. By using modeling, you can help to ensure that your organization's focus does not become too narrow by becoming dependent on the details of one particular implementation. You can focus on your customers' needs—not just your products. In this way, you can adapt to the inevitable changes in technology and the marketplace more readily and thereby help to ensure the viability of your business for the long term.

Information Representations and Modeling

We have seen how class and object-based models can be used to provide an abstract representation of a particular problem domain. However, this is just one type of information that is found in a typical business enterprise. Information that is important to the enterprise exists in many forms: system and application programs, databases, process descriptions, technical manuals, regulation guides, and a host of others. What is needed is not only a way to model all these disparate forms of information, but also a way for the applications that they represent to exchange data and be used together. In order to achieve this, we need to have a common way of expressing different types of modeling information. As we will see next, MOF provides a hierarchy that enables us to represent information at progressively higher levels of abstraction and define ways to express different types of models. Because XMI is based on MOF, what can be expressed in a MOF-compliant model can be represented in XMI.

XMI and MOF

In the examples we looked at earlier, we saw how XMI can be used to represent the content of object-oriented models that are expressed in UML. Although this capability is valuable in providing a standard way to represent UML models, the expressive power of XMI extends far beyond this. When we introduced XMI in Chapter 1, we explained that XMI is based on MOF. To understand the expressive power that XMI has, let's first take a look at the capabilities provided by MOF.

MOF provides the capability to represent information at multiple levels of abstraction, or *metalevels*. Information at a higher metalevel provides a more abstract representation of the information at the metalevel below it. Although this may seem like a simple idea, it is actually the capability to represent information at higher levels that gives the MOF (and XMI) its expressive capability.

For some common architectures, it is convenient to show four levels of abstraction. However, it is important to emphasize that these are examples of common architectures, and the actual number of abstraction levels can vary. In practice, your models will be at different levels depending on how they are used. It is very common to use multiple levels together. Figure 10.1 shows an example with four levels of information representation. Starting with the most concrete information level at the bottom, we'll go through each level to introduce the terminology that is used and help you to see how the information becomes more abstract as we move up in the hierarchy.

We include this taxonomy to help you to understand some of the terminology (such as metamodel, meta data, and so on) that you may encounter when working with XMI. However, if you're not interested in knowing about information hierarchies, for the purposes of this chapter all that you need to understand is that FCM provides a type of modeling that is different from UML, but both UML and FCM are similar in terms of their relationship to MOF. As with UML, models created with FCM can be represented with XMI. Tools that can read and generate XMI corresponding to these models can be used to establish integration points for the modeled applications, even if the applications being

Information Type	Example
Meta-metamodel	MOF model
Metamodel	UML, FCM (others)
Model	Car rental agency model
Data	2002 Jalopy Deluxe

Increasing Level of Abstraction ⟶

Figure 10.1   Different levels of information abstraction.

integrated are represented by different types of modeling notations. Tools also exist that can generate standard Java interfaces from models using JMI. The WebSphere Studio and XMI Framework covered in this book generate Java interfaces that match a given model. When combined with XMI, Java interfaces let you share information within and across software programs.

Model Information Hierarchy

Although the terminology for describing levels of abstraction may be new to you, the concept of representing data at different levels is something you've probably been aware of for quite some time, especially for the bottom two levels of our example. The main point to remember is that for each level you move up in the hierarchy, the metalevel (and the number of occurrences of the *meta* prefix) increases by one. As we present each level of Figure 10.1, we will give an example of the type of information that could be represented at that level that corresponds to the car rental agency model we discussed at the beginning of Chapter 6. If you have not read Chapter 6, you may want to quickly look at the car rental agency model to help you better understand this section. The relationship between any two levels is the same as the relationship between a class and an object, or the relationship between a schema (or a Document Type Definition [DTD]) and an XML document.

Let's look at the example in Figure 10.1 by starting at the bottom level. The type of information that is represented at this level is simply an instance of something. Examples of this could be the information in a column of a database record, the score you got at the golf course last weekend, or, to tie into the example we've been working with since Chapter 6, a 2002 Jalopy Deluxe—the car from the car rental agency model. Objects running in a Java program are also typically at this level.

Now let's move up a level in the example. By moving up a level, we know that the information represented here is more abstract than that in the level below it. We also know that we can name the information at this level by prefixing an additional *meta* to the name for the information in the level immediately below it. Applying this rule to the name for the bottom level—data—we call information in this level *meta data*. A more common name for information represented at this level is a *model*. An example of this is the car rental agency UML model that we presented in Chapter 6. The Java classes we have used as examples throughout this book are another example.

Now let's move up another level in the example. Information at this level has a meta relationship to the information in the level beneath it, which are called models. Therefore, information at this level is called a *metamodel*. An example of a metamodel is the UML metamodel. The UML metamodel contains the constructs that are needed to represent a UML model. However, metamodels representing other types of modeling and software architectures can also be represented at this level. For example, the metamodel for FCM, a message flow architecture that we will look at later in this chapter, is represented at this level. Models for programming languages such as Java, C++, and COBOL are at this level, too[1]. The models for these languages are part of the EDOC and EAI specifications. Also, models of other software architectures such as EJB, which is a component architecture, are also at this level.

Finally, let's move up to the top level in the example. Just as with the previous levels, information at this level is more abstract than the information in the level beneath it. Because that information was called a metamodel, information at this level is sometimes referred to as a *meta-metamodel*. An example of this is the MOF model. Although we chose to use four levels of information abstraction in this example, the number of levels is arbitrary. Also, the same information may be considered to be at a different level of abstraction depending on the application. Finally, regardless of the level of abstraction at which you view your objects to be represented, the objects can freely reference information at any of the other levels of abstraction.

The more abstract concepts of meta data and metamodels may initially seem strange since most people are more comfortable dealing with concrete entities. However, once you understand the basic idea, you will understand what makes MOF (and XMI) so powerful as a means to represent information in a standard way. Because MOF provides the capability to describe many different types of metamodels, software developers have many kinds of modeling at their disposal that they can use to build software that is used throughout all areas of their businesses.

Now that you have seen the information representation capabilities of MOF, you can see why XMI is also so powerful. Because XMI is based on MOF, it is able to express information at *any* of the levels in the MOF hierarchy. Therefore, models that you create that are based on MOF can be represented in XMI. This provides a standard way to represent all of the different types of MOF-based models that you utilize in developing the architecture of your business's software. The XMI representation is expressed using XML—another industry standard. As a result of this standardization, information represented in XMI can be created and exchanged in the suite of tools you use to develop your applications. Further, because XMI is an open standard, any software tool developer can create tools to read, manipulate, and generate XMI. This common way of expressing information enables tools that work with XMI to work together.

What we have talked about up to this point is mostly theoretical. We explained what gives MOF (and XMI) the capability to represent disparate types of business information and share that information across multiple tools. We will now look at a more concrete example of MOF's expressive power by examining another type of modeling—modeling with FCM. In doing this, we will see how XMI can be used to represent information that is different from the examples we have seen thus far, which used only UML.

The Flow Composition Model (FCM)

FCM is used to describe flows of information among components of an application. FCM enables complex interactions to be broken down into simple flow components. Similarly, it enables simple flow components to be composed into more complex flow models. Like UML, FCM is a MOF-compliant metamodel. We utilize the elements of the FCM metamodel to create models of problem domains. Further, because FCM is a MOF-compliant metamodel, we can generate XMI for the FCM models that we create, just as we have done for the UML models that we have seen thus far. FCM is the model for WebSphere MQ (for Message Queueing), IBM's message flow/workflow middleware for exactly-once delivery of messages. When an FCM system is running, the message flows are at the data level in the hierarchy in our example.

FCM supports models that represent different levels of granularity. The more coarse-grained flows at the top level—termed *macroflows*—may be the result of a business process analysis. These macroflows can then be described in greater detail by *microflows*. For example, in a banking scenario, the macroflow may represent a workflow process, such as opening an account.

This process, in turn, may be broken down into more detailed microflows, such as identifying the customer, determining the type of account to open, accepting the initial deposit, and so on.

FCM supports the modeling of complex flows in different runtime environments. Because a complex flow may be made up of subflows that are deployed in separate runtime environments, an FCM model can be used to model integration among domains that have software running in different application runtimes (for example, a Java application, a COBOL application, and a relational database, such as DB2). In this chapter, we will see how FCM can be used to model an extension of the car broker application described in Chapter 4 that spans different runtime environments.

We will not look at the entire FCM metamodel, but will examine a simple example showing how you can model data and control flows to get an idea of how this type of modeling differs from the modeling that is done with UML. If you are interested in learning more about FCM, a more extensive treatment is provided in the EDOC specification (OMG, June 2001).

Using FCM with the Car Broker Application

In Chapter 4, we introduced an application involving a car broker and a car dealer. You may recall from that application that the car broker and car dealer decided to implement a computer application to facilitate the exchange of information that occurs during the purchase negotiation process. To quickly review, the process works as follows:

1. The broker examines the cars the dealer has for sale.

2. For a car that the broker wants to purchase, he submits a bid to the dealer.

3. The dealer examines the bid and either accepts it or proposes a higher price. If he accepts the bid, the car is sold, and the negotiation process ends. If the dealer proposes a higher price, he notifies the broker. The broker can then submit a higher bid or end the negotiation process. If he submits a higher bid, the process continues until either the car is sold or the broker decides not to bid anymore.

The broker and the dealer have each hired a programmer to implement his part of the system. The broker has hired a programmer named Bob, and the dealer has hired a programmer named Dave. In Chapter 4, Bob and Dave developed a model to represent the information that they wanted to exchange during the negotiation process, and then they generated an XMI schema based on this model. Figure 10.2 shows the model they developed.

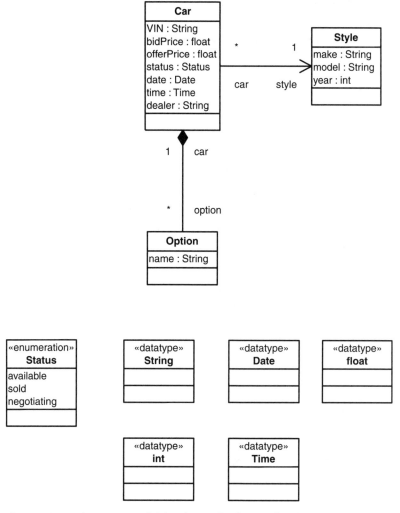

Figure 10.2   The UML model for the car broker application.

Up until this point, Bob and Dave have focused on developing the format of the information that they would like to exchange. Having used a model to accomplish that, they would now like to take the next step toward implementing the application software that will utilize the information that they have agreed on. To do this, they first have some more discussions about how they will implement their respective sides of the application. For example, from Dave's point of view, he needs to figure out how he can access the dealer's inventory so that he can respond to queries by Bob's application for information about what cars are for sale on the dealer's lot. Since both have already agreed on the format of the data that they are going to exchange, each of them can now implement his side of the application. We'll focus on how Dave implements the dealer's side of the application in this chapter.

Dave is pleased with how modeling and XMI helped him and Bob to agree on the format of the data to exchange. Now that this has been decided, Dave needs to implement the dealer's side of the application, which consists of the following two parts:

- A component that handles the bids the dealer receives from the broker. This component should enable the dealer to either accept the bid or return a counter-offer to the broker.

- A component that accesses the dealer's car inventory database and retrieves a list of the cars available for sale. The dealer already has a legacy COBOL application that manages the database. Dave would like to be able to use the COBOL application from his new Java application to obtain the cars available for sale to send to the broker.

After each of these components is implemented, Dave will need to implement the logic to enable them to work together and interact with the broker's side of the application. Because this logic involves control flow, Dave would like to create a model for the integration using FCM and follow an MDA approach to developing his part of the application. This should not only help him in successfully developing the application, but it will also help to ensure that the application can be updated and enhanced in the future.

The dealer already uses a DB2 database to manage the inventory on his lot. He also has an existing COBOL application that he uses to perform queries on the database. Up until this point, the COBOL application has worked well for the dealer. He and his sales staff are able to submit real-time queries to the database using an application with a graphical user interface (GUI) that runs on the workstations in their offices and on the floor of the showroom. The application provides a template that mirrors the fields of an input record named *INV-REQ-IN*, for Inventory Request Input (we will look at this record in detail later in the chapter). They are able to fill in the information corresponding to their queries and then submit them to the COBOL application. The output of a query is presented in a formatted file that they can view online or send to a printer to create a hardcopy. They currently perform these manual queries to check if a car is available for a customer or to respond to requests from the car broker mentioned earlier. If they implement this capability as a Web service, the results of a query can be returned directly to the broker. The dealership also runs a monthly inventory accounting program that queries the database. The inventory application reconciles the monthly sales, the new shipments received, and the inventory on hand at the end of each month. Figure 10.3 shows the different clients of the inventory application. Because this application is already in production and serving many clients, the dealer would like to make minimal changes to the application to accommodate requests from the broker.

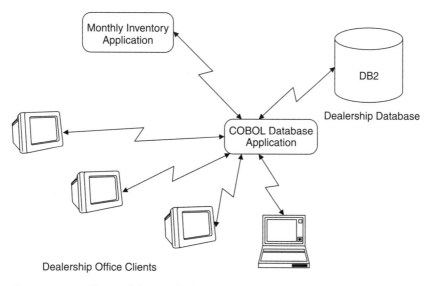

Figure 10.3 Clients of the car dealer's inventory application.

Now that the dealer and broker plan to work together, Dave would like to find a way for a query from Bob's application in the broker's office to reach the database and return the results. This will permit the broker to see what inventory the dealer has on hand before submitting a bid on a car. Dave and Bob have decided to implement their respective parts of the application in Java and use the Internet to deploy their application as a Web service. Dave's application will accept inventory requests from Bob's application. After authenticating that the request is legitimate, he would like to make a request that the COBOL application can understand. He would like the results to be returned to his Java application, so that he can then send them to Dave's application over their Internet connection. The ability to accept these requests for processing is the dealer's Web service.

Dave decides to use the FCM modeling capability of IBM's WebSphere software to create models of the control and information flows for the two application components on the dealer's side—the component that handles the negotiation process and the component that queries the dealer's inventory. When the application is complete, Dave will use WebSphere Studio to publish the application as a Web service. To do this, Dave can utilize another Web-Sphere Studio tool to generate a Web Services Definition Language representation that describes this service.[2]

We'll look at an FCM representation for the negotiation component to introduce the FCM methodology. Then we'll look at an FCM representation of the inventory component and see how it can be represented in XMI. Although we will introduce some of the notation and terminology used in FCM, what is important for you to understand is the general idea of how an FCM model can be used to model the flow of an application. Then, by focusing on a particular part of the example, you will see how an FCM model can be represented in XMI.

Figure 10.4 contains an FCM model of the component that will implement the negotiation process on the dealer's side of the application. The flow diagram in Figure 10.4 is what is known as an FCMComposition. An FCMComposition defines the flow of control and the flow of data between FCMNodes. The solid lines in the flow diagram represent FCMControlLinks and show the flow of control. The dot-dash lines represent FCMDataLinks and show the flow of data. In an FCM model, control flows route the data flows. Both FCMControlLinks and FCMDataLinks are specialized FCMConnections. The node labeled *Check Availability* is known as an FCMFunction. An FCMFunction can be thought of as being analogous to a programming language statement that makes a procedural call or invokes a transaction.

Each of the two diamond-shaped nodes in the flow diagram is an FCMDecisionNode. The leftmost node (labeled *Bid*) is known as an FCMSource. This node acts as a public entry point into the composition and defines the input for the operation of submitting a bid on a car. The rightmost node (labeled *Bid Response*) is the corresponding FCMSink, and it defines the results. Although in this example the composition has just one FCMSource, in general, it can have more than one, each acting as another public entry point. Although the flow diagram shows the steps in the bid and negotiation process, to an external user the FCMComposition simply provides the operation of submitting a bid and receiving a response.

Let's examine the flow diagram in Figure 10.4 to see the data and control flows that occur from the point of receiving a bid from the broker to returning a response. Beginning at the left, a bid for a car enters the flow composition through the FCMSource node labeled *Bid*. The FCMControlLink that goes from the *Bid* node to the *Check Availability* node triggers the activation of the *Check Availability* node. The data representing the bid flows from the *Bid* node to the *Check Availability* and *Assess Bid* nodes, as indicated by the FCMDataLinks in the flow diagram.

From the *Check Availability* node, control transfers to the *Car Available?* FCMDecisionNode. The result of this decision determines whether control flows to the *Assess Bid* or *Respond "not available"* FCMFunction nodes. If the car being bid on is not available, control flows from the *Respond "not available"* node to the *Bid Response* FCMSink. If the car is available, control flows to the *Assess Bid* FCMFunction node, where the bid is evaluated. From here, control flows to the *Bid OK?* FCMDecisionNode. If the bid is not acceptable, control flows to the *Send Counteroffer* FCMFunction node, where a counteroffer is determined. From there, flow transfers to the *Bid Response* FCMSink. If the bid is acceptable, control flows from the *Bid OK?* FCMDecisionNode to the *Accept Bid* FCMFunction node, and from there, to the *Bid Response* FCMSink.

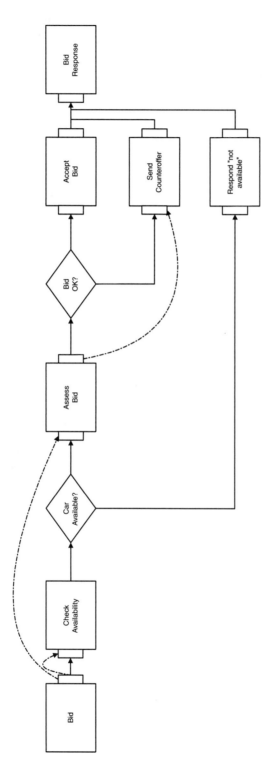

Figure 10.4 FCM model for the dealer's negotiation component.

A key feature of FCM is *hierarchical composition*—the ability to use flow compositions to create new flow compositions. For example, the FCMComposition in Figure 10.4 could be bound as the implementation of an FCMComponent in a more complex car purchasing scenario. In this way, compositions can be used together hierarchically to build more complex flows.

In Figure 10.5, we show an FCM model of the component for the inventory query. This model is somewhat simpler, consisting of just three FCMNodes. The leftmost node, labeled *Inventory Request*, is the FCMSource. The rightmost node, labeled *Inventory Response*, is the FCMSink. The node labeled *Check Inventory* is an FCMFunction node. The model flow involves receiving a request from the broker, checking the inventory, and finally issuing a response back to the broker.

XMI Example 10.1 contains a segment of the XMI file corresponding to the FCM diagram shown in Figure 10.5. This is a representation of the kind of output you would get from a tool that supported FCM modeling and had the capability to generate the corresponding XMI representation of an FCM model. We provide an explanation of this next.

The *FCMFunction* XML element corresponds to the FCMFunction node in the model in Figure 10.5. Note that the value of the *name* attribute corresponds to the label on the node in Figure 10.5. The *inbound* elements correspond to the data and control links that enter the FCMFunction node in Figure 10.5; the *outbound* elements correspond to the data and control links that leave that node. The *FCMOperation* element corresponds to the *inventory* entry point in the COBOL inventory application. The *inputs* and *outputs* elements contained in the *FCMOperation* element correspond to the inputs and outputs of the COBOL *inventory* entry point. Each contains an XML element named *languageElement* that contains an *href* attribute that links it to an XMI representation of the input and output to the COBOL application. Before we look at the XMI representation of the input and output, let's examine the format of the input and output that the COBOL application expects to receive.

Figure 10.5 FCM model for the dealer's inventory query component.

```
<FCMFunction xmi:id="Function_1" name="checkInventory">
   <inbound xmi:idref="ControlLink_7"/>
   <inbound xmi:idref="DataLink_6"/>
   <outbound xmi:idref="ControlLink_8"/>
   <outbound xmi:idref="DataLink_7"/>
   <invokes xmi:idref="FCMOperation_5"/>
</FCMFunction>
<FCMOperation xmi:id="FCMOperation_5" name="inventory">
   <inputs xmi:id="FCMParameter_10">
      <languageElement
         href="COBOLINV-REQ-IN.xml#Element:INV-REQ-IN"/>
   </inputs>
   <outputs xmi:id="FCMParameter_10">
      <languageElement
         href="COBOLINV-REQ-OUT.xml#Element:INV-REQ-IN"/>
   </outputs>
</FCMOperation>
```

XMI Example 10.1 Segment of an XMI file for an FCM model.

The inventory application accepts a COBOL record with the following structure as input:[3]

```
01  INV-REQ-IN.
            03   INV-REQ-TYPE        PIC X.
            03   INV-CAR-INFO.
            05   CAR-TYPE.
                 07   CAR-MODEL  PIC X(5).
                 07   CAR-MAKE   PIC X(5).
                 07   CAR-YEAR   PIC X(4).
            05   CAR-VIN         PIC X(20).
```

The *INV-REQ-TYPE* entry indicates the type of query that is being submitted. For example, the dealer may want to find all the entries that match a particular query or just the first one that matches. The *INV-CAR-INFO* entry
contains a *CAR-TYPE*, which holds the make, model, and year for a car in the
CAR-MODEL, *CAR-MAKE*, and *CAR-YEAR* record entries, respectively. It
also contains a *CAR-VIN* entry, which holds the vehicle identification number
for the car. You will note that some of this information is similar to that
described in the UML model that Bob and Dave developed. The fields following the names of the record entries (for example, *PIC X(5)*) indicate the format
of the data for the entries. The numbers preceding the entries in the record are
known as level numbers and are used to indicate the relative nesting of one
entry to another in the structure of the record. For the purposes of this example, the only thing you need to understand is what the names in the record
represent.

The dealer may want to perform a query that returns all the cars in the inventory with a particular make, model, and year. In this case, the dealer would specify the query type to return all the records that match, along with the make, model, and year of the cars he wants to see. In this case, he would not specify a vehicle identification number, since he would like to get records for all the cars that match. The results of a query are returned in a record with the following structure:

```
01   INV-REQ-OUT.
     03   INV-REQ-MATCHES     PIC 999.
     03   INV-CAR-INFO OCCURS 1 TO 999 TIMES
                 DEPENDING ON INV-REQ-MATCHES.
         05   CAR-TYPE.
             07   CAR-MODEL  PIC X(5).
             07   CAR-MAKE   PIC X(5).
             07   CAR-YEAR   PIC X(4).
         05   CAR-VIN        PIC X(20).
```

The output record *INV-REQ-OUT* has a numeric entry, *INV-REQ-MATCHES*, which indicates the number of records that were found that match the information in the query that was submitted. The *INV-CAR-INFO* entry contains the same information that is in the input structure. This information is repeated for as many matches as have been found that match the input query. This is indicated by the *OCCURS* clause for the *INV-CAR-INFO* entry. For example, if the dealer had submitted a query for cars of a particular make, model, and year, the application would return an *INV-CAR-INFO* entry for each car the dealer has of that make, model, and year. Each entry would also include the vehicle identification number for the car it represents.

Now that we know the structure of the information that the COBOL application expects for input and output, let's return to our discussion of the XMI segment for the FCM model in XMI Example 10.1. We are now ready to see the information that is contained in the files that are referenced through the *href* attributes for the language elements we looked at before. The *href* attributes point to files that contain an XMI representation of the COBOL input and output records. If the data representing the broker's query is represented using the format specified by these XMI files, then an adapter program can convert the data in a query from the broker into the required COBOL parameters to call the COBOL program. In this way, the functionality of the COBOL application can be extended to a new client without changing the application. The XMI representation of the COBOL input record, *INV-REQ-IN*, is shown in XMI Example 10.2. This XMI document was created according to the COBOL model defined in the EAI specification (OMG, September 2001). The COBOL model provides a way to represent COBOL data structures using standard XMI rules. Next we will explain the format of this file and how it maps to the COBOL *INV-REQ-IN* record we saw earlier.

```
<?xml version="1.0" encoding="UTF-8"?>
<xmi:XMI xmi:version="2.0" xmlns:xmi="http://www.omg.org/XMI"
   xmlns:COBOL="COBOL.xmi" xmlns:TypeDescriptor="TypeDescriptor.xmi">
<COBOL:COBOLElement xmi:id="Element:INV-REQ-IN" name="INV-REQ-IN"
   level="01">
   <sharedType xmi:idref="Type:INV-REQ-IN"/>
   <instanceTDBase href="TDINV-REQ-IN.xml#AggregateInstanceTD_1"/>
</COBOL:COBOLElement>
<COBOL:COBOLComposedType xmi:id="Type:INV-REQ-IN">
   <element xmi:id="Element:INV-REQ-IN/INV__REQ__TYPE"
     name="INV__REQ__TYPE" level="03">
     <sharedType xmi:idref="Type:INV-REQ-IN/INV__REQ__TYPE"/>
     <instanceTDBase href="TDINV-REQ-IN.xml#SimpleInstanceTD_1"/>
   </element>
   <element xmi:id="Element:INV-REQ-IN/INV__CAR__INFO"
     name="INV__CAR__INFO" level="03">
     <sharedType xmi:idref="Type:INV-REQ-IN/INV__CAR__INFO"/>
     <instanceTDBase href="TDINV-REQ-xml#AggregateInstanceTD_2"/>
   </element>
</COBOL:COBOLComposedType>
<COBOL:COBOLAlphaNumericType xmi:id="Type:INV-REQ-IN/INV__REQ__TYPE"
   usage="display" pictureString="X" synchronized="false"
   justifyRight="false"/>
<COBOL:COBOLComposedType xmi:id="Type:INV-REQ-IN/INV__CAR__INFO">
   <element xmi:id="Element:INV-REQ-IN/INV__CAR__INFO/CAR__TYPE"
     name="CAR__TYPE" level="05">
     <sharedType xmi:idref="Type:INV-REQ-IN/INV__CAR__INFO/CAR__TYPE"/>
     <instanceTDBase href="TDINV-REQ-IN.xml#AggregateInstanceTD_3"/>
   </element>
   <element xmi:id="Element:INV-REQ-IN/INV__CAR__INFO/CAR__VIN"
     name="CAR__VIN" level="05">
     <sharedType xmi:idref="Type:INV-REQ-IN/INV__CAR__INFO/CAR__VIN"/>
     <instanceTDBase href="TDINV-REQ-IN.xml#SimpleInstanceTD_2"/>
   </element>
</COBOL:COBOLComposedType>
<COBOL:COBOLComposedType
   xmi:id="Type:INV-REQ-IN/INV__CAR__INFO/CAR__TYPE">
   <element
     xmi:id="Element:INV-REQ-N/INV__CAR__INFO/CAR__TYPE/CAR__MODEL"
     name="CAR__MODEL" level="07">
     <sharedType
       xmi:idref="Type:INV-REQ-IN/INV__CAR__INFO/CAR__TYPE/CAR__MODEL"/>
     <instanceTDBase href="TDINV-REQ-IN.xml#SimpleInstanceTD_3"/>
   </element>
   <element
     xmi:id="Element:INV-REQ-IN/INV__CAR__INFO/CAR__TYPE/CAR__MAKE"
     name="CAR__MAKE" level="07">
     <sharedType
```

XMI Example 10.2   COBOL *INV-REQ-IN* record expressed in XMI.

```
         xmi:idref="Type:INV-REQ-IN/INV__CAR__INFO/CAR__TYPE/CAR__MAKE"/>
       <instanceTDBase href="TDINV-REQ-IN.xml#SimpleInstanceTD_4"/>
     </element>
     <element
       xmi:id="Element:INV-REQ-IN/INV__CAR__INFO/CAR__TYPE/CAR__YEAR"
       name="CAR__YEAR" level="07">
       <sharedType
          xmi:idref="Type:INV-REQ-IN/INV__CAR__INFO/CAR__TYPE/CAR__YEAR"/>
       <instanceTDBase href="TDINV-REQ-IN.xml#SimpleInstanceTD_5"/>
     </element>
  </COBOL:COBOLComposedType>
  <COBOL:COBOLAlphaNumericType
    xmi:id="Type:INV-REQ-IN/INV__CAR__INFO/CAR__TYPE/CAR__MODEL"
    usage="display" pictureString="X(5)" synchronized="false"
    justifyRight="false"/>
  <COBOL:COBOLAlphaNumericType
    xmi:id="Type:INV-REQ-IN/INV__CAR__INFO/CAR__TYPE/CAR__MAKE"
    usage="display" pictureString="X(5)" synchronized="false"
    justifyRight="false"/>
  <COBOL:COBOLAlphaNumericType
    xmi:id="Type:INV-REQ-IN/INV__CAR__INFO/CAR__TYPE/CAR__YEAR"
    usage="display" pictureString="X(4)" synchronized="false"
    justifyRight="false"/>
  <COBOL:COBOLAlphaNumericType
    xmi:id="Type:INV-REQ-IN/INV__CAR__INFO/CAR__VIN" usage="display"
    pictureString="X(20)" synchronized="false" justifyRight="false"/>
</xmi:XMI>
```

XMI Example 10.2   COBOL *INV-REQ-IN* record expressed in XMI. (*Continued*)

The XMI file shown in XMI Example 10.2 represents the hierarchical structure of the COBOL *INV-REQ-IN* record in XMI. Starting at the top of this file, we'll step through a few of the elements so that you can get the idea for how this is done. Although we will refer to the elements and attributes by the names used in the file to help you identify them, do not be overly concerned with the names that are used for these constructs. What is important to understand is how the hierarchical structure of the COBOL record is represented, along with the types of the record entries. As we go through the first few entries of the file, you may want to refer back to the definition of the *INV-REQ-IN* record to see that the XMI file represents the corresponding hierarchical structure.

The first element following the *XMI* XML element has a tag name of *COBOL:COBOLElement*. This type of element is used to represent data elements. Note that both the *xmi:id* and the *name* attributes are based on the name of the level *01* record entry *INV-REQ-IN*. Correspondingly, the *level* attribute has the value *01*. The *sharedType* element that it contains has an *xmi:idref* attribute with a value that matches the *xmi:id* of the *COBOL:COBOLComposed-Type* element a few lines down. The *sharedType* element is used to represent the type of a record entry. This indicates that the *COBOL:COBOLComposedType* element has information about the type of the *INV-REQ-IN* record entry.

Looking now at the *COBOL:COBOLComposedType* element, we see that the *xmi:id* contains the value of the *xmi:idref* of the *sharedType* element contained in the *COBOL:COBOLElement* we saw previously. A *COBOLComposedType* is used for nested declarations that contain additional entries, which the *INV-REQ-IN* entry has. Nested within this element in the file is another element that has the tag name *element*. A few lines below that element is another element that also has the tag name *element*. These two elements correspond to the two level *03* record entries in the COBOL *INV-REQ-IN* record—the *INV-REQ-TYPE* and the *INV-CAR-INFO* record entries.

If you examine the values for the *xmi:id*, *name*, and *level* attributes of these two elements, you will see that they correspond to those two record entries in the *INV-REQ-IN* record. Thus, these elements represent the first level of nesting in the hierarchy. Each of these elements has a *sharedType* element that has an *xmi:idref* that points to its type. For the element of the *INV-REQ-TYPE* entry, the value of the *xmi:idref* corresponds to the value for the *xmi:id* of the *COBOL:COBOLAlphaNumericType* element a few lines down in the file. This type of element is used to represent a COBOL string of alphabetic and numeric characters. In this case, the *COBOL:COBOLAlphaNumericType* element corresponds to the *PIC(X)* type of the *INV-REQ-TYPE* entry. The value of the *xmi:idref* attribute in the *sharedType* element belonging to the element for the *INV-CAR-INFO* entry corresponds to the next *COBOL:COBOLComposedType* element in the file. As you would expect, this element has two XML elements with the tag name *element* that correspond to the two record entries nested in the *INV-CAR-INFO* record entry—*CAR-TYPE* and *CAR-VIN*. This same pattern continues throughout the file as it completes the representation of the *INV-REQ-IN* COBOL record.

As we stepped through the XMI file in XMI Example 10.2, you may have noticed some elements with the tag name *instanceTDBase* and wondered what they represented. These elements are used to describe the low-level representation of the data in a language-independent way. Although the file in XMI Example 10.2 represents the structure of the data in terms that a COBOL program would, we also need a way to describe the actual data itself. By providing this complete description, an application development tool can generate a program (called an *adapter*) that can read the low-level bytes of data and convert them into a format that the COBOL application can understand.

Each of the *instanceTDBase* elements in the XMI file we looked at has an *href* attribute that points into another XMI file—*TDINV-REQ-IN.xml*. This file contains type descriptions for the low-level data representation that are language-

```
<TypeDescriptor:StringTD
    xmi:id="StringTD_1" addrUnit="byte" width="8" alignment="1"
    nickname="NT_string" bigEndian="false" encoding="8859_1"
    lengthEncoding="fixedLength"
    maxLengthFormula="1" checkValidity="false" format="X"
    stringJustification="leftJustify" paddingCharacter=" "
    characterSize="1"/>
```

XMI Example 10.3 Element from the *TDINV-REQ-IN.xml* file.

independent. To get an idea for what is contained in this file, let's look at XMI Example 10.3, which contains an element from the *TDINV-REQ-IN.xml* file. The element shown, *TypeDescriptor:StringTD*, is a type description for the language-independent representation of a string. If you look at the attributes for this element, you should recognize some that are commonly used to describe the important aspects of a string, such as its length and justification.

As we mentioned earlier, to convert the information from the broker's query into the parameters for a call to the COBOL inventory application, they need to be converted into a format that the COBOL program understands. To do this, we need code that converts data represented in one language (Java) into a form that the another language (COBOL) can understand. We will use an adapter to do this. Fortunately, the adapter code for our example can be generated by a WebSphere tool using the XMI representation, so this process is completely automated. All that Dave needs to do is use the XMI file shown in XMI Example 10.2 as input into this tool, and he can generate the code that will convert the information supplied by the broker's query into parameters to the COBOL application. Similarly, adapter code would need to be generated to reverse this translation when sending the information back from the COBOL application to the broker's program.

Finally, if the dealer is happy with the application once it is up and running, he may want to expand the number of clients that his dealership can serve. As mentioned earlier, to do this Dave can utilize another WebSphere Studio tool to generate a Web Services Definition Language representation that describes this service. This will enable the dealer to make the service that is currently available to just one broker a public service available to other brokers who want to use it. In this way, he can expand the number of clients that can buy cars through his dealership using this automated application.

In Figure 10.6, we show an illustration of how Dave's implementation could provide a public Web service that could accommodate multiple car brokers. In this scenario, multiple brokers who want to query the dealer's inventory to see which cars are available can do so. As shown in Figure 10.6, a broker could submit a request using XMI to a WebSphere server that is running the dealer's service that Dave implemented. From here, the request would be routed

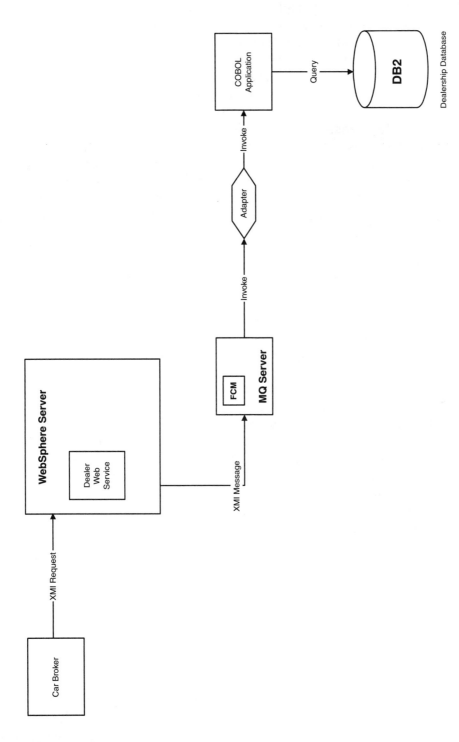

Figure 10.6   The inventory query application as a Web service.

through an MQ Server to the legacy COBOL application via the data adapter. Finally, the COBOL inventory application could query the dealer's DB2 database and return the result to the broker in the reverse direction.

This section has provided examples that show how XMI can be used to provide integration points for a diverse range of technologies, both old and new. It can be used to represent FCM models, since FCM models are MOF models. It can also be used to represent programming language data structures, language-independent datatypes, and, of course, much more. Although we looked at examples of some actual XMI files, what is important to understand is not the details of those examples, but the integration capability that XMI can provide for you through application development tools that can read and write XMI. Because of its versatility as a standard way for representing so many types of data, XMI provides a foundation on which tools can be built that realize the MDA approach to software development.

Summary

The MDA approach is the future direction of software development. Modeling provides a way to develop an application design that can be easily kept up-to-date with the software that implements it. Additionally, it facilities integration of new applications with existing ones in a way that does not require extensive changes to them. A model, as a representation of an application design, can be shared not only with members of the development team, but others in the organization who are involved in the development and delivery process. Further, modeling leverages the open standards provided by the OMG and enables the long-term preservation, enhancement, and integration of a business's software assets. As we have seen through the extension of the car broker application in this chapter, XMI, by providing a standard representation for data (and meta data), enables data sharing and interchange, and it serves as a fundamental standard in enabling the development of enterprise software systems using the MDA approach.

CHAPTER 11

A Real-World Use of XMI: WebSphere Studio Application Developer

The examples we covered earlier in this book were based on real-world domains, but they were designed to be relatively simple to enable you to focus on the XML Metadata Interchange (XMI) concepts that they demonstrated. Although this is a good way to learn about XMI, before you make the decision to use XMI in your own development projects, you probably want to know how it is being used in existing, real-world applications. In this chapter, we will examine just that by looking at how XMI is being used in IBM's WebSphere Studio Application Developer, a suite of integrated tools built on open standards that supports end-to-end development, testing, and deployment of e-business applications.

WebSphere Studio Application Developer (referred to as WebSphere Studio in this chapter) provides an advanced development environment for Java 2 Platform, Enterprise Edition (J2EE) applications. It includes the following:

- A powerful Java development environment that includes support for Java Development Kit (JDK) 1.3, a configurable runtime, an incremental Java compiler, a scrapbook, dynamic debugging, and a Java text editor.

- Advanced Web, Java, and Extensible Markup Language (XML) development tools.

- A Relational Schema Center (RSC) focused on relational database design and database administration tasks, such as importing and mapping schemas and other advanced functions.

- Web services tools to quickly develop, describe, and deploy Web services-enabled applications based on open, cross-platform standards like Universal Description, Discovery, and Integration (UDDI), the Simple Object Access Protocol (SOAP), and Web Services Description Language (WSDL).

Many of the tools in WebSphere Studio utilize XMI to provide their functionality. However, as a user, you may often not even be aware that XMI is being used. WebSphere Studio was developed using the Model Driven Architecture (MDA) approach that we described in Chapter 10. Many of the tools use models that define the data they work with. The XMI files used by the tools conform to those models. In fact, many of the tools were developed by generating code from the corresponding models.

In this chapter, we will first look at one of the many tools that use XMI in WebSphere Studio—the XML to XML mapping editor. After that, we will look at how XMI is used in WebSphere Studio with Enterprise JavaBeans (EJBs). By looking at these uses of XMI, you can get an idea of how XMI can be used in real-world applications. Further, by reading this chapter, you may come up with ideas for how you can use XMI in your applications as well.

The XML to XML Mapping Editor

The XML to XML mapping editor is a visual tool that enables you to specify a mapping from one XML schema to another, or from one XML DTD to another.[1] The mapping that you create is stored in an XMI file. A representation of the relationship between this mapping in memory and the corresponding files is shown in Figure 11.1. You can use the mapping to generate an eXtensible Stylesheet Language: Transformations (XSLT) script. This is contained in an XSL file. Using this XSL file, a transformation processor, and an XML document that validates with the first schema, you can generate an XML document that validates with the second schema.

The XML to XML mapping editor is useful because you often need to work with XML files that are not in the format your application requires.[2] Rather than changing the application to support multiple formats, you can transform XML documents in one format into the format your application understands. That way, your application needs to support only one format.

The XMI file containing the mapping uses several models within the same file. One of the models is a generic mapping model that enables you to store mappings from inputs to outputs, where the inputs and outputs themselves are defined by other models. This generic mapping model is used by many of the tools in WebSphere Studio that perform mappings, not just the XML to XML mapping editor. For the mapping editor, the inputs and outputs are

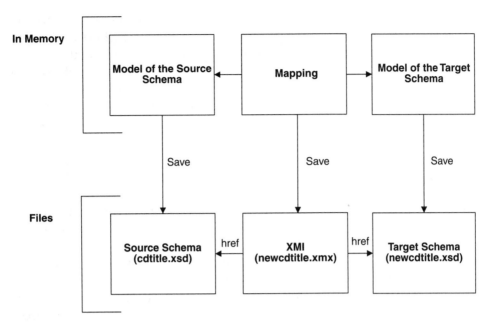

Figure 11.1 The relationship between a mapping in memory and the corresponding saved files.

defined by a model for XML that includes XML elements, XML attributes, and other parts of XML documents.

WebSphere Studio provides many examples of how to use the XML to XML mapping editor. In this chapter, we will look at one of the examples and examine the XMI file that contains the mapping. You may want to look at the example in more detail in WebSphere Studio. You will be able to see the steps that you need to follow to create the mapping and generate the corresponding XSL file.

The CD Example

The example we will look at involves starting with an XML document that describes a musical CD library and generating a second XML document that validates with a different schema. The generated XML document contains most of the same information as the first, but in a slightly different format. This example illustrates how you can use the mapping editor to map between XML elements, or to map an XML element to an XML attribute. In this discussion, we'll refer to the first document as the *source document*, and the second document as the *target document*. Similarly, we'll refer to the schemas for those two documents as the *source* and *target schemas*.

The information about each CD in the source document includes the title, the recording artist, the format (such as whether it includes two physical CDs), and a description of its content. The target document contains just the title, the artist, and the description; the format information is not included. Also, the information in the target document is in a slightly different format than it is in the source document. The artist, represented as an XML element in the source document, is represented as an XML attribute in the target document. The differences in the formats of the two documents are defined by their schemas. We'll look at these differences in more detail as we examine the source and target schemas.

The Source Schema

The schema that validates the source document is shown in Schema 11.1. The schema shows that the content of a valid *CDLib* element consists of one or more *CD* elements. Each *CD* element is made up of an ordered sequence of up to four elements, three of which are required to occur at least once. An *artist* element must be present, occur at most once, and be the first element contained in a valid *CD* element. This is followed by one or more *title* elements. A single *format* element may follow the last *title* element, but is not required. Finally, a single, optional *description* element is last. The type for the *artist*, *title*, *format*, and *description* elements is the *string* schema datatype, as shown near the end of Schema 11.1.

One of the sample XML documents provided with the example is shown in XML Example 11.1. This document validates with the schema in Schema 11.1 and is used as the source document in the mapping example. This document represents a CD library of three CDs. The CDs are represented by three *CD* elements that are contained in a *CDLib* element. Each of the three *CD* elements contains the required *artist* element and one *title* and *description* element. The third *CD* element in the document also contains a *format* element.

The Target Schema

The schema that validates the target document is shown in Schema 11.2. XML documents validated by this schema represent much of the same information as those described by the source schema. However, some differences exist in both the information that can be included and the way it is organized. The outermost element declaration in this schema is called *Collections*. Each valid *Collections* element can contain exactly one *Library* element. A valid *Library* element is made up of *CD* elements. There must be at least one *CD* element, while the maximum number of *CD* elements is unbounded. Each *CD* element contains one or more *title* elements, followed by at most one *description* element. The type for both the *title* and *description* elements is the *string* schema datatype. Finally, each *CD* element has a required attribute named *artist* that has a type that is also the *string* schema datatype.

```
<?xml version="1.0"?>
<xsd:schema xmlns:xsd="http://www.w3.org/2001/XMLSchema">
  <xsd:element name="CDLib">
    <xsd:complexType>
      <xsd:sequence>
        <xsd:element ref="CD" minOccurs="1" maxOccurs="unbounded"/>
      </xsd:sequence>
    </xsd:complexType>
  </xsd:element>

  <xsd:element name="CD">
    <xsd:complexType>
      <xsd:sequence minOccurs="1" maxOccurs="1">
        <xsd:element ref="artist" minOccurs="1" maxOccurs="1"/>
        <xsd:element ref="title" minOccurs="1" maxOccurs="unbounded"/>
        <xsd:element ref="format" minOccurs="0" maxOccurs="1"/>
        <xsd:element ref="description" minOccurs="0" maxOccurs="1"/>
      </xsd:sequence>
    </xsd:complexType>
  </xsd:element>

  <xsd:element name="artist" type="xsd:string"/>
  <xsd:element name="title" type="xsd:string"/>
  <xsd:element name="format" type="xsd:string"/>
  <xsd:element name="description" type="xsd:string"/>
</xsd:schema>
```

Schema 11.1   The schema for the source XML document.

The target schema differs from the source schema in a few subtle but important ways. In the target schema, the *CD* elements occur in a sequence that is nested inside a *Library* element, which is itself nested inside a *Collections* element. In the source schema, the *CD* elements are nested inside a *CDLib* element. However, the *CDLib* element is *not* nested inside another element. The *CD* elements in the target schema do not contain a *format* element. Also, although the name of the recording artist is placed in an *artist* element in the source schema, this information is stored in the value of an *artist* attribute belonging to a *CD* element in the target schema.

The Mapping

WebSphere Studio provides an easy-to-use wizard and a visual mapping editor to create the mapping between the two schemas. Figure 11.2 shows what the visual mapping editor looks like in WebSphere Studio. Notice that the two panes in the upper-right portion of the view contain tree representations of the

```
<?xml version="1.0"?>
<CDLib xmlns:xsi="http://www.w3.org/2001/XMLSchema-instance"
       xsi:noNamespaceSchemaLocation="cdtitle.xsd">
  <CD>
    <artist>Vonda Shepard</artist>
    <title>Ally McBeal</title>
    <description>Songs from TV show Ally McBeal</description>
  </CD>
  <CD>
    <artist>Annie Lennox</artist>
    <title>Medusa</title>
    <description>Theme song from the movie "The Net"</description>
  </CD>
  <CD>
    <artist>Madonna</artist>
    <title>Evita</title>
    <format>2 CDs</format>
    <description>Complete motion picture music sound track</description>
  </CD>
</CDLib>
```

XML Example 11.1   The source XML document.

source and target schemas. You can use these together to easily create a mapping between the components of the two schemas. The documentation provided with WebSphere Studio details how to do this. You may want to try this or other examples included with the copy of WebSphere Studio on the CD-ROM to see how this works for yourself.

XML Example 11.2 contains the target document, created by mapping the information from the source document into the format validated by the target schema. As you can see, the *CD* elements in this document are contained in a *Library* element, which is itself contained in a *Collections* element. Although each *CD* element in the source document contains an *artist* element, here the information from each *artist* element is contained in an *artist* attribute. The *title* and *description* elements have the same content as those that were in the source document, but the *format* element contained in the CD by Madonna has not been included.

Now that you have an idea of how to create and use the XML to XML mapping editor in WebSphere Studio, let's take a look at the actual mapping that is created for the CD example. This will show you how XMI can be used to represent the information that describes a mapping like this.

In the XML to XML mapping editor in WebSphere Studio, the XMI file containing the mapping from a source schema to a target schema has an extension of *xmx*. This file is shown in XMI Example 11.1. To make this file easier for you

```
<?xml version="1.0"?>
<xsd:schema xmlns:xsd="http://www.w3.org/2001/XMLSchema">
  <xsd:element name="Collections">
    <xsd:complexType>
      <xsd:sequence>
        <xsd:element ref="Library" minOccurs="1" maxOccurs="1"/>
      </xsd:sequence>
    </xsd:complexType>
  </xsd:element>

  <xsd:element name="Library">
    <xsd:complexType>
      <xsd:sequence>
        <xsd:element ref="CD" minOccurs="1" maxOccurs="unbounded"/>
      </xsd:sequence>
    </xsd:complexType>
  </xsd:element>

  <xsd:element name="CD">
    <xsd:complexType>
      <xsd:sequence minOccurs="1" maxOccurs="1">
        <xsd:element ref="title" minOccurs="1" maxOccurs="unbounded"/>
        <xsd:element ref="description" minOccurs="0" maxOccurs="1"/>
      </xsd:sequence>
      <xsd:attribute name="artist" type ="xsd:string" use="required"/>
    </xsd:complexType>
  </xsd:element>

  <xsd:element name="title" type="xsd:string"/>
  <xsd:element name="description" type="xsd:string"/>
</xsd:schema>
```

Schema 11.2   The schema for the target XML document.

to read, we have reformatted it slightly by changing the indentation and putting the *Mapping:MappingRoot* attributes on separate lines. Some of the longer *href* attribute values span more than one line in XMI Example 11.1, but are one line in the actual file created in WebSphere Studio.

As you may notice, the format of the *href* XML attribute values is somewhat complicated.[3] However, you do not need to understand all the details about them. It is sufficient to have a general understanding of the XML elements and XML attributes that are being referred to. The values of the *href* attributes use a hierarchical naming convention to point into the source and target XML schema definitions. Figure 11.3 contains a graphical representation of the information in this file. You may want to refer to this figure as we describe the contents of the file in detail in the rest of the chapter.

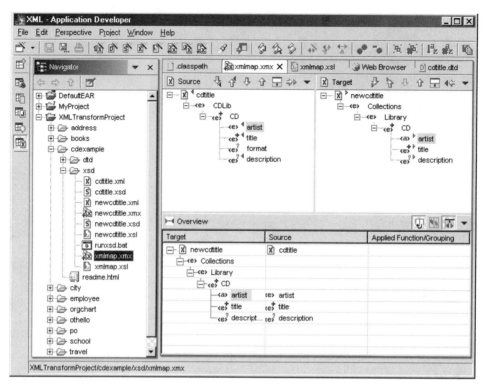

Figure 11.2 The XML to XML mapping editor.

```
<?xml version="1.0" encoding="UTF-8"?>
<Collections>
 <Library>
  <CD artist="Vonda Shepard">
   <title>Ally McBeal</title>
   <description>Songs from TV show Ally McBeal</description>
  </CD>
  <CD artist="Annie Lennox">
   <title>Medusa</title>
   <description>Theme song from the movie "The Net"</description>
  </CD>
  <CD artist="Madonna">
   <title>Evita</title>
   <description>Complete motion picture music sound track</description>
  </CD>
 </Library>
</Collections>
```

XML Example 11.2 The target XML document.

```
<?xml version="1.0" encoding="UTF-8"?>
<Mapping:MappingRoot
    xmi:version="2.0"
    xmlns:xmi="http://www.omg.org/XMI"
    xmlns:Mapping="Mapping.xmi"
    xmlns:XML="XML.xmi"
    xmi:id="MappingRoot_1"
    outputReadOnly="true"
    topToBottom="true">
 <nested xmi:id="Mapping_1">
  <nested xmi:id="Mapping_2">
   <inputs xmi:type="XML:XMLElement"
      href="cdtitle.xsd.CDLib.dtdxml#1:CDLib.1:CD.1:artist"/>
   <outputs xmi:type="XML:XMLAttribute"
      href="newcdtitle.xsd.Collections.dtdxml#1:Collections.1:Library.1:
CD.2:artist"/>
   </nested>
   <nested xmi:id="Mapping_3">
    <inputs xmi:type="XML:XMLElement"
      href="cdtitle.xsd.CDLib.dtdxml#1:CDLib.1:CD.1:title"/>
    <outputs xmi:type="XML:XMLElement"
      href="newcdtitle.xsd.Collections.dtdxml#1:Collections.1:Library.1:
CD.1:title"/>
   </nested>
   <nested xmi:id="Mapping_4">
    <inputs xmi:type="XML:XMLElement"
      href="cdtitle.xsd.CDLib.dtdxml#1:CDLib.1:CD.1:description"/>
    <outputs xmi:type="XML:XMLElement"
      href="newcdtitle.xsd.Collections.dtdxml#1:Collections.1:Library.1:
CD.1:description"/>
   </nested>
   <inputs xmi:type="XML:XMLElement"
      href="cdtitle.xsd.CDLib.dtdxml#1:CDLib.1:CD"/>
   <outputs xmi:type="XML:XMLElement"
      href="newcdtitle.xsd.Collections.dtdxml#1:Collections.1:Library.1:C
D"/>
   </nested>
   <inputs xmi:type="XML:XMLDocument"
      href="cdtitle.xsd.CDLib.dtdxml#9"/>
   <outputs xmi:type="XML:XMLDocument"
      href="newcdtitle.xsd.Collections.dtdxml#9"/>
</Mapping:MappingRoot>
```

XMI Example 11.1 The XMI document containing the mapping.

cdtitle.xsd.CDLib.dtdxml　　　　　　newcdtitle.xsd.Collections.dtdxml

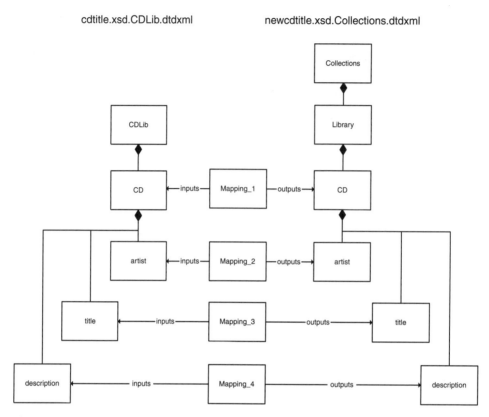

Figure 11.3　A graphical representation of the mapping XMI file.

The *Mapping:MappingRoot* XML element contains one *nested* element, *Mapping_1*. In turn, *Mapping_1* contains three *nested* elements itself: *Mapping_2*, *Mapping_3*, and *Mapping_4*. The *inputs* and *outputs* elements inside the *MappingRoot* element denote the root elements for the mapping: the *CDLib* element from the source schema, and the *Collections* element from the target schema. These elements are located at the end of the file, following all of the *nested* elements. They also indicate that one XML document is being mapped to another XML document.

Mapping_1 describes the mapping from the *CD* element in the source schema to the *CD* element in the target schema. The *inputs* element for this mapping refers to the *CD* element inside the *CDLib* element in the source schema. The *outputs* element for this mapping refers to the *CD* element inside the *Library* element that is inside the *Collections* element in the target schema. This means that the *CD* element in the source schema is mapped to the *CD* element in the target schema, where it is placed inside the appropriate container elements.

Mapping_1 also has three nested mappings inside it. These describe the mappings of the *artist*, *title*, and *description* elements. *Mapping_2* describes the mapping from the *artist* element in the *CD* element in the source schema to the *artist* attribute of the *CD* element in the target schema. *Mapping_3* describes the mapping from the *title* element in the source schema to the *title* element in the target schema. *Mapping_4* describes the mapping from the *description* element in the source schema to the *description* element in the target schema.

The Mapping Metamodel

The relevant parts of the metamodel used for the mappings are very simple. Figure 11.4 shows that each mapping consists of inputs and outputs, and possibly nested mappings as well. A *RefObject* is a generic representation of an object in WebSphere Studio. A *RefObject* is not exposed to an end user of the WebSphere Studio tools.

Figure 11.5 shows one kind of mapping that is called a *MappingRoot*. The *MappingRoot* is the top-level mapping. Typically, a mapping is specified with a

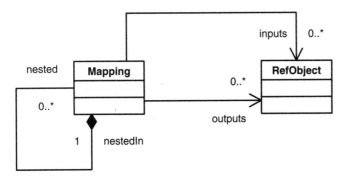

Figure 11.4 The *Mapping* and *RefObject* classes.

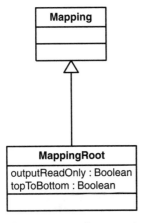

Figure 11.5 The *Mapping* and *MappingRoot* classes.

MappingRoot that contains all of the other mappings nested inside it. From looking at the XMI file containing the mapping for the CD example, you should be able to see how these parts of the metamodel correspond to elements in the file.

Using Models and EJBs

Now we'll take a look at how XMI is being used in another area of WebSphere Studio: EJB. EJB is a component architecture defined by Sun Microsystems for the development and deployment of object-oriented, distributed, enterprise-level applications. We do not cover EJB concepts in detail here, but you should still be able to follow this discussion and see how XMI is used with EJBs in WebSphere Studio, even if you've not worked with EJBs before.

The J2EE 1.2 and EJB 1.1 specifications were a big step forward for enterprise Java developers. They introduced a concept that enterprise applications had been missing for some time: that the meta data of a J2EE application could be read and written in a simple, easy-to-understand format, which is essentially plain text. Through its WebSphere software, IBM has become an industry leader in EJB tools, services, and middleware. This has some ramifications for developers working with WebSphere Studio.

As we have seen throughout this book, models can be used to describe the parts of an application that aren't code, but describe the code and how it fits together with other code. A model can contain information about a resource, such as an EJB or servlet, and information about how it can be used by other J2EE resources. In this way, models are used to represent meta data. An example of meta data is the EJB 1.1 Deployment Descriptor, which is described in the Enterprise JavaBeans Specification (Sun Microsystems, 1999).

Let's say you're building a simple EJB *.jar* file for deployment to WebSphere 4.0. The *.jar* file contains a single container-managed persistence (CMP) entity bean that represents a person. CMP means that the EJB's container manages how the bean is stored, or persisted, in a relational database. The deployment descriptor in XML Example 11.3 (named *ejb-jar.xml*) is contained in the META-INF directory of our EJB *.jar* file and describes a *Person* EJB.

This simple deployment descriptor defines the parts of this EJB—such as the home interface, the remote interface, the bean class, and the CMP fields—the fields in the bean class that will be container-managed. In other words, they will be stored and retrieved from a relational database by code generated

```
<!DOCTYPE ejb-jar PUBLIC "-//Sun Microsystems, Inc.//DTD Enterprise
JavaBeans 1.1//EN" "http://java.sun.com/j2ee/dtds/ejb-jar_1_1.dtd">

<ejb-jar>
 <enterprise-beans>
   <entity>
      <ejb-name>PersonEJB</ejb-name>
      <home>com.ibm.demo.ejbs.PersonHome</home>
      <remote>com.ibm.demo.ejbs.Person</remote>
      <ejb-class>com.ibm.demo.ejbs.PersonBean</ejb-class>
      <persistence-type>Container</persistence-type>
      <prim-key-class>java.lang.Integer</prim-key-class>
      <reentrant>False</reentrant>
      <cmp-field><field-name>id</field-name></cmp-field>
      <cmp-field><field-name>name</field-name></cmp-field>
      <cmp-field><field-name>age</field-name></cmp-field>
      <cmp-field><field-name>educationLevel</field-name></cmp-field>
      <primkey-field>id</primkey-field>
   </entity>
 </enterprise-beans>
 <assembly-descriptor>
   <security-role>
      <description>
          Everyone can gain access to this EJB.
      </description>
    <role-name>everyone</role-name>
   </security-role>

   <method-permission>
    <role-name>everyone</role-name>
    <method>
        <ejb-name>PersonEJB</ejb-name>
        <method-name>*</method-name>
    </method>
   </method-permission>

   <container-transaction>
    <method>
        <ejb-name>PersonEJB</ejb-name>
        <method-name>*</method-name>
    </method>
    <trans-attribute>Required</trans-attribute>
   </container-transaction>
 </assembly-descriptor>
</ejb-jar>
```

XML Example 11.3   An EJB deployment descriptor.

during deployment. Finally, the deployment descriptor contains other information such as the container transaction settings and the EJB security roles defined for this bean.

This information is used by WebSphere in a number of ways, such as determining how to handle transactions (an example would be deciding whether to start a new transaction for each method or to "flow" existing transactions through each EJB method). It's also used by the WebSphere security system to determine if a user (who is mapped by WebSphere to one or more J2EE roles) can access a particular EJB method. However, the part we are interested in is that WebSphere also uses the meta data to determine how to generate the code for CMP persistence that will actually do the work of storing and retrieving information from a relational database.

So far, this section has presented examples of deployment descriptors that you can find in other books and articles. We won't rehash what all the various tags in a deployment descriptor mean. Instead, let's find out what other meta data WebSphere uses in conjunction with EJBs, and how you can use that meta data in your own projects.

Meta Data in WebSphere Studio

Let's begin by examining what happens when you generate the deployment code for this EJB using the WebSphere Application Assembly Tool (AAT). Remember that there are two forms of an EJB JAR:

Undeployed form. This contains only the remote and home interfaces, the bean implementation class, and the deployment descriptor.

Deployed form. This contains the classes that are necessary to support persistence, transactions, and distribution, as well as the classes that are generated by the application server during deployment.

We won't cover how deployment is done in WebSphere in this chapter, since that is covered in the product documentation as well as in Brown, 2001. What we want to do here is to examine some of the information that WebSphere uses in this deployment process. WebSphere Studio supports three methods for mapping CMP EJBs to a database:

Top-down. Here the information in the EJB is used to create a database table that corresponds to the managed fields of the CMP EJB.

Meet-in-the-middle. Here the mapping is between existing EJBs and RDB schemas.

Bottom-up. EJB fields are created for the columns in a database table.

The key point here is that WebSphere requires additional meta data beyond the EJB deployment descriptor to perform these mappings. The meta data is used to drive the code generation process for the classes that actually execute specific SQL statements and then copy information out of the database tables into the EJB and vice versa. If you can understand the meta data generated for a top-down mapping, then you are well on your way to understanding how to use WebSphere to map CMP EJBs to database tables via the meet-in-the-middle or bottom-up method.

If you use the WebSphere AAT to generate deployment code for an EJB JAR file, or deploy an undeployed EJB JAR file using the WebSphere Administration Console without specifying any additional information about database mapping, it will perform a top-down mapping. So, if you open the JAR file that contains this descriptor (attached) in AAT, generate the deployment code, and then expand the JAR into a directory, you will see that the META-INF directory now contains the following files:

```
/META-INF
    ejb-jar.xml
    MANIFEST.MF
    Map.mapxmi
    Table.ddl
    /Schema/schema.dbxmi
```

One of these files is expected, the MANIFEST file, which is part of any JAR file, so we won't pay special attention to it. The other files are the interesting ones:

ejb-jar.xml.   The same as the one we saw before, but it is modified by AAT to contain additional identification tags.

/Schema/schema.dbxmi.   Contains an XMI representation of the database schema and table that the CMP EJB maps to.

Map.mapxmi.   Contains XMI that shows how the CMP fields in the ejb-jar.xml file map into the database schema in the schema file.

Table.ddl.   Contains the necessary SQL to create the table described in the schema file.

In WebSphere Studio, we have models of all these key parts: Enterprise JavaBeans, relational databases, and generalized mapping.

Let's begin by looking at what changed in the *ejb-jar.xml* file. The part of the file here shows what has changed:

```
<ejb-jar id="ejb-jar_ID">
  <enterprise-beans>
```

```
    <entity id="ContainerManagedEntity_1">
        <ejb-name>PersonEJB</ejb-name>
        <home>com.ibm.demo.ejbs.PersonHome</home>
        <remote>com.ibm.demo.ejbs.Person</remote>
        <ejb-class>com.ibm.demo.ejbs.PersonBean</ejb-class>
        <persistence-type>Container</persistence-type>
        <prim-key-class>java.lang.Integer</prim-key-class>
        <reentrant>False</reentrant>
        <cmp-field id="CMPAttribute_1">
            <field-name>id</field-name>
        </cmp-field>
        <cmp-field id="CMPAttribute_2">
            <field-name>name</field-name>
        </cmp-field>
        <cmp-field id="CMPAttribute_3">
            <field-name>age</field-name>
        </cmp-field>
        <cmp-field id="CMPAttribute_4">
            <field-name>educationLevel</field-name>
        </cmp-field>
        <primkey-field>id</primkey-field>
    </entity>
</enterprise-beans>

    ...

</ejb-jar>
```

As you can see, a few things have been added. AAT has added an *id* attribute to the following tags:

- *ejb-jar*
- *entity*
- *cmp-field*

These *id* attributes uniquely identify each CMP field within each Entity EJB contained in the JAR. As we will see in a moment, this unique identification is crucial for WebSphere to operate correctly on the other meta data files.

The next file to become familiar with is not really a meta data file, but a file that WebSphere generates for your convenience. This is the *Table.ddl* file, which contains the SQL to create the table for the top-down mapping:

```
CREATE TABLE PERSONEJB
    (ID INTEGER NOT NULL,
     NAME VARCHAR(250),
     AGE INTEGER,
     EDUCATIONLEVEL INTEGER);

ALTER TABLE PERSONEJB
    ADD CONSTRAINT PERSONEJBPK PRIMARY KEY (ID);
```

If you carefully compare this file to the previous EJB deployment descriptor, you will see that the table that corresponds to this EJB has the same name specified in the content of the *ejb-name* element in the deployment descriptor, and that the columns of the table match the names in the previous *cmp-field* elements. Finally, the column corresponding to the content of the *primkey-field* elements has been declared NOT NULL (since it will be the key for this table), and a primary key constraint has been added for this column as well.

You may be wondering how WebSphere knows what datatypes to use to create this table. The answer is simple: There is a fixed mapping of datatypes in the database to the Java language types of the container-managed attributes defined in the code of your EJB Bean class. This mapping varies from database to database, which is why you must select the database type in either the AAT or the WebSphere Administration Console when you deploy the EJB to WebSphere.

Now that you've seen the *Table.ddl* file and understand how WebSphere derived it from the code of your CMP EJB and the meta data in the EJB deployment descriptor, the next file to investigate is the *schema.dbxmi* file held in the *Schema* subdirectory of the *META-INF* directory. The *schema.dbxmi* file is shown in XMI Example 11.2.[4]

This file uses XMI. In fact, what it's describing is WebSphere's internal means of representing the database schema for this EJB.[5] Although it may initially appear complicated, it's not that hard to understand once you study it for a few minutes. Immediately after the opening XMI tag that describes the version and namespaces used by this file, you see the following tags:

```
<RDBSchema:RDBDatabase xmi:id="RDBDatabase_1" name="TopDownDB"
        tableGroup="RDBTable_1">
  <dataTypeSet href="UDBV7_Primitives.xmi#SQLPrimitives_1"/>
</RDBSchema:RDBDatabase>
```

The only important thing about this group of tags is that it specifies that this particular schema uses the DB2 UDB 7 mapping to map Java types to database types.

The next segment gets more interesting. Notice that these tags have the following structure, as shown in Figure 11.6.

As you can see, there is a *RDBSchema:RDBtable* element that corresponds to the table defined in the previous CREATE TABLE SQL. There are *columns* elements for each of the columns defined in the table as well. Finally, each *columns* element contains type information that describes both the originating type and the type of the column. The *originatingType* element provides information on the primitive database type (numeric and so on), while the *type* element shows how the originating type is extended for this particular column (by providing length, scale, or precision information).

Here we have an XML definition of the table. At first glance, this doesn't seem useful, because it is very similar to the information in the *Table.ddl* file.

```
<xmi:XMI xmi:version="2.0" xmlns:xmi="http://www.omg.org/XMI"
        xmlns:RDBSchema="RDBSchema.xmi">
  <RDBSchema:RDBDatabase xmi:id="RDBDatabase_1" name="TopDownDB"
          tableGroup="RDBTable_1">
    <dataTypeSet href="UDBV7_Primitives.xmi#SQLPrimitives_1"/>
  </RDBSchema:RDBDatabase>
  <RDBSchema:RDBTable xmi:id="RDBTable_1" name="PERSONEJB"
          primaryKey="SQLReference_1" database="RDBDatabase_1">
    <columns xmi:id="RDBColumn_1" name="ID" allowNull="false"
          group="SQLReference_1">
      <type xmi:type="RDBSchema:SQLExactNumeric"
          xmi:id="SQLExactNumeric_1">
        <originatingType xmi:type="RDBSchema:SQLExactNumeric"
            href="UDBV7_Primitives.xmi#SQLExactNumeric_1"/>
      </type>
    </columns>
    <columns xmi:id="RDBColumn_2" name="NAME">
      <type xmi:type="RDBSchema:SQLCharacterStringType"
          xmi:id="SQLCharacterStringType_1" length="250">
        <originatingType xmi:type="RDBSchema:SQLCharacterStringType"
          href="JavatoDB2UDBNT_V71TypeMaps.xmi#SQLCharacterStringType_250"/>
      </type>
    </columns>
    <columns xmi:id="RDBColumn_3" name="AGE">
      <type xmi:type="RDBSchema:SQLExactNumeric"
          xmi:id="SQLExactNumeric_2">
        <originatingType xmi:type="RDBSchema:SQLExactNumeric"
            href="UDBV7_Primitives.xmi#SQLExactNumeric_1"/>
      </type>
    </columns>
    <columns xmi:id="RDBColumn_4" name="EDUCATIONLEVEL">
      <type xmi:type="RDBSchema:SQLExactNumeric"
          xmi:id="SQLExactNumeric_3">
        <originatingType xmi:type="RDBSchema:SQLExactNumeric"
            href="UDBV7_Primitives.xmi#SQLExactNumeric_1"/>
      </type>
    </columns>
    <namedGroup xmi:type="RDBSchema:SQLReference"
        xmi:id="SQLReference_1"
        name="PERSONEJBPK" members="RDBColumn_1" table="RDBTable_1"
        constraint="Constraint_PERSONEJBPK"/>
    <constraints xmi:id="Constraint_PERSONEJBPK" name="PERSONEJBPK"
        type="PRIMARYKEY" primaryKey="SQLReference_1"/>
  </RDBSchema:RDBTable>
</xmi:XMI>
```

XMI Example 11.2   The *schema.dbxmi* file.

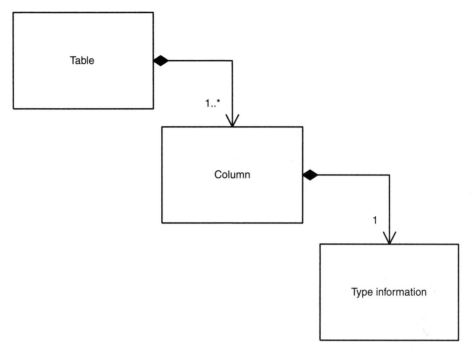

Figure 11.6 Database tag structure.

However, the next file, *map.mapxmi*, brings everything together and helps all this make sense. This provides another instance of the mapping we described in the previous section. The *map.mapxmi* file is shown in XMI Example 11.3.[6]

A few things are key to understanding how WebSphere EJB to RDB mapping works. We wouldn't expect that you would be able to generate this file from scratch, but we'll explain what it does so that you'll be able to make small changes to this file (and the others we've covered) in order to handle simple challenges in CMP mappings with WebSphere.

Let's start several lines down in this file:

```
<inputs xmi:type="ejb:ContainerManagedEntity"
        href="META-INF/ejb-jar.xml#ContainerManagedEntity_1"/>
<outputs xmi:type="RDBSchema:RDBTable"
        href="META-INF/Schema/Schema.dbxmi#RDBTable_1"/>
```

Here we have the first indication of what is going on. As you can see, these two lines link a specific EJB reference in the *ejb-jar.xml* file (*ContainerManaged-Entity_1*, which was the *id* of the PersonEJB we saw earlier) with a particular database table defined in the schema (*RDBTable_1*, which is the *PERSONEJB*

Chapter

</

```
<ejbrdbmapping:EjbRdbDocumentRoot xmi:version="2.0"
  xmlns:xmi="http://www.omg.org/XMI"
  xmlns:ejbrdbmapping="ejbrdbmapping.xmi" xmlns:ejb="ejb.xmi"
  xmlns:RDBSchema="RDBSchema.xmi" xmlns:Mapping="Mapping.xmi"
  xmi:id="EjbRdbDocumentRoot_1" outputReadOnly="false"
        topToBottom="true">
<helper xmi:type="ejbrdbmapping:RdbSchemaProperies"
    xmi:id="RdbSchemaProperies_1" primitivesDocument="DB2UDBNT_V71">
  <vendorConfiguration
    href="RdbVendorConfigurations.xmi#DB2UDBNT_V71_Config"/>
</helper>
  <inputs xmi:type="ejb:EJBJar" href="META-INF/ejb-jar.xml#ejb-jar_ID"/>
  <outputs xmi:type="RDBSchema:RDBDatabase"
        href="META-INF/Schema/Schema.dbxmi#RDBDatabase_1"/>
<nested xmi:type="ejbrdbmapping:RDBEjbMapper" xmi:id="RDBEjbMapper_1">
  <helper xmi:type="ejbrdbmapping:PrimaryTableStrategy"
        xmi:id="PrimaryTableStrategy_1">
    <table href="META-INF/Schema/Schema.dbxmi#RDBTable_1"/>
  </helper>
  <inputs xmi:type="ejb:ContainerManagedEntity"
        href="META-INF/ejb-jar.xml#ContainerManagedEntity_1"/>
  <outputs xmi:type="RDBSchema:RDBTable"
        href="META-INF/Schema/Schema.dbxmi#RDBTable_1"/>
  <nested xmi:id="PersonEJB_id---PERSONEJB_ID">
    <inputs xmi:type="ejb:CMPAttribute"
        href="META-INF/ejb-jar.xml#CMPAttribute_1"/>
    <outputs xmi:type="RDBSchema:RDBColumn"
        href="META-INF/Schema/Schema.dbxmi#RDBColumn_1"/>
    <typeMapping
        href="JavatoDB2UDBNT_V71TypeMaps.xmi#Integer-INTEGER"/>
  </nested>
  <nested xmi:id="PersonEJB_name---PERSONEJB_NAME">
    <inputs xmi:type="ejb:CMPAttribute"
        href="META-INF/ejb-jar.xml#CMPAttribute_2"/>
    <outputs xmi:type="RDBSchema:RDBColumn"
        href="META-INF/Schema/Schema.dbxmi#RDBColumn_2"/>
    <typeMapping
        href="JavatoDB2UDBNT_V71TypeMaps.xmi#String-VARCHAR"/>
  </nested>
  <nested xmi:id="PersonEJB_age---PERSONEJB_AGE">
    <inputs xmi:type="ejb:CMPAttribute"
        href="META-INF/ejb-jar.xml#CMPAttribute_3"/>
    <outputs xmi:type="RDBSchema:RDBColumn"
        href="META-INF/Schema/Schema.dbxmi#RDBColumn_3"/>
    <typeMapping
        href="JavatoDB2UDBNT_V71TypeMaps.xmi#int-INTEGER"/>
  </nested>
```

XMI Example 11.3   The *map.mapxmi* file.

```
    <nested xmi:id="PersonEJB_educationLevel---PERSONEJB_EDUCATIONLEVEL">
      <inputs xmi:type="ejb:CMPAttribute"
            href="META-INF/ejb-jar.xml#CMPAttribute_4"/>
      <outputs xmi:type="RDBSchema:RDBColumn"
            href="META-INF/Schema/Schema.dbxmi#RDBColumn_4"/>
      <typeMapping
            href="JavatoDB2UDBNT_V71TypeMaps.xmi#int-INTEGER"/>
    </nested>
  </nested>
  <typeMapping xmi:type="Mapping:MappingRoot"
    href="JavatoDB2UDBNT_V71TypeMaps.xmi#Java_to_DB2UDBNT_V71_TypeMaps"/>
</ejbrdbmapping:EjbRdbDocumentRoot>
```

XMI Example 11.3   The *map.mapxmi* file. (*Continued*)

table previously seen in the schema file). In fact, if this were a multiple-table mapping (one where some columns came from two or more tables), you'd see multiple *outputs* elements, each referring to a different schema file and table within that file.[7] This same principle continues throughout the rest of the file, as the next section indicates:

```
<nested xmi:id="PersonEJB_id---PERSONEJB_ID">
  <inputs xmi:type="ejb:CMPAttribute"
  href="META-INF/ejb-jar.xml#CMPAttribute_1"/>
  <outputs xmi:type="RDBSchema:RDBColumn"
  href="META-INF/Schema/Schema.dbxmi#RDBColumn_1"/>
  <typeMapping href="JavatoDB2UDBNT_V71TypeMaps.xmi#Integer-INTEGER"/>
</nested>
```

In this segment you see the connection between a particular container-managed field defined in the *ejb-jar.xml* file (*CMPAttribute_1*, which is the field id) and a particular database column defined in the schema (*RDBColumn_1*, which is the ID column). After the input and output mappings are defined, the final piece to this puzzle is the type mapping, which (as you can see) maps a Java type (*Integer*) to a relational database type (*INTEGER*). This kind of mapping is repeated for all of the CMP fields in the EJB.

If you're familiar with converters in VisualAge for Java EJB support, you'll recognize that the *typeMapping* element is used to pick the default converter. If you need a different conversion than what is specified (say, a specialized converter that knows how to convert the special *Strings* Yes and No to a *boolean*), you can specify this through a *helper* element at this point.

Figure 11.7 shows the interaction between these three primary XML files and their constituent parts.

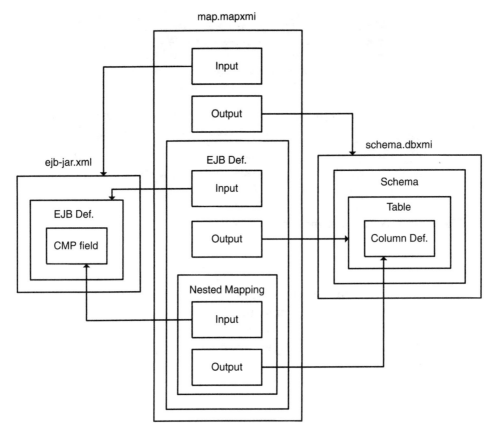

Figure 11.7   Meta data file relationships.

EJB XMI Mapping Example

Now that you know about the existence, structure, and interrelationships of these XML files, the question is, what do you do with them? If you are a tool builder who wants to generate your own entity EJBs using this information, consider using the documented Application Developer tool APIs to construct these files.

There are a couple of instances where directly changing the XML can be the easiest way of updating your EJBs. For example, many corporate environments have different database tables set up to support development, testing, and production. In some cases, these databases may be hosted on the same instance of DB2 or Oracle, and only differ by schema name (you might have DEV.PERSONEJB, TEST.PERSONEJB, and PROD.PERSONEJB). How would you write your code so that it doesn't have any dependencies on a certain environment? In the case of CMP Entity EJBs, WebSphere makes it simple. All you need to do is change the name of the schema in the schema tag, and then deploy the EJB JAR file to the different WebSphere instances used for the three environments. For example, for DEV, your tag might look like this:

```
<RDBSchema:RDBDatabase xmi:id="RDBDatabase_1"
name="DEV" tableGroup="RDBTable_1">
```

While for PROD, your tag might look like this:

```
<RDBSchema:RDBDatabase xmi:id="RDBDatabase_1"
name="PROD" tableGroup="RDBTable_1">
```

The great thing about this simple substitution is that you can automate it with tools like AWK, SED, or even ANT, which could also be used to invoke the appropriate WebSphere command-line tool (SEAppInstall on Advanced Single Server Edition, or WSCP on Advanced Edition) to generate the deployment code and install the resulting application.

In this case, you'd start with an undeployed EJB JAR file, deploy it once, and then copy the meta data files described previously back into the build tree of your project so that they become part of the undeployed JAR file. When you deploy the JAR, WebSphere picks up the meta data files and generates the deployment code appropriately.

Another simple change you can make is to update the XML to perform a minimal meet-in-the-middle mapping when either the EJB definition or the database schema changes. For instance, suppose you decide later in the project to change the name of the *educationLevel* CMP field to *edLevel*. You'd only need to update the *ejb-jar.xml* file to change the field like this:

```
<cmp-field id="CMPAttribute_4">
   <field-name>edLevel</field-name>
</cmp-field>
```

Keep the *id* the same, because (as we saw earlier) the *id* is actually used to map the CMP field to the corresponding column in the schema. As you can imagine, a corresponding change in the database would involve keeping the *ejb-jar.xml* the same while updating the *schema.dbxmi* file appropriately. Again, in either case, redeploy the EJB JAR file after editing the XML.

Summary

The example we saw with the XML to XML mapping editor shows just one use of XMI in WebSphere Studio. However, from this example you have seen how XMI is being used in a real-world product, and how the models corresponding to the XML to XML mapping editor demonstrate the use of the MDA approach in its design. Similar to the example we presented in Chapter 10, this demonstrates another way that the expressive power of XMI enables it be used to represent many different kinds of information in a programming application.

In the example with EJBs, we examined the use of XMI in model-based enterprise architectures using EJB, Java, and a relational database, as well as the mappings between these models. We described how the *ejb-jar*, *schema*, and *map* files interoperate, and how the tools that operate on these files function. This information can help you make better use of the WebSphere tools for CMPs and plan the best way to handle automated configuration and deployment issues involving CMPs.

We encourage you to try out the XML to XML mapping editor, the EJB creation and deployment tools, and the other tools that are included in the copy of WebSphere Studio on the CD-ROM. This is the best way for you to see the benefits that XMI and MDA are already bringing to the world of software development.

The XMI Framework:
Supplemental Documentation

The purpose of this appendix is to describe the Framework capabilities in a systematic way so you can effectively use the Framework. It provides you with information about all the Framework capabilities, not just the ones used by the programs in this book. Some of the material in this appendix will be familiar to you if you have read Chapters 7, 8, and 9. Sometimes we refer back to material already covered in those chapters, rather than repeating it here.

You do not need to read this appendix to understand the programs in Chapters 7 through 9; those chapters explain enough about the Framework for you to understand the programs in them. For example, this appendix describes how to use the Framework with XML Metadata Interchange (XMI) 1.0 and XMI 1.1, as well as XMI 2.0, but the rest of the book only discusses XMI 2.0. In addition, in this appendix we explain parts of the Framework object model that are not covered in the rest of this book because they are not used by the programs in the book.

We begin our explanation of the Framework by explaining its purpose, and then we provide an overview of some of the most important aspects of the Framework. After that, we provide advice on how to use it. Then we explain the Framework object model, which enables you to represent your objects and classes in a generic way. Once you understand the object model, you can begin to learn how to load and save XMI files, generate Document Type Definitions (DTDs) and schemas, and generate code from models.

Other sources of Framework information are Chapters 7 through 9, the Javadocs for the Framework application programming interfaces (APIs), and the examples that are provided with the Framework (the Javadocs and Framework examples are included on the CD-ROM). This appendix supplements those sources of information. Depending on how you learn best, you might want to examine the Framework examples, and then consult this appendix or the Javadocs for further information.

Purpose

The purpose of the Framework is to enable you to learn about XMI. The Framework is designed to let you begin to work with XMI without becoming an XMI expert.

The primary capabilities of the Framework are as follows:

- Reading and writing XMI files
- Creating XMI DTDs
- Creating XMI schemas

You can use the Framework to learn about the following topics:

- XMI 1.0, XMI 1.1, and XMI 2.0, and how XMI has evolved
- The capabilities that XMI software provides
- How to use XMI in your applications

You can even get ideas for how to implement your own XMI software.

The Framework is designed to enable you to work with XMI at a higher level of abstraction than Extensible Markup Language (XML) elements and attributes. The Framework uses an XML parser, but you can use the Framework without being an XML expert. You do not need to learn how to use the Simple API for XML (SAX) and the Document Object Model (DOM) to use most of the Framework functionality, although some advanced Framework capabilities enable you to use SAX if you understand it.

You should be aware of some basic XML issues though, especially what a legal XML tag name for an XML element is, and what a legal name for an XML attribute is. It is possible to use the Framework to create illegal XMI files, DTDs, and schemas. If you do so, XML parser errors occur when those files, DTDs, and schemas are used. The Framework reports parser errors to you.

Overview

The numerous classes and interfaces in the Framework are grouped into four major parts. The four parts are as follows:

- The Framework object model
- Classes that represent XMI files, DTDs, and schemas
- Adapters
- Helper classes

We provide a brief summary of each of these parts of the Framework in this section. Figure A.1 contains the entire Framework object model. Figure A.2 contains the most important classes for the other parts of the Framework.

Framework Object Model

The Framework object model is a generic representation of objects and classes. This generic representation enables you to specify all the information necessary to serialize objects using XMI and to create XMI DTDs and schemas from classes. There are two major parts of the object model. The first part supports objects and their values. The second part supports packages, classes and their features, and datatypes. Packages, classes, features, and datatypes are called *declarations*.

Both parts of the Framework object model consist of interfaces and implementations of the interfaces. The names of the interfaces are related to the names of the classes that implement the interfaces. Each class that implements an interface has a name that consists of the name of the interface followed by the suffix *Impl*. For example, you will learn that the *XMIObject* interface represents an object. The class that implements this interface is named *XMIObjectImpl*.

You use the Framework interfaces and implementation classes representing objects and their values to create XMI files. The Framework uses the interfaces and implementation classes by default to create objects and values when it loads XMI files. However, the Framework is capable of creating instances of other classes when it loads XMI files, as we explain later. You can use the Framework to make objects without making corresponding classes.

Packages, classes and their features, and datatypes are Framework declarations. You can put declarations into a Framework *model*. You can create XMI DTDs and schemas from Framework models.

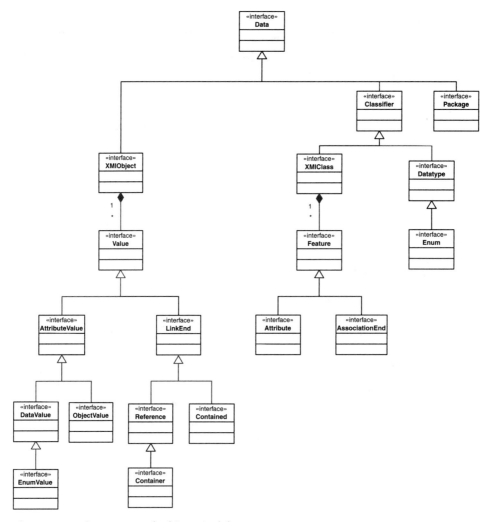

Figure A.1   The Framework object model.

XMI Files, DTDs, and Schemas

Several classes represent XMI files, DTDs, and schemas. The *XMIFile* class is a representation of an XMI file; you use it to create an XMI file. When you load an XMI file, the Framework makes an instance of this class so you can access information about the file and the objects the Framework created when the file was loaded. You use the *XMIDTD* class to create an XMI DTD, and you use the *XMISchema* class to create an XMI schema. There are also other classes for creating DTDs and schemas.

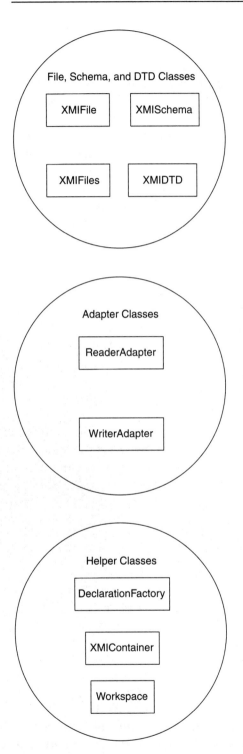

Figure A.2 The parts of the Framework apart from the object model.

Adapters

Adapters enable you to connect your Java objects and classes with the Framework. By implementing an *object writer adapter,* you enable the Framework to write your Java objects to an XMI file. By implementing an *object reader adapter,* you enable the Framework to restore your Java objects from an XMI file. In both of these cases, the adapters you write enable you to work with your Java objects rather than representations of them based on Framework objects and values. Finally, by implementing a *declaration writer adapter,* you enable the Framework to use your Java classes to create XMI DTDs and schemas.

You do not need to write an adapter to work with XMI files, DTDs, and schemas, but you can do so if you want to avoid representing your objects using the interfaces in the Framework object model.

Helper Classes

Helper classes provide useful functionality when using the Framework. One helper class is the *XMIContainer* class. You can put *XMIObjects* into an *XMIContainer* and print the container. Doing so gives you a list of the objects and their values. This capability is useful for determining which objects and values the Framework created when it loaded an XMI file. The *XMIContainer* class also enables you to obtain an *XMIObject* by using its uuid and obtain all constructs with a given XMI name.

Another important helper class is the *Workspace* class. It enables you to register one or more models with the Framework so they are available when the Framework saves and loads XMI files. By using this class, you can ensure that the Framework properly interprets the contents of an XMI file. We explain this topic in more detail later.

Suggestions for Using the Framework

There are several ways to use the Framework. This section presents some possible ways of using the Framework and the pros and cons of each way.

If you want to work with XMI files that contain data conforming to a specific model, create a Unified Modeling Language (UML) model for your data, and then use the *UML2Java* class in the Framework to generate Java classes that you can use to work with your data. (You can also generate a DTD and schema from your model if you wish.) Generating classes this way enables you to work with XMI 1.0, XMI 1.1, and XMI 2.0 files if you load the XMI files using a workspace. A major additional advantage of using this approach is that your users do not need to keep track of XMI names; the generated Java classes hide details about XMI names and the Framework *Data* hierarchy from your users. This approach is best for people that do not want to learn a lot about XMI.

If you know about XMI, you can use the implementation classes provided for the *Data* hierarchy to make XMI files regardless of your problem domain. You can also use the *Data* hierarchy to represent objects from XMI files even if you do not know the model they conform to. You can use the *XMIClass* and *Package* implementations to create XMI DTDs.

You should use a workspace for loading XMI files if you want to preserve the value types of object values; otherwise, when you load an XMI file, the value types of the new *Value* objects will not match the original value types. You need to create a model for your objects and add the model to the workspace before loading XMI files for this approach to work.

You can implement adapters if you want to connect your objects or classes to the Framework without having those objects or classes inherit from the Framework or implement Framework interfaces.

Framework Object Model

The Framework object model provides a generic representation of objects and classes. The purpose of the object model is to provide the Framework with the information it needs to save and load XMI files and create XMI DTDs and XMI schemas. Although it is not a standard, the object model has concepts that are similar to the concepts in the UML and Meta Object Facility (MOF) object models, so learning it can help you learn those standards. You can also learn what information is required by XMI by learning the Framework object model.

As explained previously in this appendix, there are two major parts to the Framework object model: objects (and their values) and declarations. Declarations consist of packages, classes and their features, and datatypes.

We explain how to represent objects and their values first. Next we explain how to represent classes and their features, and then packages. We explain details about the interfaces that are used to represent these concepts. Finally, we explain aspects of the object model that apply to many of the parts of the object model; some of these aspects are XMI names, namespaces, tag values, and definers.

Objects and Values

The root interface of the Framework object model is called *Data*. All the other interfaces in the object model directly or indirectly extend the *Data* interface. The *Data* interface contains methods for getting and setting an XMI name, a definer, a namespace, and sets of tag values, which can be used to store additional information for a construct. We explain more details about these concepts later in this appendix.

The *XMIObject* interface represents objects. Objects have values, which are either object values or data values. The *XMIObject* interface does not let you represent the behavior of objects, so there is no *Method* or *Operation* interface in the object model. The purpose of the object model is to represent the state of an object so the Framework can save the state in an XMI file and restore it when loading an XMI file (it also represents the structural features of classes so XMI DTDs and schemas can be generated). Because methods and operations are not part of an object's state, they are not included in the Framework object model.

The *Value* interface represents one or more values for an object. It enables you to specify all the information required by XMI to save a value in an XMI file: the name of the feature corresponding to the value, the kind of value, and the data values and object values themselves. Data values are represented by Java *String* objects, and object values are *XMIObjects*. A *Value* object holds one or more data values and object values, as we explain later.

The interfaces for objects and values extend the *Data* interface, as shown in Figure A.3.

XMIObjects

Unlike Java, which requires you to make a class before you can make an instance of the class, you can make an *XMIObject* and set values for it without making a corresponding *XMIClass*, the Framework representation of a class. The reason you can do this is to make it easy for you to create a Framework representation for your objects and save them in an XMI file so you can learn how XMI handles your objects.

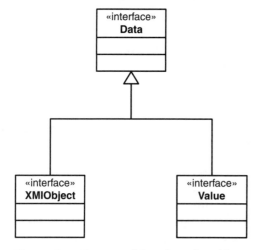

Figure A.3   Framework interfaces for objects and their values.

You can make *XMIObjects* using the Framework in several ways:

- You can make instances of the *XMIObjectImpl* class.
- You can load an XMI file.
- You can invoke one of the *makeXMIObject()* methods in the *FactoryAdapter* class.
- You can create instances of Java classes that implement the *XMIObject* interface. You can create these classes yourself, or you can use the Framework to generate Java classes that implement the *XMIObject* interface from your models.

You use the *XMIObject* interface methods to add, get, remove, and set values; set the XMI identity for an object; and work with XMI extensions. The XMI identity of an object consists of the XMI id, uuid, and label. XMI extensions are described in the *XMI Extension* section of Chapter 8.

Attribute Values

As explained previously, each *Value* object enables you to specify the kind of value. The Framework has several interfaces that extend the *Value* interface. Some of these correspond to different kinds of UML attribute values, and some correspond to UML link ends. The *AttributeValue* interface represents three kinds of UML attribute values. Each *AttributeValue* object represents one or more attribute values. In both UML and MOF, you can specify a multiplicity for an attribute that defines the number of legal values that a attribute can have in an object. An *AttributeValue* object represents *all* the attribute values for a particular attribute in an object if the multiplicity is greater than *1*.

Three interfaces extend the *AttributeValue* interface. These three interfaces correspond to three different kinds of UML attribute values. The *DataValue* interface represents data values for an attribute in an object. The *EnumValue* interface extends the *DataValue* interface and represents enumeration literals in an object. The *ObjectValue* interface represents object values for an attribute in an object. These interfaces and the relationships among them are shown in the hierarchy in Figure A.4.

The types of values are specified using constants in the *Value* interface. The type of a *DataValue* is *Value.DATA*. The type of an *EnumValue* is *Value.ENUM*. The type of an *ObjectValue* is *Value.OBJECT*.

The *EnumValue* interface is included in the Framework object model so the Framework can support XMI 1.0 and 1.1. In those versions of XMI, enumeration literals are saved in a different format than other data values. In XMI 2.0, enumeration literals are saved in the same format as other data values.

Each *AttributeValue* object represents one or more attribute values. In both UML and MOF, you can specify a multiplicity for attributes to define the

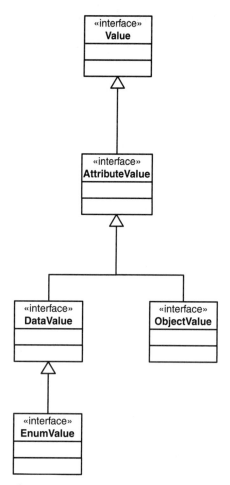

Figure A.4 Framework interfaces for attribute values.

number of legal values that an attribute can have in an object. An *AttributeValue* object represents all the attribute values for a particular attribute in an object.

Link Ends

We saw previously the three kinds of Framework values that represent attribute values. The other category of Framework values is represented by the *LinkEnd* interface. A link end is an instance of an association end. A *LinkEnd* object represents all the instances of a particular association end in an object. Each *LinkEnd* object relates one or more linked objects to the object that has the *LinkEnd*. The relationship may have composition semantics. By composition, we mean that the linked objects are parts of the object that has the

LinkEnd, and if the object that has the *LinkEnd* is deleted, the linked objects are deleted as well.

There are three kinds of link ends, each represented by an interface. The *Reference* interface represents one or more link ends with no composition semantics. The *Contained* interface represents one or more link ends with composition semantics; the linked objects are contained in the object that has the link end. The *Container* interface represents a link end whose linked object is the container for the object that has the link end; it is the link end across from a *Contained* link end in an object diagram. An object can only have one container, so an *XMIObject* can only have one *Container* link end, and that *Container* link end can have only one linked object. These interfaces are shown in Figure A.5.

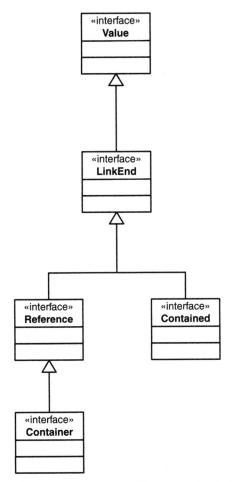

Figure A.5 Framework interfaces for link ends.

Each link end has a Framework *value type* that indicates what kind of link end it is. The type of a *Reference* link end is *Value.REFERENCE*. The type of a *Contained* link end is *Value.CONTAINED*. The type of a *Container* link end is *Value.CONTAINER*.

Creating and Setting Values

You can create *Value* objects and set the values for an *XMIObject* in several ways. A given *XMIObject* can have many *Value* objects, but each must have a unique name. It is not legal for more than one *Value* object for an *XMIObject* to have the same name. Here are the ways you can get and set *Value* objects in the Framework:

- You can create an instance of the *ValueImpl* class yourself (or one of its subclasses) and add it to an *XMIObject*.

- You can use the *setXMIValue()* and *addXMIValue()* methods of the *XMIObject* interface to create any of the six kinds of values, add additional values to a *Value* object, or replace values of a *Value* object. In this way, the *XMIObject* interface serves as a factory for creating values.

- You can use the *makeValue()* method of the *FactoryAdapter* class to make a *Value* object and then add it to an *XMIObject*.

- You can use the *getXMIValues()* method in the *XMIObject* interface to obtain all the *Value* objects for an *XMIObject*.

- You can use the *getXMIValue()* method in the *XMIObject* interface to get the *Value* object with a given name belonging to the *XMIObject*.

- You can use the *getXMIValueOfValue()* method in the *XMIObject* interface to obtain the data values, object values, or linked objects for a *Value* object with a given name.

We recommend that you use the *setXMIValue()* and *addXMIValue()* methods in the *XMIObject* interface to create values.

Here are some examples of using objects and values. How do you create two dogs, one named Sparky and one named Lassie? Here's the code:

```
XMIObject dog1 = new XMIObjectImpl("Dog");
XMIObject dog2 = new XMIObjectImpl("Dog");
dog1.setXMIValue("name", "Sparky", Value.DATA);
dog2.setXMIValue("name", "Lassie", Value.DATA);
```

In the previous example, *dog1* is named *Sparky* and *dog2* is named *Lassie*. Note that you do not need to have an *XMIClass* to make objects. You might use the following code to obtain the two names, assuming the names have already been set:

```
System.out.println("dog1 name: " + dog1.getXMIValueOfValue("name"));
System.out.println("dog2 name: " + dog2.getXMIValueOfValue("name"));
```

Note that in the previous example, if you used the *getXMIValue()* method rather than the *getXMIValueOfValue()* method, the *Value* object that holds the dog's name is returned rather than the dog's name itself.

Using the *XMIObject* interface, the *Value* objects for each dog can be obtained and then processed as in the following example for getting the *name* value of *dog1*:

```
Iterator values = dog1.getXMIValues().iterator();
while (values.hasNext()) {
  Value v = (Value) values.next();
  if (v.getXMIName().equals("name"))
    System.out.println("dog1 name: " + v.getXMIValue());
}
```

Consider how to represent a car, its owner, and its engine in the Framework. This code creates a car that contains an engine and is owned by a person:

```
XMIObject car    = new XMIObjectImpl("Car");
XMIObject engine = new XMIObjectImpl("Engine");
XMIObject person = new XMIObjectImpl("Person");
car.setXMIValue("engine", engine, Value.CONTAINED);
engine.setXMIValue("car", car,    Value.CONTAINER);
car.setXMIValue("owner",  person, Value.REFERENCE);
```

This example demonstrates the use of all three types of values that correspond to UML link ends. Since the engine is physically contained inside the car, the car has a *Value* whose type is *Value.CONTAINED,* and the engine has a *Value* whose type is *Value.CONTAINER.* Finally, the car is related to its owner by a *Value* of type *Value.REFERENCE.*

To obtain the objects related to the car object created previously, you can use the *getXMIValueOfValue()* method of *XMIObjectImpl* as follows:

```
XMIObject carOwner  = (XMIObject) car.getXMIValueOfValue("owner");
XMIObject carEngine = (XMIObject) car.getXMIValueOfValue("engine");
```

You can also use the *getXMIValues()* method in the *XMIObject* interface to obtain the *Value* objects for the car and then process each one if you wish.

The following example shows how to represent a person that has two cars, and how to obtain the objects representing the cars from the object representing the person:

```
XMIObject person = new XMIObjectImpl("Person");
XMIObject car1   = new XMIObjectImpl("Car");
XMIObject car2   = new XMIObjectImpl("Car");
```

```
person.setXMIValue("car", car1, Value.REFERENCE);
person.addXMIValue("car", car2);
Collection cars = (Collection) person.getXMIValueOfValue("car");
```

The *getXMIValueOfValue()* method in the previous example obtains the linked objects for the *car* reference of the *person* object.

The *addXMIValue()* method obtains an existing *Value* object with the given name, if one exists, and adds the given value to that *Value* object, creating a *Collection* to hold the values if necessary. If a *Value* object with the given name does not exist, one is created. In the previous example, the *cars* collection contains *car1* and *car2*.

You can also create values yourself and then add them to objects. The previous example could also be created with the following code:

```
XMIObject person = new XMIObjectImpl("Person");
XMIObject car1 = new XMIObjectImpl("Car");
XMIObject car2 = new XMIObjectImpl("Car");
List l = new ArrayList();
l.add(car1);
l.add(car2);
Value reference = new ReferenceImpl("car");
reference.setXMIValue(l);
person.add(reference);
```

Classes and Features

Classes and their features are represented by the *XMIClass* interface and the *Feature* interface, respectively. The features of a class define the legal values that objects that are instances of the class can have. Figure A.6 shows part of the Framework interface hierarchy containing the *XMIClass* and *Feature* interfaces. We explain the *Classifier* interface later.

Features

There are two kinds of features: attributes and association ends. Attributes are represented by the *Attribute* interface; association ends are represented by the *AssociationEnd* interface. A Framework attribute corresponds to a UML attribute, and a Framework association end corresponds to a UML association end. Both of these interfaces are shown in the part of the Framework interface hierarchy in Figure A.7.

Each feature has a name, a multiplicity, a type, and a value type. The multiplicity defines the number of values the feature can have in an object. The type is a *Classifier*; there are two kinds of *Classifiers* in the Framework: *XMIClass* and *Datatype*. A Framework *Datatype* corresponds to a UML datatype. In addition, the *Enum* interface represents an enumeration and extends the *Datatype* inter-

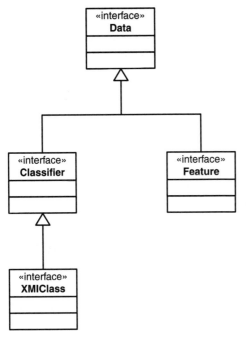

Figure A.6   Framework interfaces for classes and features.

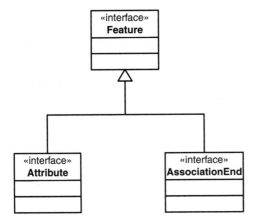

Figure A.7   Framework interfaces for attributes and association ends.

face. These interfaces are in the part of the Framework interface hierarchy shown in Figure A.8.

Because a feature has a type, you may wonder why it needs to have a value type as well. There are several reasons. First, it is not always possible to determine what kind of value a particular feature has in an object based on its type alone. Consider an *XMIClass* named *C* with an *AssociationEnd* named *end*. The

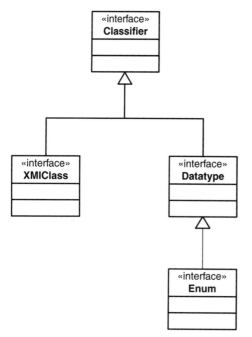

Figure A.8   Framework interfaces for classifiers.

type of the *AssociationEnd* is another *XMIClass*, C2. From this information alone, you cannot determine whether link ends in an object corresponding to this association end have types of *Value.REFERENCE, Value.CONTAINER,* or *Value.CONTAINED*. Second, in some cases you can save the effort of setting an attribute's type if you set its value type first. Rather than creating a datatype and then setting an attribute's type to that datatype, you can simply set the value type of the attribute to *Value.DATA*. The values of this attribute in objects will be correctly written. This attribute will be treated correctly when the Framework generates an XMI DTD for a model that contains the attribute. The attribute's type is mapped to the schema *string* datatype when a schema is generated for a model that includes the attribute. You can set the type of an attribute to a datatype you create, if you wish.

The following example demonstrates how to create a class for dogs if each dog has a feature for the name of the dog:

```
XMIClass dog = new XMIClassImpl("Dog");
Feature name = new AttributeImpl("name");
name.setXMIValueType(Value.DATA);
dog.add(name);
```

Since the value type of the attribute is *Value.DATA*, it is not necessary to set the attribute's type, although you can create a datatype and set the type of the attribute to it if you wish. We could also have used the *FeatureImpl* class in the previous example rather than the *AttributeImpl* class.

The following example illustrates how to create features corresponding to UML association ends and how to add them to classes. The classes represent a car, a person, and an engine. A car contains an engine, an engine is related to the car it is in, and a car is related to the person(s) that owns it. The classes are shown in Figure A.9.

In this example, note how the type, value type, and multiplicity are set for the features that represent the relationships among the three classes. You should see that the way these are set corresponds to the relationships that the classes have to each other through the association ends that the features represent:

```
XMIClass carClass = new XMIClassImpl("Car");
XMIClass engineClass = new XMIClassImpl("Engine");
XMIClass personClass = new XMIClassImpl("Person");

Feature engineFeature = new FeatureImpl("engine");
engineFeature.setXMIValueType(Value.CONTAINED);
engineFeature.setXMIType(engineClass);
engineFeature.setXMIMultiplicity("1");
carClass.add(engineFeature);

Feature carFeature = new FeatureImpl("car");
carFeature.setXMIValueType(Value.CONTAINER);
carFeature.setXMIType(carClass);
carFeature.setXMIMultiplicity("1");
engineClass.add(carFeature);

Feature ownerFeature = new FeatureImpl("owner");
ownerFeature.setXMIValueType(Value.REFERENCE);
```

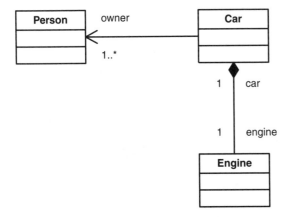

Figure A.9 *Person*, *Car*, and *Engine* classes.

```
ownerFeature.setXMIType(personClass);
ownerFeature.setXMIMultiplicity("1..*");
carClass.add(ownerFeature);
```

Inheritance

Framework classes may have subclasses and superclasses. You add superclasses and subclasses to Framework classes using the *addSuperclass()* and *addSubclass()* methods in the *XMIClass* interface.

If you are working with animals, mammals, dogs, and cats, and mammals inherit from animals, while dogs and cats inherit from mammals, the following code creates Framework classes representing the situation:

```
XMIClass animalClass = new XMIClassImpl("Animal");
XMIClass mammalClass = new XMIClassImpl("Mammal");
XMIClass dogClass = new XMIClassImpl("Dog");
XMIClass catClass = new XMIClassImpl("Cat");

animalClass.addSubclass(mammalClass);
mammalClass.addSuperclass(animalClass);
mammalClass.addSubclass(dogClass);
mammalClass.addSubclass(catClass);
dogClass.addSuperclass(mammalClass);
catClass.addSuperclass(mammalClass);
```

Definers

So far, we have explained objects, values, classes, and features. Although you don't need to create an *XMIClass* to create an *XMIObject*, you can relate an object to its class. You can also relate a value to its feature in a class. You do so by using the *setXMIDefiner()* method in the *Data* interface. Table A.1 shows the definers for objects and their values.

If the definer is set for a construct, the Framework uses the XMI name of the definer as the XMI name of the construct.

Setting the definer for an object or a value makes it possible for semantic checking to be performed for that object or value. Currently, the Framework

Table A.1 Definers

CONSTRUCT	DEFINER
XMIObject	XMIClass
AttributeValue	Attribute
LinkEnd	AssociationEnd

does not perform semantic checking, but you can write code that does. For example, if the definer for a value is set to a feature, you can determine whether the values are legal ones by checking the type of the feature. You can also examine the number of values and compare it to the multiplicity of the feature to determine whether the number of values is legal.

When you register a model with a workspace and then load an XMI file, the Framework matches the objects and values in the XMI file to the classes and features in the model, setting the definers in the process.

Packages

The Framework *Package* interface represents a UML package. A package can contain classes, datatypes, or other packages. You use packages to group related classes and datatypes.

Models

The Framework *Model* class represents a model. It contains Framework declarations, which are packages, classes, features, and datatypes. The *toString()* method of the *Model* class creates a *String* that enables you to see the contents of a model. The *Model* class contains methods that enable the Framework to match objects and values in an XMI file with the classes and features that define them when an XMI file is loaded. A *Model* contains packages, classes, and datatypes. You add models to a workspace to register the models with the Framework.

XMI Names

Each package, class, feature, datatype, object, and value has an XMI name; if a construct has a definer, its XMI name is the XMI name of its definer. In the following discussion, we indicate how to create the XMI name for a construct from its name in a model.

In XMI 1.1 and 2.0, it is no longer necessary to use fully qualified names of constructs as their XMI names, because you can use namespaces to distinguish constructs with the same names. In the Framework, you can attach a namespace to any construct in the Framework object model, and the Framework will use the namespace prefix as appropriate in XMI 1.1 files, XMI 1.1 DTDs, or XMI 2.0 files and schemas. The namespace prefix may be the empty string, but cannot be *null*.

In XMI 1.0, the XMI name of a construct is fully qualified, similar to the fully qualified name of a Java class. The fully qualified name includes the name of the construct, the name of the construct's owner, and the name of the construct owner's owner, and so on, up the ownership chain. These names are then written in a dot-separated sequence beginning with the name of the uppermost construct in the ownership chain. For example, for a class C contained in a package $p2$, which itself is contained in a package $p1$, the fully qualified name would be $p1.p2.C$. The XMI name of an object is the XMI name of its class.

In XMI 1.0, the XMI name of a feature is the fully qualified name of the class that the feature belongs to, followed by a period (.) and the name of the feature. The fully qualified name of a local value of an object is the fully qualified name of the object followed by a period and the name of the value. However, the fully qualified name of an inherited value of an object is the fully qualified name of the class the value's definer belongs to followed by a period and the name of the value. For example, consider a class Sub that inherits from class $Super$. Class $Super$ has a feature whose name is a. What is the fully qualified name of value a belonging to an instance of class Sub? The fully qualified name of the value is not $Sub.a$, but rather $Super.a$. This is because the definer of value a, which is feature a, belongs to class $Super$, not class Sub.

As another example, to represent a dog, you might create an XMI object and give it an XMI name Dog. If you create another dog, its XMI name is Dog also. Each XMI object is an instance of the Dog class. If the Dog class was in a package called $Mammals$, which was in another package called $Animals$, the XMI name of each object for XMI 1.0 would be $Animals.Mammals.Dog$. For XMI 1.1 and 2.0, the XMI name would just be Dog if there were no other packages or classes named Dog.

Now consider a model containing a package p that contains two other packages, $p1$ and $p2$. Both $p1$ and $p2$ contain classes named C. In XMI 1.0, the XMI names of the two classes are $p.p1.C$ and $p.p2.C$. In XMI 1.1 and 2.0, the name C cannot be used as the XMI name because that is not unique. You should assign a different namespace to both packages and set their XMI names to C; this way, the namespace prefixes in the XMI names of the classes enable you to distinguish between the two classes.

If objects and values have definers, they can be saved in either XMI 1.0, XMI 1.1, or XMI 2.0 files. If an object and its values do not have definers, and the XMI 1.1 (and XMI 2.0) names for that object and its values differ from their XMI 1.0 names, it is not possible to save that object in all XMI formats without changing its XMI name.

To support all XMI versions whenever possible, set the XMI names of constructs as follows (some of these rules are rather complicated if you do not set the definers for an object and its values):

- For a class or a package, use its name as the XMI name, and use namespaces to distinguish among classes and packages with the same names. When working with XMI 1.0, the Framework computes the fully qualified name of a package or a class using its sequence of owners. For

XMI 1.1 and 2.0, the Framework uses the XMI name you assign to each class or package, ignoring its owners.

- For a feature, use its name as the XMI name. The Framework will use the feature's sequence of owners to compute the fully qualified name, if necessary.

- For an object that does not have a definer, use the fully qualified name of the class for XMI 1.0. Use the class name for XMI 1.1 and XMI 2.0.

- For a local value that does not have a definer, use the value's name as the XMI name. The Framework will use the XMI name of the object that holds the value (the value's owner) to compute the name if necessary.

- For an inherited value that does not have a definer, and whose type is either *Value.OBJECT* or *Value.CONTAINED*, use the XMI name of the class that the value's definer (a feature) belongs to, which is followed by a period and the value's name. Set the value's owner to *null* so the Framework does not use the XMI name for the object that has the value.

- For an inherited value that does not have a definer, and whose type is neither *Value.OBJECT* nor *Value.CONTAINED*, use the value's name as the XMI name for XMI 1.1. For XMI 1.0, use the XMI name of the class that the value's definer (a feature) belongs to, followed by a period and the value's name. Also, for XMI 1.0, set the value's owner to *null* so the Framework does not use the XMI name of the object that has the value.

When using XMI 1.1 and 2.0, set the namespace if desired to enable the Framework to use XML namespaces.

The Framework automatically assigns the correct XMI names to classes and packages if it makes them from a UML model. Then you can make objects and set the definers of the objects and their values to the ones the Framework created to ensure that the XMI names are correct. The Framework also assigns correct XMI names to objects and values when you use the classes generated by the *UML2Java* program. The Framework sets the definers for objects and their values when loading XMI files if you use the *Workspace* class.

Because the XMI name of a construct becomes either an XML tag name or an XML attribute name when the construct is saved in an XMI file, the XMI name must be a valid XML tag or attribute name. See the XML 1.0 specification for more details. In general, letters and numbers are allowed in names, but spaces and punctuation marks, except for hyphens and periods, are not allowed.

Namespaces

The use of namespaces in the Framework is covered in the *Namespaces* section of Chapter 8. Please refer to that section for details on using namespaces with the Framework.

Encoding Non-XMI Information

There are two ways to specify additional information for constructs in the Framework object model. One way is to use tag values; the second way, which applies only to *XMIObjects*, is to use XMI extensions.

You use tag values as a shortcut rather than using the *Extension* interface to create XMI extensions for *XMIObjects*. You also can use them to specify the XMI file an object will be saved in. A possible future use for them is to tailor schemas by setting tag values for declarations. The current version of the Framework does not do this, but a future version might.

The *XMI Extensions* section of Chapter 8 discusses using tag values to create XMI extensions for *XMIObjects*, and also describes the use of the *Extension* interface.

Implementing Framework Object Model Interfaces

All the interfaces and implementation classes for the data hierarchy are public, so you may extend and implement any of them. Although you can use the code-generation capability of the Framework to generate subclasses for you, we include an example here to help you write your own subclasses. The following is an example that demonstrates how you can write subclasses of *XMIObjectImpl* being used to represent cars engines, and persons, where each car has a value for the model of the car, and a value for the engine. Each engine has a value for the car it is in, and each person has a value for the cars the person owns. This situation is illustrated in Figure A.10.

The classes that implement this functionality are displayed in Source Code A.1.

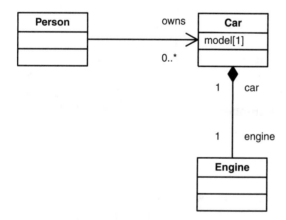

Figure A.10   A second model containing *Person*, *Car*, and *Engine* classes.

```
// Car.java
import com.ibm.xmi.framework.*;

public class Car extends XMIObjectImpl {
   public Car() {
     super("Car");
   }

   public void setEngine(Engine e) {
      setXMIValue("engine", e, Value.CONTAINED);
   }

   public Engine getEngine() {
      return (Engine) getXMIValueOfValue("engine");
   }

   public String getModel() {
      return (String) getXMIValueOfValue("model");
   }

   public void setModel(String model) {
      setXMIValue("model", model, Value.DATA);
   }
}

// Engine.java
import com.ibm.xmi.framework.*;

public class Engine extends XMIObjectImpl {
   public Engine() {
     super("Engine");
   }

   public Car getCar() {
      return (Car) getXMIValueOfValue("car");
   }

   public void setCar(Car c) {
      setXMIValue("car", c, Value.CONTAINER);
   }
}

// Person.java
import java.util.*;
import com.ibm.xmi.framework.*;

public class Person extends XMIObjectImpl {
```

Source Code A.1 Subclasses that inherit from *XMIObjectImpl*.

```
    public Person() {
      super("Person");
    }

    public void addCar(Car c) {
      addXMIValue("owns", c, Value.REFERENCE);
    }

    public Collection getCars() {
      java.lang.Object v = getXMIValueOfValues("owns");
      if (v instanceof Collection)
         return (Collection) v;
      List l = new ArrayList(1);
      if (v instanceof XMIObject)
          l.add(v);
      return l;
    }
}
```

Source Code A.1   Subclasses that inherit from *XMIObjectImpl. (Continued)*

This example demonstrates that you can write your own subclasses of the *XMIObjectImpl* class. This enables you to use the methods that you implement, rather than using only those in the Framework interfaces.

XMI Files

This section describes how to create XMI files using the Framework. It focuses on the *XMIFile* class. Many aspects of creating XMI files were covered in earlier chapters. Rather than repeating those discussions here, we provide references to them so that you can review them if you like. The two primary things to do with an XMI file are to create a new one or to load an existing one. We start by discussing how to create simple files and load them; then we discuss how to work with information that describes a document and how to create more advanced XMI files.

Creating Single XMI Files

To create an XMI file, make an instance of the *XMIFile* class and then use the *write()* method to write your XMI objects to the file. Before calling the *write()* method, call the *setXMIVersion()* method if you want to create an XMI 1.0 or 1.1 file; the default is XMI 2.0.

When you create an *XMIFile* object, you indicate the file to create, the entry to make in a ZIP file, or the output stream to use. This enables you to write a new XMI file, create an entry in a ZIP file, or write objects to an open output stream, respectively. If you want to create an entry in a ZIP file, you are responsible for opening a ZIP output stream and providing the name of the entry for the ZIP file. The Framework will create an entry in the ZIP output stream, write the objects in that entry, and then close the entry. It will not close the ZIP output stream though, because you might want to save other files in the ZIP file. If you specify an open output stream when creating an *XMIFile* object, the Framework will not close the output stream after it writes the objects. This enables you to write additional information to the output stream after the Framework uses the output stream.

The *write()* method takes two parameters: an iterator for the objects to write to the file, and an option. Chapters 7 and 8 provide examples of using the *write()* method with the *XMIFile.DEFAULT* option. This method throws an exception if the file cannot be written.

Default Write Option

When using the *XMIFile.DEFAULT* write option, the Framework does the following things when the *write()* method is invoked:

- Writes all top-level objects to the file.

- Writes values of type *Value.OBJECT* (attribute values) or *Value.CONTAINED* (link ends with composition semantics) to the file. This is done recursively.

- Creates an XMI identifier (the value of the *xmi:id* attribute) for each object if it has not already been given one.

- Identifies itself as the creator of the XMI file by specifying *XMI Framework* for the *exporter* and *1.2* for the *exporter version*.

- Throws an exception if an object is referenced, but is not written to the file.

- Throws an exception if an object is written twice.

We present some examples of this behavior and some errors that can occur. Consider a container that has a part. We can represent the container and the part as *XMIObjects*. The *XMIObject* for the container has a value whose value type is *Value.CONTAINED* with the part as the linked object. Here is a segment of code where we create the objects and the value, and serialize them in an XMI file:

```
// Create the two objects, and make the container contain the part.
XMIObject container = new XMIObjectImpl("Container");
```

```
XMIObject part = new XMIObjectImpl("Part");
container.setXMIValue("part", part, Value.CONTAINED);

// Prepare to write the objects in this example by putting them
// in an ArrayList.  We only need to put the container object in
// the list, since it already contains the part object.
ArrayList myObjects = new ArrayList();
myObjects.add(container);

// Write the objects.
XMIFile f = new XMIFile("container.xmi");
f.write(myObjects.iterator(), XMIFile.DEFAULT);
```

Notice that we did not add the *XMIObject* for the part to the collection. The reason is because it is serialized when the *Container* is serialized. The file *container.xmi* has the following contents:

```
<?xml version="1.0" encoding="UTF-8"?>
<xmi:XMI xmi:version="2.0" xmlns:xmi="http://www.omg.org/XMI">
    <xmi:Documentation>
      <exporter>XMI Framework</exporter>
      <exporterVersion>1.2</exporterVersion>
    </xmi:Documentation>
  <Container xmi:id="_1">
    <part xmi:id="_1.1" xmi:type="Part"/>
  </Container>
</xmi:XMI>
```

Now consider what happens if both the part and the container are in the collection of objects to write. To do this, we add the part to *myObjects* and also add the container:

```
// Create the two objects, and make the container contain the part.
XMIObject container = new XMIObjectImpl("Container");
XMIObject part = new XMIObjectImpl("Part");
container.setXMIValue("part", part, Value.CONTAINED);

// Prepare to write the objects in this example by putting them
// in an ArrayList.
List myObjects = new ArrayList();
myObjects.add(container);
myObjects.add(part);

// Write the objects.
XMIFile f = new XMIFile("container.xmi");
f.write(myObjects.iterator(), XMIFile.DEFAULT);
```

The Framework throws a *ContainmentException* in this case because *part* would be written twice, once as a value of *container* and once as a top-level object.

Now consider the case where a *Car* object and a *Person* object are related via a reference, but only the *Car* object is added to the collection of objects to be written to an XMI file. Here is a segment of Java code showing how we would do this:

```
XMIObject car = new XMIObjectImpl("Car");
XMIObject person = new XMIObjectImpl("Person");
car.setXMIValue("owner", person, Value.REFERENCE);
List myObjects = new ArrayList();
myObjects.add(car);
XMIFile f = new XMIFile("car.xmi");
f.write(myObjects.iterator(), XMIFile.DEFAULT);
```

In this case, the Framework throws a *NoIdException*. The Framework assigns an XMI identifier to each object to be written, in this case the *Car* object. When it serializes the *owner* value, it attempts to create a cross-file reference to the *Person* object because the *Person* object is not included in the *car.xmi* file. Because the *Person* object does not have an XMI identifier, and the Framework does not assign one (because the *Person* object is not in *car.xmi*), it throws the exception. Cross-file references are explained in the *Cross-file References* section of Chapter 8.

When you use the default write option, it is your responsibility to make sure that objects are not included twice in the file. You also need to ensure that referenced objects are in the collection of objects to write, or that you provide enough information for them so the Framework can create cross-file references to them.

Other Write Options

There are other write options in addition to the default option. The options are *OBJECTS_ONLY*, *PRESERVE_WHITESPACE*, and *REFERENCES_AT_TOP*. These options are not mutually exclusive. You can specify more than one by using the logical OR operator (|). For example, the following invocation of the *write()* method specifies both the *PRESERVE_WHITESPACE* option and the *REFERENCES_AT_TOP* option:

```
xmiFile.write(someCollection.iterator(),
            XMIFile.PRESERVE_WHITESPACE | XMIFile.REFERENCES_AT_TOP);
```

The *OBJECTS_ONLY* option suppresses the serialization of the *XMI* XML element and the header information. You will probably use this option most often when you want to serialize objects to an open output stream, and you want to serialize only the objects, not the header information.

If you use the *PRESERVE_WHITESPACE* option, then any attribute value that has whitespace in it will be serialized in the content of an XML element, even if it could be serialized as the value of an XML attribute. By default, the Framework serializes attribute values in XML attributes when it can. This can result in the loss of whitespace because the XML specification requires that an XML parser normalize XML attribute values and eliminate whitespace. If you want to preserve whitespace in your applications, you should specify this write option.

The *REFERENCES_AT_TOP* option causes the Framework to serialize all objects related to the objects in the collection of objects to write, not just those objects and objects contained in them. The Framework serializes related objects that ordinarily would not be serialized as top-level objects. This option enables you to serialize all objects related to a given object in an XMI file without regard for whether the related objects are contained or not.

We saw in the previous section a *Car* object that was related to a *Person* object with an *owner* reference value. If the default write option is used, and only the *Car* object is in the collection of objects to write, the Framework throws an exception. However, if you use the *REFERENCES_AT_TOP* option, the Framework serializes the *Person* object as a top-level object. Here is a segment of code to create the objects, set the value, and serialize the objects in an XMI file using the *REFERENCES_AT_TOP* option:

```
XMIObject car = new XMIObjectImpl("Car");
XMIObject person = new XMIObjectImpl("Person");
car.setXMIValue("owner", person, Value.REFERENCE);
ArrayList l = new ArrayList();
l.add(car);
XMIFile f = new XMIFile("car.xmi");
f.write(l.iterator(), XMIFile.REFERENCES_AT_TOP);
```

The contents of *car.xmi* are as follows:

```
<?xml version="1.0" encoding="UTF-8"?>
<xmi:XMI xmi:version="2.0" xmlns:xmi="http://www.omg.org/XMI">
    <xmi:Documentation>
      <exporter>XMI Framework</exporter>
      <exporterVersion>1.2</exporterVersion>
    </xmi:Documentation>
  <Car xmi:id="_1" owner="_1.1"/>
  <Person xmi:id="_1.1"/>
</xmi:XMI>
```

Note that the *Person* object is serialized as a top-level object.

Loading Single XMI Files

You use the static *load()* method of the *XMIFile* class to load a single XMI file; the Framework creates an instance of the *XMIFile* class for you that you can use to get the top-level objects from the file. To load from a file, you use the *load()* method with three parameters:

- The file name.

- The load option; the default option is DEFAULT.

- A *boolean* value indicating whether to perform validation.

When you use the default option, the Framework loads the file and reports any XML errors. If you specify *true* for the validation parameter, it reports any validation errors the parser detected when it loaded the file.

To properly interpret the contents of an XMI file, you need to know the model that defines the objects and values in the file. Chapter 7 contains a code example of how to do this. The Framework makes assumptions when it loads a file without knowledge of the model. These assumptions are as follows:

- Each XML attribute value is a data value of value type *Value.DATA*.

- Each contained object is a value of value type *Value.OBJECT*.

- Each XML element that has *String* content is a value of value type *Value.DATA*.

Notice that the Framework does not create values with value types other than *Value.DATA* or *Value.OBJECT* if it does not know the model. Consider the following file:

```
<?xml version="1.0" encoding="UTF-8"?>
<xmi:XMI xmi:version="2.0" xmlns:xmi="http://www.omg.org/XMI">
    <xmi:Documentation>
      <exporter>XMI Framework</exporter>
      <exporterVersion>1.2</exporterVersion>
    </xmi:Documentation>
  <Car xmi:id="_1" owner="_1.1"/>
  <Person xmi:id="_1.1"/>
</xmi:XMI>
```

We created this file by creating an *owner* value of value type *Value.REFERENCE* and setting the linked object to be the *Person* object. However, when the Framework loads this file without knowing the model, a *Value* object is created for the *owner* value with a value type of *Value.DATA* and with a value of the string _1.1. If the Framework knows the model, the *Value* object that is created would be of value type *Value.REFERENCE*, and the linked object would be the *Person* object.

Header Data

XMI defines header data that can be put in each XMI file. For XMI 1.0 and 1.1, this information was put in an *XMI.header* XML element; for XMI 2.0, this information is put in the *xmi:Documentation* XML element. To put header data into an XMI file, use the accessor methods in Table A.2 to set the header data before calling the *write()* method of the *XMIFile* class. To get header data from an XMI file, use the accessor methods of the *XMIFile* class to get the header data after loading the XMI file. Table A.2 shows the accessor methods for each kind of information.

For XMI 1.0 and 1.1 files, you can use the *setDTD()* method before calling the *write()* method so the Framework writes a reference to the DTD in the XMI file. You can also use the *setTimestamp()* and *getTimestamp()* methods to set and get the timestamp in an XMI 1.0 or 1.1 file. By default, the Framework sets the timestamp to the current time when it writes an XMI 1.0 or 1.1 file.

For any version of XMI, you can use the *setEncoding()* method to set the XML encoding for an XMI file, and you can use the *setIndent()* method to control the indentation of nested XML elements. By default, the encoding is *UTF-8*, and the Framework indents nested XML elements two spaces from the containing XML elements. If you invoke *setIndent()* with a parameter of *0*, the Framework does not indent nested XML elements.

Related XMI Files

You can write your objects in multiple XMI files with cross-file references between related objects in different files. The *Cross-file References* section of Chapter 8 explains how to create these files and how to load them.

Registering Models with the Framework

You register models with the Framework using the *Workspace* class. The *Reading an XMI Document* section of Chapter 7 explains how to do this.

Table A.2 Header Data Accessor Methods

DATA	ACCESSOR METHODS
Exporter	*getExporter(), setExporter()*
Exporter version	*getExporterVersion(), setExporterVersion()*
Notice	*getNotice(), setNotice()*
Contact	*getContact(), setContact()*
Owner	*getOwner(), setOwner()*
Long description	*getLongDescription(), setLongDescription()*
Short description	*getShortDescription(), setShortDescription()*

XMI DTDs

To create XMI DTDs, you create classes and packages and pass them to the *write()* method of an *XMIDTD* instance. If you want to create an XMI 1.1 DTD, call the *setXMIVersion()* method with a parameter of *1.1* before using the *write()* method. Here is a code segment that shows how to use the *XMIDTD* class:

```
XMIClass dog = new XMIClassImpl("Dog");
XMIClass cat = new XMIClassImpl("Cat");

Feature name = new FeatureImpl("name");
name.setXMIValueType(Value.DATA);
dog.add(name);

Feature friend = new FeatureImpl("friend");
friend.setXMIValueType(Value.REFERENCE);
friend.setXMIType(cat);
dog.add(friend);

ArrayList classes = new ArrayList();
classes.add(dog);
classes.add(cat);

XMIDTD dtd = new XMIDTD("dog.dtd");
dtd.write(classes.iterator());
```

XMI Schemas

XMI schemas are more powerful than XMI DTDs. The Framework contains an *XMISchema* class, which produces XMI schemas using the final version of the W3C schema specification. The use of the *XMISchema* class is similar to the use of the *XMIDTD* class, as illustrated by the following code segment:

```
XMIClass dog = new XMIClassImpl("Dog");
XMIClass cat = new XMIClassImpl("Cat");

Feature name = new FeatureImpl("name");
name.setXMIValueType(Value.DATA);
dog.add(name);

Feature friend = new FeatureImpl("friend");
friend.setXMIValueType(Value.REFERENCE);
friend.setXMIType(cat);
dog.add(friend);

ArrayList classes = new ArrayList();
classes.add(dog);
```

```
classes.add(cat);

XMISchema schema = new XMISchema("dog.xsd");
schema.setURI("http://MyCompany.com/dog.xsd");
schema.write(classes.iterator());
```

Code Generation

The *UML2Java* class has been significantly improved from previous versions of the Framework. It correctly handles packages in UML models and provides more options for generating code. It also handles multiple inheritance in UML models if the *-interfaces* option is used. *UML2Java* will then generate both a class and an interface for each class in the UML model; the interfaces will extend each other to reflect inheritance in the UML model, but the generated implementation classes do not inherit from each other. This enables one generation pattern to support multiple inheritance.

The *UML2Java* class produces subclasses of *XMIObjectImpl* from UML models. This capability will help you create subclasses of *XMIObjectImpl* automatically, so users of your code can work with your classes, rather than the Framework classes. The *UML2Java* class also creates a factory that can be registered with the Framework, so the generated subclasses are instantiated by the Framework when loading XMI files.

To use the *UML2Java* class, invoke it with the following options from the command line:

-model.   Use this option to indicate which XMI file to use. The file must be an XMI 1.0 file containing a UML 1.1 model. If you get no output, check whether the *uml11i.dtd* file is in the directory the file is in. An example of the use of this option is *java com.ibm.xmi.framework. UML2Java -model umlModel.xmi.*

-dir.   The directory to put the generated code in. If not present, the current directory will be used. An example would be *java com.ibm.xmi. framework.UML2Java -model umlModel.xmi -dir e:\generatedCode.*

-package.   The top-level Java package. All the code will be generated into this package or in packages within this package. If you do not specify this option, Java classes corresponding to UML classes that are not in a package are put in the default Java package. An example of specifying a package would be *java com.ibm.xmi.framework -model umlModel.xmi -package com.mycompany.mypackage.*

-namespaceName.   The namespace name for the model. XMI 1.1 and 2.0 enable you to assign a namespace name to a model. You do not need to specify this option. If you specify this option, the Framework will attach

a namespace to each construct in the model in the generated *UserFactory* class.

-namespaceURI.   The namespace URI for the namespace you assign to your model. It will be used when writing XMI 1.1 and 2.0 files.

-interfaces.   If present, an interface and an implementation class will be generated from each class in the UML model. For example, if there is a class *A* in your UML model, the Framework will generate *A.java* and *AImpl.java* for class *A*. *A.java* will contain an interface for the class; *AImpl.java* will implement the interface. An example of this option's use is as follows: *java com.ibm.xmi.framework.UML2Java -model umlModel.xmi -interfaces*.

-ignorePackages.   If present, any packages in the UML model will be ignored. All the generated code will be put in the default Java package, with classes renamed as necessary to avoid name conflicts. You only need to use this option if you do not want the Framework to make Java packages from the UML packages in your model.

-oneConstructor.   If present, the Framework will only create one constructor for each generated class. By default, the Framework makes two constructors, one of which lets you set each attribute of the class. If a class has a large number of attributes, it is not likely that this constructor will be used though. If you specify this option, only a no-argument constructor will be made for each generated Java class.

The *Code Generation* section of Chapter 8 contains more information about using the Framework to generate Java code.

Using the Framework by Implementing Adapters

The Framework adapters are explained in detail in the *Creating an XMI Document* and *Reading an XMI Document* sections in Chapter 7. The Java Object Bridge (JOB) is an example of adapters.

DeclarationFactory Class

The Framework converts UML models saved in XMI files into classes and packages if you use the *DeclarationFactory* class. The Framework converts UML packages into Framework packages, UML classes into Framework classes, UML attributes into features of Framework classes, and UML association ends into features of Framework classes.

Table A.3 UML to Framework Mapping

UML	FRAMEWORK
Class	*XMIClass*
Package	*Package*
Attribute	*Attribute*
Association end	*AssociationEnd*
Datatype	*Datatype*
Enumeration	*Enum*

If the type of a UML attribute is an enumeration, the Framework sets the value type of the corresponding *Feature* to *Value.ENUM* and the type of the *Feature* to an *Enum*. If the attribute type is a UML class, the Framework sets the value type of the corresponding *Feature* to *Value.OBJECT* and the type of the *Feature* to the *XMIClass* corresponding to the UML class that is the type of the UML attribute. If the attribute type is not an enumeration or a UML class, the Framework sets the value type of the corresponding *Feature* to *Value.DATA* and the type of the *Feature* to a Framework *Datatype* corresponding to the UML datatype.

The Framework makes features from UML association ends. For UML association ends that are compositions, the Framework sets the value type of the *Feature* to *Value.CONTAINED*, and the value type of the *Feature* corresponding to the opposite association end to *Value.CONTAINER*; otherwise, it sets the value type to *Value.REFERENCE*. The Framework sets the type of the corresponding *Feature* to the *XMIClass* corresponding to the UML class that is attached to the association end.

Table A.3 summarizes the mapping from UML to the Framework.

The Framework assigns subclasses and superclasses of Framework classes to reflect the inheritance between classes in the UML model. It also assigns XMI names to the packages, classes, and features based on the names in the UML XMI file.

Currently, the *DeclarationFactory* class supports UML 1.1 models saved in XMI 1.0 format.

To create Framework classes and packages from a UML XMI file, load the XMI file and get the top-level objects, as explained in the *XMI Files* section. Then make an instance of the *DeclarationFactory* class and invoke one of the *makeDeclarations()* methods, passing the objects from the XMI file. See the Framework example provided on the CD-ROM in the *UML2Classes* directory for more details.

Notes

Chapter 1

1. As explained in the Introduction, XMI works with Meta Object Facility (MOF) models. As this book is being written, there is ongoing work in the OMG to align UML and MOF. If this work proceeds as we expect, UML models can be transformed into equivalent MOF models transparently to users of XMI. If this alignment does not succeed, UML models need to be transformed into MOF models for use with XMI. In this book, we treat MOF and UML as if they are aligned. We refer primarily to UML.

Chapter 5

1. The XMI specification describes how to reverse engineer Meta-Object Facility (MOF) models from XML documents, DTDs, and schemas. We describe how to reverse engineer UML models from XML. As we explain in the Introduction, we believe that UML and MOF will be aligned by the time this book is published. If this happens, the UML models created by the algorithms in this section will be equivalent to the MOF models created using the procedure specified in the XMI specification. If this does not happen, the UML models need to be transformed into MOF models. Also, please note that some of

the refinements to the basic algorithms presented here are not included in the XMI specification. We describe them to help you make the most useful models possible.

Chapter 6

1. The *Option* object is an object value of the *option* attribute in the *Car* object, so the tag name in the XMI file is *option* and not *Option*.

2. We set the object attribute value *option* in CRAHandler4, where we also set references.

Chapter 7

1. Splitting the lines as we have done does not change the semantics of the XML document, but we mention it so that you are aware of the difference between the output shown in the book and the output of the book software. In general, if you observe that software output has longer lines than the output shown in this book, it is because we formatted the output to fit the page width.

2. In the Framework, a reference is one kind of link end. Since it is the only kind of link end that we will use, we will not explain the other kinds.

3. Attribute values and references are the types of Framework values that we use in this chapter. The classes that implement the Framework interfaces that represent attribute values and references include fields for a name, a type, and a value. Because the term *value* could be used in a couple different ways, if the meaning is not clear by context, we specifically state which value we are referring to.

Chapter 8

1. Splitting the lines as we have done does not change the semantics of the XML document, but we mention it so that you are not surprised if you run the program and see slightly different output. In general, if you run the book software and observe longer lines than that shown in this book, it is because we formatted the output to fit the page width.

Chapter 9

1. Splitting the lines as we have done does not affect the semantics of the XML document, but we mention it so that you are not surprised by differences

between the output of the book software and the output shown in this book. In general, if you run the book software and observe differences in the length of lines, it is because the output shown in this book has been formatted to fit the page width.

Chapter 10

1. The terms model and metamodel are sometimes used loosely. Strictly speaking, the models we're referring to here would be considered metamodels as we've described them in this example.

2. The Web Services Definition Language is a specification that has been submitted to the W3C.

3. We provide an explanation of this record later so you do not need to be a COBOL programmer to understand the ideas in this chapter.

Chapter 11

1. For a complete discussion of the capabilities of the XML to XML mapping editor, refer to the documentation contained with the version of WebSphere Studio included on the CD-ROM.

2. As you have seen earlier in this book, using XMI helps to solve this problem.

3. The *href* attribute values are based on some historical code in the implementation.

4. In the *schema.dbxmi* file shown, we have made minor changes in the indentation so that the information is easier for you to read.

5. The format of the *schema.dbxmi* file has changed slightly between the beta and initial versions of WebSphere Studio Application Developer. The format shown here is for the beta version.

6. In the *map.mapxmi* file shown, we have made minor changes in the indentation so that the information is easier for you to read.

7. This is because the current schema file only contains a single table in each file.

References

Architecture Board MDA Drafting Team. "Model Driven Architecture, A Technical Perspective." Review Draft Version 00-17(frame). Document Number ab/2001-01-01. www.omg.org/cgi-bin/doc?ab/2001-01-01. January 29, 2001.

Biron, P., and A. Malhotra (editors). "XML Schema Part 2: Datatypes." W3C recommendation. World Wide Web Consortium, www.w3.org/TR/xmlschema-2. May 2001.

Booch, G., J. Rumbaugh, and I. Jacobson. *The Unified Modeling Language User Guide*. Reading, MA: Addison Wesley, 1999.

Bray, T., J. Paoli, C. M. Sperberg-McQueen, and E. Maler (editors). "Extensible Markup Language (XML) 1.0 (Second Edition)." W3C recommendation. World Wide Web Consortium, www.w3.org/TR/REC-xml. October 2000.

Brown, K. "EJB Metadata in Websphere 4.0—A Tale of Four Files." International Business Machines Corporation, www7.boulder.ibm.com/wsdd. 2001.

———. *WebSphere 4.0 AEs Workbook for Enterprise JavaBeans, 3rd Ed*. Minneapolis, MN: Titan Books, 2001.

Christensen, E., F. Curbera, G. Meredith, and S. Weerawarana. "Web Services Description Language (WSDL) 1.1." W3C Note. World Wide Web Consortium, www.w3.org/TR/wsdl. March 2001.

DeRose, S., E. Maler, and D. Orchard (editors). "XML Linking Language (Xlink) Version 1.0." W3C recommendation. World Wide Web Consortium, www.w3.org/TR/xlink. June 2001.

Fowler, M., and K. Scott. *UML Distilled*. Reading, MA: Addison-Wesley. 1997.

Gosling, J., B. Joy, G. Steele, and G. Bracha. *The Java Language Specification, 2nd Ed*. Palo Alto, CA: Sun Microsystems, Inc., 2000. java.sun.com/books/jls.

Gudgin, M., M. Hadley, J. Moreau, and H. F. Nielsen (editors). "SOAP Version 1.2." W3C working draft. World Wide Web Consortium, www.w3.org/TR/soap12. July 2001.

Internet Engineering Task Force (IETF). "Uniform Resource Identifiers (URI): Generic Syntax." RFC 2396. www.ietf.org/rfc/rfc2396.txt. 1998.

Iyengar, S. "JSR 40, The Java Metadata Interface (JMI) Specification." Java Community Process, www.jcp.org/jsr/detail/40.jsp. 2001.

Le Hors, A., P. Le Hégaret, L. Wood, G. Nicol, J. Robie, M. Champion, and S. Byrne (editors). "Document Object Model (DOM) Level 2 Core Specification, Version 1.0." W3C recommendation. World Wide Web Consortium, www.w3.org/TR/DOM-Level-2-Core. November 2001.

Levitt, T. "Marketing Myopia." *Harvard Business Review*, Volume 38 (July-August 1960): 45-56.

Matena, V., and M. Hapner. "Enterprise JavaBeans Specification." Version 1.1 Final Release. Sun Microsystems, Inc. java.sun.com/products/ejb/docs.html. 1999.

Object Management Group, Inc. "Common Warehouse Metamodel (CWM) Specification." Version 1.0. www.omg.org/cgi-bin/doc?formal/01-10-01. October 2001.

———. "Meta Object Facility (MOF) Specification." Version 1.4 RTF. July 16, 2001.

———. "OMG Unifed Modeling Language Specification (draft)." Version 1.4 draft. February 2001.

———. "OMG XML Metadata Interchange (XMI) Specification." Version 1.1. www.omg.org/cgi-bin/doc?formal/2000-11-02. November 2000.

———. "OMG XML Metadata Interchange (XMI) Specification." Version 1.2. August 2001.

———. "UML™ for EAI, UML™ Profile and Interchange Models for Enterprise Application Integration (EAI), ad/2001-09-17." OMG EAI SIG joint submission. OMG Document Number ad/2001-09-17. www.omg.org/cgi-bin/doc?ad/2001-09-17. September 2001.

———. "A UML Profile for Enterprise Distributed Object Computing." Joint final submission, Part I, Version 0.29. OMG Document Number ad/2001-06-09. www.omg.org/cgi-bin/doc?ad/2001-06-09. June 2001.

———. "XML Metadata Interchange (XMI) Response to the RFP ad/2000-01-04 for XMI Production of XML Schema." Joint revised submission. OMG Document ad/2001-06-12. www.omg.org/cgi-bin/doc?ad/2001-06-12. June 2001.

Rumbaugh, J., I. Jacobson, and G. Booch. *The Unified Modeling Language Reference Manual*. Reading, MA: Addison Wesley, 1999.

SAX Official Web site, sax.sourceforge.net.

Soley, R. and the OMG Staff Strategy Group. "Model Driven Architecture." Object Management Group, White Paper, Draft 3.2. November 27, 2000.

Thompson, H. S., D. Beech, M. Maloney, and N. Mendelsohn (editors). "XML Schema Part 1: Structures." W3C recommendation. World Wide Web Consortium, www.omg.org/TR/xmlschema-1. May 2001.

Index